D0964996

{ The Brokeback Book }

From Story to Cultural Phenomenon

EDITED BY WILLIAM R. HANDLEY

University of Nebraska Press   Lincoln and London

*Library of Congress
Cataloging-in-Publication Data*

The Brokeback book : from story to
cultural phenomenon / edited by
William R. Handley.
p. cm.
Includes bibliographical references
and index.
ISBN 978-0-8032-2664-7
(pbk. : alk. paper)
1. Brokeback Mountain (Motion
picture) 2. Proulx, Annie.
Brokeback Mountain. I. Handley,
William R.
PN1997.2.B75B75 2011
791.43'72—dc22   2010038342

Set in Scala and ScalaSans Pro by
Bob Reitz. Designed by A. Shahan.

This book is about a story and film that depict broken hearts, marriages, and lives—and generations that barely communicate across the distances. In Annie Proulx's story, the relation between fathers and sons, in particular, is one of violence passed on and inherited, little more. Proulx has a telling point, and with that in mind I would like to dedicate this book to people of generations before and after me who represent the better side of what is possible.

Descendants of nineteenth-century Mormon polygamists, my parents actively support gay civil rights. Given the history of intolerance toward Mormons, one might think that more in the Latter-Day Saints (LDS) community would share my parents' views or at least refrain from efforts to deny civil rights to others—but of course both the LDS defense of polygamy and the (so far) successful attempts of the LDS church and other religious organizations constitutionally to overturn civil marriage equality in California and elsewhere stem from religious belief. In my teens I heard each of my parents speak before our LDS congregation in Connecticut against racial prejudice and against prejudice toward those whose sexual orientations are different. I do not know what makes them the way they are, but like any son or daughter, I've long observed what my parents do. With many of their friends in their seventies and eighties, in Salt Lake City where they now live, they work to make progress toward a more civil, healthy, and humane society—on issues from gay rights to gun control, from health care to environmental conservation—despite a recalcitrant state legislature and a large church influence. Dixie and Bob Huefner, Ann and Gale Dick, Norma and Ron Molen, Millie and Gary Watts, my parents Kate and Ken, and many others represent to me what is best about westerners—courageous stewards of the future who deal cheerfully and persistently against difficult odds, and who do not forget the past.

I dedicate this book to them and to others like them—and to a mountain man and environmental and civil rights activist out West, Dave Stalling (whom this book allowed me to know after so many years since junior high school), and to his personal hero, his son Cory.

Contents

List of Illustrations   x

Acknowledgments   xi

Introduction: The Pasts and Futures of a Story
and a Film   1
WILLIAM R. HANDLEY

**Part 1. Gay or Universal Story? Initial Debates and
Cultural Contexts**

1. Men in Love: Is *Brokeback Mountain* a Gay Film?   27
DAVID LEAVITT

2. An Affair to Remember   31
DANIEL MENDELSOHN

3. Response to "An Affair to Remember"   39
JAMES SCHAMUS

4. The Magic Mountain   42
ANDREW HOLLERAN

5. Backs Unbroken: Ang Lee, Forbearance,
and the Closet   52
MUN-HOU LO

Part 2. Miles to Go and Promises to Keep: Homophobic Culture and Gay Civil Rights

6. Back to the Ranch Ag'in: *Brokeback Mountain* and Gay Civil Rights   81
   JAMES MORRISON

7. Breaking No Ground: Why *Crash* Won, Why *Brokeback* Lost, and How the Academy Chose to Play It Safe   101
   KENNETH TURAN

8. "Jack, I Swear": Some Promises to Gay Culture from Mainstream Hollywood   103
   CHRIS FREEMAN

9. "Better Two Than One": The Shirts from *Brokeback Mountain*   118
   GREGORY HINTON

10. American Eden: Nature, Homophobic Violence, and the Social Imaginary   123
    COLIN CARMAN

11. West of the Closet, Fear on the Range   137
    ALEX HUNT

Part 3. Adapting "Brokeback Mountain," Queering the Western

12. Interview between Michael Silverblatt and Annie Proulx   153

13. In the Shadow of the Tire Iron   163
    ALAN DALE

14. Adapting Annie Proulx's Story to the Mainstream Multiplex   179
    ADAM SONSTEGARD

15. Not So Lonesome Cowboys: The Queer Western   190
    JUDITH HALBERSTAM

Part 4. Public Responses and Cultural Appropriations

16. "One Dies, the Other Doesn't": *Brokeback* and
    the Blogosphere   205
    NOAH TSIKA

17. Making Sense of the *Brokeback* Paraphenomenon   229
    DAVID WEISS

18. Alberta, Authenticity, and Queer Erasure   249
    JON DAVIES

Part 5. Scenes of Work and Experience in the Rural West

19. Real Gay Cowboys and *Brokeback Mountain*   267
    PATRICIA NELL WARREN

20. Marx on the Mountain: Pleasure and the
    Laboring Body   283
    VANESSA OSBORNE

21. Personal Borders   299
    MARTIN AGUILERA

Part 6. Sympathy, Melodrama, and Passion

22. Mother Twist: *Brokeback Mountain* and Male
    Melodrama   309
    SUSAN MCCABE

23. Passion and Sympathy in *Brokeback Mountain*   321
    CALVIN BEDIENT

Selected *Brokeback* Bibliography   351
Works Cited   353
Contributors   371
Index   377

Illustrations

1. From story to cartoon in the same magazine   10
2. Ennis threatens to throw another punch   53
3. Defeated, the biker crawls—and looks—away   53
4. Yet someone continues to look up to Ennis   54
5. Poster for the Taiwanese release of *Lust, Caution*   58
6. A 忍 (*ren*) scroll hangs from the rafters   66
7. A shirt sports the same 忍 character   67
8. Complete the ensemble with a skirt   68
9. Empty shirts full of meaning   106
10. The film's iconic one sheet   232
11. Tom Delay and Jack Abramoff star in "Kickback Mountain"   234
12. Secrets on a national scale   235
13. Gumby plus Pokey makes pudding   237

Acknowledgments

I am very grateful to Jesse Matz, who suggested this book and helped to get it off the ground; to Matthew Carnicelli, who shepherded it; and to Ladette Randolph, who brought it home even on her way to Boston. Kristen Rowley, Susan Silver, Courtney Ochsner, Sara Springsteen, and others at the University of Nebraska Press have guided it expertly to publication. Susan Kollin helped to make this a better book with her thoughtful suggestions. In addition to being generous friends, Ann Pellegrini and Michelle Latiolais are fine editors who took the time to cast their keen eyes so helpfully on my introduction. None of its faults belongs to them.

Focus Features and NBC-Universal generously granted permission to reprint images from the film and the movie poster; I am grateful to James Schamus, Korin Mills, Alex Jade, Jean Nolte, Roni Lubliner, and Peer Ebbighausen for their assistance in those and other matters. The deans of the College of Letters, Arts, and Sciences at the University of Southern California made available research funds that have been of assistance in completing this book.

My greatest debt of gratitude is to this book's contributors for their excellent essays, their patience, and their reliable dedication. It has been my pleasure to work with them and to read their work. I speak for many of us in expressing gratitude to Annie Proulx for her story, to Larry McMurtry and Diana Ossana for their screenplay, and to Ang Lee and the many others who made the film *Brokeback Mountain*, not least for giving us so much to think and write about.

I also gratefully acknowledge the following for permission to print or reprint their work:

David Leavitt's "Men in Love: Is *Brokeback Mountain* a Gay Film?" was originally published in *Slate Magazine* (www.slate.com), December 8, 2005. © 2005 by David Leavitt. Reprinted with permission of The Wylie Agency LLC.

Daniel Mendelsohn's "An Affair to Remember" was originally published as a review of the film *Brokeback Mountain* in the *New York Review of Books* 53.3 (February 23, 2006). © 2006 by Daniel Mendelsohn. The version of the essay published in this volume is from his collection of essays *How Beautiful It Is and How Easily It Can Be Broken* (HarperCollins, 2008). Reprinted with permission of the author.

James Schamus's "Response to 'An Affair to Remember'" was originally published in the *New York Review of Books* 53.6 (April 6, 2006), in "*Brokeback Mountain*: An Exchange." © 2006 by James Schamus. Reprinted with permission of the author.

Kenneth Turan's "Breaking No Ground: Why *Crash* Won, Why *Brokeback* Lost, and How the Academy Chose to Play It Safe" was originally published in the *Los Angeles Times*, March 5, 2006. © 2006 by *Los Angeles Times*. Reprinted with permission.

Michael Silverblatt's interview with Annie Proulx aired on National Public Radio station KCRW's show *Bookworm*. © 2006 by Michael Silverblatt and published with his permission.

Patricia Nell Warren's "Real Gay Cowboys and *Brokeback Mountain*" was originally published online in Outsports.com, then in *The Lavender Locker Room: 3000 Years of Great Athletes Whose Sexual Orientation Was Different*, by Patricia Nell Warren (Wildcat Press, 2006). © 2006 by Patricia Nell Warren. Reprinted with permission of the author.

The Brokeback Book

Introduction

The Pasts and Futures of a Story and a Film

WILLIAM R. HANDLEY

So much happens so quickly in one short story. Twenty years fly by in the fictional lives of Ennis del Mar and Jack Twist, two young ranch hands in Wyoming who fall into an episodic twenty-year love affair after their summer in 1963 working together on Brokeback Mountain. Then Jack dies, and Ennis discovers Jack has memorialized his love for Ennis and their idyll by entwining in his closet two shirts they had worn that first summer, a summer cut short by weather and by a boss who knew too much, and too little.

And something singular had happened, seemingly in a flash: *The New Yorker* had published a *Western* story of same-sex love in its October 13, 1997, issue. Readers, as if they were miners spying precious minerals, were riveted to the story's sentences across those fleeting twenty years, but the story was tough to extract as its minerals were rare and pure, unyielding. Unable or unwilling to forget Ennis and Jack, many readers might not have known how to talk to them if they were real. Even so, in response to Annie Proulx's mix of gritty realism and fantasy sprang a well of inchoate feeling: longing, sympathy, and passion for and on behalf of Ennis and Jack, combined with a suppressed rage toward the indifferent or violent American West from which Proulx, through her scrupulously unsentimental recognition of human limitations and ends, had made their story inseparable.

The story is about human ends, not fate—certainly not fate. It is just an accident with a blown tire that killed Jack Twist, some readers believe, in the version Jack's widow, Lureen, recounts to Ennis. Others

1

find it more likely, following Ennis's conviction, that he was murdered for being gay. For some, reading the story is a vicarious experience of something past and long regretted, nostalgic despite or perhaps because of the tragic end, whatever its cause. For others, it is a reminder of a past that uncannily resembles the world they still live in: no pleasant haunting, but a haunting allowed in order to challenge life—or the worlds in which life is lived—and to refuse to succumb to what life often passes for: fate.

Proulx's literary naturalism, her sense of environmental determination, soon seemed borne out by experience. On October 6, 1998, exactly a year after Proulx's story first appeared, two young Wyoming men, who resembled physically and socioeconomically Proulx's depictions of Ennis and Jack, pistol-whipped and left to die the equally young college student Matthew Shepard outside of Laramie, in no small part because he was gay; he died six days later. Shepard's murderers (one a Mormon priesthood holder) tied his dying body to a log fence, a western crucifixion that seemed a perverse parable of the victim's name. The brutal killing seemed linked with Proulx's story and made it feel even more urgent. In the summer of 2001, Judy Shepard, Matthew's mother, flew to Cortez, Colorado, to comfort the grieving mother of Fred Martinez, a *nádleehi*, or "Two-Spirit," sixteen-year-old Navajo boy who was fatally bludgeoned in the head in a hate crime, his body left near sewer ponds. (A recent documentary, *Two Spirits*, explores his life, death, and culture.)

Just days after "Brokeback Mountain" was published, Larry McMurtry and Diana Ossana bought the film rights for the story from Proulx. Their screenplay garnered an Oscar in 2006. Ang Lee directed the film, for which he also won an Academy Award (the first Asian director to do so), and Jake Gyllenhaal and Heath Ledger turned Jack Twist and Ennis del Mar into "the stuff of Hollywood history," as Manohla Dargis, in her early review of the film, called Ledger's "wrenching" performance ("50's Pinup"). Ennis and Jack "roared back" into Proulx's mind, "larger and stronger than they had ever been." "I realized," she writes, "that I, as a writer, was having the rarest film trip: my story was not mangled but enlarged into huge and gripping imagery that rattled minds and squeezed hearts" ("Getting Movied" 136, 137). The film largely surpassed the heated expectations surrounding it and proved, to most, an exception to the frequent presumption that Linda Hutcheon challenges, that "an adaptation is likely to be greeted as minor and subsidiary and certainly never as good as the 'original'" (xii)—especially when the original is an instant classic.

Where so much happened so quickly in the short story, the film broke with Hollywood convention by having very little happen—even very little dialogue—in the film's first twenty-five minutes. Ang Lee's mastery of cinematic time was so subtle that some impatiently overlooked the teeming interest his patient eye revealed. But so much happened so quickly *around* the film. There was the iconic and much riffed-on movie poster; the seemingly incessant late-night talk-show jokes ("Brokeback" had entered the vocabulary); the hyperactive blogosphere; the upset for Best Picture at the Oscar ceremony on March 5, 2006, about which Kenneth Turan writes in this volume; and a swirl of academic writing the next year. *Film Quarterly* was just one of the journals that had a special feature on the film (see the selected *Brokeback* bibliography at the end of this book). Then Heath Ledger died in 2008, making those iconic shirts seem truly empty. He could not accept his Oscar the following year for portraying the Joker in the film *The Dark Knight* (Christopher Nolan, 2008), a film that seemed to capture, even more than *Brokeback Mountain*, the anxiety of the time: how Americans are kept hostage to fear and terror and to the violent machinations that are supposedly required in response. After *The Dark Knight*, Ledger's penultimate film, appeared, there was yet another mashup of the *Brokeback* movie poster online, with Ledger's Joker paired with Batman in the iconic image of their near embrace while looking past each other, which was inspired by the graphics of doomed love in the *Titanic* movie poster. Mark Turner's "Brokeback Gotham" has more than just the *Brokeback* idiom in common with other such images that B. Ruby Rich has written about (see "Brokering") and that David Weiss discusses in this book. The images often share, whether intended or not, a sense of the interesting bedfellows American political culture can make, whether in cahoots or in apparent opposition to each other. Six months after Ledger's death, the New York City Opera commissioned Charles Wuorinen to compose an opera based on *Brokeback Mountain*, scheduled to premiere in the spring of 2013. The story is far from over.

That this cursory description of the story, the film, and all that surrounded and resulted from them is so well known may suggest how little the phenomenon was understood. *The Brokeback Book* is a contribution to understanding what arose in the wake of this story and film. I say "wake" because so much of the cultural response to the film, from the adulatory to the mocking, had the quality of trauma, and of people working through trauma, as if there had been some rending of the seams of the culture, which for the trauma to be contained or understood, needed mending. But the restitching was odd, strange, and took the form of descriptive phrases that are reductive and tonally suggestive of impossibility. Most particularly is the phrase "gay cowboys," a seeming oxymoron that distorts the story and the film and represses much of what they are about: *not only do we all know there is no such thing as a gay cowboy, let alone a Western with gay cowboys, "they" certainly would not actually love each other.* While some of the film's viewers wrote extensively online about prolonged states of mourning and tremendous life changes, others tittered and sneered; what wounded one person's heart was the butt of another's jokes. Or, perhaps even worse, others seemed completely indifferent. "Why do some people walk out of the movie and go to dinner and talk about the weather while others walk out of the theater to find the horizon has been erased?" wrote one viewer in the largest *Brokeback* forum, on Dave Cullen's Web site, which had millions of views, thousands of posts, and dozens of threads (Members 31).[1] In the wake of the film, melodrama, tragedy, and spoof all took the cultural stage and acted themselves out.

Those three make appearances in this volume—albeit under critical lenses—alongside some of the political questions the film has raised, the passionate personal responses it has engendered, and the several cultural contexts in which one can illuminatingly situate this film. Noah Tsika's examination of the blogosphere's response to the film and Weiss's essay about *Brokeback* parodies and spoofs together suggest how inseparable the personal and political responses to the film are. Gregory Hinton and Martin Aguilera explore their personal responses to the film in the context of growing up in the rural West, as does Patricia Nell Warren, who writes about "real" gay cowboys in the West. The book explores some of the political questions raised by the film's depiction of both external and internalized homophobia. Whether or not *Brokeback Mountain* is indeed an "issue" film, without a doubt its depictions of two characters so taken to heart by many viewers and so caricatured by others is another demonstration of how the personal is ineluctably both cultural and political. Even as the signs of the closet are everywhere evident in the film, Mun-Hou Lo's illuminating essay reads this repression within the Chinese embrace of forbearance as a positive virtue. Lo's essay is not the only one to situate the film outside of U.S. culture, political or otherwise: so does Jon Davies's discussion of how Alberta's tourism board sought to capitalize on the film while erasing its queer affiliations. Several essays, such as those by Chris Freeman, Colin Carman, Alan Dale, and Judith Halberstam, situate the film within resonant literary and cinematic contexts, including the history of gay cinema and the Western.

These various contexts illustrate a rich paradox about the cultural significance of this groundbreaking film, one that Andrew Holleran describes in his essay: "A director raised in Taiwan, an Australian lead, a Mexican cinematographer and an Argentine composer have made a Western filmed in Canada that puts gays into the central American narrative." In a correspondingly diverse vein, the essays in this volume range from the personal to the theoretical and include writers, journalists, and critics to represent the cultural breadth of response to *Brokeback Mountain* and to engage anyone interested in this film and its many contexts.

Brokeback Mountain's cultural wake is as broad as it has been unusual in film history. When else have responses included four months of late-night talk-show jokes about a film that others have seen not only as no laughing matter but as life-altering, shattering, and unshakeable? In his essay here, Weiss is not making a false historical or moral equation between the Holocaust and homophobia when he notes that late-night jokes about *Schindler's List* did not occur when that film came out. When has a U.S. president been asked if he had seen a film, a film that academics published more about in the few years since it appeared than about any other film in a similar time frame? Suggesting it belongs to a category of its own, no other film has even competed with *Brokeback Mountain* to be one of the top grossers in the Western genre *and* the top-grossing drama in the gay or lesbian category.[2] Indeed, the categories "gay" and "Western" obscure something remarkable about Ang Lee's film, which the film shares with Proulx's work more generally: *Brokeback Mountain* not only represents rural working-class people but also makes the conditions of work the very conditions of its plot. In the film, Ennis tells Jack during their last outing together, "It's likely November before I can get away again, after we ship stock and before the winter feedin' starts." When Jack explodes with frustration, Ennis tells him, "I got to work. Them earlier days I used to quit the jobs. You forget how it is, bein' broke all the time. You ever hear of child support? Let me tell you, I can't quit this one. And I can't get the time off." Such everyday concerns are in a film that Christian critic Ted Baehr dismisses as "neo-Marxist propaganda," a comment that is the starting point for Vanessa Osborne's analysis of Ennis's laboring body.

For all that is rare and groundbreaking about it, *Brokeback Mountain* and the responses to it are not ruptures in time: they are historical revisitations of deeply familiar cultural problems and tropes, most particularly—as Halberstam explores here—the gender and gender-bending of the Western and the complex relations among masculinity, violence, and American identity that the Western has screened (in both senses of the term) from its inception. If that web of often contradictory associations is the assumed background that made one short story in particular leap off the page, it is also part of the terrain of Larry McMurtry's Western fiction that made him and his partner Diana Ossana astute adapters of this short story for film. The Western on the screen has a distinctly larger life in cultural fantasy than it does on the page today, because film is our dominant art form, as Proulx observes in Michael Silverblatt's interview of her, published here for the first time. In his concluding essay, Calvin Bedient argues for the artistic truth of the film over the story. Adam Sonstegard and Alan Dale see the film, in contrast, as a compromise of the story's ambiguities.

Because of the film's dominance culturally as an artistic medium and the freighted matter of representing gay and lesbian lives at a time of ongoing political tension surrounding gay civil rights, the possible future of *Brokeback Mountain* is a continuing and open question. Has this film opened doors, changed hearts and minds, created the possibility for new kinds of cinema—even new ways of seeing and living social bonds? At the end of her essay, Halberstam raises some provocative, nonrhetorical questions, among them, "why does the spectacle of cowboy love entice us now, in this historical moment of U.S. supremacy?" The answers to this and similar questions *The Brokeback Book* raises will prove quite different over time. For one thing, as Dale argues in his essay, "the alleged achievements of ameliorist movies tend to fade with time," and perhaps those of *Brokeback Mountain* will also. Will the film come widely to be viewed, as James Morrison argues it is, as "something like the *Uncle Tom's Cabin* of Hollywood movies about gay experience"?

A related question—"What Ever Happened to Ennis del Mar?"—was raised in the title of an event in December 2009 at the Autry National Center for the American West in Los Angeles. The question wants to rescue Proulx's character from an Uncle Tom status, but more importantly, to rescue gay men and women from such tragic representations and to open up other possible futures. The panelists, including myself, never got around to answering that question, and not because it is a hypothetical one about a fictional character. That this was the inaugural event for the Autry's Out West series—created and organized by Hinton—which explores LGBT contributions to, and representations in, the American West, suggests how fiction and reality bleed into and remake each other. In a sense, so do the famous entwined shirts that Tom Gregory bought for charity and loaned to the Autry for display. Freeman's essay considers the huge investments in these vestments, as do Hinton's remarks in this volume, which he gave on the occasion of their installation. Representations and even the remains of a film production can open up what we know or think we know. The panelists could not answer the question "What Ever Happened to Ennis del Mar?" because it remains necessarily open and undecided. This openness to different possible futures may also describe the actual set of affairs for gay and lesbian lives at a time when we see both progress and backlash in the American West and in the United States on LGBT issues.

As one example of how western states are places of both retrenchment and innovative change with regard to gay civil rights, consider the state of Utah, whose Mormon citizens in large numbers financially supported the successful "Yes on Proposition 8" campaign in California to overturn the right for same-sex couples to marry there by amending its state constitution in 2008. ("Stay out of my state!" many liberal Californians felt, complicating the political valence surrounding states' rights.) Utah citizens had already amended their constitution to ban not just gay marriage but also any legal recognition of, or protections for, same-sex relationships such as civil unions or domestic partnerships (seventeen other states have similar amendments). Yet within what is a daunting political climate for Utah's gay citizens, fascinating coalitions are clearing paths to progress on a number of civil protections and rights—and not just for gay couples. New coalitions formed among disparate LGBT groups, and there has been unprecedented political dialogue among LGBT activists, conservative state legislators, and the Mormon leadership. Equality Utah, in the Common Ground Initiative (CGI), asked opponents of gay marriage to demonstrate that their stance on that issue is not antigay and that they truly support nondiscrimination in other arenas such as housing and health care for all citizens.

In her article in *The Nation* called, punningly, "What's Right with Utah," Lisa Duggan, a New Yorker who had spent a season in Salt Lake City, details the hopes for the CGI and its limited successes so far. In a political arena like Utah's, she states, "queer flamboyance and tough-minded seriousness have to coexist to get anything done." Charting the future and taking stock of the past, she writes, gay activists "should look to Salt Lake City for pointers instead of Boston and New York." Further complicating the picture of an easily stereotyped western state, and seeming to defy bans on gay marriage, a recent UCLA study found that among the five states with the highest percentage of same-sex spouses (those who claim they are "married" or "spouses" as opposed to "domestic partners" or "couples") are Utah and Wyoming (Gates 4).[3] Whether this is a gay version of western radicalism or of tradition is hard to determine. But within the conditions of Proulx's story and the world of the film, it is unimaginable.

Beth Loffreda recalls that when she wrote *Losing Matt Shepard*, she had noted that the typical impulses in the analysis of his murder "swung between characterizing Wyoming as utterly different—qualitatively more homophobic, more primitive, more violent and hate-filled than the rest of the nation—and Wyoming as 'just like everywhere else.' I thought, and still think," she writes, "that neither was right." The Wyoming she inhabits is now "a mundanely, fitfully contradictory place, a place where forgetfulness and remembrance, othering and embrace, commingle"— much like the West itself ("Scheduling Idealism" 159). When *Brokeback Mountain* came out, she heard that a group of students at the University of Wyoming had started a page on Facebook to decry the very idea of gay cowboys: "an impossibility, they claimed, since cowboys are irrefutably the apotheosis of American masculinity in all of its heterosexual splendor." The University of Wyoming's sports teams are all called the Cowboys, and Loffreda heard another report that students shouted "Brokeback cowboy" at a basketball game to any player on their team who missed a shot. *Brokeback Mountain*, "in all of its queer sympathy and beauty, provided a new lexicon and a new set of opportunities for the old poetics of homophobic expression" at the university (170). Yet Loffreda concludes with a different kind of observation: the heterosexual bar The Cowboy "got queered around the same time *Brokeback Mountain* queered the cowboy on a national level," when a friendly crowd came to watch a drag show. If regionalism, she writes, "traditionally has entailed a retreat from the differences and the complexities of the present into a mythic and monolithic past, then what we can see in Laramie is the inchoate beginnings of a new regionalism, a struggle between the nostalgic form of regional identity and a queer remaking of it." "The poetics are up for grabs," she concludes. "And that's a West that, while still volatile and unpredictable, is finally starting to grow as spacious as it should be" (170, 171). *Brokeback Mountain* straddles this growing spaciousness. Although set in the rural West, the story's and the film's embrace by metropolitan readers and viewers suggests a more porous exchange between here and there than usually imagined, one traditionally negotiated for eastern readers by the figure of the tenderfoot, the most famous being Owen Wister's narrator in *The Virginian* (1902), who says of Wyoming, "What world am I in? . . . Does this same planet hold Fifth Avenue?" (36).

A *Brokeback*-inspired cartoon appeared in *The New Yorker* shortly after the film, thus completing the cultural trajectory the magazine had launched when it published Proulx's story. It shows a presumably urban, gay couple in their bedroom (see figure 1).

"And what if I don't want to be Jack or Ennis?"

1. From story to cartoon in the same magazine. *The New Yorker*, December 26, 2005. © William Haefeli/Condé Nast Publications/www.cartoonbank.com.

Donning a cowboy hat and long underwear, one of the men tosses a cowboy hat to his partner, who's already in bed but at work on his laptop. The supine partner responds to the tease for role-playing by saying, "And what if I don't want to be Jack *or* Ennis?" It's a telling and complicated joke, not just about sexual positions. Coming so soon after the film's release in urban environments, the cartoon suggests how gay identity is shaped and limited by its representations, and how they travel. But more directly, with that laptop and the freedom to play cowboy, it sends up the divide between rural and urban gay lives and class experience in the United States, or rather the ease with which that distance seems to be crossed just by going to the movies.

This volume explores that divide but in no way overcomes it. There is increased interest in academic queer studies about rural and urban divides and interrelations, for which the response to *Brokeback Mountain* offers a kind of case study.[4] While the film premiered in New York, Los Angeles, and San Francisco, it also played in such places as Wyoming and El Paso, Texas, which made all the difference for Aguilera, who writes about his hometown. Along with an in-depth look at Proulx's art, Alex Hunt's essay explores rural experience and rodeo, while Tsika's essay about online responses to the film might suggest they are a kind of Rorschach test about urban and rural experience. Despite what Scott Herring describes as the "universalizing mass public spheres" that *Brokeback Mountain* inhabits, this film also complicates such a picture, opening up a space between its setting and its contemporary audiences: while some may find the film "a socially conscious 'issue' film that invites nothing but pure escapism" ("*Brokeback Mountain* Dossier" 93, 94), many contributors to Dave Cullen's forum on the film suggest just how hammered by reality—their own in relation to the film—many rural viewers are.

We might come to learn that the rural West is filled with as much tolerance as intolerance and is characterized as much by political and communal innovation and progressivism as it is by conservatism and long-standing antifederalism. The American West has long been a complicated, paradoxical region—America writ large. Those perched in urban centers often do not appreciate its subtleties and complexities or how parochial urban folk may seem from a rural perspective. Noah Tsika told me that when he saw the film in New York, among the many gay men who had dressed up as cowboys for the occasion, one was heard to complain on the way out of the theater, "I didn't realize they [Jack and Ennis] were going to be white trash!" One cannot underestimate the extent to which class is as important a consideration as gender, sexual orientation, and geographic location in understanding the range of viewers' responses to the film. It was important to Ang Lee, a master of creating whole cultural worlds—eighteenth-century England; Fairfield County, Connecticut, in the 1970s; a Taiwanese family and wedding banquet—to spend time in the West and to talk to westerners when he scouted for locations with Larry McMurtry. In an interview with Carlo Cavagna, Lee said he wanted a "realistic" West, "which is quite unfamiliar to the world's population, even to a lot of Americans I know from the cities." The mystery of what he calls conservative places, for him, is that they are filled with "nicer" people than one finds elsewhere: "I felt guilty that I was going to do a tough movie about them," he said. Their eccentricities, their tragic stories, their loneliness, wariness, and hospitality intrigued him—as did the wind, one of those aspects of western rural life unknown to those who have not lived there, but unavoidable to those who live with it. "They've got space and time," Ang Lee said. "They've got a lot of wind. Drives you crazy, constant wind. It's on the screen the whole time. . . . Just stand there for a year in the wind, and you'd go shoot yourself."

If it was important to Ang Lee to put the real West in the film, it is equally important to put *Brokeback Mountain* into the context of the literary and cinematic West. Groundbreaking as it is, the film is not without precedents. For his part, Ang Lee decidedly did not consider his film a Western in any traditional sense. But it is ineluctably read as one, just as the ranch hands Jack and Ennis do not consider themselves queer while their viewers claim them as "gay cowboys." Lee's distinction is an important one. *Brokeback Mountain* is not a conventional Western. Yet it is a Western to the same extent that *Thelma and Louise* (Ridley Scott, 1991) and Wister's *The Virginian* are—neither involves battles between cowboys and Indians but both are studies in gender difference within a nationalized landscape, which might be a broad description of Westerns. These and other Westerns merit brief discussion to explore some of the literary and cinematic contexts in which so innovative an avatar of the genre as *Brokeback Mountain* can seem groundbreaking while having precedent. In addition to the many films Halberstam canvasses in her essay, one could add *Shane* (George Stevens, 1953), with its barely concealed homoeroticism, and with Shane's advice to the young boy who adores him about how to grow up "straight." In the nineteenth-century literary West, among other examples that Chris Packard explores in *Queer Cowboys*, Bret Harte's stories "Tennessee's Partner" and "In the Tules" could be claimed as antecedents of Proulx's story. These are stories of otherwise inexplicable devotion between men. Tennessee's partner's devotion to him outlasts Tennessee's life, as he longs to meet him in the afterlife—even though Tennessee had run away for a time with his partner's wife. Harte's stories of male intimacy offer only that "there is an intuition of friendship that is nearly akin to love at first sight," as the narrator says in Harte's "In the Tules" about Martin

Morse's immediate captivation by Captain Jack, who leaves Morse's hand "warm and tingling from his sudden soft but expressive grasp, as if it had been a woman's" (152).

In the twentieth century, as Alan Weltzien demonstrates, Thomas Savage's much neglected 1967 novel, *The Power of the Dog*, for which Proulx wrote an afterword when it was republished in 2001, is a powerful pairing with "Brokeback Mountain." Both are concerned—as Wister's novel decidedly is not—with the actual *work* of ranching and with the corrosive consequences of internalized homophobia. Set in 1924 in Montana, Savage's novel depicts the unforgettable character Phil Burbank, who exhibits all of the repression of homosexual desire that Heath Ledger's portrayal of Ennis del Mar does—and a great deal more. Such internalized repression is the continuing thread of William Haywood Henderson's strangely beautiful, mournful, and narratively complex novel *Native*, published four years before "Brokeback Mountain." A twenty-three-year-old ranch foreman, Blue, is attracted to his ranch hand, Sam, but he cannot let himself realize the dream that haunts him of an Edenic domestic space for them in Wyoming's Wind River mountains after he and Sam are separately attacked and Sam is nearly killed by the same man for seeming queer. The novel's title refers to Blue's search for a securely inhabited place in which he can reconcile his love both for the West and for Sam, but it also refers to the third gay character in the novel, the Native American Gilbert, who has other, mystical ways—within the Two-Spirit tradition—of healing the exiled self.[5] (This character may have been inspired by Tom Spanbauer's 1991 novel *The Man Who Fell in Love with the Moon*.) That search for an "elsewhere," where one can invulnerably belong (one of the subjects in Freeman's essay) is a hallmark of these Western stories, particularly Proulx's, and is so brilliantly evoked in the final shot of Ang Lee's film, as the postcard of Brokeback Mountain returns to Ennis's closet and the viewer glimpses the outside world through the dark frame of his trailer's window.

The Virginian is an instructive contrast and companion to Proulx's story because of what its 1902 readers seem not to have recognized—though, as Proulx points out, some reviewers of Savage's novel did not recognize the subject either. Wister's novel is often cited as the "origin" of the popular Western, after the dime novel. Yet it little resembles so many formula Westerns on-screen, while barely concealing the central and tragic love between two men, the Virginian and his best friend Steve, the only one to know and call the Virginian by his given name, Jeff. That friendship is mirrored in the unnamed male narrator's reverential and physical attraction to the cowboy hero that is the psychosexual frame for his heroism and for his ultimate, sacrificial assimilation into the heterosexual marriage plot (see Handley 67–96). When he first met the Virginian, the narrator tells the reader, he saw him as a "slim young giant, more beautiful than pictures" and imagines, "Had I been the bride, I should have taken the giant, dust and all" (4). But since marriage is the only thing that might bring women into their lives and hence separate them, it's also the last thing either wants or can imagine: "Nothing's queer," the Virginian had said, "except marriage and lightning."

This wildly popular Western's first reading audience did not seem to recognize the deep well of same-sex desire at work in it, but a modern reader can readily see it: "his mind took one of those particular turns that made me love him," the narrator says at one point (63). One of the rich paradoxes of Proulx's "Brokeback Mountain" is that it is a story about suppression, hiding, and denial, and yet it is so open and revealing about what is usually encoded in the genre—indeed, in its revised form first published in *Close Range*, the story is framed entirely by Ennis's subjectivity rather than by any vaunted "objective" gaze that frames so many Westerns. Absent from Wister's 1902 Western, of course, is a quick fuck, which happens in *Brokeback Mountain* (as it does in the story). What a difference that makes for any assessment of the cultural significance and impact of this unexpectedly successful Hollywood film. *Brokeback Mountain* inserts into the culturally symbolic Western a literal sexual act at emotional odds with the genre's most recurring and violent gesture: a man penetrating a man with a bullet. And it does so with a nod to that tradition: after Jack takes Ennis's hand and puts it on his erection in their pup tent, the reaction is almost violent, and through a brief but elaborate choreography of aggressive ambivalence, Ennis gives in only by making Jack give it up. What had before seemed implicit in some nineteenth- and early twentieth-century literary examples like *The Virginian*—but also in twentieth-century film Westerns such as *Shane* or *Red River* (Howard Hawks, 1948)—is made not just explicit in *Brokeback*

Mountain but also irreducibly personal, which is to say primarily character-specific as opposed to archetypal or formulaic. This specificity may explain why so many viewers have claimed in the blogosphere that they cannot shake these characters; for the same reason, Proulx claimed she was reluctant to face them eight years after she created them.

In psychoanalytic terms, one might say that instead of elevating the phallus (the sign of patriarchal power) over the penis in the form of a gun, as innumerable Westerns have done, *Brokeback Mountain* reveals and levels that cultural metaphor, as when Proulx's character Jack gasps, "Gun's goin' *off*" during their first sexual encounter. That line is not in the film, whose visual generic conventions could have rendered it only as an inflated joke.

While the homoerotic content of *The Virginian* was lost on most of its readers, and the sexual content of *Brokeback Mountain* was impossible to ignore and became the focus of the film for those who complained there was not enough or too much, women and guns became the distracting locus of *Thelma and Louise*. Perhaps the reason Thelma (Geena Davis) and Louise (Susan Sarandon) landed on the cover of *Time* magazine is that they used literal guns against phallic masculine power. In contrast, Jack and Ennis, like the gay man's castrated and murdered body that Ennis's father showed him, were lambs before either slaughter or internalized, soul-crippling fear—or perhaps both, given the ambiguous circumstances of Jack's death. The gay-male version of *Thelma and Louise*—two men in potentially violent rebellion against a heterosexual world—has yet to hit the megaplex.[6] *Brokeback Mountain* was a greater cultural phenomenon than *Thelma and Louise*, but when one compares the degrees or qualities of shock that these two revisionist Westerns produced, perhaps the greater outcry, including from feminists, was over women behaving as a violent law unto themselves. Two guys getting off in a pup tent were, in contrast, most notably fodder for repeated jokes on late-night talk shows.

It is not difficult to understand both the similarities and divergences between the responses to *Thelma and Louise* and *Brokeback Mountain*: both are explained by a culture's privileging of masculine authority or power *within* the structure of heterosexuality. *Thelma and Louise* explicitly regenders violence by portraying women as sympathetic outlaws and *Brokeback Mountain* substitutes the homo for the hetero. The former deviation says that neither the male nor the heterosexual relation is of chief importance; the latter is less shocking by half because it still participates within a masculine code in which straight men exert power through violence. Consternation over the sympathetic rendering of a woman's murder of a rapist was one common response to *Thelma and Louise*. A homophobic trivialization through repetitive jokes was a common response to *Brokeback Mountain*, a film in which at least one man is murdered for being gay.

To see the difference that gender makes in response to these films another way: one might reasonably imagine that some American heterosexual males of a certain conservative inclination could enjoy both *Butch Cassidy and the Sundance Kid* (George Roy Hill, 1969) and the erotic lesbian Western *Desert Hearts* (Donna Deitch, 1985) but respond to the homosexual love story of *Brokeback Mountain* and the denigration of men in *Thelma and Louise* with something between indifference and contempt. Without having seen *Brokeback Mountain* and insisting he would not, Tony Curtis, one of the most famous cross-dressers in Hollywood film history, said on Fox News, "This picture is not as important as we make it. It's nothing unique. The only thing unique about it is they put it on the screen. And they make 'em cowboys." He then lent a certain cultural authority to his point but added little clarity by saying, "Howard Hughes and John Wayne wouldn't like it" (Hirsen).

"They make *'em* cowboys"; "they put *it* on the screen": Tony Curtis's sense of the only unique *thing* in the film falls on an indeterminate "it" (man-on-man action?) and an ambiguous "'em." *Them* cannot mean Proulx's Ennis del Mar and Jack Twist; it probably means "gay men": gay men appear uniquely as cowboys in this film, but gay men in movies is nothing new. Two online journalists tried to resolve Curtis's ambiguous pronoun with interpolations: "they made 'em [gay] cowboys" (Jack and Ennis used to be straight?) and "they made [the gay male lovers] cowboys" (Jack and Ennis weren't cowboys in a previous film?). Neither clarifies Curtis's point. The ambiguous pronoun is very much to the point and raises interesting questions: did the film, which adds to the story key scenes set during Thanksgiving and the Fourth of July, masculinize and Americanize homosexuality, or did it queer the Western and the mythic nation it often stands in for? Or both?

One of the most distinctive differences between Proulx's story and the film's screenplay is the far greater extent to which the film depicts the married, domestic lives of Jack and Ennis in contrast to their outdoor idylls together. At first glance *Brokeback Mountain* offers a twentieth-century version of the nineteenth-century notion of women's and men's "separate spheres," an ideological and social buttress of Manifest Destiny, as Amy Kaplan has argued. But here, the public and domestic spheres for action become the spheres of play and work, of men drinking in the mountains and women stuck with dishes and kids. As Paula Cole's sardonic post-Western feminist says in her song "Where Have All the Cowboys Gone?": "I'll go do the dishes / You go grab a beer."

But there's a "twist" in the film. Almost entirely absent in the story but prevalent in the film is a regendering of—or rather a gender confusion around—domestic roles, even in the masculine wild. In scenes that Susan McCabe describes in her essay in this book as the insertion of the maternal into male melodrama, Jack and Ennis take turns cooking and doing laundry while the other is the shepherd; Ennis recoils both from Jack's nursing and his desire for intimacy but enters, like a shy bride, the pup tent where Jack is reclined in his domain. In one scene of marital domesticity, Jack Twist is more a traditional mother than his wife is: as she does the business accounting, he once again raises his concern about their son's schooling. An entire essay remains to be written on carving Thanksgiving turkey in this film: who does it, why, and with what instruments. Few films have ever so subtly and repeatedly displayed the fluid performance of gender beneath its naturalization and nationalization. The queerness of same-sex domestic scenes in *The Virginian* is similarly disguised by a naturalizing western setting and cloaked within a denigration of the New Woman. *Brokeback Mountain* recognizes separate spheres, but they are not women's and men's. They are heterosexual and homosexual—and the homosexual is no more at home in the wild than he is at home (whether as a child or as a husband in a heterosexual marriage). No amount of Thanksgivings or Fourth of July fireworks or cowboy clothing can make a home, any more than those trappings and settings can make heterosexuality natural rather than an artificial performance of power arbitrarily held.

Some feminist and gay critics object to *Brokeback Mountain*, arguing that it returns Ennis to heteronormativity as he promises to go to his daughter's wedding, that it represents a wife's borderline rape as the consequence of marrying a closet case, or that it disparages women as domestic traps. Yet one of the largest audiences for *Brokeback Mountain* was heterosexual women, and if the number of those who, after seeing it, came to question their marriages or their homophobia is an indicator, the film's popularity among women was not simply a product of false consciousness. One thread in the "Ultimate Brokeback Forum" is by and for straight women and attests to the film's extraordinary, heartfelt, and still ongoing impact among many women. The marketers of the film knew it had the potential to reach this audience and pitched it to them, but the intensity and extent of the responses suggest that something more than marketing notions about women and romantic melodrama were and are at work. If the evidence suggests anything, it is that the film's gaze is certainly not just a straight man's, neither is it simply a woman's, and perhaps less certainly, neither is it a queer perspective. As in *Thelma and Louise*, the film's cultural divide mimics its visual divide between the national *as* the heterosexual domestic and a natural landscape that seems to offer a dream of escape from cultural imperatives. But since that landscape is iconic by virtue of its many representations in Westerns, it only returns the dream to the national imaginary, with the trace of a failed utopian desire to imagine away the nation that surrounds the outlaw pairs of Thelma and Louise, and Jack and Ennis. One might call this the nostalgic sublime: a seemingly natural nostalgia for something beyond the social from which it is derived. The sense of tragic failure in not finding a landscape of escape endlessly circulates pain and pleasure for the viewer. The distance between hope and fear is not bridged; it feeds on itself. Such innovative avatars of the Western as *Thelma and Louise* and *Brokeback Mountain* do not so much revise the genre as they expose—by deliberately and subtly bringing it out into the wide open—the cultural work regarding gender, power, and the national imaginary that the American Western has long framed.

I call this version of the sublime "nostalgic" because of the ambiguous and ambivalent relation to history that Western films often assume. *Brokeback Mountain* begins in 1963—before the riot at the Stonewall bar in New York City in 1969 that has come, accurately or not, to be marked as the birth of the gay civil rights movement—and in the twenty years in which it takes place, the film seems to exist outside of any kind of gay history, as Sonstegard observes. Some viewers, as Holleran notes in his essay, ask the hypothetical: why didn't Jack and Ennis just move to San Francisco?—which is akin to asking, why didn't they make another movie? The western rural setting fosters, as it often has, two kinds of perpetual pasts: an ongoing social and national past that feels artificial, as something staged in the cause of heterosexual role-playing (the costumes, wigs, makeup, and set designs in the films work to great effect in this regard); and the irretrievable, sublime past of an unviolated natural landscape. *Thelma and Louise* ends with an uneasy suspension between the two, as their tail-finned retro convertible is suspended over the abyss of the most ancient of visible scars in North America, the Grand Canyon—the sublime emblem in the film of the divides between nation and nature, gender and heterosexuality, the cultural imaginary and the limits of history. "We don't live in that kind of world," Louise says at one point to Thelma. As they drive through their last and most nationally iconic landscape, the one most seemingly devoid of people and most promisingly free, Thelma says to Louise, "I've never felt so awake," an echo, possibly, of the naturalist ending of Kate Chopin's 1899 feminist novel *The Awakening*, as the heroine Edna Pontellier swims into the Gulf of Mexico, beyond the continent, where she presumably drowns. Proulx's "Brokeback Mountain" ends with a description of Ennis sleeping, dreaming, and waking—alternating between a blunt sense of Jack's loss and the "joy" of his memory—as the "open space between what he knew and what he tried to believe" (283).

The ambiguity of Proulx's ending speaks to one of the central interpretive ambiguities in the film, which contributors to this volume see in different ways. The central dilemma of interpretation in the film concerns Jack Twist's death: Was it murder with a tire iron? Was he killed for being queer? Or was it a roadside accident? The film risks resolving the decided ambiguity of Proulx's story in this regard because of its use of what look like flashbacks, as Daniel Mendelsohn argues they are, as opposed to what they could also be, flashes in Ennis's mind, which is how Mun-Hou Lo reads the scene. Many viewers resolve the ambiguity, as does Ennis in the story, and argue that he was killed. Others have put the question to Proulx for her to resolve, which she refuses to do. Ang Lee and Anne Hathaway, who plays Jack's widow, Lureen, agreed to keep secret their own interpretations, according to the actor Graham Beckel, who plays her father, L. D. Newsome (personal interview). The decided ambiguity is not a question of whether Ennis is "merely" paranoid *or* whether the world is in fact that brutal. After, all, we do know that Ennis's father took him when he was a boy to see the savagely murdered body of a homosexual man. Lesson learned: men who love men have violent enemies, and the enemies may be their own fathers (Ennis suggests his father may have been the murderer).[7]

That knowledge, however, is of a kind different from what Ennis experiences after he hears, in Proulx's story, Lureen's narrative of Jack's death as an accident. As he is hearing it, he at first thinks, "No . . . they got him with the tire iron." But then, as the "huge sadness of the northern plains rolled down on him . . . [h]e didn't know which way it was, the tire iron or a real accident, blood choking down Jack's throat and nobody to turn him over. Under the wind drone he heard steel slamming off bone, the hollow chatter of a settling tire rim" (278). Notice how *feeling* determines what can be known rather than the reverse: paranoia leads him at first to contradict the "knowledge" being passed on to him, but then, in the "huge sadness" of the personified wind, he does not know one thing from another as true or false, and his senses settle briefly on the cruel indifference of an accident. It is only later that his aesthetic perception—his having turned wind into steel—becomes, through another memory, a form of traumatic knowledge whose truth lies in the real effects of actual trauma rather than in the unknowable, specific facts and circumstances of Jack's death. He meets Jack's father, who tells him that Jack was going to set up a ranch with another man after splitting with his wife. Immediately Proulx writes, "So now he *knew* it had been the tire iron" (280; emphasis added). The line subtly recalls what Ennis had last said to Jack (in both the story and the film) regarding his sexual infidelities: "What I don't know . . . all them things I don't know could get you killed if I should come to know them" (275). Now he perceives an infidelity worse than Jack's tricks in Mexico: the "knowledge" that he had been replaced in their dream of a ranch together. In both instances, feeling shapes but cannot govern the oscillation between knowing and not knowing, which, like the question of "truth" and "falsehood," is nondualistic and *intimately beside* the emotional point.[8]

This interpretive ambiguity is instructive about the very history of gay civil rights that feels so outside of the film's diegesis, particularly at this historical moment, a time of both political progress and regress since the film came out. One of the tensions in the response to the film is whether this is (or was marketed as) a specifically gay love story or a universal one, which David Leavitt, Daniel Mendelsohn, and James Schamus discuss in their chapters. This either/or approach to *Brokeback Mountain* is an interesting mirror image of the question about gay and lesbian rights being "special" rights, as opponents of gay rights often spin it, or "universal" rights, as liberals claim. Yet, as Morrison argues in this volume, that sort of tension is enacted whenever a minority is embraced or defended by a set of "universal" majoritarian values; there is, Morrison writes, always an "inextricability of regressive and progressive claims in debates concerning minorities' civil rights waged in majoritarian public spheres." Not just viewers in the straight audience, but many in the gay audience too, may perhaps *want* to believe Jack was killed, precisely to bolster the sympathies that make an appeal to universal rights all the more compelling. Yet the paradox of universal rights is that they should not need either pity or passionate sympathy to make them universal. If they are universal, we should know them without having to feel anything particularly about those rights—or they should exist institutionally without people having to close the gap in their own hearts and minds between, as Proulx writes about Ennis, "what he knew and what he tried to believe," or in this context, between what citizens believe about homosexuality and what they ought to know about the meaning of civil equality and the lives of gay citizens. ("In my church we don't believe in homosexuals," Tony Kushner's Mormon character Harper Pitt says to the homosexual Prior Walter in *Angels in America*. Prior responds, "In my church we don't believe in Mormons" [38].) The instructiveness of Ennis's case lies in the possibility that what he thought he "knew" might only be a projection of what he once felt toward Jack ("all them things I don't know could get you killed if I should come to know them") and that what he "tried to believe" might be what he already knows is not true and will not happen: the future he could not bring himself fully to imagine, let alone have, with Jack.

Much has happened in gay cultural and political history since *Brokeback Mountain* arrived at the multiplex. Changes seem both swift and slow—in the first half hour of Ang Lee's film, in Proulx's short story, and in the long view of history. This book points to the multiple pasts and futures that *Brokeback Mountain* still straddles. My interest in putting together *The Brokeback Book* is in different kinds of "open space" from the one Ennis is left to live with, though they are not unrelated to it: the yet open spaces between the film *Brokeback Mountain* and its cultural reception and significance, and the open spaces between the past and the future that Proulx's story and Ang Lee's film so artfully challenge us to bridge.

Notes

1. The writer's moniker is "bluehorse." Not included in that book, one contributor to the forum claimed she had seen the film fifty times and that she did not know how to stop.

2. According to boxofficemojo.com, *The Birdcage* is the top-grossing gay-themed film, followed by *Interview with a Vampire* (which one might well argue does not fit the category) and *Brokeback Mountain*.

3. The states with a higher percentage of same-sex spouses than Utah and Wyoming are Massachusetts (first), Vermont (second), and Hawaii (third).

4. See Scott Herring's *Another Country: Queer Anti-Urbanism* for a reorienting of queer studies away from the metropolis.

5. While introducing a screening of the documentary *Two Spirits* on June 28, 2010, Gregory Hinton remarked, "Born in rural communities, many of us feel forced to leave our families behind to move to the city in search of identity, companionship, and safety. That said, happily, not everyone leaves. And some of us return."

6. Gregg Araki's *The Living End* (1992) could be construed as just this sort of film, but it did not receive widespread distribution beyond the art house and gay and lesbian film festival circuit.

7. Violence haunts this film far more than it does in many six-gun Westerns, a violence not of frontier life but of the heterosexual family when its domestic codes are broken. Graham Beckel also told me that many straight male friends of his could not comprehend why his character let Jack get away with berating

him—his father-in-law and purse string—at the dinner table, and so they hypothesized that, in the end, Beckel's character indeed got his retribution, with the tire iron (personal interview).

8. The terms of my observations here are indebted to Eve Kosofsky Sedgwick in her book *Touching Feeling*.

Part 1 } Gay or Universal Story?

Initial Debates and Cultural Contexts

1 } Men in Love

Is *Brokeback Mountain* a Gay Film?

DAVID LEAVITT

Big love, in stories about men, tends to be a cheat, a lost cause, or a chimera. In *Brokeback Mountain*—Ang Lee's moving, operatic film adaptation of Annie Proulx's story—it's exactly what the tagline for the film says: a force of nature. Herding sheep just above the tree line on a Wyoming mountain, two dirt-poor cowboys find themselves suddenly caught up in a passion for each other that they have no idea how to name, much less cope with. Neither thinks of himself as "queer." On the contrary, the mountain itself gets both the credit and the blame for the affair that over the next twenty years will endow their lives with an intermittent grandeur, even as in other ways it drags them to the ground.

Is *Brokeback Mountain*, as it's been touted, Hollywood's first gay love story? The answer—in a very positive sense, I think—is yes to the love story, no to the gay. Make no mistake: the film is as frank in its portrayal of sex between men as in its use of old-fashioned romance movie conventions. Its stars are unabashedly glamorous. The big-eyed Jake Gyllenhaal is a far cry from Proulx's small, bucktoothed Jack Twist, just as the blond, square-jawed Heath Ledger is nothing like her Ennis del Mar, "scruffy and a little cave-chested." Yet, even if, in their tailored jeans and ironed plaid shirts, Gyllenhaal and Ledger sometimes look more like Wrangler models than teenagers too poor to buy a new pair of boots, the film neither feels synthetic (in the manner of the abysmal *Making Love*) nor silly (in the manner of gay porn). On the contrary, his stars' outsize screen presence provides Lee with a means of bringing to vivid cinematic life what is in essence a paean to masculinity.

And masculine the film is. Ledger's astonishing performance reveals an unsuspected vein of tenderness in a character more likely to express emotion through violence than words. His Ennis del Mar is as mono-lithic as the mountainscape in which—with the same swiftness, brutality, and precision that he exhibits in shooting an elk—he fucks Jack Twist for the first time. ("Gun's goin' off," Jack grunts in response—in the story, not the movie.) Ennis's surprise at the affair—at its inconvenience as much as at its intensity—reflects a fundamental humbleness that keeps butting up against Jack's willingness to take risks. It's Jack who proposes, over and over, that they start up a ranch together, a plan Ennis counters with pragmatism (not to mention fear), even after his wife, Alma, divorces him. Instead Ennis limits the relationship to fishing and hunting trips two or three times a year. It's as if he believes they don't deserve better.

As for Jack, the same cockiness that makes him dream of a "sweet life" with Ennis also leads him to pursue sex with other men, despite his own marriage—something Ennis never contemplates. In a key scene, Jack, disappointed at learning that, even after his divorce, Ennis has no intention of making a life with him, drives to a louche simulacrum of Juárez, where he picks up a hustler and disappears with him into the literal darkness of a back alley. The scene is unsettling because it pres-ents such a stark contrast to Jack and Ennis's heady, exalted mountain-top lovemaking. For just a few seconds, we get a glimpse of the urban nightscape that was the locus of the very gay movies that might have been playing, in big cities, at the moment when the scene takes place—movies like *Nighthawks* and *Taxi zum Klo*, in which sexual profligacy is at once celebrated as a form of liberation and mourned as a pallid substitute for meaningful connection.

It goes without saying that *Brokeback Mountain* is an entirely different kind of film. Perhaps it takes a woman to create a tale in which two men experience sex and love as a single thunderbolt, welding them together for life; certainly Proulx's story is a far cry from such canonical gay novels as Edmund White's *The Farewell Symphony* or Alan Hollinghurst's *The Swimming Pool Library*, which poeticize urban promiscuity and sexual adventuring. Proulx, by contrast, exalts coupledom by linking it to nature. Her narration, with its echoes of Western genre fiction, is knobby and elliptical, driven by an engine as unpredictable as the one that runs Jack Twist's troublesome truck, with the result that it often backs into scenes that a more conventional writer would place front and center.

Though *Brokeback Mountain* may have the sheen of a Hollywood romance, it is anything but conventional. True, screenwriters Larry McMurtry and Diana Ossana have ironed out Proulx's kinks, but they haven't eliminated her eccentricities; instead, they've found a cinematic parallel in their appropriation of Hollywood conventions of masculinity. This is particularly the case in the last half of the film, which alternates scenes of quotidian domestic grief (and the rare emotional triumph) with the trips that Jack and Ennis make together into the mountains— trips during which, as they age, sex takes a back seat to bickering and what might best be described as a kind of conjugal ease. What both men want, it becomes clear, is what Ennis is afraid to let them have: the steadiness of each other's companionship. By the end, Ledger's Ennis has crow's feet, while Gyllenhaal's Jack has sprouted a prosthetic paunch and a heavy mustache. The result is a defense of gay marriage made all the more eloquent by its evasion of the banalities implied in the word "gay."

Indeed, with the one exception of the scene in Juárez, nothing in *Brokeback Mountain* cries "gay." Neither of the heroes eschews sex with women; instead, they simply assert that they prefer sex with each other. At one point in the story, Ennis asks Jack, "This happen a other people?" and Jack answers, "It don't happen in Wyomin' and if it does I don't know what they do, maybe go to Denver." Interestingly, McMurtry and Ossana leave this lone mention of possible urban refuge out of the movie, the point of which seems to be less to subvert the conventions of male bonding than to extend them. "Lover" isn't a word Ennis and Jack ever utter. Instead they call each other "friend." When they kiss, their teeth hit. Respect for some burdensome ideal of masculine struggle underlies and at the same time undercuts their ability to love each other: an idea that Ledger in particular brings home by investing his performance with the deadpan, reticent tenderness of Hollywood Western stars from the 1950s. His stoicism drives the movie, and nowhere more movingly than when he utters its signature line: "If you can't fix it you've got to stand it."

Does the fact that none of the principals involved in *Brokeback Mountain* is openly gay have anything to do with the film's happy resistance to the stale clichés of gay cinema? Perhaps. In any case, McMurtry, Ossana, and Lee deserve as much credit for their tenacity (it took them seven years to get the movie made) as for the skill with which they've translated Proulx's spare, bleak story into a film with an epic sweep that nonetheless manages to be affectingly idiosyncratic in its portrayal of two men in love. In the end, *Brokeback Mountain* is less the story of a love that dares not speak its name than of one that doesn't know how to speak its name, and is somehow more eloquent for its lack of vocabulary. Ascending from plains where they lead lives of drudgery and routine humiliation, Ennis and Jack become the unwitting heroes of a story they haven't a clue how to tell. The world breaks their backs, but in this brave film, they're as iconic as the mountain.

2 } **An Affair to Remember**

DANIEL MENDELSOHN

Brokeback Mountain—the highly praised new movie as well as the short story by Annie Proulx on which the picture is faithfully based—is a tale about two homosexual men. Two gay men. To some people it will seem strange to say this; to some other people, it will seem strange to have to say it. Strange to say it, because the story is, as everyone now knows, about two young Wyoming ranch hands who fall in love as teenagers in 1963 and continue their tortured affair, furtively, over the next twenty years. And as everyone also knows, when most people hear the words "two homosexual men" or "gay," the image that comes to mind is not likely to be one of rugged young cowboys who shoot elk and ride broncos for fun.

Two homosexual men: it is strange to have to say it just now because the distinct emphasis of so much that has been said about the movie—in commercial advertising as well as in the adulatory reviews—has been that the story told in *Brokeback Mountain* is not, in fact, a gay story, but a sweeping romantic epic with "universal" appeal. The lengths to which reviewers from all over the country, representing publications of various ideological shadings, have gone in order to diminish the specifically gay element is striking, as a random sampling of the reviews collected on the film's official Web site makes clear. The *Wall Street Journal*'s critic Joe Morgenstern asserted that "love stories come and go, but this one stays with you—not because both lovers are men, but because their story is so full of life and longing, and true romance." The *Los Angeles Times*'s Kenneth Turan declared the film to be "a deeply felt, emotional love story that deals with the uncharted, mysterious ways of the human heart just as so many mainstream films have before it. The two lovers here just happen to be men."

Indeed, a month after the movie's release most of the reviews were resisting, indignantly, the popular tendency to refer to it as "the gay cowboy movie." "It is much more than that glib description implies," Colin Covert of the *Minneapolis Star Tribune* sniffed. "This is a human story." This particular rhetorical emphasis figures prominently in the advertising for the film, which in quoting such passages reflects the producer's understandable desire that *Brokeback Mountain* not be seen as something for a niche market but as a story with broad appeal, whatever the particulars of its time, place, and personalities. (The words "gay" and "homosexual" are never used of the film's two main characters in the forty-nine-page press kit distributed by the filmmakers to critics.) "One movie is connecting with the heart of America," one ad that was part of the publicity campaigns declared; the ad showed the star Heath Ledger, without his costar, Jake Gyllenhaal, grinning in a cowboy hat. A television ad that ran immediately after the 2006 Golden Globe awards showed clips of the male leads embracing their wives, but not each other.

The reluctance to be explicit about the film's themes and content was evident at the Golden Globes themselves, where the film took the major awards: for best movie drama, best director, and best screenplay. When a short montage of clips from the film was screened, it was described as "a story of monumental conflict"; later, the actor reading the names of nominees for best actor in a movie drama described Heath Ledger's character as "a cowboy caught up in a complicated love." After Ang Lee received the award he was quoted as saying, "This is a universal story. I just wanted to make a love story."

Because I am as admiring as almost everyone else of the film's many excellences, it seems to me necessary to counter this special emphasis in the way the film is being promoted and received. For to see *Brokeback Mountain* as a love story, or even as a film about universal human emotions, is to misconstrue it very seriously—and in so doing inevitably to diminish its real achievement.

Both narratively and visually, *Brokeback Mountain* is a tragedy about the specifically gay phenomenon of the closet—about the disastrous emotional and moral consequences of erotic self-repression and of the social intolerance that first causes and then exacerbates it. What love story there is occurs early on in the film, and briefly: a summer's idyll herding sheep on a Wyoming mountain, during which two lonely youths, taciturn Ennis and high-spirited Jack, fall into bed, and then in love, with each other. The sole visual representation of their happiness in love is a single brief shot of the two shirtless youths horsing around in the grass. That shot is eerily—and significantly—silent, voiceless: it turns out that what we are seeing is what the boys' disgusted boss is seeing through his binoculars as he spies on them.

After that—because their love for each other can't be fitted into the lives they think they must lead—misery pursues and finally destroys the two men and everyone with whom they come in contact with the relentless thoroughness you associate with Greek tragedy. By the end of the drama, indeed, whole families have been laid waste. Ennis's marriage to a conventional, sweet-natured girl disintegrates, savaging her simple illusions and spoiling the home life of his two daughters; Jack's nervy young wife, Lureen, devolves into a brittle shrew, her increasingly elaborate and artificial hairstyles serving as a visual marker of the ever-growing mendacity that underlies the couple's relationship. Even an appealing young waitress, with whom Ennis after his divorce has a flirtation (an episode much amplified from a bare mention in the original story), is made miserable by her brief contact with a man who is as enigmatic to himself (as we know but she does not) as he is to her. If Jack and Ennis are tainted, it's not because they're gay but because they pretend not to be; it's the lie that poisons everyone they touch.

As for Jack and Ennis themselves, the brief and infrequent vacations that they are able to take together as the years pass—"fishing trips" on which, as Ennis's wife points out, still choking on her bitterness years after their marriage fails, no fish were ever caught—are haunted, increasingly, by the specter of the happier life they might have had, had they been able to live together. Their final vacation together (before Jack is beaten to death in what is clearly represented, in a flashback, as a roadside gay-bashing incident) is poisoned by mutual recriminations. "I wish I knew how to quit you," the now nearly middle-aged Jack tearfully cries out, humiliated by years of having to seek sexual solace in the arms of Mexican hustlers. "It's because of you that I'm like this—nothing, nobody," the dirt-poor Ennis sobs as he collapses in the dust. What Ennis means, of course, is that he's "nothing" because loving Jack has forced him to be aware of real passion that has no outlet, aware of a sexual nature that he cannot ignore but which neither his background nor his circumstances have equipped him to make part of his life. Again and again over the years, he rebuffs Jack's offers to try living together and running "a little cow-and-calf operation" somewhere: he is hobbled by his inability even to imagine what a life of happiness might look like.

One reason he can't bring himself to envision such a life with his lover is a grisly childhood memory, presented in flashback, of being taken at the age of eight by his father to see the body of a gay rancher who'd been tortured and beaten to death—a scene that prefigures the scene of Jack's death. This explicit reference to childhood trauma suggests another quite powerful reason why *Brokeback* must be seen as a specifically gay tragedy. In another review that decried the use of the term "gay cowboy movie" ("a cruel simplification"), the *Chicago Sun-Times*'s critic Roger Ebert wrote with ostensible compassion about the dilemma of Jack and Ennis, declaring that "their tragedy is universal. It could be about two women, or lovers from different religious or ethnic groups— any 'forbidden' love" ("Forbidden Love" NC30). This is well-meaning but very seriously misguided. The tragedy of heterosexual lovers from different religious or ethnic groups is, essentially, a social tragedy; as we watch it unfold, we are meant to be outraged by the irrationality of social strictures that prevent the two from loving each other, strictures that the lovers themselves may legitimately rail against and despise.

But those lovers, however star-crossed, never despise *themselves*. As *Brokeback* makes so eloquently clear, the tragedy of gay lovers like Ennis and Jack is only secondarily a social tragedy. Their tragedy, which starts well before the lovers ever meet, is primarily a psychological tragedy, a tragedy of psyches scarred from the very first stirrings of an erotic desire that, beginning in earliest childhood, in the bosom of their families (as Ennis's grim flashback is meant to remind us), the world around them represents as unhealthy, hateful, and deadly. Romeo and Juliet (and we) may hate the outside world, the Capulets and Montagues, may hate Verona; but because they learn to hate homosexuality so early on, young people with homosexual impulses more often than not grow up hating *themselves*—they believe that there's something wrong with themselves long before they can understand that there's something wrong with society. This is the truth that Heath Ledger, who plays Ennis, clearly understands—"Fear was instilled in him at an early age, and so the way he loved disgusted him," the actor has said—and that is so brilliantly conveyed by his deservedly acclaimed performance. On screen, Ennis's self-repression and self-loathing are given startling physical form: the awkward, almost hobbled quality of his gait, the constricted gestures, the way in which he barely opens his mouth when he talks all speak eloquently of a man who is tormented simply by being in his own body—by being himself.

So much, at any rate, for the movie being a love story like any other, even a tragic one. To their great credit, the makers of *Brokeback Mountain*—the writers Larry McMurtry and Diana Ossana, the director Ang Lee—seem, despite the official rhetoric, to have been aware that they were making a movie specifically about the closet. The themes of repression, containment, the emptiness of unrealized lives—all ending in the "nothingness" to which Ennis achingly refers—are consistently expressed in the film, appropriately enough, by the use of space; given the film's homoerotic themes, this device is particularly meaningful. The two lovers are only happy in the wide, unfenced outdoors, where exuberant shots of enormous skies and vast landscapes suggest, tellingly, that what the men feel for each other is indeed "natural." By contrast, whenever we see Jack and Ennis indoors, in the scenes that show the failure of their domestic and social lives, they look cramped and claustrophobic. (Ennis in particular is often seen in reflection, in various mirrors: a figure imprisoned in a tiny frame.) There's a sequence in which we see Ennis in Wyoming, and then Jack in Texas, anxiously preparing for one of their "fishing trips," and both men, as they pack for their trip—Ennis nearly leaves behind his fishing tackle, the unused and increasingly unpersuasive prop for the fiction he tells his wife each time he goes away with Jack—pace back and forth in their respective houses like caged animals.

The climax of these visual contrasts is also the emotional climax of the film, which takes place in two consecutive scenes, both of which prominently feature closets—actual closets. In the first, a grief-stricken Ennis, now in his late thirties, visits Jack's childhood home, where in the tiny closet of Jack's almost bare room he discovers two shirts: his and Jack's, the clothes they'd worn during their summer on Brokeback Mountain, Ennis's protectively encased within Jack's. (At the end of that summer, Ennis had thought he'd lost the shirt; only now do we realize that Jack had stolen it for this purpose.) The image—which is taken directly from Proulx's story—of the two shirts hidden in the closet, preserved in an embrace which the men who wore them could never fully enjoy, stands as the poignant visual symbol of the story's tragedy. Made aware too late of how greatly he was loved, of the extent of his loss, Ennis stands in the tiny windowless space, caressing the shirts and weeping wordlessly.

In the scene that follows, another misplaced piece of clothing leads to a similar scene of tragic realization. Now middle-aged and living alone in a battered, sparsely furnished trailer (a setting with which Proulx's story begins, the tale itself unfolding as a long flashback), Ennis receives a visit from his grown daughter, who announces that she's engaged to be married. "Does he love you?" the blighted father protectively demands, as if realizing too late that this is all that matters. After the girl leaves, Ennis realizes she's left her sweater behind, and when he opens his little closet door to store it there, we see that he's hung the two shirts from their first summer (Jack's now encased protectively within Ennis's) on the inside of the closet door, below a tattered postcard of Brokeback Mountain. Just as we see this, the camera pulls back to allow us a slightly wider view, which reveals a little window next to the closet, a rectangular frame that affords a glimpse of a field of yellow flowers and the mountains and sky. The juxtaposition of the two spaces—the cramped and airless closet, the window with its unlimited vistas beyond—efficiently but wrenchingly suggests the man's tragedy: the life he has lived, the life that might have been. His eyes filling with tears, Ennis looks at his closet and says, "Jack, I swear . . ." But he never completes his sentence, just as he never completed his life.

One of the most tortured, but by no means untypical, attempts to suggest that the tragic heroes of *Brokeback Mountain* aren't "really" gay appeared in, of all places, the *San Francisco Chronicle*, where the critic Mick LaSalle argues that the film is

about two men who are in love, and it makes no sense. It makes no sense in terms of who they are, where they are, how they live and how they see themselves. It makes no sense in terms of what they do for a living or how they would probably vote in a national election. . . .

The situation carries a lot of emotional power, largely because it's so specific and yet undefined. The two guys—cowboys—are in love with each other, but we don't ever quite know if they're in love with each other because they're gay, or if they're gay because they're in love with each other.

It's possible that if these fellows had never met, one or both would have gone through life straight.

The statement suggests what's wrong with so much of the criticism of the film, however well-meaning it is. It seems clear by now that *Brokeback* has received the attention it's been getting, from critics and audiences alike, at least partly because it seems on its surface to make normal what many people think of as gay experience—bringing it into the familiar "heart of America." (Had this been the story of, say, the love between two closeted interior decorators living in New York City in the 1970s, you suspect that there wouldn't be full-page ads in the major papers trumpeting its "universal" themes.) But the fact that this film's main characters look like cowboys doesn't make them, or their story, any less gay. Criticisms like LaSalle's, and those of the many other critics trying to persuade you that *Brokeback* isn't "really" gay, that Jack and Ennis's love "makes no sense" because they're Wyoming ranch hands who are likely to vote Republican, only work if you believe that being gay means being some specific, essential thing—having a certain look, or lifestyle (urban, say), or politics; that it's anything other than the bare fact of being erotically attached primarily to members of your own sex.

Indeed, the point that gay people have been trying to make for years— a point that *Brokeback* could be making now, if so many of its vocal admirers would listen to what it's saying—is that there's no such thing as a typical gay person, a strangely different-seeming person with whom Jack Twist and Ennis del Mar have nothing in common—thankfully, you can't help feeling, in the eyes of many commentators. (It is surely significant that the film's only major departure from Proulx's story are two scenes clearly meant to underscore Jack's and Ennis's bona fides as macho American men: one in which Jack successfully challenges his boorish father-in-law at a Thanksgiving celebration and another in which Ennis punches a couple of biker goons at a Fourth of July picnic—a scene that culminates with the over-the-top image of Ennis standing tall against a skyscape of exploding fireworks.) The real achievement of *Brokeback Mountain* is not that it tells a universal love story that happens to have gay characters in it but that it tells a distinctively gay story that happens to be so well told that any feeling person can be moved by it. If you insist, as so many have, that the story of Jack and Ennis is okay to watch and sympathize with because they're not really homosexual—that they're more like the heart of America than like "gay people"—you're pushing them back into the closet whose narrow and suffocating confines Ang Lee and his collaborators have so beautifully and harrowingly exposed.

3 } Response to "An Affair to Remember"

JAMES SCHAMUS

To the Editors:

Daniel Mendelsohn, in his finely observed review of *Brokeback Mountain* ("An Affair to Remember"), sets up a false dichotomy between the essentially "gay" nature of the film and the erasure of this gay identity through the marketing and reception of the film as a "universal" love story. As one of the film's producers, I am grateful for his understanding of the unapologetic and unvarnished treatment of the specifically gay story we set out to tell; but as the copresident of Focus Features, the studio that is marketing and distributing the film, I take umbrage at some of the rhetorical shortcuts Mendelsohn takes in his depiction of our work.

Mendelsohn is rightly nervous about what happens when a gay text is so widely and enthusiastically embraced by mainstream hetero-dominated culture; and it is true that many reviewers contextualize their investment in the gay aspects of the romance by claiming that the characters' homosexuality is incidental to the film's achievements. Many reviewers indeed have gone out of their way to denounce the "gay cowboy movie" label (although, to be fair, they are mainly objecting to the fact that the label was used as a derogatory joke, a point I wish Mendelsohn had more fully considered). And it is true that we have marketed the film primarily as an epic, sweeping romance between two men, and do not append the words "gay" or "homosexual" to our marketing blurbs for the movie (although you never saw a poster or ad telling you that either *Titanic* or *The Bridges of Madison County* was the "greatest straight love story of all time"). Mendelsohn selectively quotes the film's director, Ang Lee, ignoring the mountain of press utterances he's made about what he thinks of the film's specifically gay content ("*Brokeback Mountain* is more gay to me. It's a romantic love story, and sexuality is at the center. I got extra juice from the gay love story. . . . They [Jack and Ennis] are both gay, but Jack is more knowing and less denying." Etc., etc.).[1]

Mendelsohn also unfortunately mischaracterizes other aspects of our marketing too. One example: he points out that "the words 'gay' and 'homosexual' are never used of the film's main two characters in the forty-nine-page press kit distributed by the filmmakers to critics." That sounds pretty damning, as if we were trying to hide the centrality of the film's gay content. Regardless of the fact that thirty pages of the forty-nine-page kit are taken up with the list of credits and biographies of the filmmakers, I note that the press kit features the voices of two of the film's wranglers, out gay men clearly identified as such, who are active on the gay rodeo circuit. Their words are quoted at greater length and prominence than those of Heath Ledger, as it was important to us that critics understand the film directly in the context of real gay lives. And while Mendelsohn can find a couple of awards show clips or advertising images that don't highlight the two male leads' relationship, let's be serious: no mainstream film in history has been promoted with as open, proud, and insistent a celebration of the love between two men.

But Mendelsohn is correct to call our attention to a telling and disturbing logic that underlies and legitimizes a great deal of the public discourse surrounding the film, summed up in the oft-heard assertion that "it's a love story, not a gay story."

It is the "not" in that sentence, the idea of two mutually exclusive paradigmatic categories, the one replacing the other, that rightly gives pause. But I wish it were as easy as Mendelsohn appears to think it is to resolve that false dichotomy by simply asserting the gay identity of the text. To begin with, there is a very real sense in which the film is, or at least aspires to be, "universal," in just the way Mendelsohn describes it, as a "distinctively gay story that happens to be so well told that any feeling person can be moved by it."

One thing this means is that we solicit every audience member's identification with the film's central gay characters; the film succeeds if it, albeit initially within the realm of the aesthetic, queers its audience. But in so doing, it paradoxically figures its gayness not just as a concretely situated identity, but also as a profound and emotionally expansive experience, understandable by all.

The power of a cultural moment such as that signaled by the reception of *Brokeback* is that in shattering the "epistemology of the closet" we run the risk of destroying the nonuniversal, specifically gay knowledge previously hidden inside it. Think of it this way: if the phrase "You wouldn't understand—it's a gay thing" is now met with the retort "But I think I do understand!" what, we need to ask, becomes of "the gay thing" itself? You see the problem: it is not that, with *Brokeback Mountain*, we made a great gay movie and then spent the next year insistently trying to stuff it back into the closet, as Mendelsohn argues. It is that, in the process of removing gayness from the closet and "mainstreaming" it, we disturb the given sites—some closeted, some not—from which gay identities struggle for recognition. *Brokeback* appears in the midst of new, and confusing, displacements of the sites of gay and, more broadly, GLBT identities—in the vast and disorienting space between the closet and the wedding altar.

So while I do feel Mendelsohn has been unfair to us, and while I believe the simple "gay versus universal" dichotomy should be nuanced, I am nonetheless grateful to Mendelsohn for raising what is indeed a thorny issue, one I hope he will continue to interrogate. *Brokeback*'s legacy will be, I believe, a profoundly positive one, but to ignore Mendelsohn's disquiet at important aspects of its reception would be foolish.

Notes

This chapter was originally published in the New York Review of Books *53.6 (April 6, 2006), in "Brokeback Mountain:* An Exchange," *which also includes a letter from Joel Conarroe and a response from Daniel Mendelsohn to both. See also James Schamus's unpublished additional letter, "Focus(ed) Debated."*

1. www.gay.com/entertainment/news/?coll =pno_entertainment&sernum=1 139&page=2 [now defunct]. To be fair, the cast and crew do not speak with one voice—nor should they—about these issues. Some think Ennis is gay, some think he's bi, etc.

4 } **The Magic Mountain**

ANDREW HOLLERAN

Standing in line for *Brokeback Mountain* the afternoon it opened in Washington at a tiny theater near Dupont Circle, I saw two kinds of people: silent gay men of a certain age and clusters of laughing college students. For the former, the movie we were about to see was personal, crucial; for the students, I guess it was—cool. The college students were happily chattering away. The gay men were lined up, in their individual solitude, waiting to weep. As I counted the thinning hairs on the head of the man in front of me, I thought: The sadness of *Brokeback* begins outside the theater.

There had been so much buzz and praise for this film that I was proudly prepared to be the first kid on my block to hate the picture, and to be honest, it was not very long after it began that I found myself wishing Dom Deluise would burst on to the set and tap dance across the screen, like Fred and Ginger at the end of *Blazing Saddles*. There were even times when I found myself looking at my watch or thinking, the movie should end here. The relentless bleakness, the one-note, unrelieved gloom made me impatient—but then, during the last twenty or twenty-five minutes, the whole movie rose onto another plane altogether, and when it ended I wondered how most of the audience was able to stand up so quickly, gather their coats, and leave. A few of us remained in the dark theater listening to Willie Nelson sing "He Was a Friend of Mine," watching every single credit unroll until only the corporate logos remained. I was relieved to know it was already dark outside, glad I did not have to walk past a line of people waiting for the next show. I was so upset I went home and phoned a friend in New York who had seen it the previous week. It was only when he said, "I don't want to bring you down, but . . ." that I could tell I was in some sort of semihysterical reaction that was probably explained by the Christmas blues I had been hoping to escape when I went into the theater—that is, what one brought to the work of art as well as the work of art itself.

Indeed, the next person I phoned said he wasn't sure everyone would get the movie; after telling younger friends at the gym about *Brokeback*, he'd sensed an indifference to the synopsis because no one in their generation could understand why anyone would repress his or her homosexuality. But at a later screening, watching a *Brokeback* audience leave the theater while I stood there waiting for another ticket, there were several young gay men wiping tears away, which made me think it would be interesting to be there for every screening, to read the expressions on the faces of the audience as they walked out. I kept encountering people less moved than I had been, however. One friend asked, "Why didn't they just move to San Francisco?" "Because they were drinking too much to think of it," another friend replied. One couple I know in San Francisco saw the movie in different ways: the younger one glad he had escaped that life, the older (a divorced father like Ennis) so depressed he had to go to bed for a day afterward. (Surely what one brings to *Brokeback* explains one's feelings about it.)

The women who reviewed the film for the *Washington Post* and *City Paper* said the movie had not convincingly portrayed the passion on which the story was based (Hornaday T43; Glaze). Gene Shalit called Jack a "sexual predator." Then there were the jokes. Jay Leno made wisecracks almost every night, Letterman made a "Ten Ways To Tell" list, and *The New Yorker* published a cartoon of two men in bed, one handing a cowboy hat to the other, who says, "What if I don't want to be Jack *or* Ennis?" (see figure 1).

The idea of two men in love over the course of a lifetime obviously made some people nervous. The reviewer in the *Post* bemoaned the fact that 2005 had given us *March of the Penguins* (a parable of heterosexual coupling and parenthood), *King Kong* (a girl and an ape), and *Brokeback Mountain* (two guys), but nothing for the straight man and woman (Hornaday T43). There were people, on the other hand, who wanted to minimize the fact that *Brokeback* was a same-sex romance. *The New Yorker* said the film was neither gay nor a Western. (It went through gay, beyond gay, to something bigger, I presume.) I became a bit obsessed with asking friends what they thought. Like the narrator in Proust who judges people by their opinion of the Dreyfus case, I began to think how you felt about this movie described your character.

That was silly, of course; a friend accused me of putting him on the "bad team" because he'd found fault with the film and reminded me that reactions were not either/or but on a spectrum. It was my own reaction I should have wondered about. One can discuss works of art as to whether they're well made or poorly made, but I wondered why some people were devastated by the movie and others not. One friend I spoke to said the movie was okay but he had not been particularly moved because he thought the plot was one that gay people have moved beyond at this point. The next friend sent me an e-mail listing all the lines in the story that had been left out, he believed, to downplay the erotic specifics of the romance. (It was a convincing brief.) This led to the question: who *was* the audience for this movie? The reviewers' complaint that the movie had not convincingly portrayed the passion the two men felt for each other made me wonder if this film could be understood only by gay men. Would straight men want to accompany their wives and girlfriends to *Brokeback*? Annie Proulx said she thought they would, that the only men who would not were those "insecure about themselves and their own sexuality. Jack and Ennis would have trouble with this movie." (Or, it occurred to me, the men who killed Matthew Shepard.)

Among those who liked it there were still misgivings. A friend who used to herd his grandfather's sheep up into the mountains of Colorado pointed out to me that the clothes Ennis and Jack wore in the movie were too new—they should have been faded, covered in dust and dirt. Indeed, in Proulx's story, Jack Twist is so bucktoothed he draws blood during the great face-mashing scene of their first reunion and becomes, as he ages, "swollen in the hams" (buttocks). As if to mock Hollywood hype, the *New York Times* ran a story about real gay cowboys in Wyoming; the photographs of the men brave enough to let their images be made public showed that real cowboys tend to look quite ordinary. The only one close to handsome looks at the camera with an expression so wary, so vulnerable, so sad that the real beauty was not in his face but in the snow-dusted road and fields and mountains behind him.

However, even the term "cowboys" was now in dispute. "Excuse me, but it is *not* a story about 'two cowboys,'" Proulx was quoted as saying in Manohla Dargis's *New York Times* essay about the movie. "It is a story about two inarticulate, confused Wyoming ranch kids in 1963 who have left home and who find themselves in a personal sexual situation they did not expect, understand, nor can manage." They are, "if anything," Dargis confirms, "shepherds" ("Masculinity" AR13).

It's true: the romance depicted in the first half hour of *Brokeback Mountain* recalls the idylls of Theocritus—though here the shepherds' love erodes into the grim poverty, homophobia, and hardscrabble bleakness of life in the modern American West. That must be why writer Larry McMurtry (*Lonesome Dove*) snapped up the rights to the story when it appeared in *The New Yorker* (after his partner, Diana Ossana, who'd seen it first, insisted McMurtry break his rule against reading short fiction). *Brokeback* fits right into McMurtry's view of the West as something poor, bleak, and forlorn: the antimyth. It is still about the West, however; so it struck me as ironic that a story about two men who marry, have kids, and ride horses for a living should have such an impact on urban gay men who have done none of these things. When was the last time the average gay man slept with a ranch hand who beat up bikers for talking dirty in front of his wife and daughters? *Brokeback* is a very butch addition to the tradition of *The Boys in the Band*.

But, as Frank Rich pointed out in the *Times*, it was also a love story. That was the source of its power: doomed love—a theme as old as Romeo and Juliet, Pyramus and Thisbe. *Brokeback*, Rich writes, is not based, like *Philadelphia* or *Angels in America*, on AIDS. It's about two men who reduce the whole world to each other. (Is there a more painful scene than their first reunion, when Ennis's wife has to witness the kiss that leaves her in the cold?) *Brokeback* is not *Will & Grace* or any of the other series and films we've had before. *Brokeback*, it seemed to me, in some strange way, provides gay characters with what only the fight against AIDS has till now—dignity—in part because they've been inserted into the heart of American myth, the cowboy, even if they are, strictly speaking, shepherds. They are shepherds (whose work, Proulx states, cowboys look down on

["Getting Movied" 130]), but they lasso each other and ride horses and shoot rifles and enter rodeos, which means cowboy to most folk.

Some people compared *Brokeback* to films by Douglas Sirk (those melodramas designed to draw tears from a mostly female audience). In other words, the film is just another middlebrow soap opera based on the classic dilemma: love that doesn't work out. But the fact that this is a failed gay relationship drew another kind of criticism. (We have a strange sensitivity to stereotypes in this country when it comes to the portrayal of minorities, which means we are not allowed to portray an aborted gay love affair because in reality most gay love affairs are just that.) *Brokeback*, a therapist I know said, is about gay men's desire for attachment—and surely this movie is about that theme, the longing for love, and the failure of real life to live up to our ideals. Skeptics, however, argued that *Brokeback* was a wallow in self pity, like certain country-western songs—a lot more sentimental than Warhol's send-up of the same subject, *Lonesome Cowboys*—because the whole movie rests on that staple of the song writer's lyric: what might have been. But in the end *Brokeback* is not stereotypical or sentimental; it is tragic in the Greek sense because at the end the scales fall from Ennis's eyes and he is left alone to recognize, in those astonishing last scenes, the all-too-human tragedy in which he has played a part.

In a bookstore in Dupont Circle, shortly after seeing the film, I found a paperback called *Brokeback Mountain: Story to Screenplay*, published quickly, I assume, to capitalize on the impact of the movie. This work contains the story by Proulx on which the film is based, the screenplay, and three essays—one by Proulx and two by the screenwriters Larry McMurtry and Diana Ossana. Andrew Sullivan wrote that he preferred the story to the movie, but I couldn't see how. Proulx herself states in her essay "Getting Movied": "Larry and Diana were working with a short story which came with a sturdy framework. But there was not enough there. I write in a tight, compressed style that needs air and loosening to unfold into art" (134). Or, as she put it in an interview: The film "really enriched the story. Instead of a little canoe, it became an ocean liner" (Detrixhe). But praise be to Proulx, I thought, for inventing this story, even if a prose writer watching *Brokeback* must end up in awe of the power of images and music.

Brokeback continued to engender arguments in the media over what it is really about. The "urban critics" Proulx felt, dubbed this movie "a tale of two gay cowboys. No. It is a story of destructive rural homophobia. Although there are many places in Wyoming where gay men did and do live together in harmony with the community, it should not be forgotten that a year after this story was published Matthew Shepard was tied to a buck fence outside the most enlightened town in the state, Laramie, home of the University of Wyoming" ("Getting Movied" 130).

Brokeback, of course, indicts both kinds of homophobia: external and internal. As awful as the homophobes who litter the film are (from their first boss, to the rodeo clown who rebuffs Jack's offer to buy him a drink, to his father in the penultimate scene), it's equally about gay men's self-censorship, their internalization of what is expected of a man. That may be why Heath Ledger's character dominated the movie and one reason his performance was praised much more than Gyllenhaal's (which was just as good): We're with Ennis at the end, and it's his moment of self-recognition that provides the pathos. It's Ennis who is trapped by the constraints of conventional masculinity—by the life he thinks is expected of men. One of the most touching letters Proulx received, she said, from a father who'd read her story, contains this line: "Now I understand the kind of hell my son went through."

In this movie no father shows any sympathy, however. It is strangely haunted by the absence of fathers, in fact. Both Ennis and Jack seem to be fatherless from the start. Ennis lost his father when still a child; Jack's father never went to see him in the rodeos or passed on any of its secrets, and at the end he provides the final homophobic cruelty. When the two men grow up they both have kids. In the story Ennis tells Jack he wishes for a son, but it's Jack whom we see driving the farm equipment with his son on his lap. Ennis has two daughters who adore him, but he's hardly able to express affection. He's the all-American Dad, the Marlboro Man.

McMurtry saw immediately that *Brokeback* was part of "the strong, long tradition of doomed young men: *The Great Gatsby*, *The Sun Also Rises*, *Miss Lonelyhearts* and many others" ("Adapting *Brokeback Mountain*" 140). And that seems to me exactly right. One reason *Brokeback* is so moving is that it is not simply about the obstacles people in love with others of the same sex face; it is just as much a film about poverty, adultery, the miseries of family life (it is important to have women in this story, Proulx wrote ["Getting Movied" 132]), dreams one never realizes, wasted lives, and isolation. The whole movie is structured on the difference between dreams and disappointment, the invasion of the ideal by the real. Ennis lies in the street, being punched and kicked by the driver he has attacked. Cut to the breathtaking ridge on which Jack and Ennis are riding to their rendezvous. The editing and the score follow this pattern throughout, alternating the magnificence of the mountain scenery (guitar and orchestra) with the squalor of the men's domestic life (the whine of country-western songs) and the homophobia that requires the repeated escapes—because while the love between Ennis and Jack starts out as an idyll, it does not remain that for long.

Even so, others complained that *Brokeback* was ahistorical: the romance takes place in a vacuum, with no reference to anything outside the relationship. The longing of Jack and Ennis for one another, though set in the early 1960s, seems to unfold in its own little world— the way love does, actually. I suppose had Ennis and Jack been allowed to live together and grow old, their romance would have devolved into arguments over dish washing, channel changing, drinking, and depression. Maybe they would have moved to San Francisco or started doing threesomes. But in the movie they do not. Their love lives on after you leave the theater because it is never consummated, in the fullest sense. There is at the end one crushing revelation that Jack has transferred his dream of running his folks' ranch with Ennis to a man in Texas, and that news is just one more nail in the coffin of Ennis's loss. Yet it's this that makes *Brokeback* so moving: it's a never-resolved argument between two men, one who wishes to live freely with the person he loves and one who believes society will not let them, having witnessed something as a child that instilled that message in him in a terrible way.

One day it struck me that friends and I were discussing Ennis and Jack as if they were real people—wondering who was the top and who was the bottom and whether Jack was gay, but Ennis gay only with Jack. One of the truthful things about the two sex scenes in the tent—a place the camera stayed out of for the rest of the movie, to one friend's consternation (but then how much gay sex can a mainstream audience take?)—is that the first time, Ennis is on top and the second, Jack rolls onto Ennis. Exactly. Gay men are constantly in flux between the two— Jack the bottom and Ennis the top. They are both Jack the romantic and Ennis the realist, Jack the optimist and Ennis the pessimist, Jack longing for love and Ennis withholding it—though one thing they've all struggled with is the message that Ennis's father passes on: that two men do not lie (or live or love) with one another.

It seemed to me that this was what lay beneath so much of the criticism that didn't hold up (no passion?) and the jokes. Yet this is the most American of themes, what Leslie Fiedler was writing about under his famous title "Come Back to the Raft Ag'in, Huck Honey!" *Brokeback* eroticizes male friendship. Jack and Ennis are both best friends and lovers, fishing buddies who bring home no fish. Nothing in the film is more touching than the way Jack prefaces his remarks to Ennis with the word "friend"—or the Bob Dylan lyrics Willie Nelson sings over the credits in "He Was a Friend of Mine." *Brokeback* is right at the center of our ideas of masculinity: fathers, or the absence of them, and friendship between men.

No wonder Letterman—the national frat boy—made jokes: after years of watching gay subject matter come into the light, it was still shocking to see one of the oldest genres of American art, one of its fundamental tropes, being used to tell what it feels like to be gay. Even if you agree with the claim that cowboy movies have always had a homoerotic ingredient simmering under the surface—or on top, in Warhol's *Lonesome Cowboys*—the cowboy is our national icon, which is why some historians have made an effort to show that there were African American cowboys too. It's our central self-image. Whether Jack and Ennis are cowboys, shepherds, or ranch hands, the camp they set up, the horses they ride, the rifles they shoot, the boots they wear are all transgressive when the two begin to make love. This is the irony: a director raised in Taiwan, an Australian lead, a Mexican cinematographer and an Argentine composer have made a Western filmed in Canada that puts gays into the central American narrative.

I went back to see the movie the *Washington Post* had deprecated as "self-serious" a second time to see if it could possibly have the same effect. I saw it differently of course and considered seeing it a third time to free me of its spell but decided not to. Nor did I want to watch it on DVD when that came out. I could not imagine seeing that horseback ride along the ridge on a television screen. But I did read the book with the screenplay and the essays by Proulx and the screenwriters. Proulx got the idea for her story one night when she saw a man in a bar watching some other men play pool; that was all it took, though the story went through sixty drafts and eight years before it became a movie. I also went to Ang Lee's next movie—*Lust, Caution*—to try to understand his amazing achievement in *Brokeback*. I'd been going to lots of Japanese movies at the Freer Gallery that year and had learned that U.S. movies rush forward, but Asian cinema is not afraid to take its time. But in trying to analyze *Brokeback* I was only attempting to create a distance between myself and the movie. (Ledger and Gyllenhaal were doing the same thing, it seemed, in their appearances on talk and awards shows; only once—at the Golden Globes—did they seem to insult what they had accomplished. Most of the time they bore the waves of feeling their movie had unleashed with admirable patience.)

But with a film like this such distance was impossible. Seeing *Brokeback* for the first time in a little theater off Dupont Circle would always have a meaning I would not understand. Ledger and Gyllenhaal went on to make other movies, of course, in part, the gay viewer suspected, to secure their heterosexual bona fides. (Look how fast the former's *Casanova* followed *Brokeback*.) But they had done such good work it was out of their hands. In great movies the characters exist independent of reality; they live eternally in that movie, and the movie lives in us.

That's why, for weeks afterward, though *Brokeback* is too painful a movie to watch many times, I listened a lot to the soundtrack, which alternates between the pastoral beauty of Gustavo Santaolalla's theme—a few notes on the guitar, so spare, so haunting—and the raucous country-western music of the bars, where Matthew Shepard met his killers. And that's why, though the little theater in which I'd seen *Brokeback* closed a few years later, every time I walk by the entrance I think of the movie. There was plenty of passion in the story of Jack and Ennis—passion that had made the sex obsession many gay men settle for seem so meager. Some movies give us a kind of courage, make us want to change, which of course is much easier to do on-screen than in real life.

Brokeback, for all its pathos, was one of those; even if, as time passed, it seemed to revert to more of a confirmation of why one cannot. The impact *Brokeback* has had on people can be ascribed to many factors. But in the end I think the power of this film has a lot to do with its being what McMurtry calls it: "a tragedy of emotional deprivation" (Proulx, McMurtry, and Ossana 142). This is surely a universal experience but at a certain point in their lives most gay men seem to conclude that it's the particular fate of being gay.

Notes

A version of this essay previously appeared in Gay & Lesbian Review Worldwide 13.2 (2006): 12–15.

5 } **Backs Unbroken**

Ang Lee, Forbearance, and the Closet

MUN-HOU LO

I.

A sequence that takes place just about halfway through *Brokeback Mountain*—thereby tempting us to call it the movie's centerpiece, especially since it is not in Annie Proulx's source story—gives us occasion to contemplate the film's relation to the closet. Ennis del Mar goes with his family to a Fourth of July picnic, but the fun that everybody in the community is having is disrupted by a couple of drunk foul-mouthed bikers. Ennis tries shushing them but gets an epithet in return for his trouble. So he hands his daughter to Alma, gets up just as the first burst of fireworks goes off on the soundtrack, and wallops the two men. At this point the camera assumes the position of the downed bikers as Ennis asks them if they want to lose their teeth; the audience therefore also looks up at a victorious Ennis, as fireworks explode behind him (figure 2).

But then something peculiar happens with the perspective. The bikers admit defeat, and in the next shot, we see one of them crawl away, tail between his legs, to help his friend, who looks like he might have passed out or been knocked unconscious (figure 3). At this point, Ang Lee's camera cuts back to Ennis, still backlit by fireworks, to conclude the sequence. Though the biker has long since looked away, the camera persists in framing Ennis from below: a shot that is therefore no longer from the troublemakers' perspective but *has apparently passed on to being Lee's* (figure 4). Despite the fact that Alma fearfully cowers in one corner

2. (top) Ennis threatens to throw another punch after kick-boxing a biker—from the biker's point of view. Courtesy of Universal Studios Licensing LLLP.

3. (bottom) Defeated, the biker crawls—and looks—away. Courtesy of Universal Studios Licensing LLLP.

of the tableau, it is hard not to read Lee's shot, literally and figuratively still looking up to a man in a cowboy hat as he continues to be framed by patriotic fireworks, as expressing a certain admiration for Ennis, the very picture of American manhood.[1]

4. Yet someone continues to look up to Ennis. Courtesy of Universal Studios Licensing LLLP.

But even as we catch, in this sequence, Lee sneaking a worshipful glance at one of his protagonists, *what* he admires in Ennis is not perfectly clear. The film, by this point, has set in motion what is arguably its chief narrative: Ennis is living life in the closet. Prior to the picnic incident, for example, we get a scene—obviously meant to signify denial and repression—in which Ennis takes his wife in bed as if she were a man. (For contrast, this scene is sandwiched between two in which an expressive Jack Twist seeks to return to Brokeback Mountain but is rebuffed by Joe Aguirre, and then fruitlessly tries to pick up a man at a rodeo bar.) Is Lee here signaling, therefore, an endorsement of Ennis's constitution, his repressive abilities? And yet *within* the narrative of Ennis's repression, the incident with the bikers might also appear "out of character." After all, the scene shows Ennis—in contrast with the rest of his life in which he tries as much as possible not to give voice to his feelings—letting it all out through his fists. Might Lee be admiring Ennis when he is *least* repressed? Then again, maybe not: although we could read the picnic violence as atypical of a buttoned-up Ennis, we are also familiar with the cultural narrative that suggests how a life of sexual repression can erupt into violence, in which case this act would be *logical* instead of atypical. Indeed, we are familiar with this narrative not least because the film has alluded to it: when Ennis and Jack part after their idyllic summer on Brokeback Mountain, Ennis throws up in an alley and then reacts with further oral violence ("What the fuck are you looking at?") when a passerby stops to witness the spectacle of a man who cannot express himself any other way.

It is therefore not easy to know how exactly to read this iconic scene, how to comprehend, in other words, Lee's relation to the closet. This essay, which is first and foremost a close reading of *Brokeback Mountain*, begins by situating the film within Lee's canon. Given Lee's obsessive concern with desire and its negotiation, it is natural to read *Brokeback Mountain* as a tale—cautionary or otherwise—of sexual repression. Yet if we choose to see the film this way, we also have to acknowledge that Lee's work, given the fates it deals to its two protagonists, cannot unambiguously be said to be against such repression. However, there is an alternative lens through which to comprehend not just *Brokeback Mountain* but many of Lee's films: the lens provided by the idea of "forbearance," a term for which I provide two interrelated contexts (one social/religious/cultural and the other cinematic). My thesis, however, is not simply that forbearance is the "true" theme of *Brokeback Mountain*; rather, I argue that Lee's interest in forbearance—manifested in the film's inordinate concern with time—overlaps with, but does not map directly onto, the specific issue of sexual repression, which is why the film is, ultimately, a profoundly ambivalent one. By this reading, the Fourth of July scene, as well as a pivotal exchange between Jack and Ennis I discuss later, would therefore be symptoms of this ambivalence, moments in which Lee, and perhaps his audience, does not and should not quite know what to think.

II.

Although Roger Ebert and Robin Wood are very different types of film critics, they both found themselves flummoxed when trying to make sense of Lee's body of work. "Has he produced a coherent *oeuvre*?" Wood asks, and then, distracted by Lee's genre hopping, answers in the negative: "I have been drawn to his films from the outset . . . but the more he makes the more difficult it becomes to see a pattern" (29). Ebert was similarly puzzled, but his audience lent him a helping hand: "Failing to find the connecting link between such Ang Lee films as 'Sense and Sensibility,' 'Brokeback Mountain' and 'The [sic] Hulk,' I was quickly corrected by readers who said, obviously, all his films are about people trying to realize their essential natures despite the constraints of society" (Rev. of Lust, Caution).

We can reframe this observation by noticing that Lee's films tend to center on desire and its disruptive effects—and thus, just as often, on how best to negotiate such desires. Think, as Ebert prompts us to, of Sense and Sensibility (1995), or The Wedding Banquet (1993) and The Ice Storm (1997), or even the film that is usually considered a misstep, Hulk (2003): in Lee's version of the story, it is not so much anger that Bruce Banner has to fight. Tellingly, the most famous line from the comic and TV series—"You wouldn't like me when I'm angry"—is postponed until the very end of the film. Though in some ways this turns it into the movie's punchline, it also transforms the subject of anger into something resembling an afterthought. Instead, what troubles Banner is his *desire* for that anger: "But you know what scares me the most?" the character reveals at a pivotal point. "When I can't fight it anymore . . . when it takes over . . . when I totally lose control. . . . *I like it.*"

Lee's frequent figuration of desire as dangerous—desire for something, desire in itself—came into even sharper relief in 2007 with the release of Lust, Caution, a film based on the short story of the same name by Eileen Chang. Even in its English form, the title alone would suffice to signal Lee's continuing fascination with the risk of desire. But the original Chinese title is even more emphatic in this regard: though not a palindrome, the phrase has a weird reversibility that underlines its point. "Lust, Caution" is a reasonably literal translation of 色, 戒 (se, jie). However, if we read the phrase backward—and as any Chinese speaker knows, that is easy to do, given how *hanzi* are more traditionally written from right to left—the inverted phrase becomes 戒色 (jiese), an expression that now sounds less like a neutral yoking together of two nouns and more like an imperative command to give up or renounce desire.

"As any Chinese speaker knows": especially if he or she encounters a Chinese version of the film poster. In fact, even though the reversibility of the title is a neat trick that technically belongs more to Chang than it does Lee, it is the filmmaker who seems more inclined to play with this feature. When Chang's story first appeared in the Taiwanese journal 皇冠 (*Huang Guan*) in 1977, the two words of its title ran from top to bottom—undoubtedly because the journal itself was typeset in that traditional way, but even as an inadvertent effect, such typesetting allows for very little ambiguity. (For an image of the original journal pages, see 蔡 [Cai] 179.) In contrast, the 2007 posters for Lee's movie that were targeted at Chinese-language audiences almost seem like they were designed to *promote* ambiguity. For instance, the Taiwanese poster runs the film's title from right to left, separating the two words with a more neutral vertical bar instead of a comma. Even more strikingly, every other phrase on the poster reads in the other direction, from left to right: from the tagline ("Easy to guard against lust, difficult to prevent love"), to the actors' names and Lee's own, the latter prefaced by the titles of his other films ("*Crouching Tiger, Hidden Dragon*'s and *Brokeback Mountain*'s Oscar-winning director Lee Ang"). Though we must recognize that the right-to-left layout of the main title is an attempt to signify that *Lust, Caution* is an "olden" movie, the design makes it almost impossible not to "misread" the name of the film as 戒色 (*jiese*), a call to audiences to surrender desire (see figure 5).

In addition, since the Chinese verb 戒 (*jie*) tends to be employed to speak about vices such as smoking, drugs, or alcohol, the backward phrase would more clearly cast desire or lust as an addiction. For a final trick, the uninverted phrase in Chinese is a close homonym of 世界 (*shijie*), that is, "the world." It is as if for Lee (and Chang), almost reworking Mark 8:36—"For what shall it profit a man, if he shall gain the whole world, and lose his own soul?"—to give up desire is to gain the world.

Given Lee's proclivities, it therefore seems natural to consider *Brokeback Mountain* a meditation on desire and how best to handle, or not handle, it. In his essay about the film, Daniel Mendelsohn especially emphasizes the second half of that sentence. Taking issue with the way the film was marketed and received, which tended to universalize its gay themes out of existence, Mendelsohn staunchly recharacterizes the movie: "*Brokeback Mountain* is a tragedy about the specifically gay

5. The poster for the Taiwanese release of *Lust, Caution* compels us to renounce desire.

phenomenon of the 'closet'—about the disastrous emotional and moral consequences of erotic self-repression and of the social intolerance that first causes and then exacerbates it" ("An Affair" 12). By this reading, Lee's film is about homosexual desire, and even more so about the specific tactic of repression. After all, the "emotional climax of the film," Mendelsohn points out, "takes place in two consecutive scenes, both of which prominently feature closets—literal closets" (13).

Yet, even if the film is about what we will temporarily call, following Mendelsohn for now, "repression," is it clearly *against* such repression? Mendelsohn's reading moves seamlessly from one position ("*Brokeback Mountain* is a tragedy about the specifically gay phenomenon of the 'closet'") to the other ("about the disastrous emotional and moral consequences of erotic self-repression"), and our hearts understand why: as he styles it, the film, after all, is a "tragedy." But we can begin to complicate this view by noticing that the film's two leads exhibit such desire—and, conversely, "repress" it—very differently. Because we get more details of his homosexual lifestyle than we do Ennis's, Jack comes across as diegetically "gayer." There is, for example, a depiction of Jack's sexual tourism in Mexico, as well as a scene, already mentioned, in which he tries to pick up Jimbo, the rodeo clown. In the latter sequence, it takes only a glance, held for just a second too long, for that clown, rather smarter than his name and profession might imply, to intuit that Jack is gay. But then again, there is something about Jack, the film hints, that consistently gives away his open secret. For much of the film, we sense that Jack's father-in-law, L. D. Newsome, does not approve of him. But it is not until the Thanksgiving incident that we receive confirmation that it is Jack's deficient manhood—as opposed to, say, his inferior class or suspected gold digging—that irks Newsome. "Stud duck do the carvin' round here," Newsome declares, in the first of his emasculating gestures. For a follow-up, he turns the tv back on for his grandson over Jack's objections, telling Lureen, "You want your boy to grow up to be a man, don't you, daughter? Boys should watch football." Although Jack eventually wins that battle, the point is made for the audience: Jack's sexuality is somehow transparent to the point that we do not need any explanation of how Newsome knows. But at least Jack is sometimes able to attract the right kind of man: Randall Malone can detect Jack's homosexuality enough to make a pass. And really, none of this should startle; in an early scene on the utopian mountain, when both men grow tired of beans and go hunting for meat, the unsuccessful Jack demonstrates that, unlike Ennis, he can't even shoot straight.

Concomitantly—maybe even causally—the film does not depict Ennis just as "less gay" but as more active in his "repression." Lee himself understands the difference between his two characters in precisely that fashion: "They . . . are both gay, but Jack is more knowing and less denying" (qtd. by Schamus in Mendelsohn, "An Exchange" 68). Instead of a litany of the ways the film conveys this, perhaps we need to remind ourselves of only one feature. Of all of Heath Ledger's acting choices, none has been more arresting than his decision to let Ennis's repression "play out" on his body and even in his voice. Ledger has been praised, D. A. Miller reminds us, "for concretizing Ennis's repressed unconscious in a veritable cornucopia of psychosomatisms. If we don't read repression in the actor's pursed lips, then we read it in his evasive eyes; and should we miss it there, his rounded posture or his mumbled diction is ready to expound" (54). Even a blind person hearing *Brokeback Mountain* can pick out the repressed character: not just because Ennis sounds that way, but because he sounds that way *in relation to Jack*.

Lee has used this compare-and-contrast method before. As numerous critics have noticed, the film that broke Lee through to the Western mainstream, *Crouching Tiger, Hidden Dragon* (2000), is structured as a story of two opposed pairs of lovers (or would-be lovers). While the older Li Mu Bai and Yu Shu Lien have a relationship that is perpetually shrouded in meaningful silences, their younger counterparts, Jen and Lo, are instinctual, impetuous, and impulsive.[2] This theme is even more apparent to viewers who have a grasp on the original Chinese title of the film. Whitney Crothers Dilley rehearses this case:

> The Chinese idiomatic phrase "wohu canglong" (crouching tiger hidden dragon) is a common expression referring to the undercurrents of emotion, passion and secret desires that lie beneath the surface of polite society and civil behaviour. These subverted desires, although hidden, are very potent and mysterious, and can emerge unexpectedly, or powerfully change the course of people's

lives. For example, Jen and Lo express their desires in sudden and unpredictable ways—as they do in the desert cave—because they are young, wild and headstrong. Jen's unrestrained desires lead to trouble for the others. . . .

In contrast to this are the repressed desires of the older characters Li Mu Bai and Shu Lien, who honour their code of duty above their feelings. . . . However, in their pursuit of the foolhardy and impetuous Jen, their own "dragons," or hidden desires, are awakened. Jen's youth, energy and passion remind them both of the romance and freedom they have traded in pursuit of duty. (138)

To boost Dilley's case, we could even add that this contrast between the two main couples governs the film's visual styles. Even though it contains several fighting and flying scenes, the first hour of *Crouching Tiger, Hidden Dragon*, centering on Li and Yu, feels somewhat stifling: much of the action takes place on dark nights, in a succession of vaguely oppressive rooms and courtyards. The mood changes when Lo arrives and provokes, in Jen, a flashback sequence: suddenly, the film opens up into the vast expanse of the desert, and the visual effect on the audience can only be exhilarating and freeing. In its obvious association of "sexual freedom" with wide open spaces, *Brokeback Mountain* clearly inherits this style.

Crouching Tiger, Hidden Dragon and *Brokeback Mountain* therefore share not just an interest in desire and its regulation, but also the filmic and narrative techniques by which Lee conveys this point. But there is a crucial difference as well, one that should give pause to anyone who plans to consider the latter film a warning about the effects of "repression." In the former film, Li intends to settle his affairs before allowing himself to pursue a relationship with Yu, and the tragedy of the film, of course, lies in how he perishes before he has a chance to do so. The "repressed" couple in *Crouching Tiger, Hidden Dragon* therefore never get to consummate their relationship, while the film ends, albeit ambiguously, with the unrestrained Jen and Lo together. This is not the case with *Brokeback Mountain*, which instead punishes the member of the pair who does *not* exercise such "repression." Jack dies; Ennis lives. "It is the more effeminate, more diminutive, more expressive, and ultimately less complacent protagonist whose pound of flesh is demanded," Ara Osterweil reminds us more extensively (40), though she doesn't seem fully impressed by what this implies (in a way that, say, Vito Russo would never have been). Can the film be said to show the "disastrous . . . consequences of erotic self-repression," as Mendelsohn would have it, when the repressive character survives and the expressive character does not? Furthermore, we might even note that Jack's death, macabrely, is a fate dealt to Jack *by* Ennis: the movie frames the narrative in which Jack expires because he is gay bashed as occurring in Ennis's imagination. Of course, it might be argued that Ennis survives only in the barest and most barren of ways: doomed to a life of regret, solitude, and sadness, and reduced to playing with unwashed shirts like a kid angling to get his two favorite dolls to kiss. But tell that to the dead homosexual.

III.

Brokeback Mountain, I have thus far suggested, fits squarely into Lee's oeuvre in being concerned with desire and its dangerous effects and with the question of how such desire can best be negated—or, to follow critics from Mendelsohn to Miller—how it can be "repressed." But if we see *Brokeback Mountain* as being about sexual repression, then we have to acknowledge that it is *not* unambiguously against such "repression." Indeed, given how the film kills the man who is more expressive, the film might be seen—can *only* be seen, natch—as endorsing the closet, if not as a way of life, then at least as a survival tactic.

But let's hold our horses. "*If* we see *Brokeback Mountain* as being about sexual repression, *then* . . ." But what if we do not? Desire in Lee's universe is often a force that has to be negotiated, but have we prematurely named that negotiation? Is *repression* truly, for Lee, the privileged or de facto form of such negotiation? It is perfectly natural for critics to automatically label the way Lee's characters act, and thus Lee's theme, "repression"—we would only be following the filmmaker's lead. In a 2005 interview with the *China Post*, one of Taiwan's English-language papers, Lee, asked to identify the essence of his films, responds as follows: "Repression, the struggle between how you want to behave as a social animal and the desire to be honest with your free will. That's an important subtext in life, and a struggle for me. I also mistrust everything. Things you believe in can change just like that; that's the essence of life. . . . My point of view is a bit Taoist. When things change, you have to adapt to it. That's been our fate" (qtd. in Dilley 42). Does Lee's gloss on "repression" make sense? It is not entirely clear, first of all, if Lee is pinpointing one feature of his films, or two. He begins by confessing that he is interested in "repression"—and he "also mistrust[s]" the world and believes "things change." If the two parts of his answer are related, then presumably one effect of things changing is that our desires somehow get hindered or obstructed. Then what? "You have to adapt to it": despite the fact that "it" grammatically cannot refer to the plural "things," Lee probably means something like, "When things change, you have to adapt to the new situation." But if so, his Taoist "point of view" does not explicitly explain what happens to the "desire to be honest with . . . [our] free will." Things change and we should adapt; certainly, one way of adapting is to "repress" those desires by casting them into the unconscious. But surely another is to wait out the changes, in which case the desire would not be so much repressed as delayed, postponed, or suspended.

There is a name for this other method of negotiating desire, in which desire is not so much subdued and sublimated as held in abeyance until it can be fulfilled, and that name is "forbearance" (in Chinese, 忍 [ren]). The Chinese quality of forbearance is not a particularly easy concept to explain, and its genealogy is even tougher to trace. Nevertheless, there exist at least two interrelated Chinese traditions in which forbearance occupies a systematically important position. The first, loosely speaking, is social/religious/cultural, while the second is specifically cinematic. While there is no surefire way to determine if Lee has any interest in, or is influenced by, either of these traditions, I would venture to say, for reasons that become clearer as we go on, that he is at a minimum familiar with the second.

Forbearance is an implicit value in many Chinese religions (such as Buddhism and the religion Lee seems to see himself as closest to, Taoism) and systems of thought (such as Confucianism), especially in folk versions of such discourses. But it is a more recent Chinese movement that schematically talks about forbearance under that name. "Falun Gong," David Ownby explains in a brief but authoritative overview of the subject, "is a form of *qigong*, the general name for a set of physical and mental disciplines based loosely on traditional Chinese medical and spiritual discourses and organized around a charismatic master who teaches his followers specific techniques as well as general moral precepts, with the goal of realizing a physical and moral transformation of practitioners" ("Falun Gong" 196). Literally meaning "breath technique" or "breath work," *qigong* was invented in the 1950s as part of Chinese traditional medicine, before becoming, as Ownby describes, a loose set of "physical and mental disciplines." At times, for example, *qigong* is utilized in various forms of Chinese martial arts, or at least in their training processes. In the 1990s Li Hongzhi formulated a specific form of *qigong* called Falun Gong (meaning, literally, "technique of the wheel of law"). Since then, Falun Gong has become a highly controversial and politicized movement: the Chinese government outlawed the "heterodox sect" in 1999, though it continues to be practiced throughout the Chinese diaspora, including Taiwan.[3]

In what way does forbearance occupy a systematically important position in Falun Gong? Li, the movement's founder, who now lives in New York City, does not merely name forbearance as the overarching value of Falun Gong but also encourages people to treat his writings as important. As Ownby points out, Li "accorded far more importance to scripture (that is, his writings) than did most other *qigong* masters. The writings of most *qigong* masters either illustrated proper *qigong* technique or offered explanations of the efficacy of their practice. Li's writings were treated as holy writ" ("Falun Gong" 205). In one example of such "scripture"—the book simply titled *Falun Gong*—Li makes clear that the three principles of Falun Gong are 真 (*zhen*), 善 (*shan*), and 忍 (*ren*): truth, compassion, and forbearance. "We particularly emphasize," Li writes, "the ability of 'Ren.' Only with Ren can one cultivate to become a person with great de [i.e., virtue, especially in a Taoist sense]. Ren is a very powerful thing, transcending Zhen and Shan" (59). He then provides a clarification and an illustration:

> Being asked to forbear is not weakness, and neither is it being [foolish]. It is a display of strong will and self-restraint. There was a person in Chinese history named Han Xin [a general during

the Han dynasty], who once suffered the humiliation of crawling between someone's legs. That was great forbearance. There is an ancient saying: "When an everyday person is humiliated, he will draw his sword to fight." It means that when an ordinary person is humiliated, he will draw his sword to retaliate, swear at others, and throw punches at them. It's not easy thing for one to come and live a lifetime. Some people live for their ego. It's not worth it whatsoever, and it is also too tiring. There is a saying in China: "With one step back, you'll discover a boundless sky." Take a step back when you are confronted with problematic things. When you do, you will find a whole different scenario. (60)

Though Li is not very explicit about it, his point is that the actions of the "ordinary person" (drawing a sword to fight) are not what he would advocate; for him, that would be the "ego[tistical]" approach. Instead, Li recommends following the historical example of Han Xin: forbear. Learn to tolerate fools and enemies. Take the larger and longer-term perspective. This precept inverts an assumption: whereas we normally consider giving in (i.e., crawling) the weak and easy way out, Li suggests that it is the action of drawing swords that is cheap and foolish. In this scenario, therefore, "crawling" would paradoxically require "strong will and self-restraint" to overcome our natural and more instinctive desire to take up arms.

Falun Gong is hence the clearest textual example of a "Chinese world-view" that systematically positions forbearance as a (supreme) virtue. Short of a direct question to the filmmaker, there is no way to determine if Lee subscribes, in any kind of dogmatic fashion, to Falun Gong. (A wholehearted adherence would be a little ironic, given Li's views on homosexuality [on this, see Lubman and, more briefly, Ownby, *Falun Gong* 107, and Palmer 225–30].) But there is no real need to ask. While Falun Gong has placed the most *organized* emphasis on forbearance, it is in some ways just making explicit and systematic a value that is implied and prized by various Chinese religions—notice, in fact, how Li uses, in the previous excerpt, the Taoist term "de." Further, the significance of Falun Gong is not just in reaching back to older Chinese religions and traditions that implicitly espouse forbearance. Someone

6. In Singapore's Chinatown, a 忍 (*ren*) scroll hangs from the rafters, perhaps not accidentally next to another scroll with the character for "happiness." Photo by Mun-Hou Lo.

who walks down a street in a diasporic Chinese city—in particular, one in an enclave that is or has been designated as ethnically Chinese—just might encounter the character 忍 (*ren*) calligraphed on everything from scrolls (see figure 6) to apparel (see figures 7 and 8); in this way, Falun Gong pushes the concept of forbearance forward, popularizing or "secularizing" it. (It is probably a safe bet that neither the retailers nor buyers of the scrolls and clothes subscribe to, or even know about, the doctrinal centrality of the word and concept in Falun Gong.)

There is a second "Chinese tradition" in which forbearance plays a crucial role, and this is one tradition with which Lee is quite clearly familiar. Perusing the previous passage from Li, readers may be forgiven if they found the description of Han Xin, the general who endured humiliation, a tad cinematic. There is good reason for this, because forbearance is a discernible trope in a couple of genres in Chinese cinema. Specifically, the forbearing protagonist who endures humiliating

7. Meanwhile, at another store, a shirt sports the same 忍 character. Photo by Mun-Hou Lo.

trials because he is able to take the long view and wait for an eventual triumph should be a recognizable figure; his stomping (or crawling) grounds are *wuxia* and *kungfu* films.

In such martial arts films, our hero often undergoes great hardship, either prior to his training (in which case his forbearance of those trials serves as testimony, for his teacher as for the audience, of his determination to receive that education) or as part of it. A Hong Kong movie from 1978, Lau Kar-Leung's *The 36th Chamber of Shaolin* (alternatively called *The Master Killer* or *Shaolin Master Killer*) is a particularly illuminating example of both versions of this trope. Set during the Qing dynasty, the film follows the adventures of Liu Yu-De (a pseudohistorical figure), who is aggrieved—and after the slaughter of his family, personally pained—by the harsh Manchu rule. He craves the ability to defend himself and to teach his compatriots this ability; hence, he sets off for Shaolin Temple, both to learn the best martial arts and to persuade its monks to secularize these teachings. As critics have widely recognized, Liu's training sequence

8. Complete the ensemble with a skirt. In all three cases, the 忍 character is underlined by a proverbial verse that might be roughly translated as "Forbear a moment / Peace and tranquility / Retreat a step / Boundless sea and sky." In the story of General Han Xin in *Falun Gong*, Li paraphrases the final two lines. Photo by Mun-Hou Lo.

at Shaolin inaugurates the trope whereby the hero has to prove his worth by conquering training hardships. Stephen Teo, for instance, describes the movie as depicting "the overcoming of physical tests to determine whether or not one has achieved true kung fu skills" (225). The title of the movie refers to the way Shaolin sets up its training: the temple features thirty-five chambers (Liu would invent a thirty-sixth), each with a frankly sadistic training task that every disciple has to endure—say, carrying pails of water while sharp knives attached to your biceps ensure that you keep your arms at right angles. (My personal favorite is the chamber in which Liu's head is wedged between what looks like two giant cigarette butts.) We can even catch a whiff of this philosophy in a moment from Lee's own contribution to the *wuxia* genre. In the second duel of *Crouching Tiger, Hidden Dragon*, between Li Mu Bai and (a masked) Jen, in which he offers her a discipleship while demonstrating his superior sword skills, he rattles off a series of aphorisms that form an abbreviated version of a training sequence: "no growth without assistance," "no action without reaction," and most significantly, "no desire without restraint." If we hanker for a hint that Lee is familiar with the motif of forbearance in this tradition, here is where we would look. This trope has proven utterly influential: Jackie Chan movies, for example, feature numerous scenes showing how "Chan develop[s] the masochistic style of his brand of kung fu, where a disciple undergoes tough training (equated with physical suffering) to master the art of a particular style of kung fu" (Teo 123). The influence is not even confined to Chinese cinema, as everything from *The Karate Kid* (John G. Avildsen, 1984) to *Rocky* (Avildsen, 1976) to *Star Wars* (George Lucas, 1977) could demonstrate.

But *The 36th Chamber of Shaolin* actually offers the lesson of forbearance in a much subtler way than a critic like Teo recognizes. The film in fact uses the lesson not just as the structuring moral for the training sequence but as a framing device. Lau's film opens deceptively: we meet two men conversing in a teahouse. One is General Yin and the other is Teacher Ho—as it were, the sword and the pen. The former has all the trappings of heroism; indeed, the film sets up the expectation that Yin will be its protagonist. But this expectation is quickly defeated: Yin tries to assassinate a Manchu inspector-general, fails, and is executed. The punishment is witnessed by several of Ho's students—including

Liu, who only then emerges as the true protagonist and hero of the film. Reflecting on Yin's beheading, Teacher Ho impresses upon his students the movie's key lesson. "One must humble oneself under every rule," Ho advises, implicitly criticizing Yin's choice to fight. "Must we humble ourselves forever?" his students wonder. Ho employs a slightly grisly pun in reply: "If we don't lower our heads, then we get beheaded." But if Ho does not answer the question directly, the film does it for him: Liu, having internalized his teacher's lesson, does not seek to avenge his family's killings immediately but instead runs to Shaolin. But it is not a running *away*, merely the way of biding time that passes for forbearance in Chinese thought. And the film rewards such forbearance, since Liu becomes Shaolin's quickest learner and eventually returns to Qing society to kill (even despite his new status as a Buddhist monk) the men who murdered his family and to gather up a secular force to bring back to Shaolin to train. In a film that has become hailed as a classic and inaugurating example of the *kungfu* genre, one must not only endure the actual training tasks, but forbear the very conditions—historical, social, cultural, political—that necessitate such training in the first place. Like repression, forbearance might ask us to control or even deny our desires, but it also promises us that we will become better people for it and that the day will come when we no longer have to do so.

IV.

Armed with this understanding of what the term means in and to Chinese culture, we can hence make an argument that forbearance, rather than repression, is the key coping mechanism for the majority of Lee's characters, as well as his theme proper. This essay, however, is not the place where I can do more than gesture, in this and the next paragraph, to what such a wholesale reassessment would look like. But a particularly relevant and instructive instance occurs in *The Wedding Banquet*, a film that at some point arguably shifts from being about the gay couple Wai-Tung and Simon to focusing on the former's father. To be more exact, that point occurs when Mr. Gao, about ten minutes before the end of the film, reveals to Simon that he understands English and hence knows more about the nature of the gay relationship than he has let on. In that moment, the story essentially becomes recast as a tale of forbearance, because we suddenly grasp that Mr. Gao has lived and put up with this knowledge—and is consequently rewarded with a grandchild for his stoic endurance, as he himself recognizes. (There is an echo of this trope, though not this shift, at the end of *Brokeback Mountain*, when Ennis goes to see Jack's parents; there, however, it is the mother who is the picture of forbearance, in part because she also has to put up with the unrelenting father.) In this light, the famous final image of *The Wedding Banquet*—Mr. Gao passes through a security checkpoint in the airport and raises his arms while Lee's camera slows the scene down—makes more sense than most critics have acknowledged. Dilley has come close, though, and puts the matter in especially pertinent terms:

> Most commonly, this ending is viewed with relation to *qigong* martial arts, where the father strikes a pose (resembling a graceful crane with wings aloft) in the physical art of *qigong*. This dignified movement of *qigong* reiterates the Chinese narrative and implies that the patriarch of the family has come to terms with his son's situation [and is] at peace with his son's decision. [But] the pose . . . also (to the Western eye) looks very much like a position of surrender. In this interpretation, the father is read to have been overwhelmed by the dynamics of change caused by the modernizing global influences which force him to release his once-rigid ideology and embrace his son's choice. (64)

Dilley comprehends the scene, rather diplomatically if noncommittally, as allowing for two possible interpretations that have "basically—but not quite—the same meaning," depending, she goes on to say, on readers' "cultural lenses" (64). Mr. Gao's pose would therefore resemble the crawling image of General Han Xin that Li provided us: from one (Western) point of view, both postures look like surrender, but from another (Chinese) perspective, they more positively signify forbearance or the contentment that results. Given how much Lee focuses our attention on it, we might even go further and productively see the arresting final image of *The Wedding Banquet* not just as *permitting* two interpretations but as a comment on *why* these two interpretations are essentially sides of the same coin.

Likewise, though we previously adduced *Crouching Tiger, Hidden Dragon* to illustrate repression in Lee's movies, the *wuxia* film might more properly be considered to be about forbearance. Li Mu Bai could be said to have repressed his feelings for Yu Shu Lien, since he has not acted on them, but the film gives no indication that he and she are *unconscious* about these feelings; rather, the movie implies, the couple has not acted on their love because of their sense of loyalty and duty. Before the film begins, Yu was engaged to a man regarded as Li's brother-in-arms; when the man was killed, neither Li nor Yu felt like they could betray his memory. But the film also raises the possibility that such duty will *cease*. In part, it will cease simply because of the passage of time: after a while, no one will reasonably expect Li and Yu to hold back anymore, so they just have to forbear until that moment. The moment is depicted in the film: near its start, Sir Te is teasing and lighthearted when discussing the long-suspended relationship between Li and Yu, implying that there is no longer any social disapproval of it. In addition, Li is preparing to retire from *jianghui*, which would remove him from the milieu that holds the code of conduct that especially demands and even enforces that kind of loyalty. Jen of course is the spanner in the works: her theft of the sword that Yu was tasked to deliver means that Li has one more matter to settle before he retires. When he pointedly tells Yu, "Just be patient with me, Shu Lien," he is therefore invoking an understanding of forbearance that both of them share.

There is thus a more extensive argument to be made in which we consider what it means to view Lee's oeuvre not through the lens of repression, as is commonly done, but forbearance. What interests me here, of course, is a more specific argument about one Lee film, though the preceding discussion can aid us in understanding the role of forbearance in Lee's "gay cowboy movie." Let me, however, be clear: my argument is not simply that *Brokeback Mountain*, like *The Wedding Banquet* and *Crouching Tiger, Hidden Dragon*, is really about forbearance instead of repression. Rather, I would suggest that Lee's career-long interest in forbearance—an interest that is personal, cultural, and even "racial," albeit one that Lee himself has not been able to accurately name in English interviews—made the story of "Brokeback Mountain" irresistible to him.[4] But Lee, we might say, misrecognizes a tale of repression for one of forbearance, and this results in the deep profound ambivalence in the film.[5] The story I am telling here, in a sense, is one of cultural mistranslation.

One sign of Lee's persistent, not to say repressed, interest in forbearance—or, to be more precise, one sign that he has overmapped his interest in forbearance onto the source material—lies in the way *Brokeback Mountain* is so conscious about the passage of time. Aside from a few flashbacks—and unlike the short story, which is entirely in flashback—the film proceeds chronologically. And it is deeply aware of this chronology, a point that has gone largely unremarked. At one suggestive moment in his essay, Miller alludes to "the film's overall structure of nostalgia" (58), thinking, perhaps, about the way the movie holds up Brokeback Mountain as the space to which it seeks to return. But the movie, on the diegetic plane, *has* raised this option and scuttled it (Jack does try to go back, but learns what Aguirre knows, which effectively forecloses that possibility for good). At the very least, then, we have to recognize that the film also exhibits a desire to move toward not a past but a future, one represented by that "little ranch, a little cow-and-calf operation" Jack wants to set up and share with Ennis. In a briefer article, Martin F. Manalansan IV objects to how the film "colonizes time," by which he means that Lee positions his tale and his two characters as ahistorical, the better to universalize the gay love story. Manalansan points out that the film "bypass[es] such historical landmarks as the Vietnam War . . . the civil rights movement, explorations of the moon, and the sexual revolution," but, strangely, he supports his argument for *Brokeback Mountain*'s "ahistoricity" by noting how "the film marks the beginning of each phase of the lovers' story with calendar years." It is an odd observation and not entirely logical; after all, if Lee truly desires a "shielding of the story from the bedlam of history," then why wouldn't he omit all mention of time (98)? Why not bypass historical events *and* also refuse to number the years? Lee in fact does something like the opposite. We know, for example, exactly when two of the scenes we have already discussed take place: the Fourth of July picnic occurs in 1966 (because a public announcer's voice mentions the year), while the Thanksgiving dustup between Jack and his father-in-law happens in 1977 (another voice, this one presumably from the TV set, tells us so). Lee litters such markers throughout his film, and this is not even to mention the visual cues—graying hair on the characters or a new moustache—that make us aware of the passage of time.

Our previous discussion of how forbearance implicitly promises us a day when our desires can be fulfilled helps answer the question of why *Brokeback Mountain* is so painfully invested in the passing years. Lee's film is structured almost like a suspenseful melodrama, with this as its driving query: will Jack and Ennis ever get to a day, which a contemporary audience tends (or is even encouraged) to imagine is its day, when they can finally live in the happy present? The mentions of years therefore function like a ticking clock (we might even say a ticking bomb)—1963, 1966, 1977, 1980—with the only question being whether we will get our protagonists to, say, 2005. *Wuxia* or *kungfu* movies, such as *The 36th Chamber of Shaolin*, tend not to require that clock, because it is understood that forbearance in such films is often in the service of revenge, and any flick worth its salt (or desirous of commercial success) will never forego the payoff. *Crouching Tiger, Hidden Dragon* does not require such a clock because, as we have already noticed, the race against time is built into the narrative (will Li recover his sword, retire from *jianghui*, and live happily ever after with Yu before something happens to one of them?). But *Brokeback Mountain* has to prompt us to count, although the film's tragedy is that we never get to the time we want.

That the film prompts us but also its characters is most apparent in the exchange prone to being taken as expressing the film's, and especially Ennis's, "repressive" ethos: the now-famous utterance, "If you can't fix it . . . you gotta stand it." The line is part of a longer exchange between Jack and Ennis in the film:

ENNIS: Two guys living together? No way. Now, we can get together once in a while, way the hell out in the middle of nowhere, but . . .
JACK: Once in a while? Every four fucking years?
ENNIS: Well, if you can't fix it, Jack, you gotta stand it.
JACK: For how long?
ENNIS: For as long as we can ride it. There ain't no reins on this one.[6]

There are a few quick and simple points to notice about the scene, the first of which is the way Ennis's choice of verb places his philosophy closer to forbearance than repression. His belief is that the sole option open to them is "standing" it, which is to say, tolerating or enduring, rather than squashing, forgetting, or killing their desires. Second, the exchange notably raises the question of whether the men's forbearance will have any reward or vindication and when: "For how long?" The moment in a sense parallels *Crouching Tiger, Hidden Dragon*'s "Just be patient with me, Shu Lien," except that here, Ennis cannot even promise a payoff. All that is left for Jack to do, therefore, is to count the years in the hope that Ennis or things will change. And of course, they never do. Appropriately, then, in the last conversation the two men ever have, Jack seems to come to some new moment of resignation with this lament: "There's never enough time, never enough . . ."

But the dialogue is also important because it resembles the sequence with which we began. Like the Fourth of July set piece, the conversation between Jack and Ennis is less coherent than it first appears, and in its incoherence we can once again glean how the crossing of Lee's fascination with forbearance on the one hand, and a story about sexual repression on the other, has resulted in a deeply ambivalent film. As Jack and Ennis talk, the referent of "it" keeps shifting. Within Ennis's key line ("If you can't fix it, Jack, you gotta stand it"), there is already an ambiguity: given that the two men were examining their passion ("We can get together once in a while"), we might assume that "it" refers to sexual desire. Yet by the end of the line, "it" appears to signify something like "the situation": they have to stand (that is, endure) the conditions or circumstances, Ennis points out. Following Jack's response, however, "it" begins to inhabit a specific metaphor. When Ennis answers, "For as long as we can ride it," he likens their situation to the rodeo; accordingly, "it" transforms into a more specific referent for the sport that Jack tries his hand, but is never particularly good, at. When Ennis tags on a second comment ("There ain't no reins on this one"), "it" comes to rest on an even more precise referent: the bull, because that would be what the reins are normally attached to. But this then has the retroactive effect of conferring a double meaning on another word, "fix": whereas it first sounded like a mere synonym for mend, repair, or correct, by the end of the conversation, when we are in the midst of the rodeo metaphor, "fixing" the bull would obviously mean to castrate it.

The unconsciously ambivalent conversation, we might therefore say, pursues two not entirely compatible possibilities and narratives at the same time. In one, the problem ("it") is *desire* itself, and hence the film must direct its words and energies toward "fixing" this desire—controlling it, staying on top of it, reining it in, or as a final resort, castrating it, all of which we might think of as forms of repression. In a second narrative, the problem is not so much desire, but the *circumstances* that would prohibit or inhibit this desire. In this case, the film asks its protagonists to forbear and wait: hang on tight even though there is nothing to hang on to, ride the years out, stand it for as long as they are able. Given how much Lee is therefore asking of Ennis (not to mention himself), and how conflicted and conflicting these requests are, is it any wonder that the film ultimately cannot tell if Ennis succeeds, or even what success looks like?[7]

Notes

My thanks to Russell Heng, Martin Kavka, Daisy Ng, James St. André, Tan Pin Pin, and Paul Tschudi.

1. We might compare this sequence with three others that D. A. Miller isolates in an essay on *Brokeback Mountain* that continues his interest in the policing effects of film: when Jack first sees Ennis, when Joe Aguirre spies on the couple, and when Alma spots her husband kissing Jack. At these three moments, Miller points out, we first see "the Homosexual"—and then we realize that we are really seeing someone else (Jack, Joe, Alma) see that figure. These culminating shots therefore "render the preceding shot or sequence, given to us 'objectively,' into a 'subjective' point of view," and "the omniscient narration always has the same content: a spectacle of erotic play between Jack and Ennis" (56). The Fourth of July sequence likewise changes point of view midstream, although here the switch is from "subjective" (the bikers) to "objective" (Lee, assuming we can call the filmmaker "objective"). Miller's concern is with how the film positions its spectators; he argues that Lee's three shots "work to put the spectator at a remove from the very triangle they construct" (58). I, however, am more curious about where *Brokeback Mountain*'s filmmaker stands. Nevertheless, if I had to connect my project with Miller's, I would say—and here I would be taking a leaf from Miller's own work—that Miller's three sequences may serve as a kind of decoy or distraction: the way

they pass from objectivity to subjectivity strikes me as so marked that they serve to mask, I would suggest, the subtler passage performed by the Fourth of July sequence.

2. "I was drawn to Jen because she was the hidden dragon," Lee has said in an interview. "[T]his hidden dragon represents sexual repression, which is the hardest to tame. . . . But personally speaking, I identify more with Li Mubai and Yu Shu Lien. That's the kind of person I am—reasonable and a team player type" (M. Berry 343). Lee's phrasing is a bit confusing because it almost sounds like he sees Jen *as* sexually repressed; it should be clear from the context, however, that he is really casting her as the id-like sexual energy in Li and Yu with which they have to contend.

3. Aside from Ownby's very informative essay (and the full-length study it has been expanded into, *Falun Gong and the Future of China*), consult *Qigong Fever* by David A. Palmer.

4. Perhaps unsure of how to avoid essentialist interpretations, critics have tended not to read *Brokeback Mountain* in the light of Lee's identity as an Asian filmmaker. I hope it is clear that "race" does not have a naturalized status in my essay (nor does, of course, "culture"). One exception that does try to locate the film in a Chinese context is an essay by Chris Berry, which begins by pointing out how the film's debt to that most American of genres, the Western, obscures the fact that "just like Everest, *Brokeback Mountain* has a less well-known Chinese side." Berry goes on to place Lee's movie within two rather marginal Chinese traditions: what he calls the "family ethics" film and "popular culture stories produced for and often by straight women about love between two handsome young men" (32). But while Berry's contextualizations offer alternative or additional ways of viewing the film, they do not fundamentally change our understanding of one of the issues at its very heart, the closeting of homosexuality.

5. It is unlikely that Lee needed any help in misreading Proulx's story as one of forbearance, but the word does pop up once in the tale, albeit in a relatively minor sense. Reunited when Jack finally sends Ennis a postcard four years after their summer together, the two men debate how often they can now see each other:

> "How much is once in a while?" said Jack. "Once in a while ever four fuckin years?"
>
> "No," said Ennis, forbearing to ask whose fault that was. "I goddamn hate it that you're goin a drive away in the mornin and I'm goin back to work." ("Brokeback Mountain" 301)

6. This cinematic conversation collapses and conflates two or three moments from Proulx's short story. The first moment is already broached in note 5, because after he declares his hatred that Jack will leave soon, Ennis

continues, "But if you can't fix it you got a stand it" ("Brokeback Mountain" 301). Right at the end of the narrative, this viewpoint becomes recast in an authorial voice, as the story's final words: "There was some open space between what he knew and what he tried to believe, but nothing could be done about it, and if you can't fix it you've got to stand it" (318). Meanwhile, the metaphor of the reins comes from a separate occasion, when Ennis expresses his fears of being outed: "We do that in the wrong place we'll be dead. There's no reins on this one. It scares the piss out a me" (299).

7. In a three-page postscript, "inspired by *Brokeback Mountain*," to *Sentimental Fabulations, Contemporary Chinese Films*, Rey Chow suggests that Lee might see his film as "a bona fide reincarnation of the great Chinese theme [expressed in *Liang Sanbo yu Zhu Yingtai*, or *Butterfly Lovers*, the classic Mandarin story, opera, and film] of not being able to speak openly or directly about romantic feelings." But, she points out, *Brokeback Mountain* is also "a sentimental story in that it involves no act of social revolt or rebellion" (198). "To my mind," Chow writes, "the film's affective mode . . . seems entirely in tune with the workings of the sentimental" Chinese films she studies in her book. "With filiality as its keel, this is an affective mode whose intensity is distinguished most of all by its tendency toward accommodation and thus, ultimately, toward what in Chinese idiom is known as *weiqu qiuquan* 委曲求全—literally, stooping/bending to make compromises out of consideration for the general interest" (199).

There are definite affinities between the stance Chow identifies and the concept of forbearance I have outlined. I do think that the latter is much better known and more widespread than the former—if nothing else, 忍 is a catchy and popular word, while 委曲求全 is a fairly literary idiom. Furthermore, unlike Chow's "affective mode" (involving filiality, accommodation, and compromise), forbearance, as I have shown, is not necessarily practiced "out of consideration for the general interest." Most importantly, while Chow's brief observations are provocative, they do not register how *politically* problematic it is that a story about two gay men should involve "no act of social revolt or rebellion." Chow calls the film a success because "it dare[s] focalize on compromise" (199), but she does not notice that, from a Western perspective, this focus is "daring" in a totally different sense because it can be seen as an endorsement of the closet. She is therefore largely uninterested in thinking through, as I have tried to do in this paper, the relationship between the "Chinese" posture of forbearance (or accommodation and compromise) and the "Western" notion of repression.

Part 2 } Miles to Go and Promises to Keep

Homophobic Culture and Gay Civil Rights

6 } Back to the Ranch Ag'in

Brokeback Mountain and Gay Civil Rights

JAMES MORRISON

Asked after a routine stump speech in 2005 if he had seen *Brokeback Mountain*—at the height of the film's lightning-rod popularity—George W. Bush replied with a telling combination of studied equanimity and barely repressed embarrassment. He had not seen it, Bush answered matter-of-factly, whereupon he dissolved into a troll of sheepish giggles, exhorting the young man who had posed the question, "I hope you'll—go back to the ranch." In one sense, the meaning of this curious parry was clear enough. It implied that the notorious "gay cowboy" romance had polluted the wholesome and bucolic space of the ranch as a mythological locale, and it counseled a return to an innocent frontier unsullied by this intrusion of homosexuality.

Yet if one did not know better, one might have thought the president was reaching for a distant literary allusion. His would-be witticism, after all, recalls the title of Leslie Fiedler's 1948 essay "Come Back to the Raft Ag'in, Huck Honey!"—except that where Fiedler's bawdy title, part in joke and part double entendre, slyly proposes the return to the raft as a preslash-narrative fantasy of gay sex between two of American literature's stalwarts—Jim and Huck in Mark Twain's *The Adventures of Huckleberry Finn*. Bush's panicked remark, however, dispensed amid an effusion of debate about homosexual marriage in the United States, posits a parallel return as a *retreat* from the encumbrances of contemporary gay politics, especially the politics of civil rights. Bush's comment articulates a wish to preserve the very aspect of American sentimental life that, for Fiedler, the "existence of overt homosexuality threatens to compromise" (665)—an image of masculine fellowship, allied to an idealized wilderness and rustic male pastimes, uncontaminated by the taint of lust.

What is frequently missed in discussions of Fiedler's thesis is its role as a chapter in the postwar melodrama of civil rights in the United States. Yet it is in just that context that Fiedler considers a revived currency for the time-honored coupling of those "stock" figures, "the Negro and the homosexual." In the original version of the essay published in *Partisan Review,* Fiedler presciently notes the complex relationship that binds the two in cultural conception: "Our laws on homosexuality and the context of prejudice and feeling they objectify must apparently be changed to accord with a stubborn social fact, whereas it is the social fact, our overt behavior toward the Negro, that must be modified to accord with our laws" (665). Writing years before the Civil Rights Acts of 1957 and 1964, Fiedler already took for granted new protections for African Americans in the civil arena—perhaps having in mind the Supreme Court's ban on segregation in interstate bus travel in 1946 or Harry Truman's creation of the Fair Employment Board in 1948, the same year Fiedler wrote. Despite the archaic whiff of some of his language, Fiedler stakes out here a quite progressive position—that, once the humanity of gay people is acknowledged as "a stubborn social fact," then majoritarian homophobia cannot rightly obstruct the conferral of civil rights on this constituency, even if the granting of such rights to blacks has done little to diminish American racism. Put in these terms, Fiedler's claim describes a situation that remains essentially unchanged, despite obvious advances, some sixty years later.

Brokeback Mountain combines a progressive, urbane empathy with a Fiedleresque vision of American pastoral—just the mix that led Bush's questioner to ask him about the movie in the first place. To put it in the crude terms of modern U.S. politics, it weds the sensibility of the blue states with the imagery of the red states, and that is why it has emerged as such an important mediating object for contemporary social debates on gay rights. Set in a period of intense cultural shift from 1963 to 1985, the movie staunchly refuses any opportunity to index the most pertinent or decisive changes this era brought about, from the Civil Rights Act of 1964, through Stonewall, to the AIDS epidemic. In doing so, it places itself squarely in the mythic terrain Fiedler surveyed, a place of timeless fraternity and good fellowship, rife with masculine frolics and comradely fishing trips. It then brings to the forefront the "stubborn social fact" Fiedler was at such pains to acknowledge. Even in this Edenic landscape, this impeccably natural environment, this film insists, queer love flourishes—at least for a while.

Fiedler's essay argues that the pervasive myths of the American pastoral are rooted in hypocrisy and profound regression. Because white Americans cannot meaningfully acknowledge the historical legacies of their own violence against nonwhites, Fiedler observes, they revert compulsively to sanitized archetypes of chastened love between white males and men of color in books such as Cooper's Leatherstocking tales, *Moby-Dick*, or *The Adventures of Huckleberry Finn*. Yet these archetypes, for Fiedler, contain and encode that guilt. They depend on the white man's flight from the civilization that exacted this violence, casting him as an outcast whose self-styled alienation enables a mythic reunion with the African American or Native American other: "Our dark-skinned beloved will take us in, we assure ourselves, when we have been cut off, or have cut ourselves off from all others, without rancor or the insult of forgiveness. . . . [H]e will comfort us, as if our own offense against him were long ago remitted, were never truly *real*" (*Partisan Review* 670).

What Fiedler's work illustrates most pointedly is the inextricability of regressive and progressive claims in debates concerning minorities' civil rights waged in majoritarian public spheres. While respondents of Fiedler's own time vented their outrage about the writer's daring to impute homoerotic contents to the American classics, contemporary critics have had little difficulty in discerning the underlying homophobia of Fiedler's own work. As Joseph Allen Boone points out, "Fiedler often betrayed a biased view of 'normal' or 'correct' male development, one rooted in the psychoanalytic milieu of America in the 1950s; for, in his eyes, the freedom sought by the male protagonist 'on the run' from society *necessarily* constitutes an arrested adolescent avoidance of adult identity and hence of the mature love embodied in marital responsibility" (228). Certainly, as he himself acknowledges, Fiedler is stuck with the benighted vocabulary of his own day—as we are with ours—including words like "inversion," "pederasty," "buggery," "fag" (the last revised in a subsequent version of the essay as the presumably less offensive "queer," but both clearly intended in context as an effort to speak in what Fiedler takes to be terms of self-definition of homosexuals as a group). Though laudable as an episode of thought reform, Boone's relegation of such attitudes to a quaint and distant past, "America in the 1950s," ignores the persistence of such language into the present, in spite of its marginally successful stigmatization. Boone's supposition that changed language equals changed attitudes would not have been shared by Fiedler, who did not assume that ideas were embodied in words or that words encoded ideas in them but rather that both were carried in collectively shared myths that neither reason nor reform could easily eradicate, even if guided by the notion that localized exposure inevitably produces a greater enlightenment. What Fiedler meant by "archetype," after all, was "a coherent pattern of beliefs and feelings so widely shared at a level beneath consciousness that there exists no abstract vocabulary for representing it, and so 'sacred' that unexamined, irrational restraints inhibit any explicit analysis." Even progressive efforts to expose these damaging myths are limited by the fact that they can proceed only, as Fiedler notes, "according to the language of the day" (522).

Fiedler was not writing in what he took to be a progressive age. When he reprinted "Come Back to the Raft" in his book *An End to Innocence* in 1955, it was in the context of an excoriation of liberal backwardness from an explicitly liberal vantage. In the book's first chapter, he makes this position clear: "American liberalism has been reluctant to leave the garden of its illusion; but it can dally no longer: the age of innocence is dead. . . . It is not necessary that liberals be self-flagellants. We have desired good, and we have done some; but we have also done great evil. The confession in itself is nothing, but without the confession there can be no understanding, and without the understanding . . . we will not be able to move forward from a liberalism of innocence to a liberalism of responsibility" (24).

In the same vein, in *Love and Death in the American Novel* (1960)—a book typically read as an expansion of the themes of "Come Back to the Raft"—he confronts with ironic trepidation the very question his most hostile respondents hurled at him on the appearance of the earlier essay: "How could Antinous come to preside over the literature of the nineteenth century United States, which is to say, at a time and in a place where homosexuality was regarded with a horror perhaps unmatched elsewhere and ever?" In response, he cautions against just the sort of majoritarian homophobia that had greeted that essay: "[S]o violent a disavowal of male inversion foster[s] an ignorance of its true nature" (350). Fiedler remains silent on what this "true nature" might be—while ridiculing those who vilify it as "sin" or "crime"—but readers after the brief flowering of queer theory are likely to find the taint of homophobia in any such reference, especially to something already designated as "inversion."

All of this, however, is only to locate Fiedler's standpoint to clarify the significance of the claim he makes from it. Despite the complicating factor of his own Jewishness, he writes from what remains essentially a majoritarian position, at least in regard to sexual identity—that of straight white cold war liberalism. The nuances of his work reveal what should come as no surprise, that this position, however sympathetic to minoritarian calls for gay rights—demands that barely existed as he wrote—readily embraces what may in fact be a substantial measure of homophobia. He declares that "[o]ur laws on homosexuality . . . must apparently be changed." To reject this conclusion because it is based on the assumption of homosexuality's immutability—the "stubborn social fact"—rather than on that of its validity would be to disregard a basic feature of American civil rights movements, namely, their dependence on majoritarian assent, including that of hostile opponents.

Even more to the point is the observation that *Brokeback Mountain*, appearing at a time that many *would* call progressive, derives from a similarly majoritarian standpoint and addresses, in large part, a majoritarian audience. Above all, it is an expression of sympathy for suffering, derided, marginalized others, with little of Fiedler's provocative self-consciousness despite its wholesale adoption of both the mythos he outlines and the disapproval he ultimately vents against it. Even if this sense of otherness were not fully visible in the movie itself, it would remain vexingly audible in the words of the film's creators. As one of the actors (Jake Gyllenhaal) remarked on the prospect of playing a gay cowboy: "I was like, No way! . . . At eighteen years old, it's not something you want to be involved in" (Spines 37). Or, as the director Ang Lee commented on the difficulties of the production: "It didn't make any sense why anybody would make this movie. The place you don't know. The gayness you don't know. It's so hard it wrenches your guts" (34). In both quotations, the "you" remains blithely unexamined, but what is indisputably clear is that this "you" is decidedly not gay.

This background points to the simple fact of the film's peculiar status as a nominally gay movie by, and largely for, straight people. This hardly places it at odds with the few previous mainstream gay movies, typically designed for niche audiences or those few straights who might find some titillating satisfaction of curiosity in them, and pedaled with the same robust expressions of heterosexuality one finds in the utterances cited previously. In this sense, *Brokeback Mountain* stands outside the history of gay cinema as such, a history it ignores insofar as it duly countermands any putative "advances" of that cinema—those, say, of the New Queer Cinema of the nineties, which for all its outrage against oppression set itself devoutly against majoritarian dictates or norms. Viewed from this perspective, *Brokeback Mountain* reverts to a model in which the oppressive majority is addressed, more in sorrow than in anger, in an exhibit of homosexuality as a state of abjection seen as sadly unjust to the extent that gay people are akin to straight people. This assumption—one that few would deny, of course—comes more sharply into focus once one acknowledges that *Brokeback Mountain* is much more a film about marriage than it is about homosexuality, a fact that must account for much of the movie's mass popularity.

Why does the theme of heterosexual marriage play such a prominent role in the "gay cowboy movie"? Annie Proulx, author of the story that served as the basis of the film, ventures the following answer in terms uneasily close in its underlying assumptions to the ruminations of the movie's director and its costar: "Because this is a rural story, family and children are important. Most stories (and many films) I have seen about gay relationships take place in urban settings and never have children in them. The rural gay men I know like kids, and if they don't have their own, they usually have nephews and nieces who claim a big place in their hearts" ("Getting Movied" 132).

It is not clear what stories and films Proulx has been reading and seeing (*Philadelphia? Velvet Goldmine? Mädchen in Uniform? The Object of My Affection? Querelle?*), but her comment absents an important lineage of gay writing with rural settings from, to name only a few, Paul Bowles to Tennessee Williams, James Purdy, and Dorothy Allison—and featuring, as it happens, a rich array of children as characters. The real crux of the matter, though, appears to be this: "For both characters to marry women enlarges the story and introduces two young wives who move from innocence and happy trust to some pretty hard lessons about real life. Alma and Lureen [the wives] give the story a universal connection, for men and women need each other, sometimes in unusual ways" ("Getting Movied" 132). The straight wives, in other words, are universal; the gay husbands apparently less so. It should be kept in mind that these words were written not in benighted 1948 but in progressive 2005, by an avowedly sympathetic party. Yet for Proulx, clearly, lives without marriage are diminished at least to the extent that marriage, in her view, serves to "enlarge" them. What is most striking in these remarks, however, is that Proulx cannot understand why gay narratives would move away from the standard marriage plot, as she expresses a hunger for that plot that remains unsated, apparently, even though nearly all stories, everywhere, reproduce it. A particularly pernicious universalism is at work in Proulx's comments—as it rarely is in Fiedler's—implicitly faulting gays and lesbians for failing to achieve an estate from which society excludes them and promoting the homophobic presumption that same-sex relationships abrogate profound male-female intimacies. This is logically tantamount to arguing that marriages of "one man and one woman"—in the current antigay slogan—destructively exclude all people outside those unions, and from Proulx's assertion, it is a small step to the stereotypical claim that gay men hate women or that lesbians hate men.

A similar universalism animates conservative defenses of gay marriage by popular pundits like Bruce Bawer and Andrew Sullivan. To simplify these writers' already simple contentions, they argue that gay people are much like anyone else—the title of Sullivan's book is *Virtually Normal*—and should be allowed to marry so that they can be even more so, in the name of social order. To the extent that gay sexuality has historically arisen apart from conventional marriage, this argument amounts to a demand for the privilege of assimilation. It relates interestingly to the concept of "covering" in Kenji Yoshino's sense of that word (adapted somewhat problematically from Erving Goffman). In *Covering: The Hidden Assault on Our Civil Rights*, Yoshino discusses the difference between those with stigmatized traits who attempt to render the trait wholly invisible and those who try to render it less obtrusive—"passing" versus "covering." He goes on to sketch gay history in the twentieth century according to this distinction:

> Through the middle of the twentieth century, gays were routinely asked to convert to heterosexuality, whether through lobotomies, electroshock therapy, or psychoanalysis. As the gay rights movement gained strength, the demand to convert gradually ceded to the demand to pass. This shift can be seen in the military's adoption in 1993 of the "Don't ask, don't tell" policy, under which gays are permitted to serve so long as we agree to pass. Finally, at millennium's turn, the demand to pass is giving way to the demand to cover—gays are increasingly permitted to be gay and out so long as we do not "flaunt" our identities. (19)

Significantly, Yoshino views "the contemporary resistance to gay marriage" as a "covering demand: *Fine, be gay, but don't shove it in our faces*" (19; emphases in original). But if marriage is defined as what ensures the stability of homes, the pliability and diligence of workers, and the fertility of families—all in the name of utilitarian mandates disguised as social goods—one could argue with equal legitimacy that gay marriage might be itself a form of covering, integrating gays into a set of heterosexual norms.

Indeed, this is a tamer restatement of Michael Warner's argument in *The Trouble with Normal*, an extended rebuttal of Sullivan's position. In that book, Warner criticizes Sullivan for desexualizing gays in general and argues that the drive for gay marriage, specifically, has the purpose of domesticating gay sexuality, recuperating it under a spuriously virtuous norm. Many gays, of course, desire the civic parity marriage may be thought to confer—and if marriage is a right, there can be little doubt that gays deserve it as a function of equal protection under the law. For many others, though—for me, certainly—a clear benefit of being gay is that one is under no obligation to marry. Though this liberation is also obviously the product of a forcible exclusion, it brings to light a fact about marriage as such. If many homosexuals resent their exclusion from marriage, many heterosexuals experience marriage itself as an oppressive societal demand.

Certainly Jack and Ennis, erstwhile heterosexuals who are the main characters in *Brokeback Mountain*, marry because it is expected of them. The oppressive quality of these marriages recalls the failing, stifling unions strewn throughout exemplars of the marriage plot, including the work of writers such as Proulx and Larry McMurtry, coauthor of the screenplay for the film and also the author of numerous studies in bad marriages and soured heterosexuality, including *Horseman, Pass By* (filmed as *Hud*), *The Last Picture Show*, and *Terms of Endearment*. A study of these writers' collective work—mostly in a thoroughly heterosexual context—could make the case that marriage itself is the pertinent social problem. Certainly contemporary U.S. debates on gay marriage—from which gays are often denied any meaningful participation—are less about gay rights than about a crisis in heterosexuality, a surely unfounded fear that heterosexuality cannot hold its own in a free market. These debates function to provide conservatives with an appearance of moderation, based in the rhetorical concession that gays do deserve rights—just not this one. This specious position continually allows the rollback of fundamental rights putatively not under discussion, co-opting gay marriage, practically speaking, as a diversion on the part of the right. Such ignominious strategies are comparable to opponents' tactical shifts from large questions of general social parity to more circumscribed issues of voting rights to forestall larger gains prior to the 1964 Civil Rights Act. Playing into this manipulation, Sullivan advocates lobbying for gay marriage and then, once it is achieved, shutting down the gay rights movement. This position assumes just what George W. Bush pretends, that gay rights in the United States are already established, as part of "our" cherished freedoms. For Sullivan, too, there seems only one last battle to be won, but in practice, it will have to be fought state by state, at agonizing length, with all the petty advances and virulent backlashes decreed by the galling predictability of human behavior. The truth is that gay civil rights give every indication of being at the *start* of processes of social reification, not at the end of them. We do well to recall that, when sodomy laws were struck down by the Supreme Court—only in 2003, having been powerfully reaffirmed in 1986—dissenters from the opinion worried that it would open the door to gay marriage. Yet the triumph of that decision, if any, was that it just opened the same door some might have thought Stonewall had already thrown wide, thirty-five years before. Sixty years after Fiedler's explicit call for gay civil rights, they remain only local and nebulous. If the movement for gay marriage reminds us of how precariously stationed the rights of gay people in the United States really are and if it consolidates activism around a platform as meaningful as the 1964 Civil Rights Act—an aspiration undreamed of by too many, precisely due to the smokescreen of gay marriage—it will have been a valuable episode.

Brokeback Mountain is just the film for a cultural moment embroiled in debates such as these. Its success, therefore, is no surprise at all. Just as the movie mixes a dose of blue-state liberalism with a wash of red-state iconography, it is a post-Stonewall movie—in its frank depiction of a sex act, for instance, and its vigilant avoidance of gay stereotypes—with a pre-Stonewall heart, in which there is nary a hint of the seeming breakthroughs of New Queer Cinema. In contrast to most works of that movement, which took up questions of the politics of sexuality and the social construction of gender, Brokeback Mountain posits sexuality as the function of a deep-seated and implicitly unchangeable nature. This assumption is basic to the movie's universalizing tendency, as a nature is something we are all supposed to have. The movie's overall sensibility is even more germane to this universalist disposition, as it discards the commitments to identity politics of recent queer cinema in favor of old-fashioned appeals to pathos. By situating itself squarely in myth, it allows straight people to weep over the plight of oppressed gays without taking responsibility for their own position as oppressors.

Brokeback Mountain begins in myth and falls into time without ever making a detour through history. For nearly the first third, the film chronicles a summer season of shepherding, Jack and Ennis alone in the wilderness with their work and their flock. The movie emphasizes, in this phase, the diurnal intensity of the labor and the natural beauty of the setting, in rhythms infused with a quiet placidity, befitting a bluff arcadian parable. The moment of Ennis and Jack's coupling cannot be called unexpected—the whole episode depends on the audience's feverish anticipation of it—but it remains surprising all the same. After this turn, the film's narrative technique shifts. The two men soon part, and the film becomes markedly elliptical, crosscutting restlessly between their separate lives over a period of decades, in smooth yet clipped interludes punctuated by their periodic reunions in the wilderness. The shocking news of Jack's death truncates this long middle stretch, preparing for a final movement into a grievous stasis that answers, in negative, the pacific tones of the film's opening section. Ennis's tragic, unbending solitude, at the end of the film, unfolds in a parallel state of timelessness, attesting to adjacent forms of allegory—one tied to thwarted fantasies of flight and freedom, the other to insistent realities of consequence and bondage.

As Fiedler notes, U.S. myths of wilderness traditionally place it beyond the reach of history. In such tales, it is both vast and marginal, open and unpopulated, empty of convenience and culture but abundant in liberty for those very reasons—because it eludes the oppressive charters of civilization and is thus conceived as the only remaining site of escape. In terms perhaps more obvious than Fiedler's, such myths are mired in denial. In the U.S. West, any pretty piece of vastness, after all, might have been subject in some less mythic past to violent evacuation to secure its impressive, isolated grandeur, and any stretch of wilderness may be viewed, therefore, not so much as gloriously unpopulated as uncannily *de*populated. As an idea, wilderness may be most powerful less as the site of escape from civilization's prohibitions than as the place where these conscriptions operate under cover or where they are given a freer rein due to the widespread illusion that they are in abeyance there. Proulx herself describes her setting as "empowering and inimical" ("Getting Movied" 131). A far more self-conscious writer on the myths of U.S. wilderness, Marilynne Robinson suggests an even more sinister overtone in an essay that recommends, Fiedler-like, giving up the idea of wilderness in favor of that of responsibility. "Wilderness," writes Robinson, "is where things can be hidden" (246).

The yoking of this wilderness setting to gay and straight marriage plots is the principal claim to novelty of both the story and the film of *Brokeback Mountain*. In this respect, too, it follows tradition, since for much of the twentieth century, gay identity has been associated predominantly with the phenomenon of urbanization. John D'Emilio's study of the making of a homosexual minority in the United States in the period from 1940 to 1970 aptly represents the common approach. In that book, D'Emilio not only exclusively examines the emergence of urban subcultures but never ventures to comment on rural communities, nor to note the absence of any such discussion. Like nearly every commentator along these lines, D'Emilio assumes that the rise of homosexuality as a category of identity over the last hundred years was enabled by industrialization and its consequent production of large cities:

> During the second half of the twentieth century, the momentous shift to industrial capitalism provided the conditions for a homosexual and lesbian identity to emerge. . . . The interlocking processes of urbanization and industrialization created a social context in which an autonomous personal life could develop. Affection, intimate relationships, and sexuality moved increasingly into the realm of individual choice, seemingly disconnected from how one organized the production of goods necessary for survival. In this setting, men and women who felt a strong erotic attraction to their own sex could begin to fashion from their feeling a personal identity and a way of life. (11)

D'Emilio does not deny that same-sex attraction may precede the social forces that consolidate it, but he has almost no interest in this dimension of the issue in practice. Instead, he examines the coalescence of these forces to produce homosexuality as a category of identity and a reified lifestyle, using the backdrop of the urban setting to lay the groundwork for a discussion of the social construction of gay and lesbian identity.

By contrast, *Brokeback Mountain* departs from an urban setting precisely to challenge the idea of sexuality as social construction. Proulx's story is most direct in this regard in the description of Jack and Ennis's first sexual encounter: "Ennis ran full-throttle on all roads whether fence mending or money spending, and he wanted none of it when Jack seized his left hand and brought it to his erect cock. Ennis jerked his hand away as though he'd touched fire, got to his knees, unbuckled his belt, shoved his pants down, hauled Jack onto all fours and, with the help of the clear slick and a little spit, entered him, nothing he'd done before but no instruction manual needed" ("Brokeback Mountain" 7). The first sentence of this passage represents the folksy obliquity that characterizes Proulx's style throughout. Despite the conjunction of the two clauses with the neutral "and," the sentence still implies a causal relation. Because Ennis defines himself as conventionally masculine— propulsive, animated, "full-throttle"—he instinctively spurns Jack's lure. Yet his subsequent advance in the "active" role is equally instinctual. The next sentence piles up verbs in a rush of quick phrases that give no sense of when his automatic recoil turns into innate acceptance.

More than preserved in the film, this vision of sex-as-instinct has clear implications for the cultural politics of the movie. For all its reserved eloquence and tortured empathy, *Brokeback Mountain* is something like the *Uncle Tom's Cabin* of Hollywood movies about gay experience. Its narrative of doomed love might have been culled from the back reaches of the Celluloid Closet, but for the western garb, and its underlying sense of moral indignation is channeled stringently into a well of the taciturn pity that comprises the film's dominant affect. Like Stowe's classic work of sentimental protest, *Brokeback Mountain* exhibits individual calamities, through a lens of vicarious pathos, as indices of social injustice, while actively resisting a larger social analysis of the individuals' circumstances in favor of a direct emotional appeal. To suggest such a parallel should not be seen to denigrate the achievements of the film but to underline the fact that the movement for gay civil rights in the United States has never had its *Uncle Tom's Cabin*. Empty of significant understanding of African American experience beyond that of the white reformist's zeal, the abolitionist fervor of Stowe's book was an extreme form of what every drive for minoritarian civil rights in the United States has required to date, for better or worse—a persuasive expression in the cultural sector of powerful support from a majoritarian position.

In fact, the parallels run deeper than such shared aspirations or surface similarities. Both works, for example, counterpoint studies of two marriages, that of the Legrees and the St. Clares in Stowe's novel and those of Jack and Ennis to their respective wives in *Brokeback Mountain*. All are, in one way or another, failed marriages—and it is instructive to recall here Fiedler's treatment of the theme of heterosexual union in *Love and Death in the American Novel*. He argues that marriage, as represented in American literature, surrenders repeatedly to the same sentimental myths that produce the archetype of "innocent homosexuality," yielding a cult of specious purity on the one hand and terrible manifestations of fetishism and sadism on the other—once these myths inevitably collide with the very reality-principle they have taken root to obviate. In *Uncle Tom's Cabin*, the two marriages enact an archetypal confrontation of purity and corruption, pairing a debauched slave driver with a benign Christian, or a fallen Southern belle with an upright gentleman. In *Brokeback Mountain*, the marriages are doomed from the start by the film's proposition, both sentimentally romantic and dire, that Jack and Ennis are meant for each other, that their bouts of sex on the mountain are not merely "a way to make the time pass," as one hostile character remarks, but evidence, in the terms of the film, of something deep within themselves. This is a conviction that the marriages are portrayed at such length precisely in order to convey. Consequently, a clear implication of the film is that heterosexual marriage, contrary to conservative dogma, is endangered not by homosexual relationships but by social edicts that compel gay people into marriages running counter to their natures.

Finally, both *Brokeback Mountain* and *Uncle Tom's Cabin* turn on acts of violence meant to provoke the audience's revulsion, the murderous beating of Tom in Stowe's novel and the killing of Jack in *Brokeback Mountain*. In *Uncle Tom's Cabin*, Tom's death has about it more than a whiff of ritual penitence. Tom is punished for his lone act of rebellion, his refusal to betray a runaway slave. A spokesperson in the novel for Christian forbearance and the acceptance of one's lot, Tom must fall prey to his own passivity, demonstrating the inefficacy of this quietist position, so that the book's protest—which nonetheless invokes Christian charity as its guiding principle—may achieve its most dramatic shape. Yet the implicit call to action embodied in this painful martyrdom is displaced and absented, as Fiedler notes, by a devout return to the family romance plot, as if "to [Stowe's] bourgeois readers slavery would stand condemned only if it were proved an offense against the sacred family and the suffering mother" (*Love and Death* 266). The representation of Jack's death in *Brokeback Mountain* treads a similarly fine line. It harks back to the necrologies of mainstream cinema, so copiously tallied by Vito Russo in *The Celluloid Closet* (1981), in which the elimination of gay characters typically vents both a halfhearted pathos and the symbolic satisfaction of a righteous purgation (the death of Plato at the end of *Rebel without a Cause* [1955] comes to mind). The extent to which recent efforts to portray gay experience in the Hollywood mainstream, from *Philadelphia* (1993) to *Brokeback Mountain*, retain this underlying structure is worthy of note, even as they amplify the pathos as a mark of their greater understanding and convert the purge into a strategically necessary sacrifice now intended to signify an abject loss instead of a cathartic purification.

Perhaps to circumvent this slipknot, *Brokeback Mountain* casts a swathe of ambiguity over Jack's death. It might be either an improbable accident, the explosion of a tire, or a hate crime, an attack with a tire iron. In Proulx's story, this ambiguity enlarges a key theme: Ennis's concern with whether Jack has sex with other men and is therefore "really" gay. It is clear, in both the story and the film, that Ennis does not regard himself as "queer" because Jack is the only man with whom he has had sex. When he discovers that Jack has frequented Mexican prostitutes—a sexual recourse to racial otherness with a distinct Fiedlerian overtone—Ennis himself threatens violence against Jack, in a fit of rage: "[A]ll them things I don't know could get you killed if I should come to know them" (21). At the story's end, when Ennis visits Jack's parents after his death, he learns that Jack was planning to bring another man to live with him on the ranch in place of Ennis. In response to this revelation, Ennis's inner reflection is characteristically laconic: "So now he knew it had been the tire iron" (25). In other words, Ennis realizes in the same instant that Jack was really gay and that this was what, in Ennis's understanding, made him the victim of the murderous homophobia Ennis's lifetime of denial avoided.

The question of whether both Jack and Ennis are really gay was an object of dispute among several of the film's critics. As one writer put it, the film is "about two men who are in love, and it makes no sense. It makes no sense in terms of who they are, where they are, how they live and how they see themselves. It makes no sense in terms of what they do for a living or how they would probably vote in a national election" (LaSalle E5). Rejecting such approaches, Daniel Mendelsohn views them as indicating the urban bias in the social construction of homosexuality: "Criticisms like [these] . . . trying to persuade you that *Brokeback* isn't 'really' gay, that Jack and Ennis's love 'makes no sense' because they're Wyoming ranch hands who are likely to vote Republican, only work if you believe that being gay means having a certain look, or a certain life-style (urban, say), or politics; that it's anything other than the bare fact of being erotically attracted primarily to members of your own sex" ("Affair to Remember" 13). Both sides of this debate respond to something deep in the film, attuned as this movie is to strategies of self-denial potential in homosexual identity that pose special challenges to the achievement of gay civil rights. Jack and Ennis are indeed, in Mendelsohn's words, "Wyoming ranch hands who are likely to vote Republican," and neither conceives himself, to put it mildly, as a member of a sexual minority. After their first encounter, Ennis bluntly declares, "You know I ain't no queer," while Jack asserts, with less certainty, "Me neither." The differences between these denials point to the status of gay identity as a form of self-definition—a factor that distinguishes it from many civilly protected minority identities.

The film develops the contrast between the main characters quite systematically, even to the detriment of its own universalizing impulse. It traces the process of Jack's foiled efforts to create provisional circumstances, against all odds, in which he *could* define himself as gay, and that of Ennis's staunch, self-destructive refusal to do so. To this end, Jack is portrayed as being visibly gay throughout the film, in contrast to Ennis's more successful passing. In a bar, when Jack offers to buy a beer for the rodeo clown Jimbo, the man firmly refuses, obviously understanding this apparently "innocent" offer as an unwelcome sexual overture. Later, when he and his wife double-date with another couple, the husband, alone with Jack, proposes a getaway between them, in a voice weighted with salacious overtones: "We ought to go down there some weekend. Drink a little whiskey, fish some—you know?" The last phrase has an especially marked overexplicitness that Jack clearly comprehends as an erotic advance, but before Jack can respond, the women return.

From the start of the film, Jack is depicted as the agent, Ennis as the object of desire. As the two men wait silently in the first scene outside a remote trailer for their employer to arrive, before they have been introduced, the film emphasizes Jack's furtive glimpses at Ennis as they both awkwardly avert their gazes from each other. Later, as they begin their work on the mountain, a telling shot shows Jack in the extreme foreground, facing front, while a naked Ennis, behind him, completes his ablutions. Though Jack does not look at Ennis, his gaze remaining fixed intently ahead, the shot is fraught with a powerful sense of unspoken desire. That this desire originates with Jack is made clear by the fact that he initiates sex in their first encounter, an initiation Ennis later turns against him, accusing Jack in their last meeting of having corrupted or "converted" him: "It's because of you, Jack, that I'm like this."

As this plaint makes clear, Ennis is shaken to his core by this encounter with homosexuality. Jack, meanwhile, is profoundly validated by it. In Yoshino's terms, Ennis wants to convert while Jack wants to pass, and this difference explains why Ennis responds with rage to imputations of homosexuality, like those of his ex-wife, while Jack responds with a blithe, matter-of-fact acceptance. By the end of the film, it is clear that almost everyone has viewed Jack's sexuality as an open secret. In the phone conversation with Ennis when Jack's wife recounts the details of her husband's death, her tone makes clear that she is aware of Jack's having been gay—a disdainful knowingness that echoes that of Jack's employer earlier in the film and his father in the penultimate scene, when he says scornfully, while staring meaningfully at Ennis, "I know where Brokeback Mountain is."

Yet, though Ennis mostly escapes such expressions of knowing contempt, it is he who perceives suspicion everywhere, as a constantly lurking possibility: "You ever get the feeling," he says to Jack, "I don't know, when you're in town, and someone looks at you, suspicious . . . like he *knows*." Earlier in the film, Ennis tells of having been taken by his father to see the corpse of a gay man who had been beaten and castrated by a mob. The movie makes clear that his fear of being "queer," instilled by this primal scene, prevents his being able to accept the union Jack offers. Jack, meanwhile, accepts the fact that others recognize him as gay with a kind of poignant equanimity, because he seems to glean that this comes with the rough, unforgiving territory of self-acceptance.

What the film makes clear is that Ennis and Jack experience their sexualities in very different ways, a contrast that enables the mixture of universalizing and minoritizing discourses on which the movie's version of gay identity ultimately depends. Ennis sees sexuality as something he does, while Jack increasingly comes to understand that he must accept it as a dimension of something he is. Ennis wants to preserve a kind of "innocent homosexuality" linked to myths of wilderness and evasion of responsibility. Jack recognizes that they would need to put such myths aside to build a life together—and, in the film's saddest implication, comes to realize in the end that if he is going to try to be happy, he will have to leave Ennis behind. He makes this recognition bitterly explicit in a burst of anger during their last meeting: "Tell you what, we could have had a real good life together, a fuckin' real good life, had us a place of our own. You wouldn't do it, Ennis, so what we got now is Brokeback Mountain."

That *Brokeback Mountain* tells a story of "unlikely" homosexuality could be said, in fact, to be the raison d'être of the film: to show that homosexuality, as a "stubborn social fact," potentially occurs anywhere, among anyone of any lifestyle or social class or self-image. The myth of wilderness contributes fundamentally to this goal, providing the backdrop against which everything has been determined that has allowed no visual or verbal language, no media images or role models or possibilities for communal affiliation by which to form an image of homosexuality—one's own or anyone else's—except a destructive one. Yet homosexuality appears there all the same, irresistibly and passionately—"no manual needed." This is the very essence of the movie's universalizing impulse.

Yet the difference that the film insists on between its two main characters reveals the limits of such universalism as a position from which to argue for a minority's civil rights. That Jack and Ennis might have lived happily together according to their instincts if they had been able to free themselves from the shackles of society is a virtually unimaginable circumstance. If such freedom were available anywhere, as all the given myths confirm, it would be on Brokeback Mountain. But the obverse of the men's instinctual homosexuality, the film also makes clear, is their own internalized homophobia. Even there, in that idealized wilderness, without prototypes or paradigms, homosexuality manifests, attesting to its "naturalness"—and even there, it is powerfully inhibited. The wonder is that Brokeback Mountain, for all the stirring exotica of its setting and the muted indignation of its empathy, narrates the same tale of forbidden love and tragic consequence that had long since been rendered archetypal—if not thoroughly clichéd—by the products of urban cultures. As itself a form of mythology, a conformity of every type to the same general pattern, universalism always depends on a foundational moment of regression. No matter what "new" group emerges, however formerly unimaginable it may have been to the majority whose perpetually revitalized innocence it assaults yet again, it must subsequently be referred back to a presumed, underlying fund of commonality or "shared humanity." Brokeback Mountain is especially complicit in this structure in its propensity to make its gay characters familiar to a straight audience by adverting to regnant marriage plots that show the men's homosexuality permitting a semblance of heterosexuality that reassures as it affronts.

Brokeback Mountain ends with a beautiful song, "Maker Makes," by the gay singer-songwriter Rufus Wainwright. Its poignancy is enhanced by its consignment to a marginal position at the end of the closing credits, following Willie Nelson's moving rendition of "He Was a Friend of Mine"—and starting only after most of the audience will have left. (I saw the film in a theater on three occasions, and each time almost nobody remained in the auditorium when Wainwright's song began.) Yet the song serves not only as a heartrending gloss on the film but a plaintive comment on the Sisyphus-like character of a movement for civil rights caught between universalizing and minoritizing discourses. "One more chain I break, to get me closer to you," the lyrics begin. "One more chain does the maker make, to keep me from busting through." In a surprising turn, the song shifts to the conventions of gospel music: "Oh Lord, how I know, Oh Lord, how I see, / That only can the maker make a happy man of me." This wrenching faux-epiphany bows ironically to majoritarian authority, whether divined as an empowering God or personified as a secular "Maker."

In the space of a few lines, the singer builds a pastiche of folksong traditions, and the tune reaches its height as it trails off into a cliché of the cowboy ballad, as Wainwright sings sadly, "Git along, little dogies, git along, little dogies, git along." The extraordinary effect of a gay singer, with well-known associations of urban hipsterism, adopting the position of the archetypal cowboy, in a mode that is both affectionately campy and grievously wise, befits the end of this film. To hear what is, speaking literally, the only authentically gay voice in this movie intone these words, with their air of woozy tenderness—he could be singing for Jack and Ennis, or for any of us who must live under the spurious authority of an abstract "Maker"—is to realize the ultimate tragedy the movie stands for: how much the appearance of progress still depends on adverting to the same old myths, how much we still needed a film like this one, in the year 2005.

7 } **Breaking No Ground**

Why *Crash* Won, Why *Brokeback* Lost, and
How the Academy Chose to Play It Safe

KENNETH TURAN

Sometimes you win by losing, and nothing has proved what a powerful, taboo-breaking, necessary film *Brokeback Mountain* was more than its loss Sunday night to *Crash* in the Oscar best picture category.

Despite all the magazine covers it graced, despite all the red-state theaters it made good money in, despite (or maybe because of) all the jokes late-night talk-show hosts made about it, you could not take the pulse of the industry without realizing that this film made a number of people distinctly uncomfortable.

More than any other of the nominated films, *Brokeback Mountain* was the one people told me they really didn't feel like seeing, didn't really get, didn't understand the fuss over. Did I really like it, they wanted to know. Yes, I really did.

In the privacy of the voting booth, as many political candidates who've led in polls only to lose elections have found out, people are free to act out the unspoken fears and unconscious prejudices that they would never breathe to another soul, or, likely, acknowledge to themselves. And at least this year, that acting out doomed *Brokeback Mountain*.

For Hollywood, as a whole laundry list of people announced from the podium Sunday night and a lengthy montage of clips tried to emphasize, is a liberal place, a place that prides itself on its progressive agenda. If this were a year when voters had no other palatable options, they might have taken a deep breath and voted for *Brokeback*. This year, however, *Crash* was poised to be the spoiler.

I do not for one minute question the sincerity and integrity of the people who made *Crash*, and I do not question their commitment to wanting a more equal society. But I do question the film they've made. It may be true, as producer Cathy Schulman said in accepting the Oscar for best picture, that this was "one of the most breathtaking and stunning maverick years in American cinema," but *Crash* is not an example of that.

I don't care how much trouble *Crash* had getting financing or getting people on board, the reality of this film, the reason it won the Best Picture Oscar, is that it is, at its core, a standard Hollywood movie, as manipulative and unrealistic as the day is long. And something more.

For *Crash*'s biggest asset is its ability to give people a carload of those standard Hollywood satisfactions but make them think they are seeing something groundbreaking and daring. It is, in some ways, a feel-good film about racism, a film you could see and feel like a better person, a film that could make you believe that you had done your moral duty and examined your soul when in fact you were just getting your buttons pushed and your preconceptions reconfirmed.

So for people who were discomfited by *Brokeback Mountain* but wanted to be able to look themselves in the mirror and feel like they were good, productive liberals, *Crash* provided the perfect safe harbor. They could vote for it in good conscience, vote for it and feel they had made a progressive move, vote for it and not feel that there was any stain on their liberal credentials for shunning what *Brokeback* had to offer. And that's exactly what they did.

Brokeback, it is worth noting, was in some ways the tamest of the discomforting films available to Oscar voters in various categories. Steven Spielberg's *Munich*; the Palestinian Territories' *Paradise Now*, one of the best foreign-language nominees; and the documentary nominee *Darwin's Nightmare* offered scenarios that truly shook up people's normal ways of seeing the world. None of them won a thing.

Hollywood, of course, is under no obligation to be a progressive force in the world. It is in the business of entertainment, in the business of making the most dollars it can. Yes, on Oscar night, it likes to pat itself on the back for the good it does in the world, but as Sunday night's ceremony proved, it is easier to congratulate yourself for a job well done in the past than actually do that job in the present.

8 } "Jack, I Swear"

Some Promises to Gay Culture from Mainstream Hollywood

CHRIS FREEMAN

Promises/Compromises

In the few years since *Brokeback Mountain* had its meteoric run, several things have happened to make looking back on the film at once necessary and problematic. Foremost, of course, is the death of Heath Ledger on January 22, 2008. The widespread upset at his not receiving the Best Actor Oscar for his stunning performance as Ennis del Mar was utterly trumped by his tragic death and the bittersweet posthumous Best Supporting Actor award from the Academy for his disturbing interpretation of the Joker in *The Dark Knight*. To say that Ledger's death adds gravitas to any rereading or rethinking of *Brokeback* is an understatement. The success of *Milk* on that same Oscar Night and the escalating heat of the same-sex marriage question makes *Brokeback* seem long ago, with a new nostalgia underscoring what was already nostalgic in a film about the past made in 2005. For my purposes here, I want to look at *Brokeback Mountain* as a kind of time capsule, a moment near the end of the Bush administration, before the assault of California's Proposition 8, and before *Milk* gave gay audiences some gay Oscars.[1]

The relationship of the past to the present with this film and its concerns is utterly wrapped in nostalgia—with a combination of anger, pride, and exasperation. The world of the film seems out of time in some senses—the idyll of Brokeback as an isolated space, for instance. Add to that the removal of the characters' lives from the happenings in the world around them in the turbulent sixties and seventies, and any understanding of the film's relation to its cultural context becomes vexed. Do we treat it as an ahistorical fiction? How do we read its aftermath in the twenty-first century, in a world of "post-gay" liberation, same-sex marriage, and queer political activism? The film brings a sense of pride among many gay people, but again, it immediately raises a "Hollywood" question about representation: this is a film made by straight people about gay people. So does that representation, coupled with the financial and cultural impact of this film—undoubtedly the most successful film with such "gay" content in the history of Hollywood—satisfy, frustrate, or perhaps challenge us as readers, fans, and critics?

Gay men flocked to Ang Lee's mesmerizing film, over and over again. It showed up in *New Yorker* cartoons, late-night comedy monologues, and presidential press conferences. As film scholar and critic B. Ruby Rich has said, "*Brokeback Mountain* became a cultural phenomenon, the rare film that could jump out of the film section entirely to become hard news and editorial-page fodder, a subject of parody, a controversy, a matter of pride" (44). In some ways, the film seemed to be a referendum on the relationship between gay and straight America, and, as on almost every major issue, there appears to be about an even split in our contemporary ideological civil war.[2]

The movie's crossover success was encouraging, but the sting of the Academy Award Best Picture result lingers.[3] Fans of *Brokeback* who recall the apparent glee of Jack Nicholson when he announced *Crash* as Best Picture must surely have been surprised, and maybe felt a little consoled, by the Academy described by *Milk* winner Sean Penn as "commie, homo-loving sons of guns." They may have even felt somewhat vindicated by the moving speech by *Milk* screenwriter Dustin Lance Black, one of our own in this film about gay people by gay people—the writer, director, and producers being openly gay.

If we go back a while, to *before*, to a less "homo-loving" Academy, what do we find? Richard Schneider, publisher of *The Gay & Lesbian Review Worldwide*, editorialized, "It appears the Academy genuinely wanted to reward Ang Lee for having made the best movie of 2005, but just couldn't bring itself to endorse the precise movie that he made.[4] That Hollywood wasn't quite ready to take this step is now part of the history of the cultural phenomenon that was *Brokeback*. . . . It forced mainstream America to confront a topic that it thinks about neither frequently nor with much subtlety" (10). That is probably true about mainstream America, but what did *Brokeback* and its reverberations do for gay America? What are its promises—and its concomitant compromises—to us?

"The Ruby Slippers of Our Time"

One small—but perhaps not insignificant—part of the "cultural phenomenon that was *Brokeback*" is the headlines made the week before the Academy Awards when activist-collector Tom Gregory bought the two iconic shirts from the film for $101,100 through a charity auction on eBay (see figure 9).[5] Shortly after the auction, I interviewed Gregory at his Los Angeles home to explore what the shirts meant to him and to inquire further about some of the comments he'd made in the press. As a collector, Gregory sees the connections between the past and the present. He travels between both worlds. We were steeped in Hollywood history at his home, which was built by the architect A. Quincy Jones for Gary Cooper, an icon of the Hollywood Western. The publicity surrounding his purchase provided Gregory a platform from which he could comment about gay culture and gay lives in our time. Speaking to the Associated Press, for example, Gregory called the shirts "the ruby slippers of our time" ("For Collector"). I was fascinated by that comment and its implications, so I will use some of Gregory's remarks and some exploration of the idea of "gay icons" to try to draw some conclusions about what *Brokeback Mountain* says to gay people and to straight audiences about our lives—how and what this fiction tells us about our reality.

When I asked Gregory about his provocative comment, he said,

I think that it's a new generation. I picture the shirts sort of pushing the ruby slippers out of the way. I love *The Wizard of Oz*—I know why gay people love it and relate to it. They don't want the black-and-white world of Kansas. They wanted the pretty colors, but getting off the road brings in the lions and tigers and bears. That film was a stepping stone, but we hadn't really stepped any further. *Brokeback Mountain* got the publicity; it showed the world

9. Ennis's closet: empty shirts full of meaning. Collection of Tom Gregory. Photo by Susannah Leam/Autry National Center.

that we are still here and we walk among you. Get out of our way and we'll be okay.

Cultural icons are symbols—they stand for something larger and more important than themselves. For Gregory, the shirts are his direct link to the film and its world: "One of the reasons I wanted the shirts was that I wanted to solve this conundrum in my mind—I wanted to physically connect to the film so it would stop haunting me. It wouldn't leave me alone until I had the shirts." If anything, though, owning the shirts has meant that Gregory is inextricably linked to the film and its lore. Indeed, Gregory has since acquired other artifacts from the film, including the succinct "you bet" postcard depicting the majestic Brokeback Mountain.[6]

If we think further about gay cultural icons, we might follow Gregory down the yellow brick road to Judy Garland and her most famous role. Garland's life was grand, misunderstood, filled with pathos, and ultimately tragic. Discussing *The Wizard of Oz* as his favorite movie, author Salman Rushdie, in a compelling monograph on the film, has said that he never quite believed that Kansas—"there's no place like home"—was the right resolution to Dorothy's story. He was never convinced that once she made such an incredible journey, Dorothy could ever settle for that drab, black-and-white world. She will have to make her own home on her own journey after Oz. For gay people, the vibrancy and the queerness of Oz are certainly alluring, but as Gregory suggests, it can be a dangerous place. Any deviation from the norm has concomitant hazards, a point painfully demonstrated in *Brokeback*. As Rushdie writes, "*The Wizard of Oz* is unarguably a film about the joys of going away, of leaving the greyness and entering the colour, of making a new life in 'the place where there is no trouble.' . . . It is a celebration of Escape, a grand paean to the Uprooted Self, a hymn—*the* hymn—to Elsewhere" (23). In the world of Lee's film, Brokeback Mountain as a majestic location becomes such a place for Jack Twist and Ennis del Mar—it's their Oz, their secret, and the sanctuary for their happiness: their elsewhere.[7] It's also their fiction, in the sense that it leads Jack to imagine a future with Ennis, which the more taciturn and restrained man cannot entertain. Jack's fantasy of a life with Ennis is a dream that will not be a reality, here in this world or for many of the viewers of the film, which is of course one reason so many gay people connected so personally with *Brokeback*.

One reason that Ennis can't go to Jack's mythical ranch is that his own father provided the young Ennis with a disciplinary vision of a cowboy who was brutally murdered for being queer. This is how normalization works in our culture, and it worked existentially for Ennis. It may have worked on Jack too, as Ennis's vision of Jack's death suggests. The story Jack's wife Lureen tells Ennis on the phone is just a little too neat, and Ennis's version of reality demonstrates what Gregory suggests when he says "get out of our way and we'll be okay."

When the boss, Joe Aguirre, spies Jack and Ennis frolicking, their private relationship, which they've defined as "a one-shot thing, nobody's business but ours," becomes public. As Daniel Mendelsohn describes, "Both narratively and visually, *Brokeback Mountain* is a tragedy about the specifically gay phenomenon of the 'closet.' . . . What love story there is occurs early on in the film, and briefly. . . . The sole visual representation of their happiness in love is a single brief shot of the two shirtless youths horsing around in the grass. That shot is eerily—and significantly—silent, voiceless: it turns out that what we are seeing is what the boys' boss is seeing through his binoculars as he spies on them" ("Affair to Remember" 12). The specter of public exposure haunts both men throughout the film. Ennis even confesses to Jack that sometimes he thinks people, strangers, look at him and *know*: "You ever get the feelin', I don't know, when you're in town, and someone looks at you, suspicious . . . like he *knows*. And then you get out on the pavement, and everyone, lookin' at you, and maybe they all know, too?" (McMurtry and Ossana 71).

This is the paranoia of the closet—it constructs the closet, maintains the closet, and guarantees the closet. In his theoretical analysis of the film, D. A. Miller describes this paranoia as symptomatic of the classic psychoanalytic view of homosexuality. Miller takes the point to its limits in his usual, provocative way: "Ennis is always being watched like a hawk—if not by Jack, or Joe Aguirre, or Alma, then, in a far more continuous surveillance than theirs combined, by us spectators." Miller locates an awareness of this surveillance in Ledger's "ever-'on' performance . . . in which [the] character behaves as though *he knows he is in the movie we are watching*" (56).[8] Whether or not one wants to go as far as Miller does on this point, it's clear that this kind of disciplinary self-consciousness is devastating for men like Ennis, and that pain and constriction—strangulation—are clearly what many thousands of *Brokeback* viewers and lovers connected to in the film. As Gregory said, the pain and pathos of this relationship represents "the pain of those days but also the hope that those days are now over."

"The Pair Like Two Skins, One Inside the Other, Two in One"

The gay writer Paul Monette, in a poem called "My Shirts," describes a shirt that belonged to his best friend from college, a young man he secretly loved and who died young, tragically, in a climbing accident in China. Monette writes of the shirt he got from his friend:

> It was left, as of little worth,
> when my friend went to China, where he died.
> When he died, Death altered it, but at first
> it fit the house I had as well as his,
> and so I brought it home. In time it came
> to lie in a ball, the day's last apparel, retrieved
> at dusk (the stroke of nerves) and shaken out
> and slipped on, oh, until I slept. (8)

Here, the shirt is a memento mori, as the shirts become in *Brokeback*. Monette's parenthetical reference to "the stroke of nerves" and the longing of "oh" suggest the intense connection that this tangible remnant of his friend provides for him. Likewise, in *Brokeback Mountain*, Ennis's shirt serves this role for Jack, and then both shirts become the only relics for Ennis. First, of course, Ennis's shirt is pilfered by Jack Twist. Those bloodied shirts represent for him, as for us viewers, the men's secret life together on the mountaintop. We see, for example, Jack washing the shirts in a creek. We also see him blatantly *not* looking as Ennis strips to wash himself. The men are wearing those shirts in their first, fast sexual encounter; shirtless Jack holds the fully dressed Ennis in the second, more tender scene, flesh against cotton. Then, on the day of their heartbreaking departure from the mountain, as the pain and strain of their pending separation becomes overwhelming, the men's play turns into roughhousing and then fighting. Their blood mingles on their two shirts. Ennis changes shirts, which is when, offscreen, Jack surreptitiously steals his friend's shirt, thereby transforming the vestment into a secret treasure. Ennis, a man of few possessions, cannot fathom that he'd leave his shirt on the mountain; Jack betrays nothing of his secret theft.

When Ennis learns from Lureen of Jack's death and imagines what seems to him a more likely scenario, he goes to Lightning Flat to see Jack's parents and to try to retrieve his ashes to scatter them on Brokeback. This scene is agonizing to watch, as the staunch patriarch, John Twist, sits in near-silent judgment, knowing too well the nature of the relationship between Jack and Ennis. He does, of course, twist the knife, telling Ennis about Jack's revised plan to bring someone else to the ranch: "this spring he's got another fella's goin' a come up here with him and build a place and help run the ranch, some ranch neighbor a his from down in Texas. He's goin' a split with his wife and come back here." Ennis struggles to hold back tears, and Jack's mother kindly offers him an escape: "I kept his room like it was when he was a boy. I think he appreciated that. You are welcome to go up in his room, if you want" (Proulx, McMurtry, and Ossana 90–91).

In this solemn moment, a kind of pilgrimage, Ennis notices Jack's closet and explores it. He sees a secret nook—a closet within a closet—where he spots Jack's blue denim shirt. Pulling it out, he realizes that his own shirt is hanging inside Jack's: the two shirts have been intertwined, joined since that summer at Brokeback. Annie Proulx describes the scene:

> The shirt seemed heavy until he saw there was another shirt inside it, the sleeves carefully worked down inside Jack's sleeves. It was his own plaid shirt, lost, he'd thought, long ago in some damn laundry, his dirty shirt, the pocket ripped, buttons missing, stolen by Jack and hidden here in Jack's own shirt, the pair like two skins, one inside the other, two in one. He pressed his face into the fabric and breathed in slowly through his mouth and nose, hoping for

the faintest smoke and mountain sage and salty sweet stink of Jack but there was no real scent, only the memory of it, the imagined power of Brokeback Mountain of which nothing was left but what he held in his hands. (*Brokeback Mountain* 51–52)

The story's most devastating image, I think, is in that line from Ennis's stream-of-consciousness: "the imagined power of Brokeback Mountain of which nothing was left but what he held in his hands." As Daniel Mendelsohn writes, "The two shirts hidden in the closet, preserved in an embrace which the men who wore them could never fully enjoy, stands as the poignant visual symbol of the story's tragedy" (13).

In a curiously nonverbal exchange—almost a pantomime—which Larry McMurtry and Diana Ossana invented in the screenplay, Ennis, shirts bundled in his hands, goes back downstairs and indicates to Jack's mother that he has them. She retrieves an old grocery bag, places the shirts in it, and he leaves with them.

The final moment in the film shows the shrine—humble, sad, austere, but reverent—that Ennis has created in his own closet. The shirts, reversed now with Ennis's embracing Jack's, and the "you bet" postcard representation of Brokeback, are the only remnants of their precious time together. Ossana has pointed out that the reversal of the shirts was Heath Ledger's idea, which suggests, as Proulx has said, that Ledger "knew better than I how Ennis felt and thought" (McMurtry and Ossana, "*Brokeback*'s Big Secrets" 43; Proulx, "Getting Movied" 137). Ennis's closeted shrine is all he has left of the love shared by these two men; well, that and a lifetime's memories.

"Dedicated to a Happier Year"

What we know, as viewers with some historical and critical distance from this imaginary but all too real scenario, is that a life together for lovers like Jack and Ennis was almost unimaginable, particularly in the West of legend.[9] The pastoral beauty of the landscape of *Brokeback* is part of the iconic beauty of the American West, perhaps best depicted by artists such as Ansel Adams, Richard Prince, and John Ford. What Proulx and the filmmakers give us, though, is a competing narrative of the story of the West. As McMurtry states, "Richard Avedon realized, as did Ang Lee in his turn, how seductive Western landscape can be. . . . Look too often at those hills, lie too long beside those rippling rivers, and you may think you are hearing a love song, when actually it is a death song" ("Adapting *Brokeback Mountain*" 141–42).

Domestic gay life in big cities wasn't a great deal different: an urban gay male couple during the early 1960s, when the film's first summer is set, was a rare thing. In his memoir *My Lives*, author Edmund White notes that when he first moved to New York in 1962 and lived with his lover, "two men living together was still a new thing in those days—at least we knew only one other couple" (270). The documentary *Chris &̦ Don: A Love Story* (2007) tells the story of the iconoclastic relationship between author Christopher Isherwood and his much younger lover, artist Don Bachardy, who lived as an openly gay couple in Los Angeles beginning in the mid-1950s—and in their case, the exception proved the rule that it was almost never done. In Isherwood's 1964 novel *A Single Man*, to offer another contemporaneous example, the protagonist George and his deceased lover Jim had lived together for more than a dozen years, but they were never open about their relationship to coworkers or neighbors. A few friends knew.

Or, to go back another half century and across the Atlantic, in E. M. Forster's classic gay novel, *Maurice*, which was written prior to World War I but wasn't published until after Forster's death in 1970 (with the help of Isherwood), the two men in love flee the world of everyone else for what Forster calls the "greenwood," an imaginary space that we can read as "elsewhere" or even as Oz.[10] It's instructive, in the context of the era of *Brokeback Mountain*, that Forster wrote a new afterword in 1960 for the book he still felt unable to publish, even though the manuscript's existence was an open secret in literary circles: "A happy ending was imperative. I shouldn't have bothered to write it otherwise. I was determined that in fiction anyway two men should fall in love and remain in it for the ever and ever that fiction allows, and in that sense, Maurice and Alec still roam the greenwood. I dedicated the book 'To a Happier Year' and not altogether vainly. Happiness is its keynote—which by the way has had an unexpected result: it has made the book more difficult to publish. . . . The lovers get away unpunished and consequently recommend crime" ("Terminal Note" 250).[11]

The saga of Forster's bucolic, posthumously published gay novel is relevant to *Brokeback* in a variety of ways. First, the fact that Forster was gay, I believe, is the reason that he wanted to write a "happy" tale of gay love, one that still in the 1960s he found more likely in fiction than in the nongreenwood real world. Forster's is a prime example of gay self-representation, as opposed to the representation of gays by nongay people. And, coming in 1960, his commentary sheds contemporaneous light on the relationship between gay and straight culture, as *Brokeback* does regarding our era. Forster wrote, in a one-paragraph note on "Homosexuality" at the conclusion of his 1960 "Terminal Note," "Since *Maurice* was written, there has been a change in the public attitude toward homosexuality: the change from ignorance and fear to familiarity and contempt. . . . We had not realized that what the public really loathes in homosexuality is not the thing itself but having to think about it" (255). There can be no denying that *Brokeback Mountain* made the public "think about it"—and it showed, in its first raw sex scene, what gay men do to each other. And that makes straight America squirm, and it makes Academy members wince, or vote for the safe, feel-good film about racism.[12]

"I Swear"

Gregory asserted that, for him, one other salient factor about the film and its significance is how it demonstrates the perils of persecution. It shows how soul-destroying this kind of interference with gay lives is and has been: "I think *Brokeback* was so cathartic for my friends because it allowed them to see themselves represented in some way that they hoped, when the movie had a wider release, would make us more acceptable in 2005. It was a hopeful movie for us. For the first time, I think a lot of gay people really thought that finally, now, when people see what we're really like, this persecution of us will cease." In essence, of course, *Brokeback Mountain* is a story about homophobia and its consequences much more than it is a gay love story. Proulx has complained that "urban critics dubbed [the story] a tale of two gay cowboys. No. It is a story of rural homophobia. . . . I wanted to explore both long-lasting love and its possible steep price tag, both homophobic antipathy and denial" ("Getting Movied" 130–31).

The closing moment of the film—showing Ennis, alone and defeated, with the shirts and a postcard of Brokeback Mountain, having agreed to support his daughter's upcoming marriage—presents the man's stark reality. In my interview with him, Gregory said, "At that moment, at the closing of the film, the shirts stand as a visual representation of two men in love. That's when the shirts become beautiful as art, in my mind. They show that this kind of love won't be held down. They represent our right to love."

It's in that moment that the shirts become iconic—they represent potential, love, passion, loss, devastation. Tellingly, unlike Forster's novel, *Brokeback Mountain* gives us a tragic ending. The year 2005 was not, apparently, the "Happier Year" that Forster was imagining. As the gay writer David Leavitt, who has also written eloquently about *Maurice*, states, "In the end, *Brokeback Mountain* is less a story of a love that dares not speak its name than of one that doesn't know how to speak its name, and is somehow more eloquent for its lack of vocabulary. Ascending from plains where they lead lives of drudgery and routine humiliation, Ennis and Jack become the unwitting heroes of a story they haven't a clue how to tell. The world breaks their backs, but in this brave film, they're as iconic as the mountain."

Gregory advocates a potentially positive reading of the film, one that resists the easy, almost parodic catchphrase lure of "I wish I could quit you," suggesting instead that the cryptic closing line of the film could be a new mantra, a promise from contemporary gay people to commit to making a better future:

When Ennis says, "Jack, I swear," it is a powerful line. What was he swearing to? I swear I love you? I swear I wish it could have been different? I think it's a great slogan for gay America. *I swear*—and fill in the blank with anything positive. If you want the world to be happy and loving, be happy and loving. Swear to live your life fully and openly. I like it as our oath. It's a promise—"I swear I'll make it better for the next generation"—whereas "I wish I could quit you" is a negative thing, a renunciation, as though we'd quit if we could.

That promise—a kind of community voice vowing to be good to its kind, to help one another—is perhaps the great hope of this beautiful but heartbreaking tale of a love that couldn't be. Fictions like *Brokeback Mountain* give us truths of our history and of our historical moment. They help us imagine better futures, but we, as gay people, have to look hard and with hope to find the promise of this film at this time. Certainly, we could read *Brokeback* as a film of containment, the usual narrative of the dead homosexual articulated and criticized so forcefully by Vito Russo in *The Celluloid Closet*. Taking the film as a classic melodrama in which "Ennis and Jack must be punished in order for their essential innocence to be recognized," scholar Ara Osterweil is frustrated by the film's failure (or refusal?) to be subversive: "While in the future, we may find ourselves neatly dividing Hollywood history between its pre-*Brokeback* and post-*Brokeback* phases, we must also recognize the compromises that Hollywood continues to demand from filmmakers who wish to broach radical subjects in resolutely commercial formats. Like many Hollywood breakthroughs, *Brokeback Mountain* reveals the extent to which entry into the mainstream requires the sacrifice of countercultural subversiveness. . . . Mainstream audiences [seem to] prefer their gay sex with cathartic tears of tragedy rather than the crocodile tears of camp" (38, 42).

Granted, there's no camp in *Brokeback Mountain*, but there's plenty of truth in it, and it may have an "elsewhere." It is, still, a mainstream representation *of* gay lives, one targeted to a broad marketplace. Maybe the way we read such a text is through its elsewhere, in the margins and beyond the screen, finding our own reading of these stories of our lives. For us, perhaps in *Brokeback Mountain* we can see beauty, loss, and the vow of one man to remember another man, the man he loves.

Notes

Thanks to Tom Gregory, Joe Wittreich, Stuart Curran, and Leo Baligaya. Also, for their helpful comments on this essay, I want to acknowledge Steve Rohr, James Berg, Jane Roberts, Alex Lin, and Lisa Southerland.

1. Of course, there have been gay Oscars before, notably William Hurt for *Kiss of the Spiderwoman*, Tom Hanks for *Philadelphia*, Charlize Theron for *Monster*, and Philip Seymour Hoffman for *Capote*. Interestingly (coincidentally?) all of these are for characters who come to no good end.

2. Witness, for example, the vote on California's Proposition 8, opposing same-sex marriage, which passed with about 52 percent of the vote. In May 2009, the California Supreme Court allowed that vote to stand.

3. According to the genre chart on the Web site "Box Office Mojo," which lists the top lifetime grossing gay-themed films, *Brokeback* ranks in the top five, with about $83 million; the number one film is *The Birdcage* with $124 million. The film most comparable to *Brokeback* is probably *Philadelphia*, which earned about $77 million. The Internet Movie Database information on box office is consistent with these figures.

4. In addition to Ang Lee's Best Director Academy Award, the film also took home Oscars in two other categories: Best Adapted Screenplay (Larry McMurtry and Diana Ossana) and Best Original Score (Gustavo Santaolalla).

5. In a phone conversation with Gregory in August 2009, he explained that Focus Features had donated artifacts from *Brokeback* to an organization called Variety, the children's charity of Southern California.

6. Gregory has made an extended loan of the shirts and the postcard to the Museum of the American West at the Autry National Center in Los Angeles, in conjunction with the museum's becoming the repository for the archives of the International Gay Rodeo Association. See Gregory Hinton's remarks on the occasion of their installation in the next chapter of this volume.

7. The "elsewhere" I'm referring to here is most directly from Rushdie, but I also would invoke the brilliant lesbian-feminist film critic Teresa de Lauretis's use of what she calls "the view from elsewhere" in the title essay of her book *Technologies of Gender*. In the closing pages of that chapter, de Lauretis argues that feminist presence can be found in the "elsewhere" or the "space-off," which she locates "in the margins of hegemonic discourses." Queer representation lurks in that same space-off: "elsewhere is not some mythic distant past or some utopian future history: it is the elsewhere of discourse here and now, the blind spots, or the space-off, of its representations" (25). De Lauretis calls for the occupation of both spaces—the middle and the margins—simultaneously, where "the subject . . . is en-gendered. That is to say, elsewhere" (26). It is there that we can find ourselves and our lives, even in the mainstream, even when it's not quite entirely to our liking—perhaps especially then.

8. Miller calls himself a "conscientious objector" to the film on the grounds that he believes *Brokeback Mountain* is a sensationalized film, "a middling piece of Hollywood product" that has been mistakenly seen as "a major work of art" (50).

9. In a fascinating essay on cowboy life, a version of which is in this volume, the novelist Patricia Nell Warren, who grew up in Montana on a cattle ranch first owned by her grandfather in the 1880s, writes about how, "to combat the loneliness of this life, male-male friendships sprang up like the grass. . . . Two

single males would pair up, living in close association, sharing everything, maybe starting a business together." She notes, however, that after World War II, changes in technology and agribusiness ended this behavior ("Real Cowboys, Real Rodeos" 21). She also describes the world of rodeo in which Jack Twist earned a very modest living.

10. Wendy Moffat opens her Forster biography, *A Great Unrecorded History*, with a prologue in which she details the story of Isherwood and John Lehman receiving the manuscript of *Maurice* a few months after Forster's death.

11. In *The Cave and the Mountain*, the last major book written about Forster during his lifetime, critic Wilfred Stone basically outed Forster, stating that a "completed but unpublished novel dealing with the subject of homosexuality was produced after *Passage to India*, and at least one unpublished story. Forster apparently felt both to be unpublishable; those who have read the novel generally consider it a failure" (347n). Stone quotes a rather cryptic letter from T. E. Lawrence, with whom Forster shared his gay writings, in support of his dismissive inferences.

12. Slate.com's David Edelstein writes, "The theme is racism. Let me say that again: The theme is racism. I could say it 500 more times because that's how many times the movie says it, in *every single scene*. . . . In the end, *Crash* says, when you push a vicious racist, you get a caring human, but when you push a caring human you get a vicious racist. . . . [Writer-director Paul] Haggis wants to distill all the resentment and hypocrisy among races into a fierce parable. But the old-fashioned carpentry (evocative of '30s socially conscious melodrama) makes this portrait of How We Live Now seem preposterous at every turn." For a trenchant critique of *Crash*, see Hsuan L. Hsu's "Racial Privacy."

9 } "Better Two Than One"

The Shirts from *Brokeback Mountain*

GREGORY HINTON

Remarks at the Autry National Center, August 11, 2009, on the installation of the Brokeback Shirts:

Four years ago, on a brisk Sunday morning in December, I went over to the Grove Theaters in West Hollywood to see the first showing of Ang Lee's adaptation of Annie Proulx's powerful short story, *Brokeback Mountain*. It was opening weekend. I was alone. I parked my car and when I rounded the corner, I saw hundreds of gay men, many my age, lined up to get into the theater. I admit I came with a chip on my shoulder. You see, I come from Wyoming, and what did Ang Lee know about gay ranchers in Wyoming? Besides, I've been burned before by straight Hollywood's depiction of gay men and women. Seeing the curious and hopeful men waiting on line, I fought back tears. The fact that the twelve-year-old ticket clerk asked if I needed a *senior* ticket did not improve my mood. I hated that I loved *Brokeback Mountain*. And here we are.

I just spent a wonderful month in Wyoming, where I was invited to give a talk about my dad at the Buffalo Bill Historical Center. He was Kip Hinton, former editor of the *Cody Enterprise*, the local newspaper founded by Buffalo Bill. The chairman of the BBHC, Senator Al Simpson, sends his regards today: "Congratulations to my good friends at the Autry National Center for their wisdom in presenting this display in their beautiful museum in Los Angeles. The subject matter continues a vital conversation we began several years ago in a document I coauthored entitled *The Cody Statement*."

I never heard of *The Cody Statement*, until Al sent it to me awhile back. In it, they wrote, "We are committed to Freedom; we believe everyone should be included in America's proud progression toward full civil equality for all, without regard to sexual orientation." *Brokeback Mountain* played in Cody. Al teaches me not to draw conclusions about western people and western places.

I was born on the Fort Peck Indian Reservation in Wolf Point, Montana. Lewis and Clark, literally, slept there. I am a native son of the American West, who happens also to be gay. So too was my brother, whom I lost several years ago to cancer. In case you're wondering how my cowboy dad felt about his two gay sons, he was glad we'd always have each other. He said—and we agreed—"Better two than one."

It was a year ago that I began visiting the Autry Library to research my fifth novel, *Night Rodeo*, about a Wyoming country editor struggling to save his weekly newspaper. While looking through the databases of several other prominent western research libraries, I idly wondered what information existed on the experiences and contributions of gay men and women in the West. I found little to nothing, except here in the inclusive Autry, a 1987 quote in the *San Francisco Chronicle*, by a gay rodeo competitor named John King. "A lot of people who grow up in rural communities come to the big city and then we lose our identities. The gay rodeo is a place for us to reclaim our heritage and be ourselves. It's a place where we fit in" (Evelyn White).

That night I wrote a brief concept paper called "The Gay Rodeo Legacy Project." In it, I observed that the gay community's contribution to western culture was underserved in scholarly discussions about the American West. I also stated that the rural communities we leave behind in search for safety, companionship, and community in the cities were the poorer for it.

I then called for the inclusion of the gay rodeo archives in the rodeo collections of world-class western libraries and museums.

I wrote Brian Helander, president of the International Gay Rodeo Association, which has twenty-six member associations; five thousand members; and fifty thousand annual attendees. They are a close-knit, service-oriented, peaceful rodeo community—who love animals and enjoy the country and western lifestyle. Brian sent me a letter of support but cautioned me not to get my hopes up: "Yes, I believe we have a rich history over the last 25 years . . . but they may not want to recognize our association's contribution to rodeo."

Two days later, after a thoughtful stroll through this very gallery, I came home and asked my partner, "Whatever happened to those shirts from *Brokeback Mountain*?"

He remembered they were sold at auction for charity, so I looked them up. They were purchased by a Hollywood memorabilia collector I never met before. On New Year's Day 2009, I wrote the following e-mail to Tom Gregory's Web site: "If you ever walked through the Autry Museum, there exists an exhibit called 'The Spirit of Imagination.' I hope one day, if only temporarily, your shirts might be on display in this gallery."

Tom Gregory replied in two hours. We met for lunch. He admitted something touching that I now know is typical of Tom's empathetic character: "When I bought the shirts, I thought I'd get calls from major museums, offering to display them. I didn't hear from anybody. It sorta hurt my feelings, not for me, but for the shirts, for what they represent. Nobody called but you."

When Tom Gregory first saw the shirts in *Brokeback Mountain*, they spoke to him. By purchasing them he secured the safety of the shirts. He had a vision for the good work they could do. By contacting him, I played right into his hands. He had the shirts. I had a plan. Two heads were better than one.

In March of this year, the Autry National Center agreed to display the shirts. Thanks to the passion of curator Jeffrey Richardson, six months later, here we are (see figure 9).

This Friday the archives of the International Gay Rodeo Association are arriving at the Autry, driven here from Denver by Patrick Terry, the IGRA historian. I helped pack them myself. Eighteen boxes. A hundred rodeo posters. Rule books. Rodeo shirts. Silver buckles. Maybe a trophy saddle if I get my way. (I've been measuring display cases next door in the Spirit of the Cowboy gallery.) By inviting them, the Autry is recognizing the International Gay Rodeo Association's contribution to rodeo, and they deserve our applause for doing so.

The display of the *Brokeback* shirts and the inclusion of the Gay Rodeo archives at the Autry for me underscore the need for gay men and women who leave their rural communities to reclaim their country heritage.

It is for this reason I look forward to working with Dr. Steve Aron on "Gay in the West," the symposium we are planning with the Autry Institute for the Study of the American West and UCLA. We have some great speakers we want you to get to know, plus we want to hear your stories also.

To know us is to love us. And that is why when we quit our rural communities, they lose too. In this regard, Annie Proulx recently wrote me the following: "I wish Mr. Hinton good fortune in his work. He is tragically right when he says western rural communities lose very much when gay men and women have to leave the state. I know some gay people who have stayed. Gradually the community accepts them, but only if they are born there."

I recently returned to Wyoming with the ashes of my beloved older brother, Scotty, and of Ron, his partner of thirty years. Before he died, my brother requested that they be scattered in Crazy Woman Creek, in the shadow of the Big Horn Mountains. After life in urban Southern California, my western brother yearned for his rural past till the end.

For those of us who come from the West, it's in our blood and never lets us go.

Seated here today, in this gallery called the Spirit of Imagination, are saddle bronc riders, chute doggers, barrel racers and bull riders, some who also happen to be gay or lesbian. I look at them and ask you.

What is not to love?

When I study these intertwined shirts, like the character of Ennis del Mar in *Brokeback Mountain*, I am overcome with survivor's guilt. Lovers, brothers, a cowboy father wanting to protect his sons, when I look at the shirts, I am grateful they will always be together. It makes sense. It's what we all hope for. It's what anybody deserves. Better two than one. Better two together than two alone.

I'll close with a brief reading from Annie Proulx's short story "Brokeback Mountain" and then I have a few people to thank (remembering here, Heath Ledger):

The shirt seemed heavy until he saw there was another shirt inside it, the sleeves carefully worked down inside Jack's sleeves. It was his own plaid shirt, lost he'd thought, in some damn laundry, his dirty shirt, the pocket ripped, buttons missing, stolen by Jack and hidden here inside Jack's own shirt, the pair like two skins, one inside the other, two in one. He pressed his face into the fabric, and breathed in slowly through his mouth and nose, hoping for the faintest smoke and mountain sage and salty sweet stink of Jack but there was no real scent, only the memory of it, the imagined power of Brokeback Mountain of which nothing was left but what he held in his hands. (*Brokeback Mountain* 51–52)

I just renewed my membership to the Autry. It has certainly been a bargain for me, and I recommend that each and every one of you join before you leave today. I am so profoundly grateful to the Autry National Center and its trustees, to Jackie Autry, John Gray, Steve Aron, Jeffrey Richardson, and my friend Marva Felchlin, for hanging up the shirts from *Brokeback Mountain*. Thank you to Joan Cumming, Yadhira De Leon, and Carolyn Campbell for sorting out the details of this historical event. Thanks to Brian Helander, president of the International Gay Rodeo Association, who could not be here today, and welcome to Andrew Goodman, IGRA vice president, here in his place. Thanks especially to Scotty Shadix, president of LA Rodeo and those who traveled near and far to support what we're doing with the help of the Autry.

Thank you to my friends here, old and new, and to my partner Tom Ferris, who has been going down the road with me for over twenty years. Thank you also to the media for coming to see us today. Lastly, I must express my unending gratitude and deep affection for Tom Gregory. I haven't met anyone as wise, generous, and surprising for many years. It is my privilege to introduce him to you today.

10 } American Eden

Nature, Homophobic Violence, and the Social Imaginary

COLIN CARMAN

> Obviously Eve is punished for it . . . since she
> has access to pleasure.
> HÈLÉNE CIXOUS, "Extreme Fidelity"

> Old Brokeback got us good and it sure ain't over.
> ANNIE PROULX, "Brokeback Mountain"

Stars bite and winds hiss in Annie Proulx's "Brokeback Mountain." Over the course of this influential work of American short fiction, the forces of nature that bear down on Ennis del Mar and Jack Twist ravage the men's bodies and minds. The narrative opens with Proulx's own prose-ode to the West Wind—"rocking," "hissing," and later, booming down the "curved length" of Ennis's trailer—only to conclude with the grim sort of defeatism that best characterizes Ennis's life of quiet desperation (255). The furies of homophobic violence that boom down on Ennis and Jack are as unrelenting as the winds that startle Ennis into wakefulness in the story's prelude. "But if you can't fix it you've got to stand it," he cautions Jack after a series of unsuccessful attempts to recapture the mountainous paradise inexorably lost to them both (271). But what exactly is the "it" here? Ennis's reluctance to name both the *source* of his subjection (homophobia) and its *effect* (the homosexual as other) lies at the heart of the narrative's most salient tensions: ironies of knowing and not wanting to know, speaking and not speaking what has, in effect, already been spoken.

Homophobia is a fearsome presence in Ang Lee's film, if only in the body of Heath Ledger's character, but "it" is of course not quite named, just as the psychic and physical effects of social power are both felt throughout Proulx's tragedy without being a character. The three aspects of that unnamed "it" in "Brokeback Mountain" are the narrative's attempt to naturalize same-sex desire as both a fact and force of nature; how homophobia combats this rival force through physical violence but also through a preexisting belief system that Ennis and Jack internalize at pivotal points in their psychosexual development; and how the Edenic space known simply as "Brokeback" in the wake of Ang Lee's film revives other never-never lands in the iconography of gay culture. Proulx's own paradise may come to function as the fictionalized telos in an ongoing struggle to secure equal rights for the United States' sexual minorities. The fact that in 2008 California voters' ban on same-sex marriage *and* the well-timed release of a gay-positive film like *Milk* inspired a new wave of gay rights activists only further substantiates this faith in cinema as a catalyst for social change.[1]

Proulx approaches same-sex desire as just another kind of natural element in her story that begins in the wide-open landscape of Wyoming in the 1960s. In fact, "Brokeback Mountain" tells us something about rural gay life prior to June 28, 1969, when patrons at the Stonewall Inn in New York City rebelled against police surveillance and in the ensuing riots launched the gay rights movement. Far from the anonymity of city living, Ennis and Jack live under the constant threat of being found out. And just as winds hiss and stars bite, the desire they feel for each other takes an abrupt and powerful hold on them: "Ennis ran full-throttle on all roads," writes Proulx, "whether fence mending or money spending and he wanted none of it when Jack seized his left hand" in the hope that Ennis might reciprocate his advances up on Brokeback Mountain (261). The "it" here refers to the intimacy that Ennis originally rejects inside the men's pup tent before forcibly mounting Jack from behind; thereafter, Ennis and Jack, writes Proulx, "went at it in silence" (261). Given the comic interjection on the author's part that "no instruction manual [was] needed" to finish the act, it appears as if Ennis and Jack are already naturals. By "nature," I mean the physical world as it operates beyond human experience and perception, or what John Boswell terms "nature minus human intervention" or "animal nature" (11).[2] The repressed energy that steadily mounts throughout the summer of '63 suddenly breaks loose; the act is impersonal, even animalistically so, but the rigidity of the sexual role-play underlines how homophobia even imbues their most private moments together. Just as Ennis insists on silence during the sexual act, he empowers himself as/on top lest he catch his reflection in another man's face. Proulx adds the graphic detail that when the two reunite four years later in 1967, the men's kisses actually draw blood. Again, their lovemaking paradoxically imports the very sort of social mastery that radical desire ostensibly seeks to escape. To conclude that the personal is political presumes that a separation of the two is even possible for sexual minorities. What makes Ennis and Jack tragic is that there is simply no exit; even within the supposed seclusion of their pup tent, the men are subject to one of the subtlest stratagems of homophobia: the reinforcement of the societal through the sexual. If, as Slavoj Žižek contends, the "ideological manipulation of obscene *jouissance* has entered a new stage" by way of "soliciting, or controlling and regulating, *jouissance*," can we not, then, read Proulx's protagonists as wholly controlled, policed even, by such politics (309)? Cut from the same existential cloth as Samuel Beckett's Vladimir and Estragon, Ennis and Jack occupy a stark stage whereupon the only certainties are suffering and the requisite waiting for death.

Reunited years later in a motel, now married with children, the men discuss the possibility of escape, but a suspicion of what lies just outside the bedroom walls prompts Ennis to deliver another bit of cautionary advice: "We do that in the wrong place and we'll be dead. There's no reins on this one. It scares the piss out a me" (269). Again, the indeterminacy of "it" and "one" dominates Ennis's understanding of desire. There is doing here without the doer, dancing without the dancer. The reader should not underestimate the degree to which Ennis understands same-sex desire only in terms of physical practice—"We do that"—as opposed to a social or political personage. The "it" and "this one" here may refer merely to Ennis's own erotic attraction for Jack, but here Freud helps to unlock, and name, the nameless. To mark the 150th anniversary of Freud's birth, in the *New York Times* Mark Edmundson describes the role of the "id" in Freud's tripartite model as the "agent of pure desire [because] it wants and wants and does not readily take no for an answer" (15).[3] Accordingly, in his own analogy for the ego's losing battle against the id, Freud writes in *The Ego and the Id* that "[the ego] is like a man on horseback, who has to hold in check the superior strength of the horse" (19). The sex drive must be driven, in effect, or *broken* by the ego's social face, a face that can hardly harness the erotic and destructive energies of the antisocial id. Let us extend the simile to imagine the ego as a man on horseback, digging his spurs into the animal id, and the superego (or social conscience) as a hair shirt worn by the rider. Mediating between primal urges and societal restrictions, the ego is beset on both sides. Occupying an authoritative role within Freud's mental structure, the superego is the internalized voice of authority. The ego resorts to self-punishment (or guilt) only because it can never fulfill the demands placed on it by the superego. Analogized accordingly as a prison watchtower, the superego brings the outside in and thereafter keeps a careful watch over the ego's access to pleasure.

To many secularists, biblical prohibitions against same-sex desire (received by fundamentalist believers as truth a priori) appear merely as the codifications of age-old anxieties and primal fears. The superego, however, refuses to intellectualize such matters. With its litany of Thou Shall Nots, social law uses the mind as a battlefield on which the Thou Shalls of the id are constantly combated. Love is twisted; instinct diverted. Nowhere is this conflict more salient than in the mind of Ennis del Mar. In fact, what "Brokeback Mountain" narrativizes is the psychic quandary of saying yes *and* no to the satisfaction of instinctual urges. Proving that he can't have "it" both ways, Ennis's ambivalence in the face of both gay and straight desire leaves him tragically isolated from both men and women by the story's conclusion. Ennis's own name suggests the desolation of the sea ("Del Mar") coupled with the Gaelic ("Ennis") for island, and the character fulfills the fate that his name predicts. Just as Proulx plays on her protagonist's name, Quoyle, in her 1993 novel, *The Shipping News*, her Ennis del Mar nominalizes the notion that no man is an island.

"Brokeback Mountain" signals a deeper interiorization of the social laws contravening the nature of same-sex love. While Ennis's love for Jack is driven by a strong and inexplicable force, equally insuperable in

Proulx's narrative is the competing power of antigay ideology. As Proulx told the *Los Angeles Times* soon after her decision to leave Wyoming for good, "[The story] was about homophobia in a place," and it's this place, I'm arguing, that is physical as well as psychic (Reynolds A19). Her contribution to the decoding of homophobia in all of its discursive guises is twofold: "Brokeback Mountain" provides an account, albeit fictional, of homophobic ideology and its physical effects on the body, but beneath the body, which Foucault encourages us to read as a legible surface on which power inscribes its material effects, Proulx sketches a psychic space that is equally broken by power.[4] The narrative dramatizes the fact that for gay men in particular, the mastery of natural energies is backbreaking work. Freud is indeed justified in his interpretation of dreams as unfulfilled wishes and as expressions of the repressed. Ennis's dream, which opens the story, masks the dreamer's unshakable desire to reunite with another male body *marred* by homophobia. Upon waking, after all, Ennis is "suffused" only with what Proulx deems the "sense of pleasure," for it is homophobia that drastically reduces a man's all-access pass to pleasure (255). His only resort is to dream because, as Freud writes in his book *The Interpretation of Dreams*, the "dream can take us back every night" to paradise (207).

In 1971 French theorist Louis Althusser deemed the complex process through which the voice of authority is appropriated by subjects as "interpellation," writing that we are "always-already interpellated by ideology as subjects," or always-already hailed (164). Informed largely by Marx, Althusser attempted to account for language's material effects on the individual in political society. His scenario is well-known: as a symbol of authority, a police officer calls, or hails, his suspects into the penal role by ordering them to stop. The mere utterance of "Hey, you there!" situates both the agent *and* object of power, and by turning to hear and heed the officer's call, citizens find themselves interpellated. In short, we come when called, and the only explanation provided by the law is the familiar (and familial): "because I said so!" Language catalyzes the process whereby words and slurs obtain a life of their own. In her book *The Psychic Life of Power*, Judith Butler renews Althusser's relevance to queer theories of subjection in an uncharacteristically clear précis of his theory: "Called by an injurious name, I come into social being, and because I have a certain inevitable attachment to my existence, because a certain narcissism takes hold of any term that confers existence, I am led to embrace the terms that injure me because they constitute me socially" (104).

Steeped in the language of mastery, the mountain's very name captures the doubleness of gay desire and identity, to the extent that even the romanticized space wherein Ennis and Jack's desire flourishes without sanction appears already corrupted by the forces that struggle consistently to overrun its borders. Brokeback is not, like the mythic Garden of Genesis, a place of unalloyed innocence and pristine perfection but a place of paradoxes. As Proulx describes Ennis's feelings shortly after the men's first sexual experience: "In a disquieting way everything seemed mixed" (262). Proulx queers one of the oldest gardens in the Book as a paradise always-already broken by the civilization it seemingly birthed.

A pastoral tragedy as bleak as "Brokeback Mountain," and a fate as gruesome as Jack's, would seem only to dispirit those wishing to seize Proulx's text as an affirmation of same-sex desire. Every political group is eager to possess and promote the sort of literary text that best imagines its own goals. Engels, for example, in his *The Condition of the Working Class in England*, praises the poetical works of Shelley and Byron for satirizing the morality of the nineteenth-century bourgeoisie.[5] Readers eager for the belated vindication of same-sex love would likely point to the mythologized space of Brokeback. According to this reading, Brokeback is the uniformly warm sort of space from which Ennis and Jack—our American Adam and Steve—must fall. Brokeback is both the garden of delights and a site of sexual discovery. Accordingly, their overseer, Joe Aguirre, is the godhead who observes the boys from afar with his 10x42 binoculars. Joe also plays the snake in the garden, for he precipitates the pair's fall from paradise by bringing Jack the news of his uncle Harold's impending death. Intruding into one of the narrative's only safe spaces, Joe brings with him the knowledge of death. Proulx herself underscores the prelapsarian splendor of the mountain when she describes, after the men have come down the mountain at the end of their first summer together, the "headlong, irreversible fall" experienced by Ennis, whose feelings for Jack are thereafter suspended between attraction and repulsion (263). Up on Brokeback, Jack assumes the position of Eve once he discovers the jouissance within. And like Eve, he is punished for an instinctive attraction to Ennis's apples. Shortly after waking from his dream of Jack in the story's lyrical prologue, Ennis recalls that "old, cold time on the mountain when they owned the world and nothing seemed wrong" (255).

Why "cold" here? Why must Ennis's nostalgic return to the mountain be fraught with such an unromantic absence of warmth? Even if the traumas of child abuse predate the men's time on the mountain—a mountain described, after all, as boiling with "demonic energy" and "broken-cloud light"—why must a painful present infect even the recall of a pleasurable past? (263). If Ennis appears mixed-up in terms of his sexual identity, his refusal to self-identify is certainly understandable, given the numerous paradoxes of same-sex desire: same but different, delightful but dangerous, fruitful and forbidden. Even Jack analogizes his sexual climax on Brokeback as a gunshot. The men's lovemaking is virtually silent, writes Proulx, save for a "few sharp intakes of breath and Jack's choked 'gun's goin *off*,' then out, down, and asleep" (262). Embedded in even the men's quietest moments is the ominous sound of violence, the sound that, of course, foreshadows the circumstances of Jack's death. Such a seminal moment in "Brokeback Mountain," which is representative of life/love, is juxtaposed with death to again underscore the degree to which the men's love is always-already corrupted by homophobia.

Jack too has been shocked or *twisted* into submission.[6] Just as he expresses a wish to someday share a "little ranch" with Ennis, or what he calls "some sweet life" together, Ennis responds by recounting each disturbing detail of a local lynching that he witnessed at the age of nine (270). The language of love is met by the realities of homophobic violence. Ennis suspects that his own father had lent a hand in the grizzly torture of an older rancher (and coupled gay man) known by the locals only as Earl. His father forces him to take in the scene as some kind of obscene morality play. But it's the tool of torture that continues to plague Ennis. He suspects a tire iron was used to cudgel and castrate the man. The locals lynched him and left him for dead in an irrigation ditch. The message is clear: transgress the social order and lose your head. Years later, he still can't shake the sight of Earl's mutilated body, specifically the violent theft of the old man's sex organs. This is the intractable trauma of Ennis's early life. Seeing the castrated body is enough to deter him from ever acting upon his most closeted of desires in public.

As an instrument of power, the tire iron hails Ennis and Jack into a particular state of gay panic. (Sadly, the tire iron appears to be the gay basher's weapon-of-choice: in April 2006 two New York City journalists, Dick Jefferson and Ryan Smith, were attacked outside a bar on the island of St. Martin by three men wielding tire irons and antigay slurs; the men were flown to Miami, where they were subsequently hospitalized for brain damage.) In fact, the tire iron recurs in Ennis's imagination when he learns the mysterious details of Jack's death. Lureen, Jack's Texan wife, informs Ennis over the telephone that her husband was fatally injured during a routine tire change on his truck. Naturally, Jack's untimely death strikes Ennis as no accident at all. "No, he thought," writes Proulx, "they got him with the tire iron" (279). The phallus again takes a paternal shape in the narrative's final scene, in which Ennis faces the "angry, knowing expression" of his lover's father: John C. Twist, coming face-to-face with yet another agent of oppression (281).

The narrative's interrogation scene is tempered only by the presence of Jack's doting mother who nervously offers coffee and cherry cake. Seated across from Mr. Twist, Ennis is reminded of another painful memory that Jack had once shared. Urinating accidentally on a toilet seat as a child, Jack provokes his father's rage. At the age of three or four, Jack looks down and recognizes what Proulx calls an "anatomical disconformity" between his father's uncircumcised organ and his "dick-clipped" one (282). The boy's curiosity in how men literally measure up soon unleashes a beating. His father urinates on him to further humiliate him. Now seated before the man, Ennis recalls Jack's memory of his father tormenting him with these words: "You want a know what it's like with piss all over the place? I'll learn you" (282). The common and countrified confusion between "teaching" and "learning" is telling here to the extent that the son's fear of the phallus/tire iron is taught, and learned, at a formative age. This is Proulx's scene of interpellation, of words injuring with the same impact as sticks and stones. Ennis is left to conclude, "So now he knew it had been the tire iron," for the father's lifelong disdain for Jack's dream of someday building a log cabin signifies a fatherly sort of fear and loathing that Ennis himself knows all too well (282).

Ang Lee's film adaptation helped to institutionalize a popular and particular misreading of the original text. This reading prefers a uniformly warm and fuzzy mountain over the hot-and-cold paradoxes that preside over Proulx's paradise. The public's (mis)identification of Ennis and Jack as the "gay cowboys" marked a certain disconnect between authorial intention and public perception. On the ontology of gay identity, the story is, of course, decidedly silent, but it's this precise silence with respect to the origins of same-sex love that mobilized public perception of the "Brokeback Boys" (as one late-night comic dubbed them) as just another piece of camp. Ennis's admission, in the original story, that "I was sittin up here all that time tryin to figure out if I was—?" installs a crucial lacuna insofar as the U.S. public, once it had grabbed hold of Lee's adaptation, worked hastily to fill it in (268). The homophobia that currently mobilizes discourse in the contemporary United States dictates that a subject with an unfixed sexual taste be categorized along that hoary, ironclad binarism: hetero/homo, top/bottom, butch/femme, in or out.

While the fixing of identities—upon which both readers and viewers would like to hang their hats—may be a misreading of the text's intention, the reception of Lee's film has bequeathed a curious symbol for the ongoing struggle to secure equal rights and protections for sexual minorities in the United States. The story of two factotums, gripped before the age of twenty by an attraction they can hardly understand, let alone admit to, radically recast the cinema's most dominant paradigm for masculinity: the cowboy. Megaplex Theatres, a cinema chain in South Jordan, Utah, in fact, made news in 2006 for banning *Brokeback* from its screens (Wildman 16). Despite the facts that Ennis and Jack move from job to job, none of which they perform all that expertly, and that both men refuse to identify themselves as gay, the public's perception stuck. Among the predominately gay audience that first saw Lee's film in 2005, discussions of the actors' good looks and supposed fortitude for "playing gay" (a career move that allegedly makes or *breaks* a young actor's career) initially overpowered more discerning considerations of the film's more radical intents. For example, a specialty book club, catering to its gay and lesbian membership, advertised a newly repackaged edition of Proulx's original work as the "sensual story of two cowboys in love . . . now a stunning film starring Hollywood heartthrobs Heath Ledger and Jake Gyllenhaal" ("Club Review"). Ledger's fatal overdose on January 22, 2008, has only intensified the film's cult status.[7] Again, the past is subject to the distorting present. A recent *Frontiers* guide to the "gayborhoods" of Los Angeles promises its readers a "place to have a *Brokeback* Moment," by which the editors mean the Bigfoot Lodge, a "rustic hipster hangout" located "in the wilderness between Los Feliz and Glendale" (Brooke and Cho 93). Costumes, especially those with spurs and leather chaps, have never exactly been a hard sell in the gay community, but now that America's *Brokeback* moment has come and gone, filmic and cultural appropriations of Proulx's original narrative deserve reinvestigation.

Whereas the original narrative provides only the skeletal frame of a love affair spanning two decades, Lee's film develops many of the subplots embedded in a masterful narrative that contains, in fact, multitudes. In the hands of screenwriters Diana Ossana and Larry McMurtry, the character of Ennis's sullen and submissive wife, Alma del Mar (née Beers), is deftly expanded to better underscore the emotional fallout resulting from so-called marriages of convenience. Perhaps to attract female moviegoers, the film better explores Alma's own desolation, for it deepens the degree to which she is victimized by the ideology of homophobia. She is the closet door, unwittingly used by Ennis to preempt allegations of sexual nonconformity. Like her husband, however, she accepts the social lot dealt to her and just tries to stand it. After Ennis joyously departs with Jack after their long-awaited reunion, Alma calls his name in what is described as the young woman's "misery voice" (266). She forsakes matrimony for misery, and pleasure for Ennis's rather leaden and lonesome performances in the bedroom.

Ossana and McMurtry preserve Alma's omniscient station above the men when they reunite beneath her in the stairwell outside her home in Riverton, but they endow her with the agency and pathos that Proulx only hints at in her original story. Mrs. Del Mar's private struggle is a dimension that Lee's film helps to illuminate, but too much attention to Alma's plight runs the risk of equating her own struggle with her husband's. Like Joe Aguirre—the story's other voyeur—Alma wants Ennis and Jack to come down off the mountain, but for entirely different reasons. Given her intimate involvement in the situation, she has to confront Ennis directly; Alma dares to speak what, for her husband, remains unspeakable. In a long, lyrical sentence, Proulx combines the men's blood-drawing embrace with Alma's oversight: the "door opening and Alma looking out for a few seconds at Ennis's straining shoulders and shutting the door again and still they clenched" (266). Alma chooses consciously to closet the knowledge of her husband's affair with Jack, which only exacerbates its disastrous effect on their marriage. By effectively trapping her husband into a confession later in the story, Alma participates in the very sort of *gotcha* emotionalism that closeted men live in fear of. She ties a note to the end of her husband's fishing pole to force a confession out of Ennis. By doing so, Alma refuses to once again shut the door on the realities that have finally tumbled out of the closet (or tackle-box). Alma, whose name is Spanish for "soul," supplies an ironically grounding force in Ennis's life insofar as she pressures her deceitful husband to let go of his clandestine memories of an irretrievable past—Brokeback frozen in time in 1963—and to begin living in the present-day. As in the case of Joe Aguirre, however, Alma's newfound knowledge evokes nausea. "Jack Twist?" she presses Ennis. "Jack Nasty! You and him—" (273).

Given the strong role of revulsion in the narrative, what does *Brokeback Mountain* have to offer contemporary debates concerning gay rights in the United States? Anyone conversant with gay culture knows the enduring popularity of the fantasy film, *The Wizard of Oz*. From Elton John's "Goodbye, Yellow Brick Road" to Rufus Wainwright's "Oh, What a World" (the dying words of the Wicked Witch of the West), the MGM classic is writ large in gay iconography. But the lost paradise that is "Brokeback" has come to signify (even "feel like") something similar to what Kyle Buchanan has called the "glorious Technicolor Oz" (56).[8] In fact, this colorful musical contains all the necessary ingredients of an instant camp classic: Munchkin choruses, a swishy lion, warring witches, and of course, Judy Garland in the star-making role of Dorothy. The gay rights movement's flagging of the rainbow to symbolize its struggle (and its diversity) suggests that a better world awaits its supporters somewhere, someday, over the rainbow. Lee's *Brokeback Mountain* offers the American moviegoer something altogether new. His film reminds audiences that homophobia is the stuff that bad dreams are made of, and by eschewing fantasy for realism, Lee's film depicts a different sort of dreamer. In this respect, Ennis of Wyoming may someday soon supplant the little girl lost from Kansas.[9] His agony is explicitly political, and unlike Dorothy, he never makes it home.

The dream of a better life, which for most remains inviolably safe from the exigencies of reality, is denied to Proulx's Ennis and Jack. Ennis's own dream of a paradise lost and Jack's dream of a log-cabin paradise are menaced by competing memories of physical abuse and phallic violation. But naming the "it" as unfixable, as Ennis does twice over the duration of Proulx's "Brokeback Mountain," provides the essential first step for social and political reform, just as Alma's peeking out into the realities that enclose her suggests that indeed a better world awaits her. The mountain that remains locked in her husband's imagination may prove to be a potent symbol for a new generation of liberationists. Along the yellow-brick road to reform, Jack Twist outpaces Ennis del Mar. Jack's own struggle to recover the men's paradise lost is the single inspiring effort in a story that reminds readers and viewers alike to never say never. If the reader comes to sympathize with the men's struggle, which is no doubt Proulx's aim, the permanent potential of "Brokeback Mountain" is that it brings new rainbows into view.

Notes

1. "They're calling it Stonewall 2.0," writes Jesse McKinley, referring to the new wave of U.S. activists inspired by the legacy of Harvey Milk (member of the San Francisco Board of Supervisors), assassinated in 1978 (A22). In terms of the rainbow trope, so omnipresent in gay iconography, there were at least two gay-inflected films of 2008 that used "Over the Rainbow" in their soundtracks: first, the aforesaid *Milk*, in which the song is synchronized to protests in the Castro, and *Australia*, an exuberantly kitschy epic in which Baz Luhrmann directs Nicole Kidman to sing the ditty to an aboriginal child.

2. Boswell points out that the antinomy between "natural" and "unnatural" acts has long played a role in the intolerance for gay people. For a discussion of homosexuality and naturalness, see 11–15.

3. For a poetic meditation on Freud's theory of the psyche, see Kevin Boyle's "Id," a poem in which Boyle recalls the "lost sense" of "guiltless pleasures" (44–45).

4. See Foucault's belief that "at the level of ideology," it would be "more materialist" in a post-Marxist dimension to "study first the question of the body and the effects of power on it" (58).

5. For a history of the Chartist Movement and its appropriation of Shelley's texts, see Foot (239–45).

6. In an interview with the Human Rights Campaign, which in 2006 lavished the director and his principal actors with accolades, Ang Lee speaks to the "true" nature of the men's love: "To me, they are [gay]. It's just because Heath Ledger's character, Ennis, has so much self-denial—he is so homophobic, it is harder to tell; it's more twisted, that's all there is" (6).

7. In the wake of Ledger's overdose, what the obituaries and elegies for the actor invariably overlooked was the fact that his choice of roles was always daring and dark. In *The Order* (2003), Ledger plays a defrocked priest, Father Alex, who travels to Rome to solve a murder. Ledger stayed on the dark side in pictures such as *Monster's Ball* (2001), playing the sullen, Southern son of a prison guard (Billy Bob Thornton), and *Candy* (2006), in which he stars as Dan, a heroin-addicted poet from Down Under. His decision, meanwhile, to play Casanova (the very paragon of the heterosexual lady's man) in *Casanova* (2005) on the heels of *Brokeback* was a deliberate one: he was trying on the many, if not all, masks involved in being a man. The irony is that Ledger first made his name as a teenage heartthrob in *10 Things I Hate about You* (a 1999 dopey high school comedy based on Shakespeare's *The Taming of the Shrew* with Ledger as Patrick Verona and Julia Stiles as Kat Stratford). He reportedly swore off the heartthrob role after the film's success. Ultimately, Ledger's embodiment of Ennis and his Oscar-winning, nihilistic take on the Joker in the Batman sequel *The Dark Knight* (2008) will be the performances that endure. For more on Ledger and *Brokeback* mythos, see my "Heath Ledger and the Idolatry of Dying Young."

8. Buchanan complains that "gay film has seemed for too long to be stuck in a black-and-white Kansas rut" (56).

9. There's simply no way to tell if Garland's death did or did not compound the discontent that pervaded New York gay culture in the summer of 1969. Historian David Carter has dispelled the persistent myth that the death of Garland, who was buried on the same day the Stonewall Riots began, caused the men's agitation to mount and ultimately break later that evening. There's little doubt that Garland's Technicolor rainbow provided these men tremendous comfort in an era in which prohibitions against same-sex desire were even greater than they are now. Nevertheless, Carter devotes only two pages to this

theory in his *Stonewall: The Riots That Sparked the Gay Revolution* to demonstrate that this "great artist's tragic and untimely death could not have caused the riots" based on the fact that the "main fighters in the riots were street youths" (260–61). The reader is left to assume that these new young radicals were unaffected by Garland's demise at the age of forty-seven. For Carter, the riots marked the transition from an older order of gay men who turned vicariously to such embattled divas as Garland and Garbo for spiritual comfort to the visibility of actual gay men and lesbian women on-screen and in the press. *Washington Post* writer Teresa Wiltz recently added Garland in her list of what she calls "TWGS" (or Train Wreck Girls), which also includes Britney Spears, Lindsay Lohan, Marilyn Monroe, Dorothy Dandridge, and even Sylvia Plath and Virginia Woolf. Wiltz writes that Garland was one of the original fame-stricken ingenues whose high-speed lifestyle derailed her professional ambitions (C1, C8).

11 } West of the Closet, Fear on the Range

ALEX HUNT

In my corner of the West, as in much of the great intercoastal heartland, the progressive stance on homosexuality might be summed up in the Christian-esque slogan "love the sinner, hate the sin." In the Texas panhandle, where I live and teach at West Texas A&M, the cowboy community is far more visible than the gay and lesbian community. I have twice taught Annie's Proulx's "Brokeback Mountain" in American literature classes, once in the spring of 2002—well before the film craze—and again in the summer of 2006, just as the uproar had subsided. While the film dramatically altered student expectations in reading the story, reactions varied more dramatically from individual to individual. I had, for example, conservative Christian students of perfect attendance who were quietly absent that week. Many students joined the discussion in the spirit of open-mindedness, but deeply embedded attitudes led them to troubling conclusions; some students argued that Proulx's story was about lovers who happened to be men, or men who happened—oops!— to fall in love, rather than gay men, per se. Other students argued that the power of the story was in its insistence that homosexuality was everywhere and that gay and lesbian individuals were more diverse than the familiar stereotypes allow. One student came out to the class, confirming her lesbianism and discussing her work with the regional chapter of the LGBTA. In short, teaching "Brokeback Mountain" seems to me important because it opens up productive discussions among students who come from communities in which homosexuality is a taboo subject, synonymous with sin. Teaching this story also heightened my sensitivity to and admiration for residents of places like the Texas panhandle who are openly, bravely, gay. Plenty of people, after all, hate the sinner as well as the sin.

On the other hand, everyone loves cowboys, as I have learned in my own forays into western American culture. I have always lived in the West, but raised by professors among books in college towns, most of my western experiences have been "New West" in character: hiking, fishing, rock climbing, drinking coffee in Seattle. Growing up, I had no experience and very little consciousness of farming or ranching. As a college student at Colorado State University, however, I, who cannot really ride a horse, took up bull riding. I was not good at it. In retrospect, my four-year sojourn into first collegiate and then professional rodeos began as a thrill-seeking jaunt but ended as an exercise in embedded anthropology. I saw the West in a certain way that was valuable. I learned many lessons, some of them scholarly, others more visceral. For example, when one is riding a bull—a completely contrived, theatrical, unreal spectacle having no direct connection to cowboy work—bull riding is very real: the visceral nature and physical danger of it should be real enough for anyone.

Cowboys—even rodeo cowboys whom ranch cowboys don't consider "real" cowboys—are tough. I always think of the world champion saddle bronc rider Robert Etbauer at the 1995 Denver Stock Show and Rodeo. After disengaging himself from a stirrup from which he was dragging, he hunted around in the dirt of the arena floor until he located his thumb, severed when the horse stepped on his hand, which he then picked up and carried out of the arena. He was back riding, thumb reattached, two months later. Rodeo cowboys certainly have an iconic value of masculine toughness in popular culture. Examples abound, but the "Brokeback Mountain" phenomenon includes a Miller Lite ad in which Ty Murray (seven-time all-round world champion cowboy) is one of a male think tank drafting "man laws." Murray responds to Burt Reynolds's suggestion that it is proper etiquette when clinking bottles to "touch bottoms" by saying, "No thanks, Hollywood; I ain't into that." Murray's rebuttal of Hollywood's "attack" on cowboy straight masculinity is rather humorous, but I suspect the attitudes of most cowboys toward queer sexuality are not.

The sentiments of my former rodeo travel partner, for example, are not amusing. For him, John Wayne is the epitome of masculine honor, nothing campy about it. The film *Brokeback Mountain* is for him an abomination on both Christian and cowboy macho grounds. Needless to say, he refused to read the story or watch the film. He reported that he had heard that the state of Wyoming had sued the makers of *Brokeback Mountain* for defamation or slander—or that, if this rumor was unfounded, it was nevertheless a good idea. Our conversation about masculinity, sexuality, religion, and violence reminded me forcefully that authenticity isn't what is but what those with the greatest passion imagine it to be. And so I sit here in the Texas panhandle, far from Hollywood in more ways than one, thinking about the West and western identities as things both and simultaneously inauthentic and actual, thinking the same thing I always thought at rodeos when getting ready to get on a bull: if this is so phony, why am I scared? Like bull riding, identity may be performative, but that doesn't make it unreal or safe.

For me, the rodeo is a place where danger and fear and bravery make a performance of westernness real. My reading of Proulx's story and the phenomenon of the film version—and this has to do with the politics of being western or living in the U.S. West today—suggests that Proulx's edgy hyperrealist aesthetic responds more appropriately to concerns for authenticity than fiction with a more acceptable Western pedigree. Interestingly, my experience of teaching Proulx's Western fiction—especially *That Old Ace in the Hole*—in Texas has been that students feel that Proulx does not respect the regionally defined people she writes about, that she satirizes westerners unfairly, that, finally, her treatment of the West and westerners is inauthentic. In the case of "Brokeback Mountain," queer cowboys become an example of this inauthenticity. In these responses my students' feelings parallel those of Newfoundland people who have protested Proulx's *The Shipping News*, for which Proulx won the Pulitzer Prize in 1994. Tracy Whalen writes that, for one example, "Newfoundlanders Read The Shipping News,' a series of web pages written by fifty-five students in a Memorial University education class, interrogates many of the representations of the places in the book and, offering an 'aggressively corrective picture of life in the province,' questions the validity of Proulx's use of Newfoundland as the setting for the novel" (51).

If regional peoples here and there do not appreciate what Whalen describes as Proulx's authorial regional tourism on the grounds of its inauthenticity, western U.S. literary critics on the other hand are not necessarily pleased with Proulx's attack on western shibboleths of the sacred authentic. In his recent book *Unsettling the Literary West*, Nathaniel Lewis includes Proulx's *Close Range* as one of a number of postmodern Western texts that are admirable for their subversion of the old mythological, patriarchal, homophobic, racist West and for their move toward social activism. Still, Lewis argues, these works remain "remarkably uninteresting" and ultimately disappointing as they tend to re-assert another revised claim to authenticity, or are read that way (195). I don't think Proulx is asking to be read as revisionary and authentic. Proulx's portrayals of western places and characters are far too cartoonish—even when sinister—to be mistaken for claims to authenticity. Or, to the extent that Proulx's characters achieve a kind of authenticity, they do so despite rather than through the western identities that they wear, often awkwardly, in their difficult, often mundane, often sordid lives. The emotional truth penetrates and takes the place of the campy western false fronts of identity.

Proulx's fiction reminds us in seriousness what John Stewart's Western clips at the Oscars demonstrated in hilarious montage: cowboys have always, in a sense, been "gay." I would not go so far as Chris Packard in saying that in his historical resistance to domestic heterosexist conventions "the cowboy is queer" and is so "because the audience wants him to be queer" (12). Since the cowboy is the American hero, Packard goes on to suggest, there are connections between the cowboy's role in U.S. manifest destiny and the queer hero. Despite the decodable homoerotic subtext of cowboy narratives, it seems overwhelmingly evident that on most levels Americans do not want to imagine their masculine heroes having sex with other men. Just because an overinsistence on masculine identity easily becomes a mockery of itself, it does not follow that masculine identity is not seriously upheld. Owen Wister's *The Virginian* aside, cowboy narratives demonstrate the desire for presexual innocence, making the winning of the West not a conquest but a game, enabling Americans to imagine the West not as space of violent empire but of childlike play. In the national imaginary, in my opinion, the cowboy enjoys a prolonged latency period.

Still, there is something to the queering of the cowboy. I find truth in Brian Bouldrey's observation that the rodeo cowboy's masculinity is not straightforward: "The more manly a man is, the more a woman he is. . . . It's traditional for the woman to be noticed and admired. Today the cowboy gets to be noticed" (22). Watching the Cow Palace Grand National Rodeo of San Francisco, Bouldrey says that he cannot help but think that "all these cowboys milling around outside the ring look like they might show up at the Rawhide (or some other gay Western bar) later on" (19). In my own experience at the rodeo I was conscious that rodeo cowboys, iconically the acme of manly men, wore uncomfortably and impractically tight pants, garishly colored shirts, and chaps with bright fringe. When you think about it, unless a cowboy is riding, has just been riding, or is about to ride, cowboys' boots are just an excuse for men to wear heels. It certainly occurred to me that rodeo cowboys enact masculinity, quite consciously I'd argue, and that the exaggerated performance of masculinity defends a certain heterosexist idea of the masculine. Paradoxically, at the rodeo, the more a man exaggerates his masculine performance, the more he feminizes himself through the addition of gold belt buckles and meticulously pressed shirts. In their exaggeration of masculinity beyond the bounds of the traditionally masculine, rodeo cowboys seem to be camp.

Annie Proulx is up to something with respect to camp. I do not say this because her fiction very often includes gay and lesbian characters, whether marginal or central, nor is this fact irrelevant. But it is Proulx's hyperreal, exaggerated, often cartoonish aesthetic that makes me think of her fiction as employing camp style. In her aesthetic style, her representational mode, there is an extravagance, a kind of overwriting even when she is generally terse. Even detail that seems to lend verisimilitude seems to me not realism or claim to authenticity but a self-conscious, campy gesture toward realism or authenticity. In response to B. R. Myers's attack of Proulx (and others) as guilty of bad pretentious writing (105), I think of Susan Sontag's note that "many examples of Camp are things which, from a 'serious' point of view, are either bad art or kitsch." Sontag is quick to add that not all camp is bad art and that "some art which can be approached as Camp . . . merits the most serious admiration and study" (278). Proulx's fiction certainly maintains an ironic edge and a kind of detached eye that Sontag describes, yet Proulx is serious and political. Proulx's fiction typically concerns, as she puts it, communities and ways of life that are dying away, marginal communities exploited by larger economic interests ("Getting Movied" 129). Proulx's seriousness with respect to her content is counterbalanced by her ironic, hyperreal, campy style, complicating Sontag's insistence that camp is the antithesis of tragedy and the enemy of seriousness (287). Also, in Proulx's fiction, characters often go camping.

I think it no accident—when considering camp—that Proulx wrote a story about cowboys who shed their heterosexual masculine identities (Ennis naively, in response to his absent father) and fall into a torrid affair while at a sheep camp. First of all, it's an inside joke that a literary readership may not get. Among cowboys, mention of sheep is an invitation to snickers and talk of bestiality. I remember when, as one new to cowboy culture in Colorado, I stood around with a group of cowboys, one of whom joked that an absent fellow had gone to Wyoming to shop for his Wrangler Jeans. I asked why, not getting the joke. I was told that in Wyoming, Wranglers were equipped with quiet zippers, facilitating the stalking of sheep. I imagine that the cowboys I knew—if forced to see the movie and discuss it—would explain Jack and Ennis's homosexual affair as just the sort of thing that could happen when otherwise sound cowboys make the dubious decision to go herd sheep.

But what happens while camping? Ennis del Mar (Penis of the Sea?) and Jack Twist (Masturbator?) are hired as camp tender and herder, respectively. Jack complains to his domestic partner that he is unhappy with Joe Aguirre's commandment that the herder "SLEEP WITH THE SHEEP" (255) far from camp. Like so many suburbanites living lives of quiet desperation, Jack laments, "I'm commutin four hours a day." Ennis offers to "switch" assignments, reversing their gendered roles. Ennis seems immediately more capable as a herder, shooting a coyote with "balls on him size a apples" the first night. And Jack seems the inferior camp tender, as he warns Ennis: "I can't cook worth a shit. Pretty good with a can opener" (257). Both of these images—signaling raw animal masculinity and a kind of crude domesticity—will come back. As the summer progresses, the distance from camp to pasture grows even farther, setting the scene for the night when Ennis remains in camp with Jack, the night they "deepened their intimacy considerably" (259). The following year, Aguirre (the Wrath of God?), who had witnessed Jack 'n' Ennis *en fuego* through his omniscient binoculars, refused to rehire Jack: "you guys wasn't getting paid to leave the dogs baby-sit the sheep while you stemmed the rose" (267).

This brings us, finally, to sex. If Proulx had written a touching story about two young men who herd sheep one summer, fighting together against predators and the elements to return with a thriving flock, it would probably not have made it to the silver screen. On the other hand, if Proulx had written a sexually frank and emotionally moving story about two gay men who like to don western dress and meet at the Rawhide in San Francisco, no one would have noticed; no movie deal would have followed. No, the power and appeal of the story resides not in the raw sexual zeal and touching passionate love between two men but in the raw sexual zeal and touching passionate love between two Wyoming cowboys, each of whom maintains, as Ennis puts it in perfectly appropriate double negative, that he is "not no queer" (260).

But understatement is not Proulx's forte, anyway, as we see in the scene in which Jack 'n' Ennis first share the tent. While the two are accustomed to sleeping apart to fulfill their shepherd's duties, they often sit late eating beans from the can, drinking whiskey, and speaking of many things—family history, rodeo, and other topics including the recent sinking of the nuclear submarine the *Thresher*, lost in 1963. This social life carries on until one night when Ennis finds himself too drunk and the time too late to ride out to the herd and then shares Jack's bedroll for warmth. Then it happens. When Jack pulls Ennis's hand toward his "erect cock": "Ennis jerked his hand away as though he'd touched fire, got to his knees, unbuckled his belt, shoved his pants down, hauled Jack onto all fours and, with the help of the clear slick and a little spit, entered him, nothing he'd ever done before but no instruction manual needed" (259).

This kind of inauthentically authentic western action-sequence, suggesting rugged individualism, comradeship, a can-do spirit, and a facility with livestock (these men do what needs to be done and what is natural, and need no manual) is nevertheless complex. Proulx's language describing Ennis's reaction—he "jerked his hand away as though he'd touched fire"—suggests his fear, his inclination to reject Jack's touch at this point of no return even as he moves peremptorily into the sexual act, taking control of the situation. The fear, as Ennis will later admit, is ultimately not of the sexual act or of being homosexual. Ennis's fear is of the loss of control and its potentially fatal social consequences.

Proulx's hyperrealism takes different forms in her work. In *That Old Ace in the Hole* (2002), for example, it is a hyperrealism of grotesquely exaggerated, cartoonish characters with names such as Freda Beauty-rooms, characters like Sheriff Hugh Dough, a lifelong bed wetter whose sex life has consisted entirely of trysts with his sister, even after her marriage to Richard Head. In representing the Texas panhandle, Proulx combines rigorous regional history with unbelievable characters to create, in Umberto Eco's phrase, "a fantasy world more real than reality" ("Travels" 45). In "Brokeback Mountain," Proulx's hyperrealism is more restrained, limited to a kind of self-conscious attention to detail. Lingo and facts from the rodeo world—Ennis's comment that "you're goin a go where you look," Jack's explanation of the bull rider's forearm stress-fracture (266)—lend a credible feel of western authenticity. The discussion of the sinking of the nuclear submarine *Thresher* lends historical veracity to the story's 1963 setting, but more importantly, in invoking the death by young men confined, crushed, doomed, it obviously suggests a grim outcome for Jack and Ennis's love. At the same time, though, the submarine reference lends itself to appropriately inappropriate jokes about long, hard objects full of seamen. Even the description of sexual penetration by "clear slick and spit"—a detail preserved, to the extent possible, in the film—demonstrates this meticulous attention to well-chosen details that enhance the realism of the story. Less restrained is Proulx's attention to landscape. While the film shows the Canadian Rockies of Alberta in realist technique, the landscape of the story is hyperreal, charged with an emotion ready to strike like lightening. When Jack and Ennis, feeling mixed-up, bring the mixed herd of sheep down at the end of the season, "The mountain boiled with demonic energy, glazed with flickering broken-cloud light, the wind combed the grass and drew from the damaged krummholz and slit rock a bestial drone" (261). Pathetic fallacy be damned! Proulx manipulates landscape in a manner beyond realism, to the hyperreal extreme emotional fringes.

Proulx's language when she describes Ennis's memory of Jack through the story is worth considering here. In the opening paragraph of the story, we meet Ennis as an older man, some years after Jack's death. He is pleased because he dreamed of Jack, and as he drinks his morning coffee, contemplating those days on Brokeback, he "lets a panel of the dream slide forward" (253). Memory is figured here as still image, as something like a slide show. Panels also suggest film scenes or cartoons, and so we should be very attentive to images that recur in the story, especially images that signify Jack and Ennis's masculinity and sexuality. Remember, now, Jack's limited kitchen skills, his canned beans; remember also, Ennis's coyote with the balls the size of apples.

As Proulx flashes back to the beginning of the story, we recall that the first meal after Jack's assumption of domestic camp duties, because Jack is "pretty good with a can opener" (257) is "a can of beans each, fried potatoes and a quart of whiskey on shares" (258). Proulx's penchant for word play is at full strength: as Ennis's seducer, Jack is indeed an able can opener. Later, when Ennis eagerly awaits Jack's first visit four years after their summer together, he tells Alma—a name meaning "soul": Ennis lies to his wife, his soul mate; and to himself—that they will probably not go to a restaurant, as in his mind's eye he sees "the dirty spoons sticking out of the cans of cold beans balanced on the log" (263), an image full of connotations of penises, penetrated cans, and rough, outdoorsy sex play. Proulx's playfully humorous and scatalogically crude imagery carries through to the scene when, after their divorce, Alma accuses Ennis of his infidelity, explaining how she'd found out that the fishing trips with Jack weren't really about fishing: "said you'd caught a bunch of browns and ate them up" (270). Still later, Ennis learns from Jack's wife that Jack died while changing a tire when the tire blew up, causing him to smash his head on the tire rim. Ennis interprets Jack's death as murder, concluding for himself that Jack was beaten to death (in his imagination, with a tire iron) for his affair with his male neighbor, and not, as he had once told Ennis, the neighbor's wife. Finally, in the last paragraph of the story, as Ennis dreams of Jack and his likely murder by violent beating, Ennis sees Jack "as he had first seen him, curly-headed and smiling and bucktoothed, talking about getting up off his pockets and into the control zone, but the can of beans with the spoon handle jutting out and balanced on the log was there as well, in a cartoon shape and lurid colors that gave the dreams a flavor of comic obscenity. The spoon handle was the kind that could be used as a tire iron" (283).

It works, in the lurid, nightmarish morphings of dream imagery, to imagine a spoon becoming a tire iron, an image of sex becoming an image of death, as Jack's sexuality ultimately puts him in danger, gets him killed. It is even more compelling when we consider the connection that Ennis is making—the image of the can of beans is a mnemonic trigger for his feelings of love for Jack, a love complicit in events leading to Jack's murder. But the image is also an indictment of Jack, who could not keep tidy and organized the domestic space of the camp—he was literally a poor camp tender—just as he violated the domestic, sexual, and neighborly rules of society in Childress, Texas, by having a homosexual affair with his neighbor. The spoon/tire iron is a symbol of Jack's tendency to soil his own nest.

Ennis's coyote with "balls on him size a apples" also returns in important, and lurid, ways. The most obvious reference comes near the end when Ennis visits Jack's parents, offering to take Jack's ashes to Brokeback Mountain, as he had wished. Here Ennis finds the shirts, one nested inside the other, but Jack's father angrily—knowingly—denies Ennis the ashes. In the background to this exchange, "Jack's mother stood at the table coring applies with a sharp, serrated instrument" (282). That the "sharp, serrated instrument" could not just as well be called a "knife" calls attention to those earlier masculine apples; here the mother figure symbolically both castrates and reams her son as the father reasserts his oedipal power. Ennis, too, is symbolically castrated in this scene as he notices Jack's mother's knifework—he knows that they know, but his love cannot speak its name here especially. The knife is aimed at his apples, is also twisting in his guts. In this scene Ennis also remembers Jack's story of his father's aggression. When a child, Jack had trouble making it to the toilet and his father, in a brutal moment, urinated on his son to drive home the lesson on toilet training. In the midst of this traumatic event, Jack told Ennis, he noticed "he had some extra material that I was missin." Jack interprets his circumcision in the language of livestock: "I seen they'd cut me different like you'd crop a ear or scorch a brand. No way to get it right with him after that" (280). That Jack doesn't mention castration makes the suggestion no less evident to the reader.

Proulx's referencing of branding, ear cropping, and castration has similar connotations to and may indeed be informed by Blake Allmendinger's discussion of cowboy work. Allmendinger argues that the act of branding and castrating becomes, for cowboys, symbolic of their own economic situation: cowboys "not only were required to isolate themselves from society and to abstain from expressing 'love' for great lengths of time, but were paid to act out their isolation and abstinence by castrating stock" (51). What Ennis finds comforting in his marriage to Alma—his penchant for anal intercourse aside—is "the smell of old blood and milk and baby shit, and the sounds . . . of squalling and sucking and Alma's sleepy groans, all reassuring of fecundity and life's continuance to one who worked with livestock" (262). But like Jack, Ennis has traumatic associations as well as comforting ones. That Ennis was left orphaned at age fourteen with "twenty-four dollars in cash and a two-mortgage ranch" (254) is a kind of economic castration, ensuring that Ennis would be cheated out of his inheritance of land. Ennis is also symbolically castrated when his father takes him, as a young boy, to see the corpse of a dead man. Among other atrocities, this gay man had his genitals torn off, a sight that made a lasting impression on the young Ennis.

One of the most excellent qualities of the story is the way in which Jack and Ennis are complexly constructed with ambivalences that seem to both prop up and knock down the other. Jack seems initially more experienced than Ennis in the ways of manly love, but if Jack initiates contact, Ennis runs with it. Ennis is loyal to employers and his marriage (committed to stay, to see it through) and to Jack, which seems a positive attribute until it becomes evident that he is hiding from commitment to Jack out of fear. Jack takes other lovers and lies about it to Ennis, which seems unpardonable until we feel his frustration with Ennis's reluctance, his desperate need for love in his life. One of the most poignant moments in the story is Jack's memory of Ennis holding him from behind in an embrace before the campfire, a "silent embrace satisfying some shared and sexless hunger" (276), that is beautiful to

Jack even as he knows that "Ennis would not then embrace him face to face because he did not want to see nor feel that it was Jack he held" (277). In the end, I feel every bit as trapped and hopeless as they do about their situation, and sympathize with them equally.

But for me, Ennis's memory of Earl and Rich is the epicenter of "Brokeback Mountain." This story is crucial not only to understanding his character but to the doomed relationship between him and Jack. It is also central to my overall point concerning Proulx's achievement. In the midst of an argument concerning their potential future together, Ennis tells Jack that he is "caught in [his] own loop" and can see no way out because he "don't want a be like them guys you see around sometimes"—openly gay. Furthermore, Ennis continues, he doesn't want to be killed. As he tells Jack, referring to their uncontrollably passionate embrace and kiss upon seeing each other after a long separation, "We do that in the wrong place we'll be dead" (267): "There were these two old guys ranched together down home, Earl and Rich—Dad would pass a remark when he seen them. They was a joke even though they was pretty tough old birds. I was what, nine years old and they found Earl dead in a irrigation ditch. They took a tire iron to him, spurred him up, drug him around by his dick until it pulled off, just bloody pulp. What the tire iron done looked like pieces a burned tomatoes all over him, nose tore down from skiddin on gravel" (268). Ennis adds that not only did his father take him to see Earl's body, his father laughed about it and "for all I know he done the job" (268). The only solution, for Ennis, is to go camping in the mountains with Jack whenever they can get away. Proulx's description of the atrocity committed here is about as lurid as could be still believable.

Proulx's concern with gay identity out West and the fear of hate crime carries into her most recent novel, *That Old Ace in the Hole* (2002), set in the Texas panhandle. Protagonist Bob Dollar, newly arrived from Denver, hears it this way from his landlady: "There's that Frank Owsley and his so-called roommate Teddy Paxson moved here from Dallas in 1996 and bought the old Cowboy Rose district two schoolhouse. They fixed it up as a glassworks studio and a house" (101). One character, Rope Butt, responds that he "didn't much care for the two nancy boys" but "he was willing to live and let live, for certain bunkhouse friendships were not unknown, though little talked about" (138). Francis Scott Keister, however, "hated the two," saying, "Woolleybucket Country don't need no damn fags," and speaking of "tar and feathers and worse" (138). In my opinion, Proulx manages to tap into very real, vital issues in western U.S. culture without having to demonstrate loyalty to western ideals and shibboleths of authenticity.

I wish I could say that Proulx's treatment of the violence—the murder of gay men—is another case of her exaggerated hyperrealism, but the violence, along with Ennis's fear, seems to me the most emotionally realistic aspect of "Brokeback Mountain." James Byrd, a black man in Jasper, Texas, was dragged to death behind a pickup truck in June 1998, and in October of the same year, Matthew Shepard was beaten and left for dead, tied to a fence, in Laramie. Proulx's hyperrealism casts the fear and horror of such atrocities into sharp detail. In *Losing Matt Shepard*, Beth Loffreda writes that after listening to gay men in Wyoming, one "can begin to draw a secret map of Wyoming, one most of its residents would find unfamiliar" (69). Proulx's story demands of its readers that they acknowledge that such a map exists. That this map is necessary is irrefutable, that it must be covert is criminal.

While the film *Brokeback Mountain* is quite powerful in its own right, I think something important is lost. While Jake Gyllenhaal was very good and Heath Ledger was excellent, I thought they were still too pretty, insufficiently gawky and gangly. Hollywood tends to keep its stars pretty, however, and I imagine that the producers of the film would have thought it asking too much of audiences, and particularly the younger female demographic, I suspect, to watch unattractive cowboys kissing. The film premiered early in New York and Los Angeles, which is typical, and in San Francisco, which is less so. The *San Francisco Chronicle*, citing inside sources, reported that the decision to open early in San Francisco "only made sense": "'[I]t is very likely the gay community will attend in great numbers' and a positive response would bring the film 'important credibility.' In other words, locals could make or break 'Brokeback Mountain'" (Stein). While it makes perfect sense that the gay community should have had a strong voice in the critical and financial success of *Brokeback Mountain*, I was nevertheless struck by the fact that the "locals" who would lend "credibility" and judge the authenticity of this modern-day Western would be San Franciscans rather than Wyomingites. Fortunately, the film showed in Wyoming theaters, in Laramie and Cheyenne, at least; otherwise interested viewers may have had to do what Jack and Ennis contemplate when they consider how gay men might actually live together in safety—as Jack says, "I don't know what they do, maybe go to Denver" (269).

At the time of its release and in discussions I have overheard since, *Brokeback Mountain* has "passed," we might say, as a love story. In one sense, it is just that, and we can applaud the film for its successful claim to the U.S. public that love transcends cultural politics, conventional morality, and even sexuality itself. Gay men are somehow legitimized by these cowboys, who surely would not be lovers if they had any other choice in the matter. But herein lies the problem inherent in the "love story" billing, the problem with "passing." That audiences can identify with and cry over the doomed, impossible love between these men allows them to sidestep the brash fact of queer sexual desire that is part and parcel of Jack and Ennis's love. In this sense the critical reception echoes my students' appropriation and domestication of these men as accidental or star-crossed lovers who happen to be men, but not actual gay men. The film allows its viewers to love the sinners and still hate the sin. Because, after all, as we have long known, cowboys are not, must not be, gay. I think it important, then, to insist on the violence of the story, to claim that in truth this is no love story. It is a story of love crippled by fear, hate, and murder.

Part 3 } Adapting "Brokeback Mountain," Queering the Western

12 } Interview between Michael Silverblatt and Annie Proulx

MICHAEL SILVERBLATT: From KCRW Santa Monica, I'm Michael Silverblatt, and this is *Bookworm*. Today I'm happy to have as my guest Annie Proulx, whose collection of stories *Close Range*, I would think many of you know. They are Wyoming stories. She did a second volume of Wyoming stories called *Bad Dirt* and that's her most recent book.[1] We're here as a kind of a first for *Bookworm* because one of the stories in *Close Range*, "Brokeback Mountain," has been adapted and made into a film by Ang Lee. The screenwriters were Larry McMurtry and Diana Ossana, and it's one of those kind of, I think, heavenly events for a writer when a movie stays true and fairly close to the range of the work. As someone who's had this experience with several of your books, what has this one been like?

ANNIE PROULX: Well, that's actually a more complicated question than you might think. When I wrote that story I had a serious problem with the characters. In all of my writing I had no problems at all with characters—they do what they're told; when they're no longer useful I get rid of them. [MS laughs.] And away they go—but in this story I had to stretch my imagination to a depth I never had before. A middle-aged woman writing about two nineteen-year-old guys who are very confused about their sexuality and eventually move into a love affair is not the ordinary kind of thing that I think about, so I had a lot of very serious imagining to do. And it took months and months to write this story. If all I did was write at this pace I'd probably have a lifetime output of just maybe seven short stories.

153

[MS chuckles.] But what happened is that at the end, when the story was finally finished and the imagining could stop, it didn't, and the characters were there. And I had to write *That Old Ace in the Hole*, about the panhandle of Texas, to get rid of these guys. Because they were intrusive and they wouldn't go. And after eight years I had pretty much gotten rid of Jack and Ennis until in September when I saw the film in New York for the first time, having seen not a drop of it, not a scene, having heard nothing, did not visit the set, had no idea what I was going to see—and I sat in that theater and those characters roared up off the page and back into the screen and into my brain again, and they were there with the volume turned very, very high and once again I had to try and find an exorcist.

MS: I think that's true for readers as well because, you know, I read that story when it first appeared in *The New Yorker*—what is it, around eight—?

AP: Eight years ago.

MS: Eight years ago. And, you know, I knew your work, some, but I'm kind of reading, and it's fairly unusual for any of the stories in *The New Yorker* to occur outdoors—that's a first surprise [AP laughs]— and, you know, they're cowboys, and I'm kind of sitting there, saying—

AP: No they're not. No, no—don't say that. I'm fighting that.

MS: Ranchers?

AP: No, they're just—they're ranch hands. They're just ranch kids, really they aren't anything. They would like to be cowboys because they live in the West, but really, they're not. They try in different ways.

MS: One tries working in rodeo.

AP: Yeah.

MS: The other is working around stock.

AP: Mm-hmm.

MS: I guess a city person like me calls that cowboys.

AP: Right. Well, anybody who sees the hat and the boots says cowboy, but they're not real cowboys.

MS: And I'm saying to myself—I think these boys are falling in love with one another. [AP laughs.] And I'm thinking, no, maybe this must just be some rigging in my brain—[AP chuckles]—maybe I want them to be. And then sure enough, they are—and I don't actually check the cover to check if this is *The New Yorker*, but this is *The New Yorker*, and before long they're having sex, and I thought—my goodness, this story is causing shockwaves in me, certainly—and then when it came out in its book form there is a couple of paragraphs that aren't in *The New Yorker* story, if I remember correctly.

AP: Mm-hmm.

MS: And I'm kind of sitting there, because they—I had a hunger for them, too. There are characters that seem so complexly imagined that they overtake a short story or their duration in a book. It's like all those people who wrote versions of *Don Quixote* between book 1 and book 2 so that by the time book 2 got published by Cervantes, Quixote could read about himself. [Laughter.]

AP: It was—well, that happened—that happened with the writer, too. It got to be too much. And maybe that would happen with each story, you know, if I took six months on a story—which isn't, you know . . . you can write a novel in three months. Six months on a short story—not very cost-effective, but it was—it was a good thing to do and once I got started on it I was really compelled by something. Let's just say that a strange hand came from above and was guiding the pen part of the time. There was something in the story that was larger than I had thought it would be in the beginning—and I don't know what it is. There's a universality there that—I don't know where it came from. It just came; it just happened.

MS: Well, for me it's the longing for love that the story—

AP: Right.

MS: —captures. That there's this huge sense that these men—you know, whatever lies they tell and refusals that they make, this love seems hardwired into them and is unmitigatible, unavoidable, unignorable—

AP: And inexpressible.

MS: —and inexpressible. Yeah.

AP: The other thing that I wanted to mess with in this story, too, is to get some idea of the complex plurality of human sexuality. The unclear lines, the drifts from one pasture to another—the back and forth and interplay—instead of this very rigid construct of him/her, he/

she. It was interesting to me to put a lot of gray into the story and again—count on readers to pull from their own lives and experience and thoughts what they knew about life and sex that contradicted the clear-cut pattern that's given to us, you know—the coloring book of life that we get when we're little kids.

MS: Now, when it was announced that among the screenwriters would be Larry McMurtry, I thought, well isn't that amazing—and Diana, as well—they've worked in the realm of western history. You were trained as a historian, but McMurtry has been doing historical essays—

AP: Forever, yeah.

MS: —and has a real interest in getting things right, in not being inaccurate. When you finally saw the story transformed into film in New York, what were the surprises that were there for you?

AP: Well, you know how it came to be turned into a screenplay. Diana had a friend who handed her a copy of *The New Yorker* and said there's a story you have to read, and she has insomnia; in the middle of the night she started to read it and became quite gripped by it, reread it the next morning, continued to be gripped by it, went to Larry, and said, "You've got to read this story." And Larry said, "You know me, I never read short fiction," and she said, "Well, read this one." And he read it, and they both thought that it could be made into a film, got in touch with me, and I knew Larry because I hang out at his bookstore down in Archer City, and when I was working on various things I would be down there ferreting out wonderful books on Texas history. If it had been anybody else in the world I would not have signed a contract, but with Larry's ear and eye and deep knowledge and the fact that he's got the wonderful bookstore— I trusted him; I trusted them both to make this work. They optioned the story out of their own pockets, which is pretty unusual, and I signed the contract and three months or so later I saw their first draft of the screenplay. And there were some changes that I made, mostly in the little bit of language. And there was a difference between what would be said in Wyoming and what would be said in Texas—that kind of thing. But when I first saw that film in September? Oh, boy . . . what were the things that were different? That's—I really . . . you know, it's hard to answer that question—very hard.

MS: All sorts of friends have been asking me as the so-called literary expert, and I'd say the difference between the story and the film is that when I read the story I found myself in tears and when I saw the film I felt that the film had made me cry. That there was a kind of movie-sadness sauce that somehow got ladled over the material, whereas the story is written in somewhat of the stoic way of these men.

AP: Yeah.

MS: It's not insisting that you feel anything in particular.

AP: Right.

MS: And as a result my emotions just leaked out through me unawares. It came as a real startlement to me.

AP: Right. I'm very happy to hear that because it means that the thing works the way I had hoped it would work, that for the reader what's inside is necessary to complete this story and fill it out and put the meaning in it. The place was very important to me too, while I was writing it. Place is always important to me in everything that I write, and you know that I write about rural situations. But Brokeback Mountain itself, the idea of using the mountain as—what they call in science fiction a wormhole, where two characters go in and they come out differently—and this was a thing I wanted to play with from the beginning, and I think it worked.

MS: Well, one of the pleasures of the story, as well as of the movie, is that as you read you sense that this isn't some generalized, brand-name western accent—that what's being heard here is particular to the place, and it's Wyoming; it's not Texas; it's not—and even in the story it's noted that Jack's accent changes, that he says "cow" differently in Texas than he said in Wyoming, and "wife" becomes "wahf." [Laughter.] And one senses that the movie, too, worked carefully to make sure with dialogue coaches on the set that the tone would be the tone of Wyoming. What does it mean to you to be accurate? To capture the particularities?

AP: Everything. It means everything to me. And it should mean every-thing to every writer. I feel very, very strongly about this, and when I do make an error—and there's always, there's always the sharp-eyed reader who tells you about it—I lie awake with shame. I hurt. I really, truly do if I get something wrong. So I take pains.

MS: Well, because you know, there is that thing that happens—as reading becomes as much of a passing way of life as the western way of life—one senses as one reads some writers now that you're reading the generic version rather than the real thing.

AP: Mm-hmm.

MS: And you, the difference . . . well, the difference is so great that you almost say, well, if this is what writing is going to become, then I can accept that reading will die—

AP: Yes.

MS: —because if it's not enshrining—

AP: Right.

MS: —the deep insight and ear and eye of a writer, what is it?

AP: I agree with you entirely. The thing about the film, the story, writing, architecture—it used to be that writing and architecture were the great permanent monuments that made up culture, that made up civilization. And I think now to that we absolutely must add film. We have to. Because that's the language of our time. Not the book. Not the written word. And for a writer who takes pains and who cares, it is painful to have to admit that film is bigger. This story, when it was published, I had a lot of letters from men. Gay and straight, who said this is my story, this is why I left Wyoming. Now I know what hell my son went through. I'm not gay but I cried. I work construction but I loved this story. You know, this kind of thing were the letters I'm getting—I was getting—but, uh—the thing is that I have to say that the film does that for many people that would never have read the story and who don't like reading, wouldn't read. So some kind of a dialogue is starting in the wake of this story, which I find extremely interesting and valuable.

MS: Now, just as you say these boys are not anything, they're not cowboys; they may have wanted to be because they live in the West—is that also because the option of becoming a cowboy is unavailable to them? Are there still cowboys?

AP: I think there are. I don't think there are a whole lot of them, and in fact, one of the interesting things that's come out of this is the Wyoming Council of Arts wants to get something going in 2006 to discuss this film and the story and others that other Wyoming writers have done and to talk about what is a cowboy, you know—today. What is one? And there was a fifteen-year period in the late nineteenth century when there were cowboys associated with the trail drives up from Texas to Montana. That was it. Fifteen years. Bye-bye cowboys. But we still have them with us and they are infinitely larger than they were in 1870 or 1880. There's a wonderful book called *The Trail Drivers of Texas* which I bought from Larry a year ago at an extremely exorbitant price. [Laughter.] And he remarked—well, there is a cheap reprint out now but of course you want the first edition. [Laughter.] Yeah, right. So this question of what is a cowboy is not one that I can answer. I don't even know how to ask the right questions. I know there are a lot of people around who believe very deeply that they are cowboys and who do cowboy work. And I know that there are many people in Wyoming who think that it is definitely the cowboy state—and we have the bucking bronco on the license plate, that proves it! So, uh, I don't know. Stay tuned for the saga of the cowboy.

MS: Now, in "Brokeback Mountain." I guess those of us who see a film based on a loved piece of literature—we fear and yearn for a happy ending. And from time to time in your stories there have been magical devices—

AP: Mm-hmm.

MS: —hell holes or wishing tea kettles that make it possible for the obdurate truths about life to be superseded by the magic of wishing in literature. How do you make the decision who you'll save with literary magic? [Laughter.]

AP: Oh, the hell hole was easy. But Jack and Ennis could not be saved. The funny thing when I was working on the story is I was near tears myself many, many, many times—which I found a bit frightening. And yet I never could cry. And in eight years I haven't been able to, but I have been thinking one day I will be able to. I'll get around to it. But I can't right now. The whole question of large love that comes roaring out of nowhere and just slams you to your knees—happens. And it happens to these two. If it were just the sex it wouldn't even be a story. But there couldn't be another ending. For me the ending was there enormously and largely before I wrote "Once upon a time . . ."

MS: It rips me apart. I had the same gratitude that the film is true to the truth of the story and yet at the same time that yearning . . .

AP: A fellow came up to me last night and he just said, please—wouldn't you write a story like this with a happy ending? And I said you'll have to write that one yourself. And indeed, that's what has to happen. Somebody else has to write one with a happy ending. I can't do it.

MS: Well, I thought about two things. In the newer book of Wyoming stories, *Bad Dirt*, there's a story called "What Kind of Furniture Would Jesus Pick?"—and there is a gay son, but by this time, the time of the story or these people, that son is called "sophisticated." [Laughter.] Now no one would dream of calling Jack or Ennis sophisticated.

AP: No. No. No, it'd be almost as bad as saying "condiments." [Laughter.]

MS: Exactly. But it seems possible. And that night, the father who's been told about the "sophistication" of his son by his other son is aware that he hasn't been told, that he's been shut out about the truth about his son—but he's internalized it and accepted that it must be true. He remembers things from the boy's childhood, and in the same book there is that wonderful story—I think it's a fabulous story—what is it called? "Dump Junk."

AP: Oh, thank you. That story was sort of slighted by everyone, but I had fun writing it and I liked it.

MS: And I liked that there are two women in it who have been together for a very long time and although they are dealt an execration—at least one of them—by the woman's brother, they have had a happy life. In other words, the unhappiness of "Brokeback Mountain" isn't the author's sense of obligation—internal obligation—it's a matter of truth.

AP: Mm-hmm. Yes. Yes. And that's why I couldn't write it another way. I had maybe five or six different scenes that I had written that I finally used to start the fire because they didn't go. What's in the story is what had to be in the story and that's why it took so long. I finally felt like the balance was there and then after I sent it to my agent I realized one more sentence had to be added, which is the last sentence, and called her hastily and added it and told her to send it to a certain magazine. Not where it was published, by the way. And a very long silence followed, and we didn't hear, and we didn't hear from this magazine—and finally she gave them an ultimatum of time. We still didn't hear. She sent it to *The New Yorker* and they took it within hours. That's when Buford was the editor. So I was surprised. I'd never even thought this story would get published. It was just the thing I was going to write and it was going to be written and then it was going to be there, but I didn't think of it as being published.

MS: Now tell me, because almost everyone will be angry at me if I didn't ask—but it's completely not a literary question. When you saw these actors, Jake Gyllenhaal and Heath Ledger—were they your characters?

AP: Fifty percent. Jake Gyllenhaal made his own Jack Twist—and a very excellent Jack Twist it is, too. A complex, quicksilver, beautiful, hungry, bitterly disappointed—again and again—character who still manages to express considerable love and electricity. On the other hand, I found Heath Ledger's performance totally frightening because he got right inside my head. He got stuff that I did not know about Ennis and he got it right and I was just—I was blown away by that performance. I really was. I thought it was indescribably excellent. I don't know how he did it but he got that character to an impossible depth. He understood him incredibly well. I don't know how.

MS: It amazed me because it seemed as if he was bringing to the surface the things that people used to say were hidden underneath Randolph Scott's stoicism. You know, that kind of long-suffering look that seemed to belie the things he had to do on-screen. And here in Heath Ledger's performance it's as if somehow or other— even though it's not done with words—all of that kind of enormous anguish, interest, surprise—

AP: Inchoate longing.

MS: —inchoate longing, yeah. Well, you are the writer. [Laughter.]

AP: You ain't too bad yourself, kid.

MS: Thank you. Well, there it is and that, I think—you know, that performance—is one of the stunning things that there is to see in movies right now.

AP: Oh, I couldn't agree more. I couldn't agree more.

MS: And for a long time, too. If there were nothing else about this film the aura about him would be something that you would send people to see.

MS: I've been speaking with Annie Proulx about her story "Brokeback Mountain," which has recently been made into a film by Ang Lee. Thank you, Annie, for joining me.

AP: My great, great pleasure.

Notes

Broadcast on National Public Radio station KCRW FM on January 19, 2006. Transcribed by Martin Aguilera and edited by William R. Handley.

1. Subsequent to this interview, Annie Proulx published her third volume of Wyoming short stories, *Fine Just the Way It Is* (2008).

13 } In the Shadow of the Tire Iron

ALAN DALE

> We often think of peasants as not having had much in the way of choices, but is this in fact true? Did individual villagers ever try to fashion their lives in unusual and unexpected ways?
> NATALIE ZEMON DAVIS, *The Return of Martin Guerre*

At the beginning of Ang Lee's *Brokeback Mountain*, a ranch hand named Ennis del Mar (Heath Ledger) and a rodeo rider named Jack Twist (Jake Gyllenhaal) hire on to tend a herd of sheep in Wyoming for the summer. Off alone in the rugged, mountainous terrain, the two nineteen-year-olds start having sex with each other and, though they don't realize it, fall in love. It's 1963 and, as Annie Proulx describes them in the original story, these "high school dropout country boys with no prospects, brought up to hard work and privation, both rough-mannered, rough-spoken, inured to the stoic life," a "[p]air of deuces going nowhere," have no way to assimilate what they feel for each other (*Close Range* 256, 257). After the job ends and they separate, Ennis is so overcome he collapses in an alley with the dry heaves.

No wonder: when he was a child there were two men living together on a nearby ranch; one of them was beaten to death with a tire iron and sexually mutilated. Ennis's father, who may have taken part in the crime, showed his son the corpse as a warning that has spooked him ever since. In '63 Ennis and Jack aren't worldly enough even to *contemplate* acting on their feelings—they both marry and have kids because it's the only imaginable course. Four years later, however, Jack passes through

Ennis's teensy town and they reconnect. From then on they hook up for "fishing trips" several times a year. But they don't get together permanently before something dire happens to Jack. Ennis is told that Jack died in a roadside accident, but Ennis "knows" it was the tire iron.

Nearing sixty, Proulx had moved to Wyoming in 1994, and I would guess the story sprouted from her looking around and thinking something like, "There must always have been guys out here getting it on with each other." With remarkable discipline, reflecting her graduate training at Sir George Williams University in Montreal in the early 1970s as a historian of the Annales School, Proulx works out what two young men might have thought, felt, done, and said in the circumstances.[1]

The Annales approach has been to treat history writing as a much broader endeavor than compiling what Fernand Braudel disparaged as "diplomatic history" (19). As Carlo Ginzburg has written, "In the past historians could be accused of wanting to know only about 'the great deeds of kings,' but today this is certainly no longer true. More and more they are turning toward what their predecessors passed over in silence, discarded, or simply ignored" (xiii). Thus, at one end of its scope, Annales historiography is referred to as microhistory, discovering value in untold stories recoverable sometimes only from quantitative records and from consideration of material culture, since many of the human subjects were illiterate, unleisured, and too unself-conscious to leave written explanations of their actions.[2] At the same time, the historian recognizes that "history is at least partly determined by forces which are external to man and yet not entirely neuter or independent of him, nor, for that matter, of each other: forces which are partly physical, visible, unchanging, or at least viscous and slow to change, like geography and climate, partly intangible, only intellectually perceptible, and more volatile, such as social formations or intellectual traditions" (Trevor-Roper 470–71). The ideal is "total history"—in the words of Emmanuel LeRoy Ladurie, the historian begins "by adding up hectares and cadastral units" and ends by observing "the activities, the struggles, and the thoughts of the people themselves" (8).

In a biographical note, Proulx has written that Annales historiography, which she describes as examining "the lives of individuals against the geography and *longue durée* of events," provides "invaluable training for novel-writing and . . . set [her] approach to fiction forever." In a 1999 interview with *Missouri Review*, her description of how she gathers material for her writing shows that she applies *annaliste* research to the present day: "I read manuals of work and repair, books of manners, dictionaries of slang, city directories, lists of occupational titles, geology, regional weather, botanists' plant guides, local histories, newspapers. I visit graveyards, collapsing cotton gins, photograph barns and houses, roadways. I listen to ordinary people speaking with one another in bars and stores, in laundromats. I read bulletin boards, scraps of paper I pick up from the ground." The result is that the vitality in Proulx's three Wyoming collections, *Close Range* (1999; in which "Brokeback Mountain" was republished), *Bad Dirt* (2004), and *Fine Just the Way It Is* (2008), comes almost entirely from fictional "data": the vernacular that appears in the third-person narration as well as the dialogue; the landscape and weather and the impact, often determinative, that they have on the characters' lives; and the juxtaposition of the ways of the American West in the nineteenth and twentieth centuries.

Microhistorians have considerably expanded our notion of worthwhile subject matter, but there is always the risk that they will merely imprint on it the ideological outlook they bring to it. Proulx is not reticent, though she is perhaps unself-conscious, about this. Thus, in a 2004 article she is quoted as saying, "It's a big interesting world, so I just took rurality as my ground. Wyoming and Newfoundland and the outback of Australia are not that different—the landscapes are different, but the economic situations and the beliefs of the people who live in the places are quite similar, because they are all commanded by powers in urban centres. But because they can't see who's making the rules and the economic strategies that govern them, they continue to believe in the independent rural life, which is deliciously ironic and very sad" (Edemariam).

Proulx's posture of looking down from a Marxist height through the clouds of false consciousness that darken her rural characters' lives explains the distinctively determinist pattern of her stories.[3] Almost no one in Proulx gets the better of a political, technological, or socioeconomic change: "Peace and thermoplastic resin yarns ruined the sheep market and they went to cattle," is a typical transition (*Close Range* 122).

Later, that cattleman buys a small plane because a "truck ain't no good" "to work this big a ranch" and ends up breaking his neck while landing when the wheel catches on an abandoned tractor. When we read of this character, "He had the rancher's expectation of disaster, never believed in happy endings" (128), it's hard not to think sardonically, "This certainly is the book for him."[4]

Indeed, in the same 2004 article, Proulx is quoted as saying that the "happy ending" she gave readers "somewhat viciously" in *The Shipping News* is a "mediocre, bland settling. But that's what most people's lives are like anyway. Have you ever met any happy people? . . . Anybody who says that they're happy is lying. Nobody is happy" (Edemariam). Obviously, despite Proulx's training, we're beyond the bounds of what we expect from a historian. The cumulative problem for a reader is that her point of view seems inescapable but not convincing. Her stories are so perversely dispiriting they're best read in isolation from each other.

"Brokeback Mountain" lacks the morbidity of much of her writing, however, because it isn't just the author's depressiveness that explains why Ennis and Jack can't have an open homosexual relationship in Wyoming in the 1960s and 1970s. Homophobia, a social fact still set down in the law, is a more plausible cause for the characters' frustrated lives than you find in the other stories, in which you feel urged to mourn for the failure to attain forms of satisfaction that Proulx either doesn't value or doesn't believe to exist.

If even the most desolate of her stories isn't a drag to read, it's because the environmental details, whatever narrative use she makes of them, are accurate in themselves, and the language is incredibly vivid—unostentatiously down-home and yet so far from cliché as to have an ornate ring. Proulx is a novelistic eavesdropper and there's sheer pleasure in even such random reproduction as the scraps a lonely young woman picks up on a scanner, for example, "Hey, git doughnuts. And don't be squirtin around with twelve of em. Git a bunch. Don't be squirtin around, git two boxes" (*Close Range* 136). The narrator's voice and the central characters' dialogue are equally fresh-caught, wriggling with life. In "Brokeback Mountain," for instance, the narrator describes Jack's smile as disclosing "buckteeth, not pronounced enough to let him eat popcorn out of the neck of a jug, but noticeable" (257), and when Jack suggests he and Ennis go to Mexico, Ennis objects, "All the travelin I ever done is goin around the coffeepot looking for the handle" (277). The colorful language may result from highly conscious techniques to attain verisimilitude and so feel gathered, but it also means the story is told recognizably in Ennis and Jack's idiom, which makes it an impressive feat of literary ventriloquism.

Of course, we have nothing to measure Proulx's achievement by precisely because she's creating stories of men who evaded statistical compilation. Ennis and Jack are doubly difficult subjects for this kind of literary-historical retrieval, not only because they're unknown as homosexuals to the rest of the world but because they don't effectively know themselves either, which is a difficult condition to reproduce while seeking to offer insight into it.

Ennis and Jack don't have the mental or emotional resources to explore their feelings except under the most forceful of compulsions. They've picked up more than enough information as presumed heterosexuals, but there's no information for them as homosexuals. At one point Ennis says to Jack, "I been looking at people on the street. This happen a other people? What the hell do they do?" (*Close Range* 271). Jack suggests that other people might go to Denver but it's probably implicit in Proulx's scheme that the guys cannot make any move. Proulx accepts their paralysis as a plain fact, as a precondition of describing their feelings and experiences accurately, because if it hadn't been a fact then we'd already know about gay ranch hands from other stories and movies and from our own families and the families of people we know. They wouldn't have been invisible men.[5]

Rereading the story after seeing the movie, I was stunned by how faithful the adaptation is, stunned because the movie feels so different from the story. Every incident in the story is in the movie (except for one, in which Jack's father pisses on him as a child to punish him for missing the toilet), but director Ang Lee's traditional cinematic pictorialism changes the terms in which Proulx imagined those incidents. As a movie, *Brokeback Mountain* becomes not just a purposefully limited account of two guys taken hold of by a form of lust, and then a consequent love, that can't be accommodated by their lives or even their understanding; it becomes the lyrical-tragical telling of a great, impossible passion that we're seduced into investing with an array of conventionally heightened emotions that are much less specifically connected to the characters and plot.

To do Proulx's story justice the director would have to have an interest in observation for its own sake, a dedication to repair-manual reading to match the author's. Instead, Lee was reported in an AP news story as saying that he was bothered people were calling it a gay cowboy movie, "because it's a serious love story." He then generalized that "the more difficult, the more love is hindered, the more grand the love is" (Germain). Ross Hunter, the homosexual producer who specialized in such glamorous, masochistic soap operas as *Magnificent Obsession*, *All That Heaven Allows*, *Imitation of Life*, *Back Street*, and *Madame X*, wouldn't have put it any differently. (Especially relevant here are *Back Street*, in which the heroine is the "other woman" who puts her life on hold and remains faithful to her married lover for decades although they can never be together; and *All That Heaven Allows*, in which a wealthy widow calls off her wedding to her gardener until he suffers a nearly fatal accident and she realizes that she's almost thrown away happiness because of other people's prejudices.) "Brokeback Mountain" feels complete as Ennis and Jack's untold story because it deals with the specific constraints on them as homosexual lovers. Lee's movie, on the other hand, is only technically a gay story—the richness of its misery is entirely familiar from soap operas featuring anguished heterosexual lovers.

Lee's work isn't as lurid as the glossiest of "women's pictures," a Douglas Sirk movie, say, but neither is it spare in Proulx's manner—not when it includes a shot of Ennis standing against a night sky lit by fireworks (see figure 4). Of course, in this interpolated scene Ennis isn't with Jack but at a picnic with his wife, whom he has frightened by an outburst of violence against two foul-mouthed bikers, so the pyrotechnics are ironic. But even if intended ironically, that flaming, bejeweled sky speaks nonetheless in the rhetoric of movie romance.

Proulx's naturalism is rooted in a fact-gathering historical approach to narrative. Soap opera, by contrast, is only superficially a naturalistic subgenre, updating the romance of temptation and ordeal with the trappings of bourgeois realism. By moving the (desacralized) spiritual contests indoors, generally to the domestic sphere (e.g., *Madame X*) but often overlapping with the professional (e.g., *Imitation of Life*), soap opera has allowed contemporary female characters plausibly to assume the heroic role played by the mounted protagonists of chivalric romance.[6] In the first fifty years of feature-length moviemaking, soap opera was among the most reliably popular subgenres with female audiences, and one of its specialties, as in *Brokeback Mountain*, was the conflict between licit love that is only dutiful and true love that is passionate but illicit. In contrast to Proulx's scrupulously focused naturalism, and despite the fact that the characters perform physically active work outdoors, Lee shoots the story as this kind of domestic romance. The structural problem with his approach is that the story can't function as a romance because Ennis and Jack fail in a quest—the object of which in their case would be the openly committed relationship Jack urges on Ennis—without ever attempting to achieve it.

In a traditional movie soap opera, the heroine might finally turn away from her lover for the sake of her family, and the audience would consider it the heroic choice. The passion she sacrifices is felt to confer value on the home life she returns to. Her sacrifice is presented as self-actualization through self-denial, as ennobling. (*Brief Encounter* is the peak example, *Intermezzo: A Love Story* perhaps the most popular one with a male protagonist.) The audience for *Brokeback Mountain*, both as story and movie, doesn't believe in the nobility of that kind of sacrifice anymore, if it ever did. Not to mention, Ennis and Jack don't make a sacrifice—they don't make their marriages work; they just let them idle until they run out of gas. And the audience for this movie doesn't think that Ennis and Jack should have to make any sacrifice, anyway, but rather that they should be together, even if it means breaking up their families. Thus, since the guys don't get together or make their marriages work, they're robbed of all possible pop heroism and just seem thwarted. Rather than gaining heroic stature over the course of the romance, they start to seem smaller and drabber over the two decades the movie covers. (Gyllenhaal's Jack increasingly looks like a teenager gotten up for Halloween as a used-car salesman.)

In terms of the characters as Proulx conceived them, the Australian Heath Ledger does a notable job as Ennis, mumbling in character in an assumed foreign accent. It's an honest performance—Ledger doesn't try to look past the blocky Ennis to beg sympathy directly from the audience. He doesn't need to, however, because the movie unrelievedly elicits a single-layered, patronizing sympathy, which critically restricts the characters. Inevitably, Ennis's limitations become Ledger's.

Proulx, committed to a faithful description of reality, doesn't judge the boys' sexual activities. As she said in an interview with *Planet Jackson Hole*, "How different readers take the story is a reflection of their own personal values, attitudes, hang-ups. It is my feeling that a story is not finished until it is read, and that the reader finishes it through his or her life experience, prejudices, world view and thoughts" ("At Close Range"). But neither does she rationalize the fact that Ennis and Jack lie to and cheat on their wives, which in the real world may involve a wide range of moral choices. In contrast, by amping up the romance of the boys' impossible love, the movie implicitly justifies how they treat their wives.

The problem becomes plainer if you imagine Ennis and Jack committing adultery with *women* they found more attractive than their wives. The main point is that lying and cheating don't make people sympathetic. (In my experience they further corrode character almost regardless of the reason a person resorts to them.) When we're asked to sympathize, the matter-of-fact story is falsified and it is not homophobic to demur. I'd guess that women in the wives' position, for instance, would not react the way the movie prompts us to. And it's all juiced up in the usual Hollywood way—we hope Ennis and Jack will get together because they're played by two gorgeous stars at their youthful physical peak.[7] This essentially pornographic inducement is enjoyable in itself but impairs disinterested assessment of the characters' actions, such assessment being vital to naturalism but obviated in romance by the black-or-white moral polarity. Despite Ledger's talent and commitment, this is the drain his potentially great performance slips down.

If Ledger had been directed to play Ennis as a man responsible for his evasiveness and rage, for the brutality that comes from not thinking about your feelings and enforcing that clampdown on the people around you—while sneaking off to get what you want but can't admit to—the movie's vision would be far more penetrating than mere sympathy permits, and comparisons to Marlon Brando might have been warranted. (Brando's performance as the repressed homosexual Major Penderton in John Huston's *Reflections in a Golden Eye* would be the aptest standard.) It doesn't help that Proulx's work is more descriptive than analytical and the screenwriters haven't added the kind of material that, in the hands of a fluidly intuitive director, could suggest more going on beneath what we witness. Watching an actor embodying a naturalistic role on–screen, we hope for something closer to the half-obscure depths, unpredictability, and contradictions that people have in life. The best you can say for Ledger is that under the movie's lacquer you can clearly discern Ennis just as Proulx conceived him on paper, but no more than that.

Jake Gyllenhaal gives a more varied, appealing performance because he gets to whoop and holler and leap about to establish that he's a rodeo rider, and to bat his eyelashes to establish that he's gay. That is, Gyllenhaal gets to use the conventional means of both male and female leads. McMurtry and Ossana conceive of Jack as the sexual instigator and so give him other adventures to fill out his side of the story. It makes sense to see him cruising in a cowboy bar after a rodeo (not as subtly as he thinks) and Gyllenhaal plays it right on the edge, where Jack can disguise to himself what he's doing and still hope to get laid. But all we see is Jack getting talked about, or being led down a dim border-town alley as if to sacrificial doom, so this added material just makes him seem ill-fated, living in the shadow of the tire iron.

The damnedest thing is not that the movie is bleak, which originates with Proulx, but that it romanticizes the bleakness, as she does not. As in the risqué interracial love stories in *Love Is a Many-Splendored Thing* and *South Pacific*, we know that one of the lovers "must" die. Proulx's story is an inspired guess in the face of a necessary lack of actual data; the movie is a self-pitying downer, and downers, as movie history amply demonstrates, can be addictive intoxicants in their own right.

The movie preserves Proulx's story as its kernel but further invites gay men to see Ennis and Jack symbolically. The story, however, can support a symbolic reading of them only as martyrs, whose suffering can perhaps free the rest of us. And gay men may experience the movie as tragedy paradoxically *because* it lacks one of the key elements of tragedy, in that Ennis and Jack are presented as being in no way responsible for the bad outcome. They're unresisting victims, not tragic heroes, and they're not accountable for anything, not even how they treat their wives, because, we're to understand, they have no choice. Movie audiences of all demographic descriptions prefer protagonists they not only like but also approve of. So even a story with a bummer ending is more likely to be popular if shaped for romance rather than for naturalism or tragedy, in which the protagonists' flaws are shown without cosmetic softening. Turning "Brokeback Mountain" into romance was the smart move at the time, though possibly not in the long run.

Proulx's story—an emotional rollercoaster viewed from a fixed, distant position so that we perceive the ups and downs without experiencing them as "thrills"—reads fast. The movie prolongs the story by acting everything out, not just the stolen Ennis-and-Jack interludes but the details Proulx merely notes about their home lives as well.[8] And it does so with an excruciating deliberateness, giving these baffled, benumbed country folk all the time they need to get the screenwriters' points across. With its heightened sense of anguish over waste, the movie puts us on the rollercoaster, but a ride that takes about 30 minutes in print takes 134 minutes on-screen to cover the same length of track. As a result, though each scene is overemphatic in itself, the sequence of scenes is oddly slack. It's more movie-like than lifelike yet still manages to be plain old boring.

The female moviegoers Ross Hunter catered to loved this kind of stuff but never took it as seriously as this movie has been taken. I have literally seen women sit down with a box of tissues to watch an old tearjerker on TV, laughing at themselves for their indulgence. By contrast, *Brokeback Mountain* was hailed as an "important" work that, by making us weep over wasted love, might just make us more tolerant citizens. Thus, the question of whether the movie is any good by aesthetic standards was subsumed into the question of its sociopolitical significance, and in connection with this, whether it's a gay story or a universal one.

Daniel Mendelsohn takes issue with critics who praised the movie as "not, in fact, a gay story, but a sweeping romantic epic with 'universal' appeal." Mendelsohn counters that the movie "is a tragedy about the specifically gay phenomenon of the 'closet'" and its "real achievement" lies in telling "a distinctively gay story . . . so well . . . that any feeling person can be moved by it" ("Affair to Remember" 12, 13). [9] In the *Sunday Times*, Andrew Sullivan agrees that the movie is excellent, but for the opposite reason: because it reflects his view "that the central homosexual experience is the central heterosexual experience: love." Sullivan admires the movie because it "provides a story to help people better understand the turbulent social change around them and the history they never previously recorded."

Despite starting in opposite corners, Mendelsohn and Sullivan work backward from ideological statements about homosexuality to a justification of the movie couched in aesthetic terms. But this kind of criticism comes close to eliminating aesthetics as a discipline. In any case, the tension between these viewpoints is illusory: in "Brokeback Mountain" Proulx imagines some data specific to male homosexuals' lives, but such data are perfectly amenable to the inveterate conventions of romance narrative in the movies.

Camille Paglia splits the difference between ideology and aesthetics, stating that the movie "was certainly pioneering in the persuasive way it made a sexual relationship between men emotionally credible to a straight audience," for which "Ang Lee rightly won the Oscar." At the same time, she finds the movie "far too long, soggy, and monotonous." David Leavitt appreciates the movie for its handling of the subject matter, and not surprisingly, seems more attuned to how Proulx shaped it. Thus, he writes that "*Brokeback Mountain* is less the story of a love that dares not speak its name than of one that doesn't know how to speak its name, and is somehow more eloquent for its lack of vocabulary. . . . Ennis and Jack become the unwitting heroes of a story they haven't a clue how to tell." That's a fair, if arguable, assessment. (Tragic protagonists such as Oedipus and Lear may be unwitting and still be heroes, but, as noted earlier, Ennis and Jack aren't heroic at all.) More interestingly, Leavitt admits to liking the movie, while acknowledging that it's "as frank in its portrayal of sex between men as in its use of old-fashioned romance movie conventions."

Of all the ideological discussions, Colin R. Johnson's is the most measured and detached. Johnson, professor of gender studies, history, and American studies at Indiana University, understands that the story's value as a "historical document" is probably "negligible." Proulx may command the techniques of a historian but she is not actually working from documents, neglected or otherwise. Furthermore, the movie is scaled to move us not merely as the romance of these two men but as an epic of the difficulties all American gays face in making a place for our affections in our lives. The story, however, isn't that broadly representative. On the one hand, the timeline runs from 1963 to 1983, which is to say that two-thirds of the story takes place after the Stonewall riots in New York, and on the other, as Johnson suggests, it's not entirely clear that Ennis and Jack's story is representative even of Wyoming. Johnson points us to Alfred C. Kinsey's chapter on "Rural-Urban Background and Sexual Outlet" in *Sexual Behavior in the Human Male*, where we read:

> [T]here is a fair amount of sexual contact among the older males in Western rural areas. It is a type of homosexuality which was probably common among pioneers and outdoor men in general. Today it is found among ranchmen, cattle men, prospectors, lumbermen, and farming groups in general. . . . These are men who have faced the rigors of nature in the wild. They live on realities and on a minimum of theory. Such a background breeds the attitude that sex is sex, irrespective of the nature of the partner with whom the relation is had. Sexual relations are had with women when they are available, or with other males when outdoor routines bring men together into exclusively male groups. . . . Such a group of hard-riding, hard-hitting, assertive males would not tolerate the affectations of some city groups that are involved in the homosexual; but this, as far as they can see, has little to do with the question of having sexual relations with other men. (457, 459).

Johnson's main point is similar to Leavitt's, but more fleshed out, as he writes of the "silence at work in *Brokeback Mountain*" that "it's the stymied half speech of a certain kind of willful inarticulateness about sex's meaning that was common in many nonmetropolitan areas," that is, Kinsey's "realities" and "minimum of theory." Thus, "pleasure and passion and desire and intimacy—and all the other things that we're meant to understand are at stake in Ennis and Jack's relationship—were not so terribly, terribly contingent on an identity-based discourse of sexuality that binds us together in the present, yes, but that often has the effect of separating and exhausting us as well."

The couplings of Kinsey's informants are no more articulate than Ennis and Jack's, and more furtive and fleeting, yet there's no suggestion of tragedy in Kinsey's report. In other words, actual westerners who were actively but not openly homosexual might have had sources of satisfaction other than a publicly affirmed sexual identity, but no one associated with *Brokeback Mountain* can imagine what such sources might be. Theirs is the world of soap opera, where love is all.

Proulx did an admirable job of trying to get beyond her own viewpoint. She ultimately—inevitably—failed, but her effort has an unusually lean, tough imaginative texture. The movie changes all that, and a surprising number of educated viewers have fallen for the bait that Johnson pointed out: *Brokeback Mountain* sorrows for Ennis and Jack because they fail to have the only kind of relationship the movie's target audience can imagine finding any fulfillment in. This is the (profitable) result of transforming a rigorously naturalistic story into romance.

The seeming assumption of the movie's admirers that Ennis and Jack could live happily ever after if only the world would let them suggests that even literate admirers are projecting subliterate romantic fantasies onto the movie. What do we know about the boys' relationship except that, in their twenties and thirties, they set the motel sheets on fire during their few brief meetings each year? An experienced person in Jack's position, however, would be justified in thinking that the way Ennis treats his wife is how he'd be likely to treat *any* partner over the long, rocky haul of daily cohabitation.

I suspect that the movie seems important to its admirers because it reverses the work of Proulx the annaliste. Rather than translating the audience into the minds of homosexual westerners, it situates homosexual westerners in the world as understood by the broad-minded, upscale audience, where the boys—passive targets of masochistic romantic projection—can't help but seem woeful, pathetic. The movie derives its means, however, from weepy movies about the love agonies of heterosexual women that educated audiences have never taken so seriously, and it's hard to conceive how leftovers nuked to a bitter crust deserve the kind of praise the movie received.

Is it even accurate to claim that it *furthers* tolerance? *By design*, heterosexual women were probably the single largest demographic component of the audience for the movie, which cost $14 million and made $178 million worldwide in theatrical release.[10] Lee shot the script as a story of "hindered," "grand" love in the tradition of Hollywood soap opera and the result was what the producers, highly rational players in the market, intended: gush not solely for gay men but for any and all willing comers. So it makes more sense to say that they wouldn't have made *Brokeback Mountain* in the first place if this country hadn't already been hospitable enough to the story to make them fairly certain of recouping their investment going in.

In any case, it wouldn't have to be a good movie by any aesthetic standards to succeed on these terms, provided it manipulated viewers the way the target audience wants them to be manipulated to make the world a better place, one overstated, draggy romance at a time. The alleged achievements of ameliorist movies tend to fade with time: watch *Gentleman's Agreement* or *Guess Who's Coming to Dinner* now and see what you think. Thanks to Proulx, *Brokeback Mountain* is better in substance than most progressive best-picture contenders, but it's lame enough to tide a viewer over until the next awards season.

Notes

An earlier version of this article was published on January 9, 2006, at http://blogcrit ics.org/archives/2006/01/09/052110.php.

1. In concrete terms, the Annales School refers to "the historians whose base is in the sixth section of the École Pratique des Hautes Études in Paris, whose books appear . . . under the imprint of SEVPEN, Paris, and whose regular organ is that ample and ever-expanding periodical originally entitled *Annales d'histoire économique et sociale* and now—that is, since 1947—*Annales: économies, sociétés, civilisations.* . . . [T]hese historians now form an international élite, held together by a distinct philosophy" (Trevor-Roper 468).

2. George Rudé, the historian who was in residence at Sir George Williams University while Proulx was a student there, writes that his subjects "rarely leave records of their own," and thus he relies on "other materials," including "police, prison, hospital, and judicial records; Home Office papers and Entry Books and the Treasury Solicitor's reports; tax rolls; poll books and petitions; notarial records; inventories; parish registers of births, deaths, and marriages; public assistance records; tables of prices and wages; censuses; local directories

and club membership lists; and lists of freeholders, jurymen, church-wardens, and justices of the peace" (12).

3. Proulx's view also accounts for Paglia's objection to the movie's "bleak portrait of small-town and working-class life," which she found "condescending and offensively elitist" (Paglia). The bleakness originates with Proulx, however, not with the moviemakers.

4. There's no sustained success in Proulx's stories unless it's suspect. For example, "Shan, the younger daughter, graduated from high school, moved to Las Vegas. She took a job in the package-design department of a manufacturer of religious CDs, quickly grasped the subtleties of images: breaking waves, shafts of sunlight denoted godly favor, while dark clouds with iridescent edges, babies smiling through tears represented troubles that would soon pass with the help of prayer. Nothing was hopeless and the money came in on wheels" (*Close Range* 125).

5. As Kinsey wrote in 1948, "[B]oth Jewish and Christian churches have considered [homosexuality] to be abnormal and immoral. . . . Social custom and our Anglo-American law are sometimes very severe in penalizing one who is discovered to have had homosexual relations. . . . It is, therefore, peculiarly difficult to secure factual data concerning the nature and the extent of the homosexual in Western European or American cultures, and even more difficult to find strictly objective presentations of such data as are available" (610).

6. There is also a (less robust) tradition of soap opera with male protagonists. *The Man in the Gray Flannel Suit*, in which a businessman's wartime indiscretion is discovered by his wife, who has to learn to forgive him as he learns to win corporate battles, is a key example. Not surprisingly, *Brokeback Mountain* plays out more like the less formulaic *Lovin' Molly*, which was adapted from coscenarist Larry McMurtry's novel *Leaving Cheyenne*. In that movie, a young Texas woman in the 1920s loves two male best friends equally but marries someone else. One of the boys gets married while the other remains single, but they continue their separate affairs with Molly for decades, meeting her for occasional hookups, all of them keeping track of each other and their illegitimate children, and talking *and talking* about the odd, unsatisfying situation.

7. Neither actor resembles the far less alluring physical descriptions of the characters in the story (Proulx, *Close Range* 257–58).

8. The movie's literal-mindedness is hardest on Michelle Williams as Ennis's wife, Alma, whom Proulx didn't conceive as an independently interesting figure. She's just the dead end Ennis goes down because he believes he has to, which limits Williams to a dour little performance.

9. Mendelsohn writes that "misery pursues and finally destroys the two men and everyone with whom they come in contact with the relentless thoroughness

you associate with Greek tragedy" ("Affair to Remember" 12). This does not describe the plot accurately. Even conceding that Ennis is destroyed, which I don't see (he's thirty-nine at the end of the story), the wives certainly are not. An unhappy early marriage, even with big hair piled on top, does not make a Jocasta or Clytemnestra of a young American wife, as Mendelsohn appears to believe. More importantly, the relentlessness of Greek tragedy is associated ironically with heroic action—the more actively Oedipus seeks to uncover the crime that has blighted Thebes, the closer he comes to his own downfall. *Of course*, the *less* action that Ennis takes to be with Jack, the *less* likely it is he'll end up with him.

10. James Schamus, coproducer of the film, is reported to have calculated, "[W]e'll make [*Brokeback Mountain*] for a low budget, we'll be very conservative and have a very specific marketing plan." According to Robert K. Elder, "Integral to that plan was targeting the 'fourth quadrant,' also known as the 'women 35 and older' demographic—the 'Pride & Prejudice' audience" (3). *Newsweek* reported that "the usually coveted audience of guys 18–34 years old aren't the target this time. From early on, [distributor] Focus [Features] said [*Brokeback Mountain*] was aiming for the same female fans with upscale tastes who loved 'Titanic'" (Schrobsdorff). Financial figures available on the Web site "Box Office Mojo."

14 } Adapting Annie Proulx's Story to the Mainstream Multiplex

ADAM SONSTEGARD

The first time I experienced Annie Proulx's story "Brokeback Mountain," I read it aloud to my partner like a bedtime story. The lonesome cowboys in the story seemed to whisper in what felt like authentic western accents, and in their believable argot of the Wyoming plains, they achieved a kind of intimacy that felt particular to two men who quietly shared the ambiguities of an illicit love relationship. The second time I experienced the story, I included it on a syllabus for a class in short fiction but immediately had second thoughts and never actually had my class—sixty restive undergrads in a summer course at a well-respected public university—read the work. As we neared the week I had scheduled "Brokeback Mountain," I imagined students' shocked expressions in response to the story's more explicit same-sex references. I figured we would lose the quiet intimacy of Proulx's narration in the classroom's public and clinical, not at all intimate, space. The third time, I joined my partner and another couple at a suburban multiplex theater and watched Heath Ledger as Ennis del Mar and Jake Gyllenhaal as Jack Twist come alive in Larry McMurtry and Diana Ossana's screenplay adaptation, with Ang Lee's direction and Rodrigo Prieto's cinematography. The written story had left its mysteries unresolved; had left readers to deal with more realistic, because less definable, sexual lives; and had encouraged empathy with people other segments of society knew as "men on the down-low" or "men who have sex with men," in wording that stated the fact but drew no conclusions about it. But the film retold the story by catering to mainstream moviegoers, who were less familiar with covert affections and less likely to live with the muddled ambiguities of Ennis's and Jack's sexual lives. The multiplex theater, even with its dimmed lights, and the film's gorgeous panoramas of barren landscapes recast our original bedtime story into a narrative suited for a classroom's more mainstream, public space.

When these lonesome cowboys of Proulx's story met the mainstream mores of the movie theater, an intimate, private conversation became public for people *not* "in the know," and a story about homosexuality became a motion picture about homophobia. The film seemed afraid to risk alienating segments of the audience, unable to let its characters find their own language for expressing their affections, and reluctant to ask audiences to question pat and untroubled definitions of gay and straight identities. For all of the success of this pioneering adaptation of a stirring story to a visually stunning film, the public nature of the motion-picture experience reinforces many mainstream viewers' stereotypes about gay and bisexual men. The story alone quietly manages to leave those stereotypes somewhere in windswept Wyoming on a night Jack and Ennis spend together on Brokeback Mountain.

The prose story combines a kind of lonesome lyricism with the lingo of cowboys, leaving little doubt that this narrator and these characters speak the native tongue of the Wyoming prairie. Proulx describes Ennis's first movements on a groggy morning in the story's first paragraphs: "*He gets up, scratching the grey wedge of belly and pubic hair, shuffles to the gas burner, pours leftover coffee in a chipped enamel pan; the flame swathes it in blue*"—all to lead in to the observation that Ennis "*turns on the tap and urinates in the sink*" (253).[1] Midriff "wedges" and flames that "swath" saucepans find poetry in the coarse lives of cowboys, as when "Ennis and Jack, the dogs, horses and mules, a thousand ewes and their lambs flowed up the trail like dirty water through the timber and out above the tree line into the great flowery meadows and the coursing, endless wind" (256). The heroes drive their herd of sheep in country so empty even the wind takes up space, so expansive that "during the day Ennis looked across a great gulf and sometimes saw Jack, a small dot moving across a high meadow as an insect moves across a tablecloth; Jack, in his dark camp, saw Ennis as night fire, a red spark on the huge black mass of mountain" (256–58). Even in describing a harsh and lonely place, the prose never sounds out of place. It can sound as primal as wolves baying in the night: "Ennis, riding against the wind back to the sheep in the treacherous, drunken light, thought he'd never had such a good time, felt he could paw out the white of the moon" (258).

McMurtry and Ossana choose not to use these lines in voice-over narration; they incorporate the story's prose into the film's spoken dialogues, while Rodrigo Prieto's cinematography brings the same kind of evocative visual poetry to the screen. Windswept western shots are justly celebrated aspects of a visually compelling motion picture, but they sacrifice the gritty colloquialism of the story's narrative voice, which is not polite and vague, as a camera discretely looking away to show wide panoramas, but coarsely direct, if poetically economic, as in the description of the first sexual experience, when Ennis "hauled Jack onto all fours and, with the help of the clear slick and a little spit, entered him" (260). Proulx's narrative voice is true to the characters' own idiom. When Jack says to Ennis, "Christ, it got a be all that time a yours ahorseback makes it so goddamn good" (265), his appreciation of his lover's prowess with his hips sounds as natural as his explanation that a "[f]riend a mine got his oil checked with a horn dipstick and that was all she wrote" (266). The narrator's prose is gritty and raunchy in ways that sound authentic, unblushingly erotic. This is the voice of someone who did not grow up learning to speak a gay tongue, but suddenly found himself grown up, kissing with one; someone who finds himself having to use the same words his heterosexual peers use, to describe his homosexual affections. McMurtry and Ossana amend the colloquial vulgarity in ways that keep the adaptation within the guidelines of an "R" rating, and they try to succeed with material that promises little vocal appeal. Ossana has even said that the motion picture could not recreate the "beauty of the prose" in the story: "The dialogue is very spare. These men are from a non-verbal culture, so in the screenplay, I wanted to have the quality of [Proulx's] prose, to direct the actors in the stage directions, which is rarely done" (Shank). Directly coaching the actors, and prompting Australian-born Ledger to mumble his lines in a lazy western twang, the filmmakers try to recreate the characters' reticence. But the film supplants the cowboy's coarse argot with polite panoramas, losing the lyricism of the original story's intimate if inarticulate vernacular.

As the film silences the story's narrative voice and its raunchy eroticism, it also adds and elaborates characters who complicate the original story's limited points of view. The story treats Ennis's wife, Alma, almost hastily, remarking that his increasing emotional distance "put her in a long, slow drive and when Alma Jr. was nine and Francine seven years old, she said what am I doin hangin around with him, divorced Ennis and married the Riverton grocer" (270). While the story dispatches her in this single, dismissive sentence, the film shows actor Michelle Williams, with a cherub face and pouting lips, tending their children, struggling with her grocery-store job, and establishing extensive empathy with viewers. As for a girlfriend after Alma, "Ennis said he'd been putting the blocks to a woman who worked part-time at the Wolf Ears bar in Signal where he was working now for Stoutamire's cow and calf outfit, but it wasn't going anywhere and she had some problems he didn't want" (273). The motion picture expands this single, disparaging remark into the character of Cassie, played by Linda Cardellini, who dances seductively in a tight tube top, bonds with Ennis's daughter, and says in leaving Ennis, "Girls don't fall in love with fun." In the film, she has the most memorable parting line, but in the story, none of these events occurs.

Similarly, Lureen exists in the original story only in Jack's fleeting references to her and in Ennis's mental note that she describes her husband's death over the phone in surprisingly even, civil, but frigid tones. The film further elaborates her point of view and depicts her with a son as well as with her domineering father. Ennis's grown daughter, Alma Jr., never comes to visit him in the original story to announce her wedding date, but the film includes this moment in the closing scene, showing an aging Ennis, now living alone in a desolate trailer, to be a sensitive if distant father figure. The filmmakers develop these four female characters, making what had been a whispered dialogue of two cowboys into a more public conversation. They transform a prose story, almost exclusively about two men, into a film about their neglected families.

McMurtry and Ossana thereby increase the storyline's audience appeal and widen the angle of the film's sympathies to welcome women moviegoers, who were more prepared for a romantic tearjerker. Anyone who wishes to derive a full-length movie from a thirty-page story has to develop and invent characters and action to flesh out the story line. But the result in this case is less of a whispered chat at the margins of sexual identities and more of a mainstreamed, public conversation, with a more democratic distribution of sympathetic points of view. It is less like the bedtime story I shared with one listener and more like the public experience of teaching it to a wide range of students. Some fragile aspect of the story's intimacy would shatter if sixty students were to apply pressure to it. Something that only the cognoscenti understand from their own shadowy experiences gets dragged into the classroom's more clinical light.

Gaining broader sympathies and adding points of view also means losing some of the prose story's studied ambiguities. In the story, Jack and Ennis reunite and embrace at Alma and Ennis's Riverton home, four years after their summer on Brokeback, "and easily as the right key turns the lock tumblers, their mouths came together, and hard, Jack's big teeth bringing blood, his hat falling to the floor, stubble rasping, wet saliva welling, and the door opening and Alma looking out for a few seconds at Ennis's straining shoulders and shutting the door again and still they clinched, pressing chest and groin and thigh and leg together" (263–64). Clauses pile up in the sentence as the men practically pile up on one another; the prose refuses to pause long enough even to grant Alma her own sentence. She glimpses her husband's "straining shoulders" as he kisses another man. In the story, she sees Ennis's embrace of Jack from the back; she waits and suspects, literally for years, until she understands the depth of their affections. In the motion picture, Alma does not only see his shoulders but witnesses their kiss directly, as the film removes some of the mystery she is forced to live within the prose story. "She had seen what she had seen" (264), the story slyly says a few paragraphs later, leaving readers (and Ennis) wondering, *what* had she seen? How much does she know?

The story prompts readers to wonder the same thing later in the story, when Lureen describes Jack's death to Ennis over the phone. Ennis suspects someone has beaten him to death with a tire iron, as Ennis saw happen in his childhood to another gay man, but Lureen describes a roadside accident in which Jack had choked on his own blood. As "the huge sadness of the northern plains rolled down on him," Ennis finds that "he didn't know which way it was, the tire iron or a real accident, blood choking down Jack's throat and nobody there to turn him over. Under the wind drone he heard steel slamming off bone, the hollow chatter of a settling tire iron" (278). Ennis considers the oddly "level voice" of Jack's widow, thinks, "No doubt about it, she was polite but the little voice was cold as snow" (278, 277), and wonders, how much does she know? Is she telling the truth or covering something up? When Ennis visits Jack's boyhood home in Lightning Flat and hears the story from Jack's father, Ennis feels certain "it had been the tire iron" (280). From inconclusive evidence, he must infer his lover's fate.

Jack's father, who has the look of the "stud duck in the pond" (279), mentions offhand that Jack had planned to settle with another man, a fellow Texan, near his parents' ranch. In the story, Ennis knows enough to make inferences, to pause and wonder, whether Jack had loved this other man, whether Jack had been murdered, whether Jack's widow had known more than she let on. But viewers of the film watch Jack meet the husband of a long-winded former sorority girl in Childress, Texas, and come to know Jack has had a same-sex lover other than Ennis. They watch Lureen's pained expressions, her eyes welling up, as she describes Jack's death to Ennis over the phone. They hear Lureen's voice-over narration claim Jack had died in a roadside accident, even as they see quick shots that depict his death in a beating with a tire iron instead.[2] While readers of the story share the same whispered evidence that Ennis pieces together, make the same guesses he makes, and share his quiet grief, viewers of the film do not experience the same ambiguity. Unlike Ennis, left wondering and tearfully regretting, viewers are too often granted the luxury of knowing for sure.

With the loss of the story's ambiguity comes the loss of an ambiguous conceptual space for Ennis and Jack's sexuality. Many men of their time and place would have had to live with ongoing questions about how much their neighbors and employers knew, how deeply their same-sex partners loved their opposite-sex spouses, how near they might be to a beating with a tire iron. This is not to equate their sexuality with confusion, but to recognize the necessary secrecy, the unspoken taboo, that then surrounded, and to a lesser extent still surrounds, the lives of men who have intimate relations with both genders. After the first time they have sex on Brokeback Mountain, "without saying anything about it both knew how it would go for the rest of the summer, sheep be damned" (260). Their silence on the crucial subject continues, both men "saying not a goddamn word except once Ennis said, 'I'm not no queer,' and Jack jumped in with 'Me neither. A one-shot thing. Nobody's business but ours'" (260). "I like doin it with women, yeah," Ennis later assures Jack in bed, in a room that still smells of their semen, "but Jesus H., ain't nothing like this. I never had no thought a doin it with another guy except I sure wrang it out a hunderd times thinking about you." "'Shit no,' said Jack" in return, but, Proulx writes, Jack "had been riding more than bulls, not rolling his own" (266). The slang might imply Jack has been "riding" other lovers, and not "rolling" the "bull," like Ennis. But in their silence and separation, raunchy slang and double entendre, they never quite classify their experience.

The closest Ennis ever comes to a resolution is the reflection he has when his sheep intermingle with those of a Chilean herder, who had strayed onto the same hillside: as he counts head of sheep, "Even when the numbers were right Ennis knew the sheep were mixed. In a disquieting way everything seemed mixed" (260). Proulx winks knowingly at her readers over just how "mixed" he is, as a straight fiancé for Alma and a covert amour for Jack. (The film winks as well, as when Jack drives a huge tractor labeled "Versatile.") "Jack Twist? Jack Nasty," Alma says in finally confronting Ennis. She begins to accuse: "You and him—" (271). But, when Ennis silences her and threatens her, he leaves his 1970s same-sex affair with the status it would have had in the 1890s: it is still the love that dare not speak its name. The story's coarse narrative voice speaks the same language, allowing two cowboys to love without having the words for it, while narrating, without definitively classifying, what their love means for their sexual identities. Indeed, in the prose story—forever whispered, intimately inconclusive—their love never does speak its name.

The media surrounding the U.S. release of the motion picture never stopped speaking its name. *Brokeback Mountain* was almost always referred to as "the gay cowboy movie" of 2005. Film critics spoke of Ennis and Jack not as sexually confused youths, or as bisexual men, but as gay cowboys. Gyllenhaal's and Ledger's faces soon appeared in a still from the movie on the cover of an encyclopedia of gay and lesbian film. Commentators wondered about these actors' roles in future films, cast in the shadow of these "gay roles."

Something happened similar to what occurred with Edward "Jim" McGreevey, who proclaimed himself "a gay American" as he resigned as the governor of New Jersey in 2004. The governor did not allow himself any conceptual overlap or ambiguous middle ground between gay and straight identities. McGreevey's affair with a male staff member evidently trumps his two marriages and two kids. Jack's love for Ennis similarly erases his marriage to Lureen. Ennis's affair with Jack eclipses his marriage with Alma. They were spoken of as "gay cowboys," and the governor, his wife and child at his side, spoke of himself as a "gay American." The mainstream media accepted these categories of sexual identity, admitted no third term as middle ground, and failed to mention situational sexuality or bisexuality. One can define bisexuality a number of ways; one can argue, seemingly endlessly, about Jack and Ennis as apparently bisexual or "really" homosexual. But notice that the film and the media that surrounded it never entered into that more complex conversation; in effect they forced Ennis and Jack to choose between the severely scripted lives of heterosexual husbands or the outlawed existence of gay men. Whatever happened to youthful experimentation or to situational sexuality? However one chooses personally to define it, whatever happened to bisexuality?

The motion picture, set in the 1960s–80s, creates no conceptual space for alternative definitions; sadly, neither did the nation that received the motion picture in 2005. Jack and Ennis try to keep their spouses from knowing about secret sides of their identities. They even fool themselves to some extent, proverbially keeping their left hands from knowing what their right hands were doing. But one wonders, could they have worked to reconcile the attraction they evidently felt, to some small, unequal extent, toward members of both genders?

Could they have moved to relatively tolerant areas, as Jack tentatively plans to do in relocating to Mexico? Could they possibly have asked a counselor or confidante how prevalent same-sex encounters were among twentieth-century American men? But no one in the Wyoming of the film, over the twenty years of Jack and Ennis's relationship, has ever heard of Kinsey or Masters and Johnson; ever mentions Stonewall, Harvey Milk, or AIDS activism; or ever refers, even slightingly, to such performers as Janis Joplin, David Bowie, Elton John, or Boy George. The America of the sixties, seventies, and eighties, the decades depicted in the film, knew about bisexuality and often discussed it publicly, as part of pop culture. But the film itself, set in the remote countryside, far away from these sites of vanguard sexual experimentation, seemed as if it had not. And even more disturbingly, the America that received the film in 2005 acted the same way.

In this respect, this country's reception of *Brokeback Mountain* suggests that in the twenty-first century's opening years, Americans operate more conservatively, draw categories of sexual identity more exactingly, and suppress anomalies more restrictively, than they did in, say, 1978, a year that the film depicts. How sad that this film looks back thirty years to an America that—in some respects, for some, at least—provided more freedoms and allowed for looser categories than many now enjoy. A period piece cannot be expected to cover every important event that occurred during a historical interval, of course. But *Brokeback Mountain* risks erasing some of the 1970s' private, former freedoms from Americans' collective memories, as it publicly remembers that decade's events and as it reclassifies the sexual lives of that decade's people. The film is a sign cultural conservatism is now imposed retroactively, as the piece employs selective and revisionist history to assure viewers their parents held the same supposed family values they now hold. In a red state of George W. Bush's America, this film has quietly begun rewriting the personal history of the Carter administration.

Back in the story's fictional setting of the 1960s, when Jack and Ennis first spend a summer without any company other than sheep, neither man was twenty years old. Given the level of eighteen- and nineteen-year-olds' hormones, given the isolation they would have felt in those long summer months, given the polymorphous nature of human sexuality, it should not come as a surprise that Jack and Ennis have a sexual relationship. Americans know or have heard enough about fraternity and club initiation rituals, organized team sports, all-boys or all-girls schools, and long-term incarceration to understand and recognize sexuality responding to situations and opportunities, rather than remaining constant over time. They know enough not to be surprised that in this case, what happened to Jack and Ennis has happened or could happen to a great many of us.

What does not happen as often, evidently, is American acceptance of bisexuality in male lead characters. We Americans, sitting in suburban multiplex theaters, speak of characters such as Jack and Ennis as "gay cowboys," so we do not have to see them as two men like any other men in any remote U.S. town, any men "just like us." We banish them to a mythic Wyoming that has much in common with the legendary Old West, so we can pretend that they do not live next door to us in modern, urban America. We grant them the status of fading cowboys of the western plains, as if our enduring cultural myths can separate their world of legend from our everyday reality. We argue that gay men "were born that way," so that we do not have to admit we were all born, reared, and nurtured "that way" too. We murder them with tire irons. We cover up what we know about their deaths. We maroon them in dusty, lonesome trailers. That way, we can tell teary stories about them as larger-than-life legends, rather than shake their hands as neighbors. That way, we can assure ourselves that their alternative narratives always end tragically, reserving the triumphs, the happy endings, for our heterosexual heroes. That way, we can publicly maintain rigid categories of gay and straight sexual identities, rather than risk listening to lovers' intimate, private conversations, which might begin to suggest such ambiguous alternatives instead.

"Jack, I swear—" Ennis says after Jack is gone, "though Jack had never asked him to swear anything and was himself not the swearing kind" (283). They had not sworn allegiance to each other, forced each other to make a life together as a couple, or even insisted that the other decide between loving his same-sex partner or loving his wife. The narrow circle of the story's readers comes to share their intimacy, draw from their own private experiences, and sympathize in inconclusive silence. In Proulx's story, Ennis ultimately understands that "there was some open space between what he knew and what he tried to believe, but nothing could be done about it, and if you can't fix it you've got to stand it" (283). You live with ambiguities, you keep quiet about your same-sex affections, and you wait for more of your fellow citizens to mature and open their minds. You keep yourself mature and open-minded in turn, because "you've got to stand it." But the movie, by its public nature, amplifies this intimate conversation. It widens the circle beyond the original, sympathetic cognoscenti, but grants the moviegoing masses tidier categories, offers unambiguous conclusions, and never requires them "to stand it." It never asks them to imagine living the open-ended lives of being neither straight nor gay, but lonesome cowboys, men who are, nevertheless, "just like you and me."

Notes

Thanks to Robert Riley, Jack LaPlante, David Larson, Richard Reitsma, Pamela Demory, and David Van Leer.

1. Unless otherwise noted, all quotations are from Annie Proulx's "Brokeback Mountain" in *Close Range: Wyoming Stories*. This first quotation reflects Proulx's italicization of her story's opening paragraphs.

2. Some viewers have interpreted these scenes as Ennis's imagination of Jack's death, rather than an objective depiction of a murder actually taking place. To me, the combination of Lureen's voice-over narration, the scenes of Jack's demise, and Ennis's place as a distanced listener (who hears Lureen over the phone but does not see her) ultimately grant the visual scenes the status of objective confirmation. As she tells one version of the story and he hears and imagines another, the visual scenes seem independent of either viewpoint and thus function as more definitive depictions of Jack's death.

15 } **Not So Lonesome Cowboys**

The Queer Western

JUDITH HALBERSTAM

When *Brokeback Mountain*'s patently queer plot surfaced in the media, Christian cultural critics were quick to label it "a perfect storm of Hollywood's war on morality" and "a mockery of the Western genre embodied by every movie cowboy from John Wayne to Gene Autry to Kevin Costner."[1] Even queer critics were shocked and one prominent queer film critic wrote, "With utter audacity, Ang Lee . . . has taken on the most sacred of American genres, the Western, and queered it" (Rich, "Hello Cowboy"). I don't know how many cowboy films these critics have watched, but even a cursory glance at the genre reveals a potpourri of mutual masculine longing and homoerotic posturing. And so while the Christian commentators in the United States quickly turned to voicing their outrage over the perversion of an American genre by the spectacle of homo-love, Ang Lee's Oscar-winning *Brokeback Mountain* simply suggests, proves, and confirms that the genre was always queer or at least always homo. Andy Warhol's *Lonesome Cowboys* (1968) indeed does nothing more than capitalize, lazily in fact, on the blatantly homoerotic premise of the genre—many men, few women, heroic masculinity, fascination with guns and power—and Warhol merely shifts the emphasis within the genre to highlight rather than sideline the sexualized relations between men. Even the Oscars in 2006, when *Brokeback Mountain* was up for several awards, began with a quick montage of men admiring each other's guns, staring at each other's crotches, and declaring their undying love for one another.

The appeal of *Brokeback Mountain* then cannot be explained simply in terms of the spectacular revelation of the previously implicit and buried erotic relations between men in the genre. But nor can it be explained away, as so many critics have done, by a quick nod to the universality of love—*Brokeback Mountain*, with its wide-angled views of the open, rolling hills and its tight frames of suffocating domesticity, appeals to queer audiences and straight audiences alike because it maps the tragic narrative of thwarted manly love onto the imagined landscape of that most mythic of U.S. sites—the West. One of the most enduring features of *Brokeback Mountain* is its investigation of the loneliness of this landscape and the intensity of the intimacies that are forged within it. Cowboys are often lonely in the Western for the simple reason that women are seen as extraneous to the hardscrabble lifestyle of riding the range, fighting Indians, and marking territory. Women often disappear in the first scene, as happens in *Red River* (Howard Hawks, 1948); or they are treated as having no more value than a nice horse, as we see in *The Outlaw* (Howard Hughes, 1943); or else they are just an excuse for two buddies to extend their male bonding while confirming their heterosexuality, as we see in *Butch Cassidy and the Sundance Kid* (George Roy Hill, 1969). Loneliness is almost always resolved for the cowboy in the Western by another cowboy and not by a woman. I want to consider the homoeroticism of the genre in relation to three topics: guns, heroic and homoerotic masculinities, and women.

Guns

We don't need Dr. Freud to explain to us the meaning of a gun in the Western. The gun is a perfect excuse in many a Western for the two heroes to stare boldly at each other's crotches. It is a fetish symbol par excellence in that the male protagonist of the Western often has very little time for women and so his regular use of his gun stands in for the irregular use of his penis. Even though the low slung holsters and chaps seem to be framing the crotch area for voyeuristic fascination, time and again, our gaze is shifted from the hero's phallus to his gun— possibly, the genre proposes, the penis is just a bad gun rather than the gun being a substitute for the penis. The only men who do not have guns in the Western are too old, too young, or too weak to manage them and by implication, they are not men at all. By the same token then, a woman with a gun is a virtual man and her gender-crossing possession of a weapon requires proper subjugation. The fetishization of the gun has the uncanny effect of making gender into a system depending not on the penis but on the gun. A woman with a gun then is either mad, bad, or a big old dyke. By the time we get to *Brokeback Mountain* the gun is not central; the heroes stare at each other's crotches without the crucial alibi of the guns or the sheriffs' badges that are also sometimes pinned there, and the absence of the gun means that these cowboys are looking for the "real thing."

In *Forty Guns* (Samuel Fuller, 1957) the film explicitly marks the relationship between a man and his gun as bodily and naturalistic while the woman, in this case Barbara Stanwyck, has a more mediated and cultural relation to her gun; indeed, Stanwyck's relationship to her own weaponry is so attenuated that she needs the backing of forty "real" guns to stand up to her male rival. The classic scene in this film that constitutes the gun as a natural extension to the male's body occurs when one of the brothers gets measured by his soon-to-be wife for a new gun; the camera explicitly aligns itself with the gun, and therefore with the male, in a "down the barrel of a gun shot," and the female is cast as creator not bearer of the phallus. Significantly, the film ends with a song about Stanwyck as a "woman with a whip"—clearly the whip can be accommodated to the female body in a way that the gun cannot—and the confrontation scene between Stanwyck and her rival involves a gun-fondling scene where she asks to "hold" his gun and marvels at its weight.

Similarly in *Red River*, the fraternal rivalry between Montgomery Clift's character Matt Garth and a cocky gunslinger named Cherry Valance plays itself out in a homoerotic exchange about guns: "You know," Cherry says, handling Matt's gun, "there are only two things more beautiful than a good gun: a Swiss watch or a woman from anywhere. You ever had a Swiss watch?" The two men are set up in the film to function as rivals for the attention of the father figure, John Wayne. Fraternal bonds are a staple of the Western and the brothers either get to bond naturally under the cover of family ties or fight for patriarchal power. But Matt and Cherry in *Red River* are not real brothers and in the end they do not compete for patriarchal power at all, and so this scene serves no other purpose than to establish their mutual admiration. Matt represents emotional masculinity and is often referred to in the film as "soft," and Cherry, by comparison, is brutal and hard. But both are armed and dangerous.

In *The Outlaw*, the oedipal, pederastic relationship between Billy the Kid and Doc Holliday involves them shooting each other, or rather, Billy letting Doc shoot him. The film opens with Doc staring at the crotch of his old friend, who has now become sheriff, and it ends with Doc having passed over his old buddy for a new stud, Billy the Kid, who covets his older friend's guns. In one scene, Doc is already dead and the sheriff tries to pull a fast one on Billy by giving him Doc's old guns. Billy tries the guns on and plays with them wistfully; he measures them against his own and marvels that they are the same "size" as his. But in another scene, Doc uses the gun to caress the body of the beloved Billy. In a familiar face-off, Doc and Billy are finally going to have a showdown, but Billy cannot bear to hurt Doc, and Doc uses his guns delicately and sadomasochistically to play with Billy's body, with the possibility of castration.

There are of course a whole host of other films with suggestive gun references: in *Ride the High Country* (Sam Peckinpah, 1962), for example, two older men take a younger man along with them on a mission to transport gold from the mountains to the town. There is much emphasis on the wildness of this young man and his inability to keep his gun in its holster or keep it clean. In Clint Eastwood's *Unforgiven* (1992) again, we have the same triangle as in *Ride the High Country*, two older men and a younger man: the phallic white guy, Eastwood, has a good gun and can shoot; the black guy, Morgan Freeman, has a gun but won't shoot; and the young guy has a gun but cannot see well—all allegorical in their relation to weaponry and violence and masculinity. Such films establish the metaphoric chain that links phallic power to the gun and the gun to homoeroticism, substituting violence for sex.

Heroic Masculinity

The two heroes of *Brokeback Mountain* are a completely conventional feature of the Western. While both John Wayne and Clint Eastwood pioneered the image of man alone battling the landscape, the hostile forces of nature, Native Americans, and destiny itself, the Western hero almost always demands a sidekick or foil of some kind. The male hero may begin and end his quest alone, in other words, but he often has male company along the way. In the classic captivity narrative *The Searchers* (1956) by John Ford, for example, John Wayne begins and ends the film as the mysterious outsider, but he spends almost the entire span of the movie, a five-year period, in the company of another man, Martin Pauley, who is part Cherokee. The tension between Wayne's character, Ethan, and Martin alternates between overt racism on the part of Ethan and begrudging mutual respect. Ethan is framed in the movie's beautiful opening shots as the quintessential Western hero—Ford obsessively frames Wayne through tight shots in doorways; he is always viewed from the inside as the outside to domesticity, home, peace, and the family. The classic Western hero can never come home, can never be civilized and tamed; he is of the wild and his glorious Christian sacrifice, like Jack Twist's in *Brokeback Mountain*, makes the world a safer place for those he leaves behind.

The Western, of course, tells the story of heroic masculinity as the narrative of white male exploration. And the shifts and turns in the Western narrative over time, from the early Westerns of the 1930s to the classic Westerns of the 1940s and 1950s, mark a changing and complex narrative about the United States, manliness, nationalism, race, and space. The basic components of the Western link the flawed but courageous actions of a lone hero to the fate of a tightly knit and industrious community. The individual separates from the community to protect the community from all that lies outside of it. And in the process, he becomes part of that wild outside, part Indian, part animal, part divinity, part and parcel of the majestic landscape that frames him, and apart from the nuclear family that beckons him. This neat division between the domestic and the foreign, the wild and the tamed, the violent and the pacifist allows the Western, as a genre, to explore complicated issues in remarkably complex ways and so while the genre is littered with racist characterizations and crude imperialist aspirations, it is also able to highlight the contradictions between the democratic state and the violence of westward expansion, the supposed naturalness of the family and the decimation of native tribes, the doctrines of civilization and the materialist grubbing for gold that ensues.

The Western hero is often, then, a mightily conflicted fellow—he might be returning from the Civil War and unfit for marriage or domesticity; he might be a law unto himself and therefore a threat to local and national law; he guarantees a future to the community he protects but he represents an anachronism that the community must surpass. The Western hero is quite literally born to die. As far as the homoerotic elements of the genre goes, what Ang Lee exploits is not a small seam of clearly queer insinuations but rather a rich and vast archive teeming with father-son dynamics, fraternal rivalry and love, racially inflected competition, generational struggle, and masculine enterprise. No Western is without its homoerotic inflections if only because the genre demands that men leave their women to become men and that they spend huge amounts of time with another man in a relationship of surrogate marriage. Sometimes the dynamics between men function within a group, sometimes a dyad; often they are triangulated and occasionally there is a four-way, but no matter what these relations are infused with a heady brew of intimacy, desire, and admiration that far exceeds the kind of attention that any of the men display toward any of the women.

Father-son pairings are the most conventional forms of coupling for men in the Western. These bonds are almost always infused with the specter of pederasty, and the oedipal dynamics that they are supposed to capture are so sexualized as to give way upon close scrutiny to intergenerational love. John Wayne and Montgomery Clift fight and make up as an intergenerational couple in *Red River*, and in *The Outlaw* a couple of old friends, Doc Holliday and Sheriff Garrett, fight over a younger man. The two older men are reunited when Doc comes to town searching for a "pretty little horse" that has been stolen from him. When it turns out that a young stud, Billy the Kid, has stolen the horse, the two older men hunt Billy down. But Billy manages to turn the tables on Garrett and he and Doc team up instead. In a final showdown, Garrett accuses his old friend of throwing him over for a younger man.

Brokeback Mountain, of course, resists the father-son dynamic in favor of a sexual relationship between peers. This bond between men of the same age is often contained in the Western by making both men older or it is framed by mediating the relations between men with a woman. The radical charge of the male bonding between Matt and Cherry in *Red River* has to do with the fact that they have no alibi for their relationship—neither brothers nor rivals for the same woman, the two men seem genuinely interested in each other, or at least in each other's guns; in this case, the homoeroticism has to be paid for when Cherry takes a bullet for Matt. In *Butch Cassidy and the Sundance Kid*, Paul Newman and Robert Redford have an allegiance only to each other and they play out a "til death us do part" narrative of derring-do, reveling in their friendship, squabbling like intimates, risking death together, and sharing a horse . . . and a woman. Despite the sexiness of the first encounter we see between the Sundance Kid and his teacher-girlfriend, in which he breaks into her house and forces her to undress at gunpoint, after which we find out that they are already lovers, the relationship is mostly emptied of romance, and it is Butch who romances Etta while Sundance just has sex with her. This division of labor is mirrored in their lives together as outlaws—Sundance is the "gun man" and Butch is the brains and passion of the operation. But ultimately, Etta is just in the way and when she realizes that she is never going to convince the boys to "go straight," she leaves them to their fate in Bolivia. The final scene of the film, when Butch and Sundance run out of their hiding place into a hail of gunfire, breaks the triangulation and confirms the real couple in the film as the male buddies.

In *Ride the High Country*, two older guys repeat the triangulation from *The Outlaw* but with a difference. When a tomboyish young woman diverts the young guy along the way, the two old guys relax into their own form of coupledom. Their relationship seems safe because the film has made sexuality into something that younger men get caught up in and that gets them into trouble. Older men either marry or become drunks or loners. Once the younger man hooks up with a woman, the older men are able to reminisce about the old days, sleep together, and puzzle over why neither one of them got married—without any fear of seeming "unnatural." Sexuality, apparently, has a statute of limitations in the Western—if you don't use it, you lose it, and so the old guys are depicted as past it and yet better off without it. They have cooler heads, wiser guns, and less trouble. And yet . . . the intimation of homosexuality has been made and so one of the two must die, the young man must marry, and the remaining old man remains alone after his old buddy dies in his arms, muttering, "I'll see you in the high country, pardner."

Clint Eastwood specializes in what one could call the lone wolf version of masculinity. He is rarely paired up with a woman and his laconic masculinity depends utterly on the absence of any shred of sentiment or emotionality. John Wayne is a garrulous romantic compared to Eastwood, who perfects the kind of masculinity that becomes a marker of postmodern action films such as *The Terminator* (James Cameron, 1984). You can find a trace of Eastwood in Heath Ledger's performance of Ennis as quiet, diffident, filled with unexpressed longing, tough and closed, lonely.

Heroic masculinity also establishes itself in the Western, often homoerotically, through rivalry. John Wayne is often pitched as at odds with his younger rival. In *Red River*, he is engaged in an oedipal rivalry with Montgomery Clift, which can be sorted out only by the intervention of a good woman. In *The Searchers* his rivalry is racialized, and in both films Wayne is marked as a good man gone bad and held up as a kind of caution for what can happen when a man strays too far from the civilizing influence of home. This raises the thorny question of race and the function of the Indian rival in the Western.

In *The Searchers*, Ford's self-conscious Western of 1956, John Wayne is cast as an Indian-hater and a Confederate soldier home from the war, newly defeated and possibly a criminal wanted in many states. His brother's family hosts him and he offers them protection in return; his sister-in-law clearly desires him over her more domesticated man and the two young girls love him fiercely. When Indians massacre the family and take the youngest girl into captivity, Wayne as Ethan begins a quest for vengeance that constitutes one of the most enduring plotlines of the classic Western. Almost never does the Western reference the reason that Native Americans might be burning homesteaders' land or capturing white women, and in fact the Western has traditionally presented itself simply as "history," the history of the U.S. West. *The Searchers* makes the erotics of the cowboys and Indians theme quite palpable and implies that at the heart of intense phobia—racial or erotic—lies equally intense desire.

Brokeback Mountain surprisingly and deliberately makes a detour around the issue of race. Ang Lee seems to want to shift the emphasis away from struggles between whites and Indians for possession of the landscape and toward the struggles between men for control of the meaning of desire. But in the process, he misses an opportunity to highlight the continuing racial dynamics of the Wild West in his film. The original story by Annie Proulx and apparently the screenplay both feature Ennis del Mar and his wife as Latinos. His character is a reference to the early history of cowboys as caballeros from Spain—the Spanish are credited with bringing horses to the West—and the conquered Mexicans who used horses to round up cattle were known as "vaqueros." What difference would it have made in Lee's film to have made Ennis Latino, acknowledging the racial complexity of the U.S. West from the mid-nineteenth century onward?

Women

The spectacle of two men kissing while a woman watches in *Brokeback Mountain* is astonishing more for its explicit acknowledgment of the peripheral role of the woman in the Western than for the erotic charge between men. In the genre the homoerotic bonds that tie men to one another usually develop over the course of a series of shared adventures, in their long exile from the family, or when they face and defy death together. The experiences that men and women share in the Western are few and far between. Women sometimes huddle in the back of a stagecoach during an Indian raid, or they make food and coffee when the men come home for a break. At times they are on the receiving end of male violence or explicitly provide sexual diversion as prostitutes. But men and women in these films rarely share experiences or jokes or pleasure. There is obviously a rather limited range of roles for women in the Western, but occasionally a character or an actor can break out of the generic limitations and wreak havoc. Apart from the prostitute with a heart of gold—such as Dallas played by Claire Trevor in *Stagecoach* (John Ford, 1939) or Frenchy played by Marlene Dietrich in *Destry Rides Again* (George Marshall, 1939)—there are two main generic roles for women in the Western.

One is the tomboy—and there are a lot of tomboys in the Western for the simple reason that a marriageable young woman needs to help out on the ranch and must not show too much interest in men, sex, or femininity. Femininity is a luxury that settlers and ranchers cannot afford, and so when we first see Elsa Knudsen (Mariette Hartley) in *Ride the High Country*, she is actually dressed as a boy and doing work around her very religious father's farm. Later on Elsa's tomboyish demeanor sits in stark contrast to the prostitutes in the mining community where Elsa's fiancé is working. Her distance from femininity marks her virtue and her practical and dependable nature. Similarly, Laurie Jorgensen (Vera Miles) in *The Searchers* is a high-spirited and adventurous girl who teases and bullies Martin Pawley, sneaks into his room while he is taking a bath, tells him to write to her and propose and so on. The tomboy character morphs quickly, though, into a properly but not excessively feminine wife.

And there is the tough girl: the woman with a gun is a force to be reckoned with in the Western. She is rough, tough, and bound and determined to get her way. The tough girl is sometimes a woman who has been forced through tragic circumstances to live without a man, run her own business, or manage the family ranch. She is always cast as an aberration of some kind, a rupture in the natural order of things. Sometimes she is a camp figure like Joan Crawford in *Johnny Guitar* (Nicholas Ray, 1954), sometimes she is complex but unfulfilled such as Barbara Stanwyck in *Forty Guns*, and sometimes she is just laughable like Doris Day in *Calamity Jane* (David Butler, 1953).

Mostly, the Western suggests that the woman with the gun really needs a man. In Ray's classic tough girl film, *Johnny Guitar*, Joan Crawford plays Vienna, the rough cowgirl who needs to be tamed and seduced into a mature femininity. In one scene she stands tall above her angry neighbors, dressed all in black, telling them to back off while holding a gun. "That's big talk for a little gun," says Mercedes McCambridge, her archrival and double to Emma. It is hard not to hear a Freudian admonition in here: the little gun, of course, is the woman's version of a man's big gun. When Vienna learns to be less trigger-happy, her man Johnny drops his guitar and gets his gun; gender order returns. The one remaining symbol of immature female embodiment now is Emma, and Vienna shoots her as if she is killing off her butch self and emerging triumphant, unarmed but a woman. The film's view of feminine toughness is paradoxical: on one hand, Vienna finds herself in danger whenever she takes up a feminine role and attire in the film, and it is only in masculine attire and with a tough and aggressive attitude that she can survive. On the other hand, even as she returns to her masculine self, she is forced to kill Emma and thus symbolically refuse her outlaw self. She maintains her masculinity but at a high cost. The death of Emma signifies the death of a female masculinity unmoored from male companionship and uncompromised by the marks of the feminine.

For the most part, lesbian characters in the Western are strangely absent—especially given how many outlaw women and tough cowgirls actually did roam the wild, wild West. Given how much time men spend together in the Western, there must be many women spending time without men. And indeed in LGBT film festivals there are often many great examples of lesbian directors exploiting the lonesome cowboys and lonesome cowgirls themes. In classic cinema, a great example of a beautiful woman, who the film suggests might be wasted on men, is Jane Russell in *The Outlaw*. Directed by Howard Hughes, it was given the tagline, "Sensation too startling to describe!" The sensation at the heart of film seems to be the homoerotic narrative, but for the critics of the day it was Jane Russell's startling bosom that Howard Hughes insisted must feature prominently; indeed, he even designed a special bra to better display her . . . talents. After reading a few reviews of the film, which was briefly censored, moviegoers would expect to see lots of cleavage and lots of scenes of men looking at cleavage. In fact, the two men who haggle over Russell—Billy the Kid and Doc Holliday—barely give her a second glance because they are too busy examining each other's guns and fighting over who gets to ride the "pretty little horse" that Doc owns. The breasts then remain on display, but they are never accessed through the male characters and are thus offered, without the mediation of men, to the lustful and appreciative queer or dyke gaze.

The Western in recent years has been remade as a black thing (*Posse*, Mario Van Peebles, 1993), a feminist thing (*The Ballad of Little Jo*, Maggie Greenwald, 1993), and even as a critique of its own premise of masculinity and racial vengeance (*Unforgiven*). It should be no real surprise that it has finally been recognized for what it was all along: a very, very queer thing, an age-old narrative of men being men together against the epic backdrop of nature with not a woman in sight and a campfire burning fiercely to keep them warm as they find ways to keep at bay the lonesome life of a cowboy. While the media championed *Brokeback Mountain* as a depiction of universal love, tragic love, and as a critique of homophobia in the heartland, we might ask other questions of it: why does the spectacle of cowboy love entice us now, in this historical moment of U.S. supremacy? Why did the Latino character have to be changed into a white guy? What is the purpose of the melding of melodrama and Western? What is the function of the landscape of the West now in an age of U.S. imperialism? While we enjoy the drama and the dynamism of Ennis and Jack, let's also finally admit that the Western has always been queer.

Notes

1. The quote is from Robert Knight, director of Concerned Women of America (CWA), cited in Frichtl.

Part 4 } Public Responses and Cultural Appropriations

16 } "One Dies, the Other Doesn't"

Brokeback and the Blogosphere

NOAH TSIKA

Allegedly about love, the film adaptation of Annie Proulx's short story is actually a shrewd examination of class conflict, and one of the saddest of all mainstream American movies. *Brokeback Mountain* had its premiere at a time of intense domestic conflict, yet the movie was less a reflection of strife than of sex—and effortless animal sex, at that. It seemed far *sexier* than any film I had previously seen. That I was an unspeakably naive and tittering child of twenty-two at the time, that the evening of the movie's New York premiere marked my entrée into the modern dating game, may help to explain my initially giddy attachment to *Brokeback Mountain*, a movie I considered "cool."

Viewed today, its sadness seems to me justified: two boys meet at the foot of a mountain and fuck at its summit; they spend the rest of the picture planning reunions, only to discover the mutually supportive relationship of sex and resentment. The more Ennis del Mar (Heath Ledger) resists Jack Twist (Jake Gyllenhaal), the more Jack wants to sleep with him; afterward, all Ennis can do is begrudge Jack his wealth. Each is married: Ennis to the sad-eyed Alma (Michelle Williams), Jack to the spoiled Lureen (Anne Hathaway). Probably the picture's most surprising accomplishment is to show how the lure of money, rather than the responsibilities of straight marriage, prevents these men from having sex. After Alma catches them kissing, and Ennis divorces her, the movie reveals the real schism between its gay male lovers: Jack is saved by his rich, sophisticated wife, whose family's company supports him, while Ennis is brought to his knees by child support—he literally can't afford to cohabitate with Jack, can't, in the excuse of so many middle Americans, "get off work."

Tailored to reflect the blue-collar anomie of *Hud* (Martin Ritt, 1963) and *The Last Picture Show* (Peter Bogdanovich, 1971), the script by Larry McMurtry and Diana Ossana emphasizes the details of small-town life—the prized apartments located above laundries, the Independence Day celebrations with tattered blankets spread out like magic carpets on a hillside. Thrillingly, the film reflects the pessimism of the Iraq War era, and individual scenes—Jack singing the ominous "Water-Walking Jesus," Jack flirting with a rodeo clown and facing social ostracism—are startling in unexpected ways (the former represents a caustic courtship routine, the latter an abortive and disastrous one). Jack, whose childishness is just a put-on (he knows what he wants and how to get it), is by far the most fascinating character; Ennis, the spoilsport, is the enigmatic blonde love object, and severely depressed.

A packed New York theater, the site of the film's premiere, seemed to supply prototypes of both personalities, and many more. Even before the theater doors were opened, there manifested among the attendees a sense of intense anticipation, as dozens of sprucely dressed men stood in the lobby and shouted that they wanted in, while others were similarly "acting out" by announcing, quite insistently, that Jake Gyllenhaal was just about the cutest young star in all of Hollywood. Some men, bravely, given the early December frost, wore white tank tops, or T-shirts two sizes too small, the better to show off their muscled physiques. My own date, older than I and wiser, a true New Yorker, whispered in my ear, "These men are here to cruise."

Promptly, I measured the legitimacy of that opinion by the wandering eyes, occasional smiles, winks and nods of certain of the men in the lobby. One man, speaking to the tense anticipatory mood of the queers in the queue, cried, "Give it to me! Give it to me *now!*" and in so doing managed to reflect both the unbearable suspense of waiting on *Brokeback*, along with the sexually charged atmosphere of the space between the concession stand and the closed screening-room doors. Some men laughed at the comment, but others quite visibly winced. A hallowed movie-house lobby, at a specific historical moment, was suddenly a place for the simultaneously awkward and thrilling transmission of queer community values.

If I seem to be describing the typical Saturday-night crowd at the local gay club and if such sexualized behavior seems surprising and entirely inappropriate given the "family friendly" mandate of most urban multiplexes, consider that Brokeback's opening weekend had long been predicted to be, by gay and straight cinephiles alike, the social event of the season, a happening. And like those staged by John Cage and Jim Dine for the purposes of advancing artistic expression, this particular happening, largely effectuated by gay men lucky or pushy enough to acquire advance tickets, had as its purpose—or so it seemed to me at the time—the testing of queer communal waters at the dawn of a new cultural moment. For Brokeback, some men said when I asked them, was a first: a gay mainstream film, they told me, though they hadn't yet seen it.

Knowing firsthand the difficulty, even the occasional impossibility, of locating "firsts" in film history and recognizing also the doubly slippery and perhaps wholly faulty nature of "gay mainstream" as a general critical designation, I still managed to agree.[1] Looking back, I agree still. Weeks before the film's official release, those of us interested in such matters had conducted Web searches to locate some advance reviews and had surely happened upon an online piece by B. Ruby Rich, who writes, "Quite simply, despite the long careers of Derek Jarman, Gus Van Sant, John Waters, Gregg Araki, Todd Haynes, Patricia Rozema, or Ulrike Ottinger, there has never been a film by a brand-name director, packed with A-list Hollywood stars at the peak of their careers, that has taken an established conventional genre by the horns and wrestled it into a tale of homosexual love emotionally positioned to ensnare a general audience. With Brokeback Mountain, all bets are off" ("Hello Cowboy"). By the date of that essay's publication—Friday, September 23, 2005—I had already seen the film twice at separate screenings, but my acquaintances, after reading Rich's words, seemed prepared to publicize her argument and didn't bother to seek my opinion of the finished film: Brokeback would, they told me, teach heterosexist mainstream society that rising young movie stars could "go gay"; it would be a movie first for continuing to attract so much specifically queer advance attention. So concurred a number of the men in the Loews lobby on opening night. Said one, "I'm proud to be here. It's going to be one hell of a ride."

After the screening, on the sidewalk outside, some men and a few women were willing to linger and discuss why they liked or didn't like the movie. One, a young man, complained of a lack of "hot sex," and when I suggested that the one (gay) sex scene was hot enough, he told me, "I wanted more." My date, a relatively new acquaintance, asked me to name the one man, Jake or Heath, with whom I most closely identified. I said, without pausing to reflect, "Heath." My date said, "Jake. For me, it's Jake," and proceeded to tell me why. It was our first "personal" discussion, though it was anything but private. We joined a chorus of voices debating not merely the sex appeal of one star over the other, but the recognizably queer and affirmative—or desperately misleading and offensive—aspects of the movie. These men, and I was one of them, were not expressing their complaints and concerns through the relative safety of the written word or anonymously through fictive alter egos. They were talking publicly, to strangers in some cases, of the impact of *Brokeback Mountain*, sharing private thoughts and explaining why they related to Heath and not Jake, or Jake and not Heath, or to neither. Dramatizing the potency of such personal reception strategies, some of these men claimed to "detest" the movie, and the resentment they collectively conveyed was unmistakable: nothing less than a lifetime of exposure to cinematic killer queers and sad, suicidal queens could be heard in their complaints. Bored with the movie, one optimist yet claimed that *Brokeback Mountain*, by allegedly denouncing the deceitful actions of closeted homosexual men, could serve as a vital reminder: he himself was a "good gay."

I have attempted to characterize the complex experience of receiving the film in a largely queer-identified environment in metropolitan New York. This affirmative social space, in which queer commentators (albeit perhaps momentarily on opening night) made up the majority of voices, stands in contrast to the comparably "lawless" region of the World Wide Web, in which queer voices necessarily compete with watchful queer-hostile commentators seeking to establish the "sin" of homosexuality. If the social network of text-based online forums—in short, the blogosphere—is potentially a wholly egalitarian, even excessively queer-friendly space, then what happens when a diversity of lay film reviewers mobilize to discuss a product of the queer mainstream? This essay answers that question by examining the centrality of Web-based protest to the reception of Ang Lee's *Brokeback Mountain*. Providing a means of assessing the actual complexity and diversity of queer audiences today, this essay reveals the absence of an "idealized" or harmonized audience of gay men, and in the process suggests the faultiness of what Janet Staiger has termed "the ideal-spectator interpretive strategy," in which an audience category is "assumed to be homogenous in constituency and thus uniform in response" (*Interpreting Films* 13). Both Staiger and Martin Allor have objected to the use of such a tactic, the latter claiming that it has "tended to reproduce alternative abstractions that pivot around single planes of contradiction, such as gender, class, or subjectivity in general, rather than multiple determinations" (Allor 219). In the context of this study of *Brokeback Mountain*, the imperative to so pigeonhole an audience seems to grow out of the assumption that all gay men enjoy or admire the movie, a retrograde assumption that effectively misses the point of much recent analysis of the so-called new queer spectator but that is yet available to a multitude of online commentators expressing astonishment at the mixed responses of queer men to modern movies in general and to *Brokeback Mountain* in particular.[2] This essay follows one model of spectator studies in examining more than five hundred online reviews and commentaries on the text and topicality of *Brokeback Mountain* and addresses the readability of the film's queer themes, a readability activated, for a majority of moviegoers, by an actual or imagined conversancy in queer cultural custom.

In part, this essay exposes an apparent need to reject the tragic ending of the film, and not exclusively among self-identified gay male moviegoers. Acknowledging a positive change in the social acceptance of gays and lesbians, which includes increased visibility for queers, these reviews tend to celebrate the distribution of a queer mainstream film while expressing confusion about its tragic elements, which to many seem both outdated and completely unnecessary. Others cite the film's ultimate lack of narrative legibility, its failure to make clear the actual (rather than imagined) circumstances of Jack's death, as a reason, if not to condemn the film, then to approach it with at least some reservations. Because the death itself seems to matter so much—whether, in the manner of the old Hollywood Production Code, as punishment for sexual "deviancy" or, more likely, as a means of securing the film's intended seriousness—some commentators have connected it to the unhappy endings of a range of gay-themed films, among them *The Sergeant* (John Flynn, 1968) and *Sunday Bloody Sunday* (John Schlesinger, 1971), suggesting an alarming thematic sameness across almost forty years of filmmaking. Other less obsessively pessimistic lay critics contend that it is the queer spectator's task to "do the film's work for it" by convincingly fleshing out characters and filling in narrative holes: Jack may die, but perhaps not in vain.

As an assessment of current queer reception practice, this study suggests not only the intelligence and awareness of today's queer spectator, but also the need for representation among an increasingly visible and diverse community. It proves, above all, the sometimes painful, compound notion that *any* depiction of same-sex love, however confused or incomplete, will still, to some, ring empirically true. Crucially, however, gay-identified commentators aren't the only ones interested in equating Ennis and Jack's approaches to anal intercourse and basic behavioral traits with those of "real-life" gays: straight-identified moviegoers are equally interested in aligning themselves with the "reality" of the queer experience as they themselves conceive of it, and expressly to calculate the number of "authentic" queer moments depicted in *Brokeback Mountain*. If one gay man notes the characters' deliberate, ritualized denial of sexual deviance ("You know I ain't queer," says Ennis) as evocative of his own periodic and self-loathing disavowal of a gay identity, a straight woman denounces the movie as not representative of the queer experience of her "out and proud" son.[3]

Reader-response work on the subject of *Brokeback Mountain* answers emphatically any doubts about the movie being a gay polemic. If some viewers insist that the film is about two straight men who "just happen to fuck," they do so because they themselves represent or are familiar with so-called turnaround cases: men who enact a daily process of refusing same-sex desire. In opposition to gay-identified commentators positioning *Brokeback Mountain* as supportive of gay rights or of the delicate queer experience in general, some viewers argue that the film actually advocates queer denial and so admire it on those grounds. One writes favorably of "the growing number of ex-gays," while others list Web sites such as PeopleCanChange.com (a site authored by "men who have left homosexuality") and DrThrockmorton.com, which suggests that "cured" homosexuals "do exist" and examines the methods by which some individuals "discover" their heterosexuality. Such strikingly queer-hostile Web sites abound, and a number actually (though not surprisingly, given the movie's box-office success and status as a "cultural event") continue to discuss *Brokeback Mountain*, highlighting its "degeneracy" and alleged moral offensiveness.

If, as Elizabeth Ellsworth has suggested, "social groups use cultural forms in the process of defining themselves," they do not necessarily subscribe to a politics of tolerance and optimism, nor do the processes they enact necessarily involve familiar rhetorical strategies of affirmation (183). Rather, as in the case of the right-wing Web site FreeRepublic.com, a number of conservative and Christian fundamentalist social groups define not their own merits (which they likely consider to be self-evident) but instead detail the "indecencies" of "radical secularists" and of a movie like *Brokeback Mountain*. To alert the online user about the potentially upsetting nature of those commentaries that attack queer culture and so contain queer references, some postings insert parenthetically (in the manner of so-called spoiler alerts on other, less polemical, cinema-driven sites), the warning "GAY STUFF." But what online warning signs exist for the queer user interested in avoiding queer-hostile opinions? Significantly, a number of assertively, even violently, homophobic postings have been deleted by watchful administrators on such newsgroups as Yahoo!Movies and such Web sites as IMDB.com. Nevertheless, neither rampant heterosexism nor politically sanctioned homophobia, unlike the violent threats of neo-Nazism or the overt criminality of child pornography, are subject to cyber vigilante groups, meaning Ann Coulter can viciously attack *Brokeback Mountain* and its basic thematic in a manner that would deem her anti-Semitic—a potential neo-Nazi—were the film in question actually *Schindler's List* (Steven Spielberg, 1993).[4]

In the beginning the World Wide Web may have represented—may represent still—a safe haven for both out and closeted gay men and lesbians interested in voicing same-sex desire. Since its inception, the Internet has in many cases encouraged not merely a relatively open expression of queerness but also the personal correspondences of gays through chat rooms and message boards. If the Internet facilitates queer connection as romantic rendezvous or sexual encounter (or simply as private fantasy), it also has the capacity to mobilize politically like-minded individuals. Seth F. Kreimer identifies the Internet as a "technology of protest" whereby gay communities can counteract the domineering effects of heterosexist mainstream society. If Web-based activism would seem to exist in opposition to the function of online film criticism to evaluate, even in a sense to sell, a text to the public at large, it is yet the form that numerous gay-identified online reviews take, particularly those tackling the subject matter of *Brokeback Mountain*. Even official movie Web sites tend to adopt a polemical approach to marketing. The official site for Mel Gibson's *The Passion of the Christ* (2004) sells the movie not as a work of cinematic art but as a rare and righteous church resource, advocating "film clips and stills for live performance use in worship services." If Focus Features' unusually interactive Web site for *Brokeback Mountain* exhibits a markedly queer-receptive approach, prominently and explicitly addressing the queer spectator ("Share Your Story"), it necessarily stands in resistance to Christian fundamentalist blogs and online flash games inviting players to shoot the exposed rears of gay-identified "mountain men."

The proliferation of queer-hostile Web pages does not suggest that the Internet is suddenly a dangerous place for the queer user but rather explains why queer-identified blogs, especially those with entries on *Brokeback Mountain*, seem so combative. No longer able to ignore the heterosexist, even homophobic, influence of mainstream culture from within the asylum of the Internet, gay-identified commentators are obliged to defend against rampant bigotry. The relatively unrestricted and user-friendly spirit of the World Wide Web that has historically provided a forum for queer commentaries now, in our greatly wired present moment, gives at least equal space to the "moral majority," thus becoming not a place of complete safety for the queer user but an impassioned space of constant contention. Having lost its standing as a unique rebel activity (though the potential for noncompliance with, even criminal defiance of, certain "conditions of access" persists), navigating the "Wild, Wild Web" becomes, for the queer user, a course into potentially treacherous queer-hostile waters.[5] If the Internet initially seemed to offer limitless and wholly privileged possibilities for queer expression outside of mainstream forums, it continues to offer the promise of boundlessness, but within that stance necessarily exists a collection of sometimes fiercely divergent perspectives.

To take one more example of a Web site that caters to queer-derogating individuals, FreeRepublic.com, described on its main page as "the premier online gathering place for independent, grass-roots conservatism on the web," contains numerous postings that denounce *Brokeback Mountain* as, to quote just one, a story of "fags in lust." Other postings purport to avoid altogether the topic of the movie by quoting (not ironically) such notably queer-hostile public figures as Coulter and George W. Bush (when he denied at Kansas State University that he had seen the film). A number of commentators attack the sole, in this context bravely gay-identified, writer who argues, "'Gay' has nothing to do with lifestyle. And rather than coming out of the closet to make a declaration of individuality or identity, most of us 'come out' so that we can share the gift of love openly with another individual":

Oh this writer has GOT to be kidding! Gay has EVERYTHING to do with lifestyle. Every gay person I know, including my own sister, does everything they can to be in your face.

There is nothing normal about being gay.

I can't believe he endorses this "Backdoor Mountain" flick! Ugh!

Long before conservative pundits came to appraise *Brokeback Mountain*, both queer-identified lay filmgoers and largely queer-receptive professional critics were writing of the use-value of the movie, which in the weeks leading to its release could seem a potential teaching tool, an instance of the ultimate mainstreaming of queer desire. Focus Features's official Web site quoted an early review in *Entertainment Weekly* that positioned the film as enlightening and politically relevant. Everyday social moviegoers, especially gay teenagers, had long been writing of the "hotness" of Ledger and Gyllenhaal (whose casting was first revealed in January 2004), arguing the sex appeal of one over the other.

In September 2005 Dave Cullen, a gay writer, created a Web page he titled "The Ultimate Brokeback Guide," which contains links to related news articles and to the "Ultimate Brokeback Forum," with its many threads. "On the Mountain," a fan site for Proulx's short story, had long been in existence, and continues to function today, with 519 members as of March 15, 2008. Gay Spirituality & Culture, a site dedicated to the advancement of queer culture through blogging, was among the first sites to manifest the tension of sustaining a nonpolemical, independently queer and adulatory approach to the movie. Already committed to offering a space for those willing to argue against both determinedly secular queers and fervently queer-denouncing religious types, Gay Spirituality & Culture provides an early example of a posting that cites a "nervous" mainstream press in predicting a conservative backlash against the film; another posting argues that the straight audience "looks at same-sex love and sees only 'sodomy.'" Convincingly, that commentator goes on to assert that Ennis del Mar represents "the 23-year-old version of me." Using fictive alter egos on newsgroups and online message boards, other queer commentators have been assessing the "historical truth" of the movie, a truth that seems "timeless" to some, since many of the so-called queer issues of the 1960s remain relevant today.

In one of the first professional reviews of the film (published online by *Guardian Unlimited*), B. Ruby Rich argues that the aggressively site-specific (but, in the parlance of movie marketing, "universal") *Brokeback Mountain* "reads the history of the west back through an uncompromisingly queer lens" ("Hello Cowboy"). In keeping with such an approach, which sees this period film as somehow responding to empirical history, the majority of online commentators surveyed for this essay assume a historian's task in arguing that the film either is or isn't evocative of lived reality—of, say, the recorded historical events of 1963. A number of actual residents of Wyoming or the West in general, in union with a number of actual cowboys, evaluate the film as either true to or hopelessly divergent from the "real experience" of that geographic region. Still others insist that the film is in fact timeless by pointing not to the commonness of the phrase "timeless romance" in professional reviews and in the movie's press kit but rather to those aspects of the production design (tawny jukebox bars, beat-up trucks, a family clothesline) and soundscape (Steve Earle in a saloon, Mary McBride for a community dance, Emmylou Harris on a car radio) that seem as faithful to the here and now as to bygone eras.

In addressing "the logic of alternative readings," Staiger has used the case study of Judy Garland and *A Star Is Born* (George Cukor, 1954) to argue that gay men, as casual moviegoers, tend to judge film characters "by standards not of verisimilitude but of experiential similarity." While pointing out that this particular alternative response "may be peculiar to the Garland phenomenon," Staiger nevertheless speculates that such a reception strategy (in which "personal messages of significance to private lives matter") may actually be "quite common among not only gay men but other groups of alternative readers" (*Interpreting Films* 176). Conversely, my study begins to suggest the popularity among *all* movie-goers—including, surprisingly, obsessively straight-identified and queer-hostile ones—of using these very standards of "experiential similarity" to expressly evaluate the queer codes of *Brokeback Mountain*. Consonant with the rise in queer visibility, lay moviegoers, regardless of sexual ori-entation, maintain a relationship to queers or to a perceived notion of queer culture in general, the better to evaluate a queer mainstream film like *Brokeback Mountain*. If gay males regard the accuracy or inaccuracy of the film in terms of specifically personal experiences, so straight moviegoers are willing to align themselves with queer-identified indi-viduals (a gay son or brother, a lesbian daughter or mother) to assess the truthfulness of the movie's depiction of queerness. If both approaches suggest the tolerance of moviegoers willing to discuss queerness from a personalized vantage point, they sometimes signal a markedly conserva-tive, even antagonistic, approach to perceived queer-subject positions. To take both straight and gay examples, a heterosexual woman, speaking to me at the film's premiere, revealed that her ex-husband, whom she had only recently divorced, is gay, and gleefully recalled naming his "sneaky [male] lover" as corespondent. Her critical task was to endorse the "truthful" nature of a "hideous" and "wife-abusive" movie, which depicts adultery as practiced among married gay men. By contrast, a gay male teenager, in loudly countering that *Brokeback Mountain* is in fact *not* "true-to-life," said of the movie, "It makes us seem like we're spiteful to women, and we're just not."

The lay, activist-oriented online reviews of *Brokeback Mountain* referenced here indicate that there are four distinct audience types interested in commenting on the film. These comprise men and women who self-identify as straight and openly reject the queer task of the movie (because it seems to them "dishonest"); men who self-identify as gay, enjoy the movie, and openly endorse its queer task; men who self-identify as gay and reject the movie, its tragic elements, and seemingly faulty queer task; and women who self-identify as straight and take pleasure in the physical attractiveness of the movie's male stars, missing altogether (or plainly refusing to accept) the very possibility of a queer task because—openly identifying with actual gay men and with a remarkably persistent gay male stereotype—to them only "eye candy" matters. Of the four audience types, all demonstrate a similar approach to reception in that they attempt to read the film through the lived experiences of real-life gays. Curiously, the survey did not reveal a single viewer who identified as lesbian, bisexual, or transgendered, something that begins to suggest the overwhelming lack of representations of these communities in both mainstream and alternative forms of cinema and also *Brokeback Mountain*'s apparent failure to engage with unconventional modes of queer expression. As Amy Taubin has argued, queer cinema has mainly been concerned with constructing male desire; as long as it continues along these lines, showing partiality toward homosexual men and rejecting women and the transgendered community, it can only be considered "queer by half." As my brief textual analysis has already suggested, *Brokeback Mountain* offers a problematic approach to its straight female characters; it remains to be seen if the film has much to offer a lesbian or transgendered audience.

Of the approximately two hundred negative reviews authored by self-identified straight commentators, fifty-three characterize the movie as "sick," twelve as vomit-inducing, nine as something that should not be played "in my town" or "in the red states," five as "gay recruitment" and/or "propaganda," three as something to openly boycott, and two as "crap." For others, the film is "devilish" and "a freak show," "unbelievable," "anti-Bible," "anti-God," "a footnote in cinematic history," "crud," a movie "shittin' on the West," "scary," "fucking crazy," "idiotic," "not homosexual," "wrong," "horrible," "freakin' nasty," "not for straight people," "Brokedick Mountain," "a joke," and "funny." Scarily, some of these responses seem to bear out Ennis's fears of retribution. One employs bullying language in an attempt to prove that "the red states just won't go for this movie": "I've cut back my movie theather [sic] attendance considerably because of the social issues you try to back. It's not gonna work and you better wake up." It is unclear whether this "you" is meant to address the gay audience, Hollywood, or both. Another review, similar in tone and redolent of schadenfreude, directs its threats at the filmmakers themselves: "This story of two faggot cowboys makes me want to hurl. . . . I hope this movie flops big time (like hulk [sic]) and whoever is attached to making the film has a shitty career in Hollywood." One viewer, who identifies himself as both straight and a cowboy, solemnly relates the bare facts of his own nonqueer life, seeking to establish the "misleading" nature of the film. As if preparing a libel suit, he writes, "You can rest assured that the gay lifestyle is not practiced in Wyoming cow camps. To suggest otherwise is just Hollywood's effort to normalize that lifestyle in the eyes of the public. In other words it's propaganda disguised as entertainment." Remarkably, however, the vast majority of these hostile reviews pointedly reference actual (albeit hated and denigrated) gay male acquaintances, men who, while not cowboys per se, still reside in the red states. Even aggressively queer-abusive commentators must, however grudgingly, acknowledge that self-identified gay men *do* (as the film argues) choose to live out West. That movie screens should be so widely reserved for gay material is another matter entirely, one these particular writers decry.

Not surprisingly, gay men are eager to respond to these remarkably queer-hostile commentaries. To a posting titled "I used to think heath ledger was cool (did he need the money THIS bad?)," there are seventeen responses condemning the homophobic aggression of the poster, each demonstrating the semantic precision and emotional acuity of a community accustomed to struggle. Symptomatic of its gay author's awareness of oppression, one queer-positive commentary asks, "Isn't anyone else nervous that some jerks will sneak in during a showing of BBM just to verbally trash it in front of the audience members who do want to see it?" Movingly, another concurs: "In some theaters, it is going to be so BAD for this movie. I'm cringing already. People can be awful . . . especially if they have nothing else to do and want to sneak in a showing, just to get some of their homophobia out." Nevertheless, one gay man writes, "Nothing man made can keep me from seeing this movie." He does, however, agree that queer-hostile moviegoers are and have always been antagonistic to the queer spectator, a greater problem (because of the possibility of physical violence) than even the most offensively heterosexist film text. Taking a broader approach while amusingly adopting the language of a classic queer-hostile argument, one man rightly notes that "natural selection may keep the truly hostile out . . . as they are cowardly to the point of not wishing to be thought of as one of 'those people' by association." The fairness of this assumption is confirmed by a number of like-minded commentators, though a few touchingly reverse the argument, confessing a fear of "getting looks of disgust" from ticket vendors.

Others reveal the degree to which the arena of online fandom can feel queer-hostile. Responding to a deeply odious—and since deleted—commentary that concluded with the declaration "call me anti-animal i dont [sic] care but i'm never kissing a pig," one queer commentator wrote:

Hell, yep, I wish the world were a nicer place . . . and we could just get back to talking about the movie and all the great storylines, themes and people in it. Sometimes I come back though, because I know there's another round of trolls I feel (personally) I have to deal with. I know that sounds odd, but I feel every now and then that I have to defend this film against needless and idiotic hatred. I have got used to confrontation on these boards, just because I won't be dictated to by fools or even worse, supposedly "Christian" adults who use religion to peddle a message that gay = evil.

This posting is right to point out the preponderance of queer-hostile commentators who identify as Christian and who receive the film as propaganda (when they themselves are often peddling the Christian company line, at the expense of an entire community of queer specta- tors). Some of the more fiercely oppositional, negative reviews authored by self-identified Christians have been deleted by administers of Internet message boards—on the grounds, it would seem, that they constitute harassment. Regrettably, however, queer writers occasionally take up the violence inherent in these commentaries: "I swear if I see you on the street I would beat you to *death* you f**cking stone headed republican f*ck." Another suggests the queer community take arms against those who seem especially queer-hostile. However objectionable, these kinds of queer commentaries simply reflect the aggressive, reactionary tactics of the kind of viewer who writes of Ennis and Jack, "People who do what those people did get the death they deserve."

Less hostile but equally straight-associated commentators tend openly to disavow the language of queer representation, similarly referring to the movie as a universal story of love between "people" (never between men): "The way I understood the story is that they're not 'gay' necessarily . . . just in love with each other . . . a love that hit them and stuck." This male viewer goes on to confess, "I'm certainly no expert"—a statement that suggests the cultural pressures associated with the movie's complex and potentially illegible representation of gay male sexuality—and adds, to be clear, "I'm not gay." Curiously, though, he reveals his ambivalence about these issues of gay visibility with a closing statement that would seem to contradict his earlier argument: "I'm not saying that they aren't gay." In direct response to this review, a gay male commentator argues, "First [and] foremost, this is a movie about two specific GAY men who fall deeply in love. After that is acknowledged and accepted, the universal aspect can be explored."

Though gay male viewers seem the most eager to evaluate the film in terms of the experientially "honest" elements of queer life depicted or ignored therein, straight-identified viewers are not averse to this particular reception strategy. Lay critic Pam, a straight woman who disliked the film, revealed an eagerness to read it through her own marital experience: "I saw this movie with my husband earlier this week at the Toronto Film Festival. I didn't think it was good at all. It turns out that this movie is nothing but a perverted gay love story. I didn't know that before we saw it. My husband, on the other hand, couldn't stop raving about how great it was and how it really opened his eyes. Last night, he told me he wanted a divorce, and he was moving in with his best friend Karl. I think this movie turned him gay!"

Initially, Pam's response seems to suggest, in a rather oblique way, the value of the film as a kind of eye-opener for the latent homosexual, something to effectively position it as a work of affirmation. She continues, "I am so upset. [My husband] has never indicated anything about being gay, or behaved in a gay manner. When he found out that a friend of ours from church might be gay, we stopped talking with him. That's how straight he was! We had a great sex life as well. I know this movie changed him. When is Hollywood going to stop peddling this kind of corrupting perverted garbage? I'm sure this will win an Oscar or something and now I have to start my life over because it made my husband turn gay."

It would be too easy to chide this woman for her inability to understand the dynamics of the closet, too difficult even for some queer writers fully to comprehend.[6] What her negative response suggests, more than anything, is a straight viewer's lack of familiarity with basic presumptions of gay life. Identifying with the straight mainstream, then elevating herself with a mention of her "great sex life," this female viewer seems to have missed the film's austere, candid depiction of two marriages of mismatched sexualities. Failing to recognize herself in either of the film's two major female characters (which itself suggests cinema's uneasy association with the female spectator, its difficulty addressing and positioning her), Pam aligns herself with those firmly straight-associated viewers rebuking the movie as gay propaganda. Worryingly, Pam is not alone. Lay critic Kevin, a gay man who disliked the film for its apparent sanctioning of marriage between gay men and straight women, writes, "I am almost angry at what seems to be the story line of men going back and forth, not being able to make up their minds about their sexuality! First they are together, then they get married and have children, then they yearn for each other again! I'm all for gay romance but do NOT agree with getting married, ruining the women involved's [sic] lives and those children!" Though gay, this viewer seems resistant to understanding the complexity of the closet and misses the film's attempt to call attention to that complexity, however ugly or ruinous it may seem and be to some (see Benshoff). He goes on: "I am a gay man and have been from birth. I never gave any woman false hope, nor have I been with one. I know what I am and who I truly am."

A number of other related commentaries echo the particularities of these attempts to reclassify the closet, which becomes in such confused accounts not a self-protective, historically oppressive structure but, reductively, representative of nothing more than a lifetime of selfishness, lies, and deceit. The latent homosexual eventually emerges from this structure at the expense of his straight spouse, as openly gay, attached, and happy, and eager to divorce the woman he has effectively left behind (see Sedgwick, *Epistemology*). A straight female viewer who "hated" the film wrote, "My husband is having an affair with a friend of mines [sic] husband and us wives are trying to pick up the pieces of our lives. If you want to be gay be gay, do not marry a women [sic] who doesn't know and have 3 kids. . . . It is not a gay issue it is one of moral character and high standards."

This last concept of "moral character and high standards" is not limited to the comments of queer-hostile viewers. On an Internet message board, an openly queer-friendly mother wrote of her desire to use the movie, which she admired, as a teaching tool, raising the possibility of a positive, family oriented reception tactic for a queer mainstream film: "I will be brief. My brother is gay. Our parents were very hard on him. To this day, they haven't spoken in about 15 years now. Because of this, I've decided to bring my 12 year old son and 14 year old daughter to see this film. I want to further educate my children that being gay is ok." This woman's username, "Macysaddict5," helps to underscore just how representative she is of the ideal consumer. Notably, she is rare among straight-identified commentators, not in her enjoyment of the movie but in the way she writes of it, avoiding considerations of star discourses and focusing instead on issues of gay representation.

A great many positive reviews do concentrate on the stars, the lithe muscularity of their bodies and the Oscar-baiting extent of their acting talent, though not necessarily at the expense of a broader queer thematic. What effectively sets queer-identified commentators writing positive reviews apart from their straight-identified female counterparts is a conflicting set of approaches to the star discourses of Heath Ledger and Jake Gyllenhaal. As part of a threaded discussion, one gay-identified lay critic asked his peers to designate a "dream cast" for *Brokeback Mountain*, suggesting the potential for dissatisfaction among queer audiences mindful of Hollywood casting protocol. A survey of responses to this question reveals not merely a naming of celebrities of far greater renown than Heath Ledger and Jake Gyllenhaal but also a realization of the camp possibilities of several straight-associated big names "going gay": Tom Cruise and Brad Pitt, Mel Gibson and John Travolta, Antonio Banderas and Vince Vaughn, Joaquin Phoenix and Matt Damon, Johnny Depp and George Clooney; the list goes on. These are, of course, excepting two or three, some markedly straight-associated, names (and, in the cases of Mel Gibson and Tom Cruise, some markedly queer-hostile ones). But to what extent were Ledger and Gyllenhaal straight-associated star types at the time of the film's release? Neither, up to then, had an extensive gay following. Ledger's star image had largely been associated with the aggressively heterosexual swashbuckling hero, typically in historical adventure narratives such as *The Patriot* (Roland Emmerich, 2000) and *A Knight's Tale* (Brian Helgeland, 2001).

Gyllenhaal's image, while not explicitly gay receptive prior to his involvement in *Brokeback*, was significantly less conventional than Ledger's. The cult hit *Donnie Darko* (Richard Kelly, 2001), a deliberately amorphous Christ allegory set in a Los Angeles suburb, did much to position Gyllenhaal as representative of a specific brand of American outsider. An indication of the level of cult success of the film, *Darko* was rereleased in a director's cut version in the fall of 2004, with Gyllenhaal appearing to great fanfare at a number of the premieres. And yet in the online reviews sampled for this essay, there is no mention of the cult of *Donnie Darko* or of Gyllenhaal's perceived solidarity with nonmainstream, perhaps oppressed, and rather "dark" young American males, the actor's area of representational expertise in the films he made before *The Day after Tomorrow* (Roland Emmerich, 2004), of which *Donnie Darko* is perhaps the paradigmatic example. In the online reviews of *Brokeback Mountain*, this particular blank space is suggestive of, on the one hand, a willingness to forget or discard the lower-budget, cultish successes of an actor's past and, on the other, the existence of different cults in the arena of reception (gay male moviegoers may not belong to the cult of *Donnie Darko*, and so on). Born of the content of Kelly's film, the sympathies of Gyllenhaal's star image with potentially weak ideals of youthful introspection are thus sublimated to the queer spectator's desire for total acceptance.

However much their images may have matched or deviated from mainstream models, Ledger and Gyllenhaal have always been embraced as beautiful. Nevertheless, in obvious opposition to this history of intense objectification, some self-identified gay men writing on *Brokeback* claim to be interested not in the physical allure of the actors but rather in the film's subject matter, in how to place it in terms of genre, and in Ang Lee's directorial achievements. "I'm clearly not interested in seeing this movie because of 'eye candy,'" writes one gay man. "The reason I want to see the movie is because I think it is an interesting story . . . and because of the beautiful scenery." To buttress this claim, the writer adds, "Heck, I'd even go and see it if there were two cowgirls in the leads." Of those willing to address the "eye candy" aspect of the film, a great many are straight females writing favorably of the sex appeal of the two stars. "Jake Gyllenhaal reeks with sexuality!" writes one young woman. "He's an outstanding actor. I can't wait for his gorgeous blue eyes." Another female viewer writes, "I am still undecided which actor I find more sexy and attractive." Identifying with the straight mainstream while simultaneously supporting open expressions of same-sex desire, a lay critic confesses, "I think male/male erotica is sexy and I'm a straight female." Adi, a seventeen-year-old girl, writes, "I am absolutely in love with Jake Gyllenhaal and I think he is the hottest actor out there. Right next to him is Heath Ledger." Hyperbole aside, Adi's comments effectively constitute endorsement of the movie, a mainstream endorsement not merely because Adi is female and identifies as straight, but also because she plans to buy tickets.

Though straight women seem the most eager to express a "healthy" desire for Heath Ledger and Jake Gyllenhaal (while openly favoring the former, the latter being most beloved among gay men), queer viewers are not immune to this particular response. Among those gay men who do acknowledge the physical appeal of Ledger and Gyllenhaal, the ultimate goal is to promote not queer desire itself but rather the basic *actorly* appeal of the two stars. If gay male desire is conventionally deemed unhealthy, the objective of these writers is to receive the actors as healthily talented: positive reviews by self-identified gay men characterize the pair as "amazing," "brilliant," and in possession of "a talent that goes beyond looking cute." All of this would seem to suggest that the response to the movie has been overwhelmingly positive among gay men. The commentaries referenced herein, however, reveal this to be far from the actual case. A major problem for the queer spectator is the film's failure to make clear the actual circumstances of Jack's death, leaving it up to the audience to decide whether he died as a result of a simple accident or as the victim of a hate crime, or even of AIDS, present and circulating at the time the film's tale ends in 1983. The ambiguity of Proulx's story befits its elliptical nature; the ambiguity of the film, according to an almost overwhelming number of online reviews, seems an evasive tactic, a calculated vagueness the queer spectator must overcome, even solve: "If 'love is a force of nature,'" writes one, evoking the film's official tagline, "I wonder why it could not have overcome obstacles like [death]." This writer, a self-identified gay male, then relates a litany of anxieties the characters similarly "fail to overcome," thus exposing the speciousness (for some gay viewers) of the tagline: "the fear of getting killed, societal discrimination and ostracisms, and the self-imposed . . . prison of homophobia"—these the film sees as "unendurable." Suggesting that the straight-identified filmmakers lack an adequate definition of love as it applies to same-sex relationships (for gays historically *have* overcome these and other obstacles, guided by true love), this viewer goes on to argue that "it is rather incomprehensible why Ennis consistently rejected the idea of living with Jack, if there is true love (which I would like to believe) between them." The theme song from *Titanic* (James Cameron, 1997), to cite the romantic American film most often linked with *Brokeback*, promises a future life for its heroine's troubled heart, that it will effectively "go on" after the death of her male lover. But if *Brokeback*'s Jack "died of a broken heart," as at least one gay-male spectator claims, then Ennis's surviving heart, consistently coded as inadequate, will continue to break, guiltily, across years. The title and repeated refrain of *Titanic*'s theme song, "My heart will go on," is sanctioned because it refers obviously in its context to heterosexual desire, that of a woman to replace her dead male lover. Believing his contact with a gay man to be "this once-in-a-lifetime encounter" (and unable to handle even that), Ennis will by contrast continue to implode, like the unfilled shirt he clutches toward the end of the film. Even now, the cinematic gay man's heart is a lonely one, still not even a hunter: it cannot "go on."

Interestingly, even inspiringly, some reviews fight this pandering approach. Responding to the stars' claims that Jack and Ennis aren't gay ("Just two people who fall in love"), one review attempts to reconcile the text of the film with the actors' dismissal of their characters' specificity: "'Gay' means just what it says. It's empowering. Always. Claim it. Unless you want to lie. Then use a different word. Like 'liar.'" Addressed to the actors themselves, these lines indicate a didactic and confrontational reception tactic specific to the queer spectator. That they were authored by a self-identified gay man whose username is "Monty Clift" adds a devastating, in some senses awe-inspiring, polish to the strategy, as if that tragic gay actor were speaking authoritatively from the grave.

"Tragic" happens to be the word most often mentioned in an uncomplimentary context in those reviews authored by self-identified gay men. "Queermountainman," a fifty-eight-year-old from Renton, Washington, argues that the film is "psycho-drivel about two Self-Deluded People who Don't Understand Themselves or Their Relationship, Can Never Connect, it all ending in a Terrible Tragedy"—a classic example, that is, of the kind of queer movie that is ultimately queer-abusive. "What the hell is wrong with a happy ending when it comes to gay relationships portrayed on screen?" asks one review. Another positive one lauds the film while acknowledging its limitations: "The next step will be a gay-themed commercial film with a happy ending." Not surprisingly, this gay commentator goes pointedly out of his way to establish that he himself is, in fact, "happy" and that his gay acquaintances are too. Other more confrontational responses link the tragic ending to the alleged queer-oppressive method of the film. If *Brokeback Mountain* is incomprehensible in the way it forecloses the possibility of an operational and enduring gay relationship, it fails also to suggest a clear response (other than suicide and self-derogation) to harmful social forces: "If I was in Ennis' situation, I would arm myself with a few shotguns and pistols, and settle down with Jack without any hesitation," reads one review. "They are both big men after all and defending themselves against would be [sic] attackers shouldn't be too difficult (well, unless it's a surprise attack)." A gay man who enjoyed the movie writes, "Just once it would be nice if a romantic gay relationship were played out on screen in a mainstream film to show that it's just as wonderful and normal as straight love. Only then, can we move past the idea that it's taboo and realize that it's hot!" Countering such unenthusiastic responses, a gay man named Shane Madden, like so many others, openly identifies with the film's male protagonists (and in so doing effectively responds to those viewers who fail, or refuse, to understand the married gay man): "Being raised on a farm, yeah, you had to hide it. It hurt to try and hide it. There were times I used to bang my head against a wall." Continuing, Shane demonstrates a reception strategy common among queer spectators, seeing himself in at least one of the film's two gay male characters and understanding the narrative through the dynamics of personal (and also cultural) memory: "Same thing that I've gone through; I fell in love with somebody, cared for a guy and we hid it from everybody. Society told me not to do it. Met a girl. Started dating the girl. Fell in love with her. Wasn't happy because I wasn't me." Such commentaries (abundant among the sample group) seemingly indicate that to properly receive the film, one needs to have lived the story, or an aspect of it. Only in such cases can a viewer suitably judge the movie. Relating to the kind of coping tactic that seeks to discount the film's plunge into tragedy by reading it against real, positive gay experiences, the approach of personally intervening has allegedly been available, even audible, in actual movie theaters: "At the screening I attended, gay men sort of booed Heath whenever he squashed Jake's dreams," writes one gay male commentator. "I just can't understand why Ennis won't be with Jack," writes another. "But anyway it's like he was the bad guy, and people in the audience knew it, too." Such a statement suggests a certain degree of comprehension on the part of the gay male spectator: that he might understand the task of the film better than the filmmakers themselves. One viewer communicates these issues with brevity and clarity: "Because I've been in his shoes, I know Jack dies of a broken heart," he writes, convincingly discarding the ambiguity that (deliberately) occupies the thematic center of the film and that clouds the circumstances of Jack's death. "Thank you, Jake Gyllenhaal," writes another man, "you play me better than I play myself."

One writer, evasive in his own way, captures the essence of the dilemma and endorses the film as a "simple story, simply told"—endorses, that is, the very terms with which the movie was publicized by the filmmakers: "Shit happens," he writes, "especially if you're gay. Jack can dream but Ennis can't. One dies, the other doesn't." What separates this response from the party line of the mainstream press (that the movie is nothing more than a universal love story about "people") is, of course, the word "gay." This writer may be evasive, but he's also inclusive, both establishing the pervasiveness of social prejudice and pointing, however laconically, to a wide and heavily oppressed gay audience. The filmmakers, openly courting a straight female audience, had consistently avoided such acknowledgments during the film's theatrical run. "Shit happens, especially if you're gay" is a statement that could easily end with a lone pronoun: "Like me." It's a clarification this writer, writing on this topic, doesn't even need. For while the film has failed to live up to some rather idealistic expectations—to speak nobly of a social and political history of queer America while bringing audiences together under a rubric of intense romanticism—to write about it, to champion or condemn it, is to tell your own story.

Quotes from lay critics were culled from the following sites:

National Marriage Forum
Midnight Diamonds (now defunct)
Free Republic
Dave Cullen
Internet Movie Database Message Boards
Yahoo!Movies
Gay Spirituality and Culture
Official Web site for the Focus Features Release
   Brokeback Mountain

Notes

1. For a more extensive meditation on the term "gay mainstream," see Benshoff.

2. For a further analysis of this "new queer spectator," see Aron, "The New Queer Spectator."

3. The quotes are from a self-identified gay male and a self-identified straight female in conversation with the author, *Brokeback Mountain* premiere, New York, 7 Dec. 2005.

4. For more on the activities of cyber vigilante groups, see Guisnel and McLure.

5. For an analysis of the ways in which the mythologies of the western U.S. frontier have been used to explain the ever-expanding Internet, see McLure 457–76.

6. For a further commentary on the complexity of the closet, see Benshoff.

17 } Making Sense of the *Brokeback* Paraphenomenon

DAVID WEISS

Ang Lee's *Brokeback Mountain* was the surprise of the 2005–6 movie season, offering neither typical high concept film fare nor a recipe for box-office success. Of course, as we all know now, *Brokeback* challenged Hollywood's received wisdom concerning the viability of a movie about the romantic and erotic bonds between two men.

But the warm embrace offered by the moviegoing and movie-reviewing communities to the so-called gay cowboy film was not the only *Brokeback Mountain* surprise. During the first three months of the film's release, what might be called the *Brokeback* paraphenomenon—reactions that took place alongside the film and went beyond merely viewing or praising it—took on a life of its own. Devoted fans organized *Brokeback* clubs, launched *Brokeback* Web sites and logs, took out an unprecedented ad in *Variety* to publicly thank the filmmakers (Ultimate Brokeback Forum), and even conducted a search in the state of Vermont for a mountain to officially name "Brokeback." As *USA Today* columnist Susan Wloszczyna gushed in January 2006, "[A]gainst all odds, a Western romance about two men . . . corralled the cultural zeitgeist" (1D).

Mountain-renaming campaigns aside, ardent displays of fandom are not, in the scheme of things, all that unusual. Since cinema's earliest days, certain films have been able to strike a particularly deep chord with the more passionate members of their audience. A select few even inspire behaviors sometimes referred to as "cultural poaching," which happens when a film's devotees make a movie so integral to their own lives that they figuratively wrest its ownership away from its creators.[1]

Brokeback Mountain is without question such a movie, resonating with casual admirers, devotees, and more than a few poachers.

The fact that the film so powerfully and positively moved so many of its fans is attested to eloquently throughout this book and need not be further elaborated here. Rather, what I explore are the ways that the movie catalyzed a *separate* set of public responses that might be characterized as "counterpoaching." These behaviors—widespread, mass-mediated, extremely high-profile, and usually comedic—are undeniably reactions to *Brokeback Mountain* but, paradoxically, are *not* manifestations of fandom (and in some cases do not even reflect direct experience with *Brokeback Mountain* itself).

What's most striking about these responses—the seemingly endless deluge of *Brokeback* parodies, jokes, and slang terms that filled the airwaves and glutted our e-mail inboxes during the 2006 awards season—is that they require only casual awareness of (or ungrounded assumptions about) the film's key themes, basic familiarity with elements of *Brokeback*'s marketing campaign, or in some cases simple hostility toward any movie that would dare to depict same-sex attraction. In stark contrast to the Web sites, blogs, and campaigns launched by the movie's fans, many of these counterreactions to the *Brokeback* phenomenon were produced by the film's most vocal detractors, including people who defiantly vowed they would never see the film. As John Powers notes in *LA Weekly*: "The media have been filled with pieces . . . either saying 'I don't want to see *Brokeback Mountain*' or asking whether the refusal to go makes you homophobic. I don't know about you, but I can't remember an op-ed piece about not wanting to see any other movie." Yet at the same time, like "real" poachers, the counterpoachers in their way also claimed creative control over a mass-mediated phenomenon that they had no hand in originating—and, more oddly, had no interest in promoting.

The fervor, the diversity of form and content, the inventiveness, and the ubiquity (or, depending on your perspective, the relentlessness) of the *Brokeback* jokes, spoofs, and slang are breathtaking. For these reasons alone, these nonfan and antifan reactions to the film would be worth investigating, but their significance goes deeper than their breadth or even their intensity. Plunging into their various and contradictory forms, messages, meanings, and motivations casts additional light not only on *Brokeback Mountain* itself but also on the culture into which the film was thrust and, as a result, helped to construct—a culture that was, and remains, partially receptive to, partially skeptical of, and partially hostile to a surprisingly popular film about two men in love.

Visual Parodies

The most visible of the reactions to *Brokeback Mountain* takes a number of parodic forms: televised skits, posters, and movie-trailer "mashups," online videos that juxtapose elements of *Brokeback*'s trailer with scenes swiped from other films. As a whole, these parodies are generally the most good-humored—or, put another way, the least hostile or homophobic—of the *Brokeback* paraphenomenon. If *parody* can be defined (as it is in the tenth edition of *Merriam-Webster's Collegiate Dictionary*) as a literary or musical form "in which the style of an author or work is closely imitated for comic effect or in ridicule," then there were two particularly striking tendencies of the many *Brokeback* parodies that surfaced in early 2006: (1) their emphasis on comic effect rather than ridicule and (2) the fact that, when ridicule actually was the overriding objective, its target was almost always something or someone other than *Brokeback Mountain* itself.

Posters

Perhaps the most accessible parodic form is, for both parodists and their audiences, the poster. Even for those who never saw the movie, the advertising for *Brokeback Mountain*—display ads in newspapers, magazines, and bus shelters; banners online; posters inside and outside movie theaters—was practically inescapable during the winter of 2005–6.

While the Focus Features promotional campaign for *Brokeback* included a number of print executions, one in particular immediately took on iconic status and, almost as quickly, inspired a raft of parodic responses. The original poster shows Heath Ledger and Jake Gyllenhaal in medium close-up, clad in denim jackets and cowboy hats, seemingly nuzzling—Gyllenhaal's chin may or may not be resting on Ledger's right shoulder—yet looking away from, or past, each other. The two actors

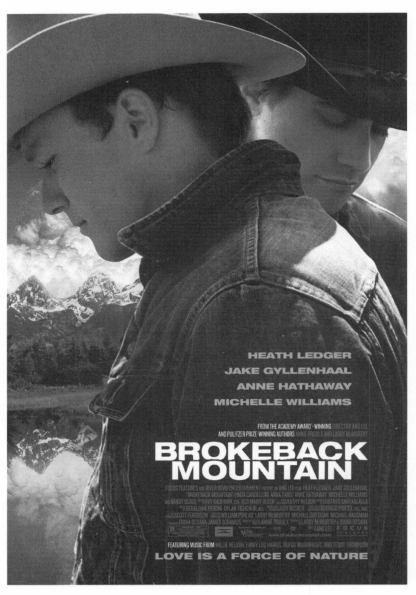

10. The film's iconic one sheet, with *Titanic* overtones. Courtesy of Universal Studios Licensing LLLP.

stand before a backdrop of snow-covered peaks and a mountain lake. Superimposed across Ledger's left arm are the film's title, the names of its four leads (Ledger, Gyllenhaal, Anne Hathaway, and Michelle Williams), and the tagline "Love is a Force of Nature" (see figure 10).

The parody posters, which for the most part circulated online, took elements of the original's layout but used them to comment on topics far removed from the thematic components of *Brokeback Mountain*. "Kickback Mountain" (see figure 11), created by Web designer Corey Anderson, digitally inserts former House Majority Leader Tom DeLay and felonious lobbyist Jack Abramoff into the Ledger/Gyllenhaal poses and outfits, places the names of Michael Scanlon and Bob Ney below DeLay's and Abramoff's, and includes the tagline "Greed is a Force of Habit." An illustrated *New Yorker* magazine cover appearing shortly after Vice President Dick Cheney's widely publicized (and presumably accidental) shooting of his hunting buddy Harry Whittington shows a rifle-touting Cheney and a nervous-looking George W. Bush striking the Ennis-and-Jack poses; its title is "Watch Your Back Mountain" (see figure 12). A similar although less politically sophisticated online execution, "Dumbfuck Mountain," features digitally modified photos of Bush and Cheney rather than illustrations ("Towleroad").

These parodies clearly would not have been created had *Brokeback Mountain* and its iconic poster not been so visible and ubiquitous. Yet they have nothing—or, at least, nothing substantial—actually to say about *Brokeback*, its themes, its stars, or its fans. Rather, the posters serve as twenty-first-century updates on the time-honored tradition of the political cartoon as social commentary; the objects of their parodies are not Jack and Ennis, but rather the public figures who were drawn or digitally inserted into the Jack-and-Ennis positions and wardrobe.

What, then, did these posters parody? All of them can be read as criticisms of the careless cowboy machismo that characterized the Bush administration's policies and their execution. Beyond that, the Bush-Cheney poster(s) mock the Connecticut-born U.S. president who refashioned himself as a Texas rancher and his "pardner," his all-too-trigger-happy vice president from Wyoming, the real-life state that, not incidentally, is the setting for the fictional *Brokeback Mountain*. Even more pointedly, the Abramoff-DeLay "Kickback Mountain" parody offers

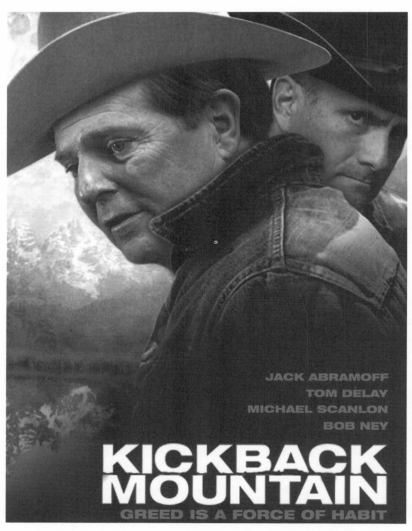

11. Political bedfellows Tom Delay and Jack Abramoff star in "Kickback Mountain." Corey Anderson/coreyanderson.net.

a critical comment on the issue of lobbyists and congress represen-
tatives being "in bed together" in the figurative sense, a political jab
sharpened by the visual reference to two characters who did, in fact,
sleep together.

Paradoxically, it is one of the more innocent looking and least

12. Secrets on a national scale. "Watch Your Back Mountain," cover of *The New Yorker*, February 26, 2006. Drawing by Mark Ulrikson. © Condé Nast Publications.

politically motivated of the posters that may have had something to say that actually relates to a theme of *Brokeback Mountain*. The widely acclaimed "Pokeback Mountain" parody positions cartoon stars Gumby and Pokey in Jack's and Ennis's cowboy garb above the tagline "Love is a Force of Pudding" (see figure 13). Unlike Bush-Cheney or Abramoff-DeLay, "Gumby Ledger" and "Pokey Gyllenhaal," as the clay characters are renamed in the "Pokeback Mountain" poster, seem to offer meager fodder for political commentary—and, in fact, the virtually criticism-proof Gumby and Pokey are not the targets of "Pokeback."[2] Rather, this parody poster may suggest that the two beloved clay creatures are themselves secretly gay, a fantastically hypothetical (and often accusatory) assumption made for decades about *Sesame Street*'s Bert and Ernie (who themselves appear in yet another *Brokeback* parody poster ["Towleroad"]) and, more recently, about both Spongebob Squarepants and the Teletubbies character Tinky-Winky. The suggestion made by the Pokeback poster, whether intended to be taken seriously or facetiously, visually links children's characters with the adult protagonists of *Brokeback Mountain*. In doing so, the Pokeback parody serves to infantilize, and even make a plaything of, gay love itself.

Of course, I may be reading much more into the undeniably gentle Pokeback Mountain parody than was ever intended. It is entirely possible that its creators hoped to evoke little more than a smile from their audience. Still, they and the others discussed here chose to make their sociopolitical comments by using *Brokeback Mountain*'s omnipresent imagery as their springboard. After all, as blogger Andy Towle observed in the *New York Times* in January 2006, "*Brokeback* has become a cultural touchstone. People have seized on the movie poster as a subversive vehicle to parody other relationships in our culture" (Ryzik).

Televised Skits

Brokeback Mountain was also parodied in a relatively small number of TV skits. The two that generated the most media attention were "*Brokeback Goldmine*," a piece on NBC's *Saturday Night Live*, and "*Brokeback Mountain: The Musical*," a segment on CBS's *Late Show with David Letterman*. Neither of these televised offerings, both still visible on YouTube.com, offer the creativity or even the satirical bite of the best of the posters

13. Gumby plus Pokey makes pudding. Posted anonymously at towleroad.com.

or the mashup trailers. If anything, the *Brokeback* musical, originated by and starring formerly closeted gay performer Nathan Lane, is at the low end of the taste and wit scale. Ostensibly developed to poke fun at *Brokeback*, the campy revue feels like a retread of the most deflated of *Carol Burnett Show* sketches (although its pantomimed male-male bum humping would never have been hinted at so broadly by Harvey Korman and Tim Conway). Featuring a quartet of young men in western garb prancing to songs sung by Lane, the spoof tosses a blunt and poorly aimed skewer in the general direction of Broadway show tunes, America's cowboy myth, gay men in general, and Lane himself in particular; ultimately, more tired gay jokes are rehashed than satirized. Similarly, *Saturday Night Live*'s spoof, featuring Alec Baldwin and Will Forte as aging prospectors in love, has little more to say than "being gay is funny." Still, these and other made-for-TV parodies offer further evidence of *Brokeback Mountain*'s ability to transcend its art-house roots and find itself entrenched as a powerful, if not necessarily universally beloved, presence in the most mainstream of popular culture outlets.

Video Parodies: Movie-Trailer Mashups, TV Spoofs, and Advertising Send-Ups

The most numerous and, often, most creative of the *Brokeback* parody forms is that of the "mashup" movie trailer. The best of these parody trailers for imagined hybrid or mashup movies marry captions (e.g., "It was a friendship . . . that became a secret" and "There are lies we have to tell") and music from the actual *Brokeback* trailer with selected scenes from other films, their actual targets. What resulted is a set of trailers for revisioned, retitled, and newly homoerotic movies such as "*Brokeback* Penguins," "*Brokeback* Fiction," "*Brokeback* Stooges," the computer-animated *Toy Story* spoof "Toyback Mountain," the *City Slickers* parody "Brokejack Palace," and even the sapphic "*Brokeback* Angels."

The sources of the mashup trailers are as diverse as their motivations. As *New York Times* film critic Virginia Heffernan observed in March 2006, "They're made anonymously or by comedy troupes or design shops, like Chocolate Cake City and Robot Rumpus, both of which give their web addresses at the end of their parody videos. . . . If they're well made, the parodies can presumably serve as a calling card for those who sign their work [as] some of them are viewed hundreds of thousands of times." The parodies typically use Gustavo Santaolalla's sexy, mournful theme from *Brokeback Mountain*, together with the title cards from that movie's trailer, to reframe clips from another movie. It works almost every time: a gay movie seems to emerge when scenes between male leads, or a male lead and a supporting actor, are slowed down, set to make-out music, and bumpered by portentous cards that say things like, "A truth they couldn't deny." All that these parodies need to do to set up the relationship is show one man's face in protracted detail and cut to the other man, who seems to watch with the same rapt attention that the viewer has been compelled to give by the slow-mo. A gay sub-text suddenly seems plain as day. At times, as many as fifty different parody trailers were available online. Not surprisingly, their technical and comedic quality varied wildly. As Heffernan notes, "Some of them are stupid. Some are droll and great. But as commentary on the forms and ceremonies of proto-gay relationships, they're surprisingly sharp, and worth taking seriously."

While most of the trailers parody well-known and often male-bonding–driven movies, television programs have also been spoofed à la *Brokeback*. On DailySixer.com alone, a visitor to the *"Brokeback* Spoofs" page could find, alongside more than twenty-five movie trailers, mash-ups of the TV crime drama *Walker: Texas Ranger*; of situation comedies such as *Scrubs*, *The Office*, and *Arrested Development*; and even of cartoons including *He-Man* and *Teenage Mutant Ninja Turtles*, as well as the more predictable targets of *The Muppets* and *Spongebob Squarepants*.

DailySixer.com and YouTube.com also posted *Brokeback*-themed advertising parodies. The *"Brokeback* Happy Meal" spot takes the form of an overly long McDonald's commercial in which three college-age men try the special new Happy Meal, complete with a set of Lego toys (cowboys, sheep, horses, and tents) that let them recreate key scenes from the eponymous movie. At the end of the commercial, the young trio appear in bed together naked, exulting over the meal's semen-like condiment, predictably called "Brokeback sauce." Much less graphic is the parodic commercial "Broke Mac Mountain," in which a frustrated Macintosh user, uttering lines from the actual *Brokeback Mountain* script (most pointedly, "I wish I knew how to quit you," directed toward his uncooperative computer), solicits help from a tech-savvy buddy. The friend solves the hero's computer problems *and* makes out with him, all to the strains of *Brokeback*'s plaintive score.

What lies beneath these various video parodies? While most of the advertising spoofs have little to say, the "*Brokeback* Happy Meal" commercial, crudely homophobic as it is, seems to have real targets, skewering as it does the artificiality of the glee exhibited by the actors in actual McDonald's commercials as well as the crass commercialization of movie tie-ins in general. Some of the movie and TV show mashups also offer meaningful commentary, bringing to the surface aspects of genuine, if covert, homoeroticism in the original productions.

The most well-aimed parody is that of *Top Gun* ("Top Gun 2: *Brokeback* Squadron"), a film that since its release has been accused of flirting with its audiences' fears of or titillation by same-sex attraction in the military. (That *Top Gun*'s uniformly handsome and well-muscled male cast is shown in locker room and shower scenes more often than strictly necessary to advance the plot certainly doesn't support a "family values" reading of the film.) Like the *Top Gun* mashup, the parody of *Goodfellas* is also effective at lampooning, or at least questioning, the nature of the male-male relationships so important to unit cohesion in the Mob, a machismo-driven subculture not entirely unlike that of the military. A similar comment is made by the *Lord of the Rings* mashup ("*Brokeback* Mount Doom"), whose target film makes much of the intense bond between two male hobbits.

Yet most of the parody trailers, TV spoofs, and advertising send-ups neither exhibit genuine homophobia nor offer serious criticisms of same-sex relationships. Mashups such as "*Brokeback* Heat," "*Brokeback* to the Future," "The Empire Strikes *Brokeback*," and so many others comment wittily on the latent (or, in most cases, nonexistent) homoerotic nature of the bonds between the characters in their target films—but do not demonize gay relationships in general or the one at the heart of *Brokeback Mountain* in particular. As Heffernan suggests, for the most part, the mashups are "nothing but labors of love, or gay panic, or both." She may have a point. At the same time, of course, these labors of love and/or gay panic do something more: They wrest creative control of *Brokeback Mountain*—its footage, its dialogue, its music, its marketing tools—from its rightful owners, a process of twenty-first-century cultural poaching that digital technology has made easier than ever to accomplish and that curatorial Web sites such as YouTube and iFilm have invested with social cachet.

Jokes

While the best and most elaborate of the online *Brokeback* parodies took time and technology to prepare, the onslaught of jokes inspired by the movie began almost as soon as the movie opened—and for four months, refused to let up. Even before the film's premiere in early December 2005, and continuing for some weeks after the March 2006 Academy Awards telecast, *Brokeback Mountain* jokes were staples on late-night television, talk radio, and the Internet. As a result of their broadcast and online ubiquity, they were told, retold, revised, and rehashed in one-on-one and group settings; collected on fan and antifan Web sites and blogs; and before long, anthologized, criticized, and even satirized in the press.

That *Brokeback Mountain* should be the inspiration for, or the butt of, humor should not be surprising or even necessarily troubling. Any political or cultural happening that is new, unusual, or "hot"—and *Brokeback* is certainly all of these—is fair game for public scrutiny, both positive and negative, both serious and humorous. As Jennifer Buckendorff observes in the *Seattle Times*, "*Brokeback* is big. Its story is sweeping. It's triumphant and tragic. It's the first film of its kind. And whenever you're a pioneer, you've got to be ready for potshots."

One noteworthy aspect of the potshots hurled at *Brokeback* is their relentlessness, something many pundits commented on. Authorities journalistic, psychiatric, and sociopolitical weighed in, in outlets as diverse as *USA Today*, *The Nation*, MSNBC.com, and *The Advocate*, with sound-bite analyses and other instant explanations of what lies behind the wave of *Brokeback* humor. Few if any of these journalists, however, notice or comment on what, to me, is the more striking and ultimately more revealing characteristic of the *Brokeback* quips making the rounds on the air, online, and around the water cooler: their diversity.

Brokeback jokes vary wildly in terms of their objectives, targets, political standpoints, attitudes, the sources of their humor, and their relevance to the film itself. For that reason, the typical journalistic framing of "*Brokeback* humor" as a monolithic genre sheds little light on the multi-faceted and often contradictory messages of the jokes or the motivations underlying their creation and dissemination. Delineating and investigating the variety of the humorous forms and messages is important if we are to make sense of the different ways in which people react to *Brokeback Mountain* and, in many cases, attempt to discipline it.

While *Brokeback Mountain* humor—as evidenced at least on late-night TV and talk radio, the most powerful and accessible of its sources—takes many forms and has many targets, one of its most noteworthy characteristics is the fact that only very rarely does it truly concern *Brokeback Mountain*. Indeed, perhaps the most one can say about the majority of *Brokeback* jokes is that they are inspired by, at best, the film and, at worst, simply homophobia.

Consider, for example, one of the most widely circulated of the comedy bits to surface in the wake of *Brokeback Mountain*'s debut: the Top Ten list read on David Letterman's December 13, 2005, broadcast of *The Late Show*. Among the "Top Ten Signs You're a Gay Cowboy" are:

10. Your saddle is Versace. . . .
8. You enjoy ridin', ropin', and redecoratin'. . . .
6. After watching reruns of *Gunsmoke*, you have to take a cold shower. . . .
2. Instead of a saloon, you prefer a salon.

This routine serves as a handy microcosm of so-called *Brokeback* humor: it appeared on the scene shortly (in this case, a mere four days) after the film opened; perpetuates tired gay cultural stereotypes; expresses facetious discomfort about gay sexual practices; pokes fun at gay lifestyle issues; winkingly refers to other allegedly gay-associated pop-culture products; dances around the supposedly oxymoronic notion of "gay cowboys"—and says absolutely nothing about *Brokeback Mountain*.

Much of the *Brokeback*-inspired humor on other Letterman broadcasts and those of his chief late-night rivals is similar, recycling old clichés while offering no commentary on *Brokeback* itself. On December 9, 2005, for example, NBC's Conan O'Brien announced, "Today, the controversial new movie *Brokeback Mountain* opens, about two gay cowboys. Apparently, you can tell the characters are gay because they're dressed like cowboys." On January 25, 2006, O'Brien included this gag in his monologue: "At a press conference in Kansas the other day, President Bush was asked if he had seen *Brokeback Mountain*. He said, no, he doesn't like Westerns where the cowboys go into town for a day spa."

Other *Brokeback*-inspired quips offered by TV and radio hosts, however, point their skewers not at gay men's supposed interests in fashion, grooming, interior design, or Broadway musicals, but instead at gay sex or male-male sexual attraction, topics that *are* actually central to the movie. Michael Savage and Don Imus, talk-radio personalities known for their antigay humor, renamed the film by incorporating into its title punning references to homoerotic acts, referring to *Brokeback* variously as "Bareback Mounting" and "Fudgepack Mountain" ("Matthews").

Although less overtly hostile, NBC TV host Jay Leno—who managed to work at least one *Brokeback* or gay cowboy reference into almost every *Tonight Show* between December 2005 and March 2006—had no shortage of his own jokes in this vein:

> The president said we must continue to find new sources of oil. The only place he doesn't want any drilling: Brokeback Mountain. (6 Feb. 2006)

> Ninety percent of men say their lover is also their best friend— which has got to be a big surprise to their wives. "Hey, hon, I'm going over to Bob's. We're catching the ten o'clock showing of *Brokeback Mountain*. Don't wait up." ("Ridin'")

Interestingly, not all of Leno's *Brokeback* cracks perpetuate gay stereotypes or otherwise put down gay people. Indeed, in a fascinating twist, two of his *Tonight Show* jokes actually reference the homoerotic content of *Brokeback Mountain* as a way of poking fun at leaders of the Religious Right:

> The cold weather continues to spread across the United States. In fact, down south, it was so cold people were shaking like Jerry Falwell watching *Brokeback Mountain*. ("Did You Hear?")

The Golden Globes were last night. It was the biggest gathering of Hollywood celebrities that wasn't an anti-Bush rally. . . . The big winners were *Brokeback Mountain*, *Capote*, and *Transamerica*—all movies with gay themes. I think this is God's way of punishing Pat Robertson. (17 Jan. 2006)

While not necessarily progay, jokes like these are at least not overtly anti-gay. They humorously acknowledge and even gently ridicule homophobia in general and cultural ambivalence about *Brokeback Mountain*'s content in particular.

Other comics went to still greater lengths in their humorous explorations of the squeamishness *Brokeback* engendered, particularly among otherwise open-minded straight males. Gay film critic Dave White published a tongue-in-cheek editorial on MSNBC.com titled "The Straight Dude's Guide to *Brokeback*," which offers "sage advice" for gay-friendly heterosexual men whose wives or girlfriends had demanded that *Brokeback Mountain* be their next date-night movie. Speaking to men who would describe themselves as "liberal" and "no homophobe," White addresses the dilemma they face when looking to please their girlfriends while watching men make out on the big screen:

You're going to see it whether you like it or not. . . . So I have some viewing tips for you, my straight brothers. . . . You have to shut up. Being silent marks you as too cool to care about how other men see you. . . . The good news: there's less than one minute of making out. It's about 130 minutes long and 129 of them are about Men Not Having Sex. So yes, maybe it will be the longest almost-60 seconds of your life, but there it is. Less than one minute.

As consolation, White promised his hetero readers, Anne Hathaway removes her blouse.

In a similar vein is the guest editorial that TV producer/star Larry David wrote for the *New York Times*. David's piece, titled "Cowboys Are My Weakness" (after Pam Houston's story collection of that name), offers a facetious retort to Dave White's "Straight Dude's Guide," while lampooning the sentiments underlying on-air comments about *Brokeback*

Mountain made by syndicated radio host Don Imus ("No, I haven't seen it. Why would I want to see that?") and similar dismissals offered by Fox News Channel's Bill O'Reilly and MSNBC's Chris Matthews on their own programs ("Matthews"; "Conservatives"). Taking direct aim at the notion that if a straight man were to see *Brokeback Mountain* he would become gay—the ungrounded fear that seems to be at the core of much of heterosexual male America's resistance to the film—David offers the following mock apologia: "I haven't seen *Brokeback Mountain*, nor do I have any intention of seeing it [much as] I love gay people. . . . If two cowboys, male icons who are 100 percent all-man, can succumb, what chance do I have, half to a quarter of a man, depending on whom I'm with at the time? Who's to say I won't become enamored with the whole gay business?" (9).

David's *Times* column may have skewered the repressed fears motivating many of the *Brokeback Mountain* jokes that flooded the airwaves, but it certainly didn't put an end to them. Indeed, for the most part, *Brokeback*-inspired humor, even after the January 1, 2006, publication of David's piece, reflected, perpetuated, and gave increasingly public voice to the prejudices and phobias mocked by David and White, rather than refuting, ridiculing, or in any other way fixing a critical lens on those feelings.

It is time now, then, to ask a number of questions that have been to this point deferred. Why, to begin with, were there so many *Brokeback* jokes, told for so many months, and with so many different targets? Why did they last as long as they did and have the ubiquity that they had?

It doesn't seem far-fetched to suggest that one of the motivators of *Brokeback* humor may well also have been a motivator of *Brokeback* resistance—something geneticist Dean Hamer calls the "ick factor." As Hamer (perhaps most famous for his claim that a "gay gene" is what predisposes some people to homosexuality) comments in a January 2006 *San Francisco Chronicle* article, "It does seem to be almost culturally universal that heterosexual men can have a deep repulsion to overt homosexuality" (Sefton). During the time of *Brokeback Mountain*'s theatrical run, some straight men, it would appear, expressed this repulsion through humor, while others did so through their rejection of *Brokeback Mountain* as a Saturday night movie pick; many, of course, likely did both. In any case, the intensity of the "ick factor," combined with the surprisingly strong critical and commercial success of *Brokeback*—which itself translated to a surprisingly long stay in cinemas, long list of awards and nominations, and intense media fascination with the film—may at least partially explain the remarkable persistence of jokes about or, more often inspired by, the movie.

The jokes themselves have a variety of targets: gay cultural stereotypes, gay men, gay sex, gay cowboys, the movie's title, and in rare cases, selected narrative or thematic elements of the movie itself. What, then, is missing from the *Brokeback*-inspired jokes? For the most part, any reference to those aspects of the film that made it more than and other than merely the gay cowboy movie is absent. Specifically, nowhere in the pages and pages of TV and online jokes do we see references to the tragic nature of the film's narrative or the more troubling of its themes.

Yes, *Brokeback Mountain* is about two men who fall in love, a fact that many *Brokeback* jokes do reference. But more specifically, the movie is about two men who fall in *doomed* love, men whose lives are made miserable by what they perceive to be the impossibility of their situation and whose marriages are destroyed by the lies they live. One of those men dies, possibly the victim of a gay bashing. The film, which ends on a note of heartbreak, is not a celebration of same-sex love but a wrenching exploration of the consequences of denying oneself the happiness that such love might bring.

In light of all this, two additional and interrelated questions come to mind: How did such a tragic film become the inspiration and/or butt of humor? And how is it that none of the film's *tragic* thematic elements are anywhere to be found in the many jokes that were made? The answer to the first question hinges on the sad fact that while jokes about racial or religious minorities (and about films featuring them and the tragedies that may befall them) have become stigmatized, jokes about gay people remain socially acceptable. This might explain why *Brokeback Mountain* inspired months of late-night comedy routines while *Hotel Rwanda*, *Mississippi Burning*, and *Schindler's List* inspired none.

Still, if antigay humor lacks the stigma that racist and anti-Semitic jokes carry, how was it that *Brokeback*'s tragic elements are not evidenced in the jokes that the movie inspired? As is the case with many of the poster and trailer parodies, it is more than likely that many of the jokes were made by people who never saw the actual film—or who, like Don Imus and Bill O'Reilly, publicly proclaimed that they never *would* see it. All that is needed to craft a *Brokeback* joke is the awareness that the film has *something* to do with homos, those time-honored targets of humor and ridicule, and that its lead characters wear ten-gallon hats. Even the ubiquitous descriptor "gay cowboy movie" reflects a lack of familiarity with the actual film; as any real *Brokeback* fan knows, Jack and Ennis are sheep wranglers, not cowboys.

People who actually *had* seen the film and were therefore familiar with its tragic content would have been *less* likely to make the sort of jokes that epitomized *Brokeback* humor during the winter of 2005–6, jokes that were for the most part simply updated versions of gay cultural clichés and had little or nothing to do with the film itself. If anything, it was probably easier to make *Brokeback* jokes (read, gay jokes or gay cowboy jokes) for those not burdened with firsthand knowledge of the actual movie. Such an excuse, however, is clearly not available for any joke writer or joke teller who had seen the film; indeed, it is unlikely that show-business insiders such as Jay Leno, David Letterman, and Conan O'Brien—or their writing staffs—would be able to find a valid excuse to miss such an important movie, even if they are personally uncomfortable with its content.

With all this said, is *Brokeback* humor all bad? Is it merely harmless fun, or has any actual damage been done to gay people? In an article exploring these questions, Associated Press writer Jocelyn Noveck argues that "most gay groups find it fairly benign, and note that in any case, the movie's overwhelming publicity can only be a good thing." To that end, Noveck quotes Susanne Salkind, managing director of the Human Rights Campaign gay lobbying group: "some of the humor may be insensitive, but even that has spurred positive conversation." Similarly, Neil Guiliano, president of the Gay and Lesbian Alliance against Defamation told a *USA Today* columnist that "when a person or a piece of artistic work reaches a certain level of acceptability, it's OK to joke about it. The whole buzz is this is a great movie" (Wloszczyna). In short, it might appear that the pros outweigh the cons. Voicing a contrary opinion, however, is Matt Foreman, executive director of the

National Gay and Lesbian Task Force, who notes that "it may be funny, but there is a real element of homophobia. It's making jabs about sex between gay men" (Noveck).

Much of the humor, however, has little if anything to do with sex. The appearance of *Brokeback Mountain*, a movie whose two lead characters are men in love with each other—and, yes, who have sex with each other—more often serves as simply the most recent, and thus most convenient, most topical, and even most hip, catalyst for the perpetuation of stereotypes many of us had hoped were heading toward extinction.

Notes

1. Anyone who has observed the clothing and behavior of hard-core fans at a *Star Trek* convention or in a multiplex ticket line on the opening day of any Harry Potter sequel has witnessed cultural poaching par excellence.

2. The "last names" given to the "Pokeback Mountain" characters reflect a slip up on the parodist's part: Pokey is placed in Ennis's position and wears his white hat and thus would logically be "Pokey Ledger." Gumby, who occupies Jack's spot and wears his black hat, should be "Gumby Gyllenhaal."

18 } Alberta, Authenticity, and Queer Erasure

JON DAVIES

> "Nothing can keep them apart. . . . Yet nothing can get them together, to help them over the pre-Stonewall hump of shame in a part of the American landscape that suffers from mythological overload: a man's gotta do what a man's gotta do, but the thing he could not do is what Wilde said three-quarters of a century earlier in London couldn't be named anywhere anyway, much less in Wyoming."
> HARLAN JACOBSON, "*Brokeback Mountain*."

"'Brokeback' Opens Up Alberta's Sweeping Wilderness," crows the lead headline on the Web site for Travel Alberta, "Canada's Rocky Mountain Playground" (Cummings, "'Brokeback' Opens Up").[1] And while the agency's particular choice of verb might conjure Ennis del Mar "opening up" Jack Twist on their first cold and lusty night tenting together, travelers would be hard-pressed to find any hint of homoeroticism—or any queer body politics for that matter—in the Canadian province's tie-in tourism campaign. Travel Alberta's substitution of *Brokeback Mountain*'s gay subject matter with the western landscape is a fascinating manifestation of the tension between artifice and authenticity that the film and the discourse surrounding it consistently draw out. Ultimately the tourism campaign serves to deauthenticate and theatricalize the very mythic rural West that it seeks to protect from contamination by the artifice and urbanity that queerness traditionally represents.

First, I would like to briefly draw some connections between the

Travel Alberta campaign's penchant for closeting, the province of Alberta's fraught relationship with queer rights, and the rise to power of an Alberta-based Conservative federal government bent on entrenching sexual conservatism. While *Brokeback* takes place in Wyoming, it was shot in Alberta, currently Canada's most affluent province and the support base for Canada's Conservative Party, which took control of the federal government on February 6, 2006. The party's leader, Prime Minister Stephen Harper, ran in the Alberta riding of Calgary Southwest and in 2006 the province was the only one to elect Conservative members of Parliament to every single seat (28 out of Canada's 308 total). While in 2006 the Conservatives formed the smallest minority government in Canadian history—with an edge of only 21 seats over the second-place centrist Liberals—they took their narrow win as a sign that the Canadian public desired substantial change in line with Conservative positions, most of which align Canada more closely with the United States in terms of everything from law and order to "family values." (I should note that the 2008 election netted the Conservatives a considerably greater edge of 66 seats over the second-place Liberals while still failing to achieve a majority government.) One aspect of this Conservative campaign was the commitment to reassess the country's legalization of same-sex marriage on July 20, 2005, by holding a free vote in Parliament, a motion that was defeated 175 to 123 on December 7, 2006. This vote occurred despite the public's widely held view that the legalization of same-sex marriage was a divisive issue that should not be revisited but instead just accepted and left alone. The Conservatives—with the support of the opposition parties—also successfully raised the age of sexual consent from fourteen to sixteen years on February 28, 2008, as part of the Tackling Violent Crime Act, Bill c-2.

Meanwhile in Alberta, Progressive Conservative Premier Ralph Klein made several unsuccessful attempts to make sure that same-sex marriage legislation never came to his province, including passing a provincial anti–same-sex marriage amendment that was in effect for five years, threatening to do away with civil marriage in the province entirely and suggesting a national referendum on the question of same-sex marriage. Among all the provinces, Alberta had earlier put up the biggest fight against amending its human rights code to include discrimination against sexual orientation and put it in line with section 15 of the federal Charter of Rights and Freedoms, which took effect in 1985. After struggling tooth and nail, the province was eventually forced to amend the legislation by a Supreme Court of Canada decision in 1998 (T. Warner 208–10). Alberta's poor reputation when it comes to gay rights was enough of an issue to warrant articles such as "Buzz and Debate Surrounding *Brokeback Mountain* Swirl in 'Redneck' Alberta, the Unlikely Location for Gay Cowboy Film," which discusses this apparent contradiction between the Alberta government's financial support of *Brokeback*'s filming and its institutionalized homophobia and reputation for being the most socially conservative province in Canada (Burroughs 1). Another commentator simply suggested that "the story of two gay cowboys getting it on in ultra-conservative rural Alberta is just so darn juicy" (Gill R1).

In light of this homophobic reputation, how do we interpret the province's tourism campaign? On the surface, the mainstream acceptance of the film has shown that queer cinema can be appreciated and lauded by straight audiences, so basing a tourism campaign around *Brokeback* is not exactly risqué—in fact, it makes good business sense. However, because the film takes place in a rural western milieu—the symbolic heart of conservative North America—it has been vilified by fundamentalist Christian forces much more intensely than other queer films that have entered the mainstream radar.[2] To craft a campaign selling the Canadian West around *Brokeback* thus does suggest a certain level of tolerance for homosexuality and liberalism, which is ultimately sabotaged by the campaign itself.

Brokeback's red-state setting is a key factor in the enormous measure of discourse surrounding it: whereas most movies churn out copious merchandising, *Brokeback* produced endless editorials, covering all the minutiae one could imagine about the film. A perusal of just the daily papers would turn up the following, above and beyond coverage of the movie's plaudits and condemnations: testimonies by real gay Wyoming and Alberta cowboys; textual analyses of the film's unflattering representation of the nuclear family; coverage of the film being pulled from a theater in Utah and banned in the Bahamas; news of its huge popularity in the form of bootleg DVDs in Beijing (where it is also banned);

essays correcting Conservative misapprehensions of the Western genre as espousing pro-Christian values; reports on the changing face of fundamentalist Christian movie reviewing; predictions of the film's success in urban, suburban, and rural markets; reproductions of Internet spoofs of *Brokeback* posters (and comparisons between its poster and *Titanic*'s); castigations of Liberal indulgence of gay minstrelsy in film and late-night television; appraisals of contemporary sexual mores and values (including a salute to the Kinsey scale); and, perhaps most importantly, interviews detailing the resolutely straight private lives of the main actors and director, more often than not emphasizing the courage of the duo of "hetero heartthrobs" for tackling such a project. Throughout this media blitz, certain ideas reappear so frequently they have become near gospel, and they help shed light on how Travel Alberta's campaign can so effortlessly efface the queerness of *Brokeback*.

One of these ideas is that *Brokeback* is a universal—even elemental—story of unrequited love between two souls and not a cri de coeur against rural economic deprivation and homophobia, that Jack and Ennis could just as easily have been a heterosexual couple whose love is forbidden. When Jake Gyllenhaal states, "These aren't gay guys, they're two souls that fall in love," one can't help but feel that he is not so much offering a queer take on the fluidity of sexual identity as making the unseemly palatable to the homophobic (Lacey). (I am more intrigued by director Ang Lee's suggestive declaration that "eventually everybody has a '*Brokeback Mountain*' in them" [Durbin 15].) In the *Brokeback* discourse, there is a prevailing unwillingness to accept that the film deals with dynamics of the closet that are specifically queer and ultimately tragic, a reality that, thankfully, writer Annie Proulx elaborates whenever she can: "Wyoming is a homophobic place. For a young guy to wonder about his sexuality, when he's been indoctrinated with homophobia from day one, is an anguished struggle, and that's what the story is about" (Winter). It has also become common to mention that Matthew Shepard's murder occurred in 1998, a year after Proulx's short story was first published. When the Travel Alberta campaign recuperates the film as purely an epic romance, the soul-destroying reality of real-world, historical, and present-day homophobia in country and city alike is minimized and the silencing of the closet that emotionally cripples Ennis is perpetuated anew.

Second, and most important for this essay, *Brokeback* hit a nerve because it transgresses the symbolic boundaries surrounding the mythology of the West. In some ways, the invitation to visit Alberta because of *Brokeback* is a call to repeat a similar invasion of the sanctified space of the heterosexual West that the chatter around the film regularly returns to: Asian American art film director and Hollywood liberal actors bring their cosmopolitanism and sodomy from the coasts—where such filthy things are permitted to flourish—to the heartland.[3] Or, as Nick Hune-Brown cleverly puts it: "It's the fact that the lovers in *Brokeback Mountain* are cowboys and not, say, NYU theater majors that Christian conservatives seem to find particularly offensive" (D1). Aiming outward, at the rest of Canada but especially at the United States, the tourism campaign dissuades fears of rural homophobia for its urbanite target audience through its choice of a relatively sophisticated cultural reference point like *Brokeback*. Yet while Travel Alberta flogs its province's connection to the film at every opportunity, the queer content is evaporated as resolutely as when anyone describes the film as a "universal love story."

Patricia Nelson Limerick describes the process of selling the West as "freezing a moment in an imagined past," disconnecting it from its context and imposing a stamp of realness to permit tourists to get back to nature in a convenient, therapeutic, and pleasurable way (46–47). Altering the land to fit desires and expectations—which are often determined by popular representations—tourism sells packaged experiences to outsiders in search of difference, in the case of the West an antiquated, preindustrial landscape made into a safe, convenient spectacle of old-fashionedness. Western tourism's desperate need for authenticity is invariably complicated when queerness enters the picture. Tourism's taming of messy, wild reality into a commodity mirrors the symbolic transformation that queering the West would engender: both pit outsider against insider, traditional rural against fickle urban. But of course, the past that tourists to the West seek is never that simple: the West has always been queer and its authenticity as much of an aesthetic construct as the most decadent and artificial urban centers. *Brokeback* offers the potential for pleasure in three forms of tourism: transporting urban and suburban audiences to the rural West, heterosexual audiences to the experience of being a closeted gay man, and twenty-first-century audiences to decades past—including before Stonewall.

Travel Alberta's campaign specifically invites tourists to find in Alberta's majestic landscape the same escape from the problems of the real world that its protagonists do, but it is rife with contradictions. In a fascinating publicity stunt, the province sent a posse of cowboys off to extol Alberta's virtues in Sodom and Gomorrah itself—New York City. Rather than unleashing the authentic rural onto the artificial urban, this stunt served to render both as fantasies by employing Ennis and Jack surrogates that were fictional on two levels—they were not actual cowboys but hired actors and they were seemingly scrubbed clean of any traces of their homosexuality. While *Brokeback*'s power originates in its bracingly and meticulously authentic portrayal of hidden gay lives in the rural West, there seems to be no qualms about the many levels of masquerade going on in the heterosexual Heath Ledger and Gyllenhaal playing gay, in Alberta dressing up in Wyoming drag, or in painting a queer film in straight colors.

What then to make of the agency hiring models and actors to play cowboys in this global mecca of queerness and artifice? This weekend-long campaign shows just how desperate the reliance on a (fragile) myth of rural, western authenticity is. Just listen to casting agent Hilary Bowers explain the details of the provincially funded Urban Cowboy plot: "She pointed out the 20 being picked in New York will only be 'fillers' to help 10 real cowboys teaching the tricks. 'We've got separate casting going on for the 10 in Canada,' she said. 'Certainly the only cowboys doing the talking and tricks in front of the camera will be real ones preferably from Alberta'" (Edwards, "Alberta Rides").

The repressed sexual desire does somewhat resurface when Bowers adds, "'Looking like Heath Ledger wouldn't hurt either'" (Edwards, "Alberta Rides"). In Manhattan, being a real cowboy means getting all gussied up, being able to do "rope tricks and cattle calls," hand out promotional cowboy-hat-shaped brochures and T-shirts, and generally sell Alberta's mythic idea of itself by promoting its place in the background of *Brokeback*. The performers were also required to test passersby about an Alberta cowboy culture that many would not know firsthand themselves. Steven Edwards describes in great detail how decidedly inauthentic these "Canadian" cowboys are, ending with the note that the group will include "rising Canadian actress and model: Xenia Siamos, 23 . . . who's just finished shooting for a film called *Push* with Chazz Palminteri, in which she plays Sasha, a strung-out model on drugs" ("Alberta Rides"). This straight-faced detailing of Siamos's acting experience serves to emphasize just how distant from the real deal these actors and models must be. In a follow-up article he describes how the event unfolded, with the thirty-strong group a mix of rodeo stars, "real" cowboys, and North American "acting hopefuls." He points out, "It wasn't hard to guess which was which after a morning of marching" and goes on to detail the boot-maimed ankles of a local beauty school student who announces "It's not easy being a cowgirl" ("Alberta Posse"). Touring Manhattan's landmarks, the group's show-stopping stunts included a twelve-year-old former Calgary Junior Miss Pageant winner lassoing CBS morning show host Harry Smith as he mooed like a cow on all fours. Of course, authenticity comes at a price, and having the stand-ins pay their own expenses and "plans to truck horses into the city" were nixed for financial and logistical (permits and poop-scooping) concerns. The article also focuses on the rural/urban culture clash, such as describing the reactions of the actual Albertans to the shock of seeing a city the size of New York, and the largely apathetic reactions of the jaded and busy Gothamites. This article barely mentions the *Brokeback* origins of the campaign at all, perhaps not surprising considering the straightness of the performers and their shtick ("Alberta Posse").

These carnivalesque machinations of the PR machine make strange bedfellows with the sense of authenticity that travel agencies must maintain for the West, a verisimilitude that *Brokeback*'s gritty realism strives on every level to capture. Many commentators have pointed out, for example, that *Brokeback* offers a deep, dramatic, and emotional counterbalance to the comic, theatrical, easily consumable stereotypes that have usually characterized gay representation. Straight-faced, seemingly preirony and decidedly not camp, these are real American men (the polar opposite of the New York speed freaks, hustlers, and pretty boys starring in Andy Warhol's queer Western burlesques *Horse* and *Lonesome Cowboys*) who have rough "high-altitude fucks" and whose feelings pack a real punch.

Travel Alberta is in a precarious position: it must indulge the mythos of the West because that is the province's primary draw as a tourist destination, but those who adhere to this constellation of myths—who do not treat it as a construct but instead seek to conserve its supposed authenticity as a space of conservative values—cannot stomach the transformation of this way of life that the public visibility of rural queers could potentially generate. That is why the central narrative and characters of the film have to be erased and cannot participate in the campaign, and Travel Alberta must focus solely on the landscape, and in the case of the Urban Cowboy campaign, on nonthreatening iconic showbiz cowboys. Just as Jack and Ennis's love had to be grafted onto a pair of shirts hidden in a closet because their real bodies one inside the other simply could not publicly *be*, so their sexual bodies are once more sublimated elsewhere—the landscape. Interestingly enough, another form of this displacement is evidenced in the article on Christian film reviewers beginning to acknowledge the technical artistry of certain films like *Brokeback* while ignoring or vilifying the content they find morally repugnant. Here gay sex is detached from the cinematic techniques used to represent it and then conveniently elided. One review of the film on Christianitytodaymovies.com had the following coda appended by editor Mark Moring: "As for the 3-star rating, that is only in reference to the quality of the filmmaking, the acting, the cinematography, etc. It is not a 'recommendation' to see the film, nor is it a rating of the 'moral acceptability' of the subject matter" (qtd. in Leland).

Another manifestation of the *Brokeback* campaign—in the form of a lengthy article on Travel Alberta's Web site—focuses on the film's Oscar wins and invites travelers to discover the real star of the film, the landscapes of Southern Alberta that are "splayed . . . on silver screens the world over" (Cummings, "Alberta's *Brokeback Mountain*"). The copy trumpets the huge boost to Alberta's publicity that the film's major presence at the Oscars—with its many millions of viewers—opened up. It goes on to describe the persistent phone calls from tourists and location scouts that the province has received thanks to the film, including fans desperate to find the real-world locations where, for example, "the two star-crossed sheep tenders, Heath Ledger (playing Ennis del Mar) and Jake Gyllenhaal (Jack Twist), jump off a cliff into a clear Rocky Mountain river." (This is just one of two vague references that Travel Alberta makes to *Brokeback's* central relationship—the other is a "soul-stirring cowboy romance.") And while most of the article extols the virtues of the landscape—mountains, lakes, bridges—it also tells the secret of which local entrepreneur rented out the bear that Ennis encounters (Doug's Exotic Zoo Farm), which perfectly captures the idea of "accessible wilderness" that the campaign is selling. These sites are close to major roads, easily accessible to tourists traveling by car. Precisely the qualities that make nature so alluring—its unspoiled grandeur and distinctness from civilization—end up being erased by promoting its closeness to modern conveniences, summed up by the line, "What looks off the beaten track is on." The writing also extols the virtues of small Alberta towns such as Cowley and Fort MacLeod, home of the "almost squalor" of Ennis and Alma's apartment above a laundromat, and Aguirre's "rusted-up, derelict trailer" where the two men meet. Rather than being disheartening, these signs of rural dilapidation are spun as evidence of the film's bewitching authenticity—which tourists can experience themselves, sort of. But they can be rest assured that they won't be staying in any "almost squalor," just stopping by.

This passage speaks volumes about the economic decline that forces so many rural areas to depend desperately on tourism, which in Alberta is an industry worth more than $5 billion a year ("Alberta Tourism"). Journalist Alexandra Burroughs claims, "The most recent numbers show that for every $10 million invested into the filmmaking industry through the Alberta Film Development Fund, the province sees $129 million in economic spinoffs." She goes on to report on the small-scale rumblings against Alberta's involvement in the film, framing it as a question of government support of homosexuality (i.e., "We shouldn't be funding things that promote the destruction of family"). As of the summer of 2006, *Brokeback Mountain* had earned about $180 million in its worldwide theatrical release, according to the Internet Movie Database; was central to the Oscars; and had become a cultural touchstone. As many commentators point out, the province's majestic presence in the film is publicity that money can't buy, and Travel Alberta has capitalized on this connection since at least January 31, 2006 (with the news posting "Brokeback Mountain to Shine at Oscars: Alberta Film Crews Building Mountains of Acclaim").

A key aspect of the campaign is the opportunity for tourists to design their very own *Brokeback Mountain* tour: "Independent travelers who want to camp out under a tarp of stars—the very ones featured in *Brokeback*—or hike along the precise ridge that swirled with 1000 head of sheep, go two-stepping in the exact cowboy bar where Jack first met Lureen (Anne Hathaway), can follow this self-guided trail" (Cummings, "Alberta's *Brokeback Mountain*"). What is so fascinating about this offer is that it gives visitors the opportunity to enjoy pursuits that could be found in any Western, but none of those that made *Brokeback* a landmark film. This is not to say that one would expect an official tourism bureau to invite people to enjoy explosive gay sex in rural Alberta, but that this invitation epitomizes how the campaign literally focuses on the background of the film while largely ignoring the plot and the big picture. Or, as journalist Murray Whyte puts it: "[D]espite the story's universality—a love story driven by class conflict, the onset of modernity and the death of the rural life—there is concern that moviegoers will not be able to see the forest for the one, giant redwood tree looming in the foreground." What is so hypocritical about Travel Alberta's stance is that it pretends that this towering giant redwood in fact does not exist at all, despite the fact that everyone is perfectly aware that it does.

The first section of the self-guided *Brokeback* tour is about Calgary, the largest city in Alberta, where some of the scenes were shot and the cast and crew spent some time. This paragraph renders in sharp relief the stark differences between gay cinematic fantasy and the harsh, often homophobic, reality of life in the rural West. Ironically, the campaign does not target—nor will it likely entice—queer tourists, for whom the idea of a closeted world with no public queer culture would not exactly be a big draw. Whereas historically queer people have fled rural areas for the cities, Travel Alberta extols a return to the wilderness in a completely heterosexist pitch that never entertains the idea of a queer readership. Even when discussing the urban center of Calgary—with a population of a million, twice that of the entire state of Wyoming—it highlights its bucolic as opposed to urban qualities and makes no reference to its large gay community (perhaps this would draw too much attention to their marked distinction from the queer cultural desert of Wyoming). The closing paragraph of the article shows how the discourse of "diversity" most often connected to the cultural plurality of the city becomes hijacked to describe the varied topography: "One of the wonders of this film," says [Derek] Coke-Kerr [the managing director of Travel Alberta], "is that the focus is not exclusively on the Rocky Mountains. Yes, they're present and they're as captivating as always but it's the sweep across Alberta's small towns and prairies that best illustrates the diversity of our landscape" (Cummings, "Alberta's *Brokeback Mountain*").[4]

Another facet of the campaign is that Travel Alberta must constantly remind anyone who will listen that Alberta is the true, real-life, indexical location of *Brokeback*, and not Wyoming, which is simply the role it is playing. (This masquerade was apparently of great concern to Lee, who initially wanted the same authentic landscapes described in Proulx's story [A. Davis].) Perhaps self-conscious of having to perform the "real" American West south of the border—the only one, statistically, to have much of an international presence in the cinematic imaginary—Travel Alberta reasserts its own geographic authenticity by jettisoning the gay ranch hands, still tainted by the suspect alienness of queerness no matter how intensely grounded they are in the West. Playing the role of the American West meshes nicely with the Canadian province's abysmal support for queer rights; one wouldn't want to give the impression to tourists looking for Wyoming that they were actually setting foot in a nation that was fourth in the world to extend marriage rights to queer people and boasts extensive antidiscrimination provisions to protect them. The province's masquerade was so successful that the U.S. state's tourism industry has been significantly boosted by Alberta's stellar performance.[5] This double mimicry was prominent enough to be noticed by Edwards, writing on the Urban Cowboy stunt: "Just as the Alberta outdoors masqueraded itself as Wyoming in the movie *Brokeback Mountain*, star-hopefuls from the United States could make up 20 of the 30 members of the provincially funded posse that will quiz Manhattanites about their knowledge of Alberta-cowboy culture" ("Alberta Rides").

A small article in the queer biweekly *Xtra!* titled "No Gay Cowboys Here" put the question of Travel Alberta's support for a queer film directly to the agency: "But while Travel Alberta spokesperson Noelle Auni is quick [to] claim Alberta's role in *Brokeback Mountain* ('We see the star of *Brokeback* as the senery [*sic*]') she stresses that that's where the connection ends. 'It was based around cowboys. Nothing more'" (19). In a similar comment given to the CBC, Auni specifies that it is the "magnificent unspoiled scenery" that is the "major star" ("Cowboys Promote"). Employing the same rhetoric in a report on the reactions to *Brokeback*'s underwhelming showing at the Oscars, Tom Cox of Alberta Film Entertainment (a coexecutive producer of the film) said, "It's also disappointing that it didn't take the cinematography award, there are so many beautiful shots and exteriors that Alberta became a character in this movie that deserved an award for her own landscape" ("Alta. Film"). (Also note how Cox casts the landscape as female, as if to reinsert a leading lady into the proceedings, detracting attention from the lead couple—too male by half.)

Without getting too melodramatic, readers can interpret these statements as evidence of a kind of colonization of queer bodies and queer space by the tourism industry. What is so ironic is how this phenomenon works in the context of the film's iconography of queer and straight space, which was provocatively outlined by Stephen Hunter, arguing that Lee constructs heterosexual space as grim, stifling, dysfunctional, and unpalatable by making "imagery of family and hearth . . . expressions of the impoverishment of the heterosexual family lifestyle." He contrasts this with the representation of Ennis and Jack's relationship, symbolized by a rushing, life-giving river: "Homosexuality in *Brokeback Mountain* is always associated with a river: It's a great torrent of nature, which cannot be controlled and which provides sustenance, nurture, satisfaction, joy." The closet—located as it is within the stifling nuclear family home and the tightly knit community—is contrasted sharply with the wide open, eternal, tolerant landscape.[6] And think of the sharp contrast between the prelapsarian beauty and freedom of the mountain and "being stuck" in the harsh wind and decrepit streets of the flat and feeble Signal, especially when the men come down from Brokeback and cannot touch each other anymore, with their aloof good-bye proving anguishing enough to make Ennis retch. This is especially evident in the juxtaposition of the postcard of the blissful mountain—now only accessible through this cheap memento—that a grieving Ennis fixes to his trailer with the barren and brutal life of deprivation he leads. As J. Hoberman concludes his review in *The Village Voice*: "The closet has never seemed more cruelly constricting than in comparison to the wide open spaces of what Americans are pleased to call 'God's country'" (48).

This is arguably what gets conservative pundits so riled up about the film: queer love and sex are deeply rooted in the land and in traditional rural life. In *Brokeback* the queers penetrate the heartland by penetrating in the heartland. *World Net Daily* editor David Kupelian's accusation that *Brokeback* raped the Marlboro Man and *Renew America* writer Andrew Longman's suggestion that homosexualizing an icon of American heroism in times of war is tantamount to treason were therefore deliciously spot on (qtd. in Hune-Brown D1). The threat cannot be contained through recourse to myths of queerness being solely an urban and thus an effete, intellectual, and culturally sophisticated phenomenon because here all traces of civilization are what keep their raw lust—freely expressible only in the isolation of nature—in check. Critic Peter Bradshaw states, "[When they have sex it] is a glorious, revelatory experience, and safe from society's disapproval on that remote Arcadian spot they are at one with their own natures and with nature itself" (7). Their unforgiving shepherding work on the mountain is certainly not utopian, but the glory of the landscape and the love and lust that it fosters transcend the horrors of backbreaking labor and deprivation. (The film's deeply romantic, instantly recognizable score takes the edge off the harsh conditions of life on the mountain, hardships that contribute greatly to crafting the image of real American men.) In *Brokeback*, the landscape is a safe haven when there is no one around, but when other humans are present—as represented through Aguirre's invasive, surveying binoculars (which we look through ourselves)—they can turn the landscape murderous. In the *New York Times* piece on real Wyoming gay ranchers, writer Guy Trebay states, "Just as chilling [as the gay-bashings in the film], perhaps, is the emotional wreckage left littering the majestic landscape, hulks of lives ruptured by intolerance and misunderstanding left rusting at the end of dirt roads" (6).[7] Perhaps this is what makes the erasure of homosexuality from the Travel Alberta campaign seem so violent: Ennis and Jack are wrenched out of their environment, pulled up by the roots to reestablish the heterosexuality and normativity of a culturally untainted wilderness that the film shows has never existed. This is why the traumatic primal scene from Ennis's childhood—witnessing the corpse of a gay man who had been genitally mutilated and left as a monument to establish what is and is not permitted in the West—is so important. It establishes that Ennis and Jack are part of a history and are not an anomaly and that not only is the West a queer space but it has been so for generations, kept concealed through violence. Lending its name to the film's discrete title, a symbol for paradise lost, Brokeback is in fact not real, but a fictional mountain—a place that Travel Alberta can never really take anyone to. This truth is echoed in a very powerful moment in the film where Lureen tells Ennis that, knowing Jack, she imagined Brokeback Mountain "might be some pretend place where the bluebirds sing and there's a whisky spring." Ultimately fanciful Jack, living in a fantasy world where two men could make a life together, is killed for his daring to dream, and Ennis must suffer on in purgatory, alone and forever regretting his inability to do anything more than "stand it."

While one tactic of the Christian conservative response to the film has been to decry its perversion of the iconic cowboy and the West, another has been simply to deny the existence of Wyoming men who have sex with Wyoming men. Matt Drudge famously trotted out an anonymous "playwright and lifelong Wyomingite" who claimed that gay cowboys do not exist in Wyoming: "Don't try and take what we had, which was wonderful—the cowboys that settled the state and made it what it was—don't ruin that image. . . . There's nothing better than plain old cowboys and the plain old history without embellishing it to suit everyone." Travel Alberta's campaign unfortunately plays right into this heterosexist-to-the-core proposition. While the film is very much about how queerness has always existed and will always exist in the rural West, Travel Alberta erases that reality and misrepresents the film. The irony lies in the fact that no matter how deeply interwoven homosexuality is with the authenticity of nature and poor, western life in the film, the queerness can still be evacuated by Conservative forces who are unprepared to deal with the possibility of a queer rural space. Claiming that the real star is the scenery manages to block out the film's narrative, characters, and themes to draw attention to its location and setting. Here gay sex and gay relationships—including, metaphorically, the validity of same-sex marriage rights—are utterly eclipsed by the campaign's focus on the pristine scenery that forms the backdrop to Jack and Ennis's now-invisible couplings. Without going too far, one could claim that, faced with a story that detheatricalizes and authenticates queerness in the West, Travel Alberta is seeking recourse in the most basic and elemental signpost for cinematic authenticity imaginable: the indexical image. The landscape will endure far longer than any queer film and their Hollywood North camera crews; for Travel Alberta the mountains are real; the river is real; the fields are real; even the bars, laundromats, ramshackle houses, and animals are real, but the actors and their characters, their fiction and even their Brokeback, are not. This erasure is especially regrettable considering that it runs counter to Alberta's cinematic cash cow's impassioned examination of the traumatic dimensions of such closeting and secrecy.

Notes

1. This headline was abbreviated to "'Brokeback' Opens Up Alberta" when the site was updated on March 6, 2006; see http://www1.travelalberta.com/canada/en/.

2. While western Canada and the western United States are very different locations, they share in a popularized iconography of "The West" that glosses over regional differences. When I refer to "The West" it is to this construct, heavily molded by cultural representation and tourism.

3. In his article on the anti-Christian bent of many Westerns, Nick Hune-Brown quotes Peter A. French's *Cowboy Metaphysics: Ethics and Death in Westerns* to show how Christian tenets such as charity and mercy were ironically constructed as weakness in an eerily similar way to how homosexuality is now: "In most Westerns, the Judeo-Christian conceptions on which much of our traditional ethical understandings are based are portrayed as impotent, useless, something belonging 'back East'" (D4).

4. An ad selling Alberta as a filming location by the Alberta Film Commission—which has also been pushing its role in *Brokeback* far and wide—similarly boasts the slogan, "Alberta: Unparalleled Diversity," while the front page of its Web site prominently featured the *Brokeback* poster in 2006 (www.albertafilm.ca).

5. Shooting in Alberta as opposed to Wyoming was, unsurprisingly, purely a business decision. Alberta has a far more developed film and TV industry than Wyoming, the least populous state in the union, and the government

of Alberta offers a significant rebate (at the time, up to $750,000) to productions within the province. Budgeted at about $14 million, the film was shot in summer 2004 (Dinoff 28). An account of *Brokeback*'s filming in Calgary scene magazine *Avenue* by Anthony A. Davis—clearly uncomfortable with the queer content himself—suggests the shoot was not immune to good-natured homophobia: "Jokes helped grease the wheels for those who found the storyline unpalatable; crew could share gay jokes on set and Lee wouldn't lynch them for it. He was known to crack a few himself, says [head wrangler T. J.] Bews" (74).

6. Manohla Dargis points out that this idyll not only separates the characters from law and society, but "most radically, the yoke of identity. On Brokeback, the two men are neither straight nor gay, much less queer; they are lovers, which probably accounts for the category confusion that has greeted the film." She goes on to suggest that they queer the iconic construct of the cowboy that is taken so literally by their homophobic compatriots: "Jack and Ennis cling to the myth of the cowboy because it offers a freedom that only really exists when they cling to each other, a freedom that remains contingent even now" ("Masculinity").

7. In his first paragraph, Trebay connects the nuclear missile silos hidden away throughout Wyoming with the explosive inner lives led by its residents: "Wyoming's wide-open spaces [have] space enough to conceal wide-open secrets, and good reasons to do so."

Part 5 } Scenes of Work and Experience in the Rural West

19 } Real Gay Cowboys and *Brokeback Mountain*

PATRICIA NELL WARREN

As *Brokeback Mountain* hit mainstream movie theaters in early 2006, the cable channel TLC launched a series about rodeo. *Beyond the Bull* profiles world champion bull riders as regular guys who are belt-buckle deep in wives, kids, girlfriends, and groupies. Was this a heterosexist propaganda ploy timed to counter the hit movie's gay cowboys, especially twenty-year-old Jack Twist, the gay rodeo rider played by Jake Gyllenhaal?

Yup, it's time to talk about rodeo and the gay people in it.

Rodeo is one of our most American sports, with roots as deep as baseball's. As an action-packed extreme sport that lends itself to TV showcasing, rodeo now gets routine coverage on ESPN. The sport reached exhibition status at the Salt Lake City Winter Olympics. Rodeo even has its own TV reality show—"Cowboy U" on CMT.

Riding high, *Brokeback Mountain* became an icon of culture overnight. The film also kicked up a political dust storm. After all, right-wingers view the cowpoke as a core symbol who embodies the purest in family values. One Christian blogger screamed, "Now they're out to destroy the American legend of the cowboy. God help us, and John Wayne forgive us!" In Congress, senators from sagebrush states are pushing a resolution declaring July 22 as "National Day of the American Cowboy."

Meanwhile, on the rodeo scene, some contestants assure the media that, in all their years around the arenas, they never met a real-life Jack Twist.

I have to smile at all this denial. I grew up on a historical Montana cattle ranch that was steeped in cowboy tradition. Back through U.S. history, few occupations were more conducive to secret man-to-man love than cowboying. Indeed, frontier men may have gravitated to this job so they could enjoy the company of other males.

If gay cowboys have never been visible in professional rodeo, it's because the sport has gone so conservative that it makes the NFL look more liberal than the ACLU. Going by what we know of other sports, there must be a few closet cases on the lists of world champions for the Rodeo Cowboys Association (RCA) and Professional Bull Riders (PBR). But so far none has dared to come out.

So instead I will profile a few rank-and-file contestants who pioneered simply by being there—by competing in mainstream rodeo when they were young and closeted. Their stories are important because they give us some texture of an ongoing gay presence in the sport. Important profiles also come from the gay rodeo circuit, which is not affiliated with PBR or RCA.

Dirty Dangerous Work

Rodeo is said to be "the only sport that grew out of an industry"—meaning the vast nineteenth-century livestock business that flourished west of the Mississippi, from Mexico north to Canada. To find the roots of gay rodeo riders—and gay rodeo itself—we have to dig in this soil of the Old West.

Already in colonial times, cattle and herders dotted the English-speaking East Coast and the Spanish-speaking Southwest. But after the Civil War (1861–65), with native tribes being slaughtered or swept onto reservations, millions of square miles of grassland in the western interior were suddenly open to grazing. The livestock industry exploded. By the 1880s there were millions of cattle on the prairies and plains. For a couple of decades, my family's ranch, the CK, was one of the big shippers—we averaged fifteen thousand steers to the Chicago stockyards every year. Beef was suddenly abundant and cheap, and Americans rushed to eat it.

To handle these millions of cattle, the cowboy proliferated too. People also called him a cattleboy, cowpuncher, cowpoke, drover, wrangler, vaquero, buckaroo, ranahan, rannie, and waddie. He was a skilled working stiff—the horseback equivalent of an autoworker or coal miner. Ethni-cally he might be white, American Indian, Mexican mestizo, Hispanic, Creole, African, Canadian Metis—or mixtures of these. "Boy" referred to his menial status, whereas the word "cowman" designated a rancher.

Cowboys did all the dirty dangerous work that made millionaires of cattle kings like my great-grandfather Conrad Kohrs. And they did it at a time when there were no unions, workers' comp, industrial safety regulations, pension plans, or health insurance. Since there was also no mandatory retirement age, a working cowboy might be seventy. An outfit's youngest rannie—usually called "the Kid"—might be fifteen or sixteen, since there were no child-labor laws.

Often a cowboy had a "past"—army deserter, former slave, criminal on the run from the law in another state. So he might introduce himself simply as Arizona Bill or Dutch Joe. Nobody asked questions. There were no Social Security numbers to track you with. All that mattered was whether you could be trusted with a horse and a lariat.

A rank-and-file cowpuncher was usually poor—he owned his clothes, horse gear, rope, and bedroll, maybe a harmonica or Colt .45. He did have pride in his person—clothes, boots, and gear were good quality. His hat varied in shape—a wide Spanish brim in sun-fried Texas, a nar-row brim on the windy northern plains. But the horses he rode usually belonged to the boss. Well into the twentieth century, his wage was forty dollars a month and board—less if he was black or Mexican.

Some cowboys banked their wages for decades, aiming to home-stead somewhere and live out the sunset years in comfort. But many a cattleboy blew his pay in the nearest honkytonk—alcohol and gambling addictions were common. He might have chronic health problems—bronchitis and rheumatism from sleeping on the ground in cold rainy weather—not to mention old aches and pains from wrecks with horses. When he got too old or broken-down to work, he sometimes wound up homeless. Suicide was not unknown among ailing elderly cowboys who didn't want to wind up in a bed at the county poorhouse. Because there was no welfare or Medicare, many ranches (including ours) took care of indigent ex-employees till they died.

One has to ask how this hard and thankless life ever got so romanti-cized. In the 1800s novelists like James Fenimore Cooper were already gilding the frontier lily. But the big romantic job started after 1900, when the art of western artists Charles M. Russell and Frederic Remington were popularized on calendars sold across America. That painted figure of the lone cowboy silhouetted against the western sky had a deep appeal and a nostalgia value as the Old West disappeared. Cowboys were also mythicized in bestselling pulp novels cranked out by Zane Grey, Max Brand, and others.

But it was Hollywood who recast the hard-drinking, rough-living nineteenth-century hired hand as a twentieth-century hero. Played by John Wayne, Gary Cooper, Ronald Reagan, Roy Rogers, and others, the cowboy became a symbol of "manly clean living" and "family values." Surely his canonization as a saint is one of the world-champion feats of public relations—culminating in the title of "Cowboy President" for Ronald Reagan. One prominent American who never bought the cowboy myth was country singer Willie Nelson. His "Mammas, Don't Let Your Babies Grow Up to Be Cowboys" told how cowboys were viewed as trash by many "nice" people in town.

Yet despite the cowboy's iffy social status, he was a proud, prickly, independent, tough-minded man. He knew how to defend his dignity. The boss couldn't run a cow business without a skilled labor force, so he learned to handle "the boys" with care.

Cowboys also knew how to make their stark lives bearable—even fun and entertaining at times. After supper, in the bunkhouse, the boys might swap yarns, play cards or dice, and howl with laughter as they played practical jokes on one another. Even on roundup, with all hands tired and busy, there might be a little storytelling at the campfire. During the daylight hours, the boys could find a few minutes for spontaneous sport—like roping a wolf for the hell of it. As Annie Proulx said, "When you live a long way out, you make your own fun" (*Close Range* 250). But the cowboy's favorite sport was the hard-core occupational variety. Like bronc riding on a cold morning.

Hang and Rattle

An ungentled horse was called a bronc (from Spanish *bronco*, meaning wild). On most ranches horses weren't ridden till they were full-grown at five to six years old. The first few rides were an athletic contest—a man matching his wits and reflexes against the wits and reflexes of a thousand-pound horse.

You ran one of those wild things into a corral. You roped him, hobbled his feet so he couldn't kick you in the nuts, and slapped a saddle on his quivering back. Then you took a deep breath, climbed on, and yanked the hobble-rope loose. Naturally the horse thought you were a mountain lion on his back. So he frantically tried to unload you in any way he could think of. Cowboys had colorful names for these moves—hogging, sunfishing, highrolling, frogwalking, corkscrewing. The horse might slam you against the corral fence, even throw himself backward to try and mash you.

Who would win—man or animal? If you "hung and rattled" (stayed on), the horse tired of the fight—and finally figured out that you were harmless. From then on, he was a dependable mount.

Sometimes the horse won and stayed an incorrigible bucker. Every big outfit had one or two of these hellions, which the boss kept around for entertainment and sporting value. Not every cowboy could ride these bad ones. It took a real buckaroo (from Spanish *vaquero*) to be a "bronc stomper." He didn't think of himself as an athlete, but he was—he had a lean build that melded core strength with lightning reflexes, instinctive timing, and balance. The combination helped him to stay ahead of a bronc's violent and unpredictable movements.

After the Civil War, these little ranch competitions began to be organized into public sporting events called "stampedes" or "round-ups." Eventually the new sport adopted the Spanish word for roundup—*rodeo*.

In 1885 Buffalo Bill Cody's Wild West Show put bucking and roping contests on the program, along with the choreographed Indian fights and stagecoach holdups. When Wild West shows disappeared in the early 1900s, rodeo stayed. Now the public was hungry for more variety, so new events like steer wrestling and wild cow milking were invented.

By World War I many a western community was building its facility for an annual rodeo—equivalent to the baseball stadiums and football fields that dotted the Midwest and East. Around the arena was a high fence strong enough to withstand direct hits by broncs. Behind the arena, corrals held the bucking and roping stock. Facing the grandstand was the dramatic row of side-release chutes for the bucking events.

Rodeo Gets Creative

Through the early 1900s rodeo mostly stuck to the traditional work-based events—roping and bronc riding. You paid an entry fee for each event. Everybody's fees went into a prize-money pot, sometimes with added money from the rodeo committee. You could win the "day money" for the best performance on that day's go-round in your event. Or you could win "best all around champion" if you swept the go-rounds in several events. In addition to the prize money—twenty-five or thirty bucks in those days—you got a trophy belt buckle with an inscription on it.

Rules were written. Timekeeping was introduced for the roping events—the fastest roper won. For bronc events, you had to stay on the horse for eight seconds. The judges scored how well you rode and how well the horse bucked.

But around 1920 one new event made rodeo history. This was Jack Twist's specialty—Brahma bull riding.

Across the southern United States, those hump-necked, droopy-eared Brahma cattle had been imported from India. They tolerate a hot climate so Southern cowmen had been using them for crossbreeding. Inevitably some creative promoter put a cowboy on a droop-ear's back and discovered that Brahmas and Brahma crossbreds were astoundingly athletic. A bull might weigh a ton, but he could jump the arena fence like a deer if it suited him. Limber as a gymnast, he could unleash high kicks, vertical leaps, belly rolls, dizzying spins, neck-snapping feints, and turns.

The cowboy had to ride him bareback, with one gloved hand wrapped tightly into a rawhide rope cinched around the bull's midsection. The rope was rosined to help his grip. The eight-second rule applied, along with judges' scores.

Bulls could be more dangerous than broncs. Once a bull threw you, he might go after you on the ground with those horns of his. Cowboys called this type a "headhunter." Worse—if your hand got hung up in that rope when you bucked off, the bull kept spinning and sunfishing with you attached. So you were flung around by one arm like a rag doll, possibly even trampled horribly, before you could be freed.

Introduced at the Fort Worth rodeo in 1920, bucking bulls quickly became the climax event of every rodeo—and the apex of machismo in the sport.

A rodeo producer now had to contract for a whole string of "rough stock" that would buck reliably well. Contestants drew their rides out of a hat, so each one had to get a fair shot at a money ride. This created a new business—rodeo stock contractor—and a steady market for misfit horses and bulls with an attitude about humans on their backs.

The most unrideable animals became celebrities. They were worth a lot of money and lived long lives with good veterinary care. Some bulls know their jobs so well that they are actually quite gentle, except for that eight seconds in the arena, when they turn into a hoofed hurricane. The minute the whistle blows or the rider is off their back, they trot calmly to the gate. Cowboys call them "union bulls."

Serious injuries and deaths did happen to rodeo stock. Humane societies complained about rodeo, so the sport finally got more proactive on animal welfare.

Rodeo was hard on humans too—not just injuries, but crooked judges who took payola, and crooked promoters who embezzled prize money. Blacks and American Indians were often denied entry. Cowboy pride ensured that these abuses wouldn't be tolerated. So in the 1930s outraged contestants formed a grassroots union that would launch athlete activism in the sport. Eventually the Rodeo Cowboys Association (RCA) took control of world-championship competition and enforced fairness to everybody (except to women, who were barred from RCA competition in the 1930s).

For the world champions, those gold or silver belt buckles—often designed by leading western artists—were equal to Olympic medals.

Around 1960, when young Jack Twist came along, he would have been a rank-and-file member of RCA, carrying his sexual secret unnoticed in and out of the arenas. The movie actually romanticized Jack—he was no Hollywood cutie like Gyllenhaal. In the original story, Proulx describes him: "Jack seemed fair enough with his curly hair and quick laugh, but for a small man he carried some weight in the haunch and his smile disclosed buck teeth."

Gay Cowboys—Yes or No?

Closet love between cowboys grew out of the loneliness and hardship in that job.

In the 1800s a fall roundup or an eight-hundred-mile trail drive meant being away from civilization for weeks or months. Even for heterosexual cowboys, female companionship was scarce. Indeed, in some areas women were still in such short supply that it was acceptable for cowboys, miners, and so on to dance together at honkytonks. Ranchers didn't want the boys fighting over women, so most had no women employees. You had to wait till Saturday night, or the end of the season, to visit the whorehouse in town. But town sex could also give you syphilis and gonorrhea—not curable in those dark days before penicillin. Like men in the army or on ships at sea, even the hetero hands may have turned to each other for sexual relief when the boss wasn't looking.

Across the northern United States the winters were long and harsh, so employment lasted only from May to October. Fall roundup was the finale of the work season. In the early 1900s when my family's ranch still had a big operation in eastern Montana with seventy-five thousand cattle ranging on free grass, our roundup might need fifty men and five hundred horses. After we got maybe fifteen thousand steers loaded on trains and shipped to the Chicago stockyards, we paid off most of the boys, keeping a skeleton crew through winter. The rest had to find a warm burrow somewhere till spring.

These circumstances tended to discourage most cowboys from marrying and settling down. Most were itinerant bachelors, "saddle bums" who drifted from ranch to ranch. According to Montana artist Charlie Russell, who cowboyed in the late 1800s, "Cowpunchers were careless, homeless, hard-drinking men" (Brown and Felton 129). Only in the Spanish-speaking southern United States did a few big outfits encourage their vaqueros to have families and live on the ranch year-round.

Most ranches had a bunkhouse where the boys slept and ate and hung out together. On our ranch the 1880s bunkhouse still stands—a long log building, with woodshed, washroom, kitchen, dining room, and dormitory room with narrow iron beds. When I was a kid in the 1940s, it was still operating in the old-time way. The place was snug but spartan, heated by wood stoves, with a table and chairs for card games.

A vintage AM radio provided news and music. Chaps and other gear hung from hooks along the log wall. Each man kept the rest of his few possessions in a box under his bed. The latrine was outside, fifty feet away—a long walk on a cold night.

To combat the loneliness of this life, male-male friendships sprang up like the spring grass. Even heterosexual bonding tended to be strong. In frontier times western men used the word "partner" for these bonds. Two single males would pair up, living in close association, sharing everything, maybe starting a business together.

There was also an economic reason for partnership: the low pay. In those days, society expected a man to own a house and prove his ability to support a family *before* he got married. But a dirt-poor cowboy could hardly afford to feed a wife and kids on forty dollars a month. As one old cowboy song put it:

When all your bills are settled,
There's nothing left for beer. (Targ 578)

Typically, a pair of men operated on the old adage that "two can live cheaper than one." They'd work the ranches for years, getting themselves hired as a team. They'd save to file on a homestead or buy a little ranch, own it as joint tenants, and maintain visibly separate sleeping quarters. Often a "Kid" paired up with an older guy so he could learn the ropes with an expert.

Traditional cowboy songs often revealed deep grief over the death of a partner in a shooting or roundup accident. In one old song, "Utah Carroll":

In the land of Mexico in the place from whence I came,
In silence sleeps my partner in a grave without a name.
We rode the trail together and worked cows side by side,
Oh, I loved him like a brother, and I wept when Utah died.

You don't have to have a PhD in sociology to realize that some of these rawhide partnerships extended into discreet sexual intimacy.

I've come to think that gay cowboy love was silently accepted by many livestock owners as an unavoidable result of the circumstances. They let some of the boys have it because it made the loneliness and hardship bearable—as long as two partners were discreet and did their jobs. Ranchers who treated men well got their pick of the best men and that could include two buckaroos who were an item. The policy of not asking questions was conveniently invoked here.

But as the West modernized, as it filled up with towns and churches, this old-time tolerance slowly vanished. After 1900 the fencing of public lands made it impossible to swing the big herds. Ranches downsized and switched to more intensive methods of producing beef. Our own ranch dropped from fifty thousand deeded acres and 2 million acres of leased grazing in 1900, to just six thousand deeded acres by 1940. Agriculture was mechanizing by then—fewer horses and men were needed.

During World War II the trend accelerated. Many a young puncher who was drafted into the armed forces and drove a tank or jeep across Europe came home to find that the newest farm machine had put him out of a job. By 1950 the bunkhouses were closing everywhere. At the ck we closed ours in 1958. For fall roundup, all we needed now was three to four hands. As a teen, I always helped my dad, my brother, and the foreman move the cow herd between summer range and the home ranch.

When the livestock industry stopped being so dependent on that big workforce, I think that many westerners started to ask nosy questions about that traditional buckaroo bachelorhood. A cowboy was now expected to marry.

Rodeo Heterosexism

It's no coincidence that rodeo went big time and commercial during the same postwar period. As ranch jobs vanished, many cowboys drifted to rodeo—it was one of the few niches left in America where cowboys could still earn with their skills.

You could get into rodeo for just a few bucks. To rope or wrestle steers, you didn't have to own a horse. You could buy rides on somebody else's horse. To ride bareback broncs or bulls, all you needed was your riggin' and a gunny sack to tote it in. You didn't even need a new wardrobe.

The plain workday chaps, the conservative white or Pendleton cowboy shirt, were fine for the arena, not to mention the resoled Justin boots, and last year's "beaver" Stetson. A rodeo cowboy might be broke, but he still wore good clothes to work.

The changing attitude toward cowboy relationships must have hit hard in rodeo. Contestants suddenly found their private lives under the harsh floodlights of gossip, kidding, and social scrutiny. Indeed, I think that the raw heterosexism of today's rodeo, with its groupies, flag-waving and pumped-up parading of family men, is the sport's effort to leave behind that time when a cowboy might be more interested in his "pard" than the cute little gal in town.

The "Brokeback" story of Jack Twist and Ennis del Mar fits this historical trend like a horseshoe fits a hoof. By 1963 the year that the story starts, real cowboy jobs on cattle ranches were so scarce that Jack and Ennis wound up herding sheep. Ennis not only felt compelled to deny his love for Jack—he also felt he had to prove his masculinity by getting married. The story unfolds Ennis's grim struggle to support a family on the few rural jobs available in Wyoming.

"I'm nothin'. I'm nowhere," Ennis tells Jack.

Jack had an option that Ennis didn't. He had rodeo. Most important, Jack had social opportunities on the rodeo scene. His curly hair and quick smile were good enough to snag a rodeo queen from a well-to-do Texas family. So Jack moved up the social ladder a little. Now he had the money to travel—not only to rodeos but to Mexico for gay sex. But he was ready to give up all this comfort if only Ennis would go live with him on their own little place.

But Ennis knew this old-time strategy for closet "partners" was now risky. So he said no.

Jack Twist "at Work"

As the sport went heavily professional, the fifties and sixties would be called the Golden Age of Rodeo. In 1963 a real-life Jack waiting his turn at the bucking chutes would have rubbed shoulders with world champions like Larry Mahan, Gene Rambo, Casey Tibbs.

Jack Twist would have been just a face lost in that celebrity crowd. Proulx writes, "He was infatuated with the rodeo life and fastened his belt with a minor bull-riding buckle, but his boots were worn to the quick, holes beyond repair." So Jack often finished out of the money. One year he got three thousand dollars, along with a list of sprains and broken bones that would have crippled a city dude.

We can imagine Jack in the chute, getting settled on the back of that hot restless bull. He's drawn a good bucker, so maybe he can make a money ride. But this bull has horns—and he's known as a headhunter. Jack wraps and rewraps that nine-braid rawhide rope around his gloved hand till the "suicide wrap" is just right. But at that moment, he sure as hell is not thinking about Ennis's body. He tries to clear his mind for those eight endless seconds ahead—what moves the bull might make, how to stay with him.

As Jack pulls his hat down tight with his free hand, his heart is pumping and his mouth is dry.

The chute gate swings open. Five seconds into the ride, the bull snakes into a reverse spin, then a high roll. Ten feet in the air, Jack and bull part company. His hat comes off. He manages to jerk his hand out of the "suicide wrap" just in time. The bull is big, so it's a long way to the ground. Jack hits hard, breath slammed out of him. Then, instinctively, he sucks in his breath and scrambles up because, out of the corner of his eye, he has glimpsed the bull veering around and charging at him.

Jack races for the arena fence with the bull's horns bumping his hip pockets. Just before the bull gives him an uninvited prostate examination, Jack climbs the arena fence like a scared cat, just in time to hear the announcer say, "And it's a goose egg [zero] for Twist."

As the bull trots off to the pen, he steps on Jack's hat with a manure-plastered hoof. Another hard day at the office.

Rainbow Rodeos

In 1983 Jack's story ends with a beating by gay bashers and his death at the age of forty-three. By that time a real-life Jack Twist could have been out of the closet and competing at gay rodeos.

The first gay rodeo in history had been held in Nevada in 1976. Reno events producer Phil Ragsdale, who was also emperor of the Imperial Court, had come up with the idea of an amateur gay rodeo as a fundraiser for the Muscular Dystrophy Association. Local homophobia meant that Ragsdale had a time hiring a stock contractor and a venue. But finally the event came off at the Washoe County Fairgrounds on October 2. The court raised thousands of dollars for charity.

Today, contrary to what some right-wingers say, gay cowboys who competed in mainstream rodeo aren't hard to find. I've been running into them for years as I travel the United States on a book tour.

Texas produces a good crop of gay cowboys. Example: my good friend Don, who is a financial consultant in Los Angeles today. Don is thirty-nine, a handsome wiry blond guy with the curly hair of a Jack Twist—but not the buck teeth. Don's teeth are picture perfect, and he shows them in a slow cowboy grin as he tells his story.

Born in 1967 on a ranch near Dallas, Don rodeoed seriously during his sophomore and junior years in high school, when he was fifteen and sixteen, and collected his share of trophies and belt buckles.

"Rodeo is part of the culture in Texas," he told me. "It's a letter sport in high school. You go out for rodeo like you go out for football. It's one of those things you do to prove your manhood the Texas way. I was an all-around guy—calf roping, bareback bronc, saddle bronc, and bull riding. Saddle bronc was the scariest, in my opinion. A horse is bigger than a bull and it's a lot farther to the ground. But the bulls could be bad. I always prayed to draw a bull with no horns.

"My older brother was a professional bull rider, so I would sneak away with him on weekends and go to all the big rodeos across Texas. I loved everything about rodeo—including the partying, everybody drunk and getting into fistfights. I'd come home with black eyes and a split lip. My dad knew what I was up to, but he'd say, 'Just tell your mother you fell off your horse.' I wasn't out yet, of course, but I had a kinda boyfriend through high school."

Don aimed to follow in his brother's footsteps—he had to be eighteen to turn professional. But during his junior year, he injured his back playing football. That finished rodeo as his number one career choice. Business was number two. When he graduated from business school at age twenty-two and got ready to move to LA, Don finally came out to his parents. They took it in stride. Don relates, "All my dad said was, 'Yeah, we used to have guys like you around. They were called confirmed bachelors.'"

Another gay son of Texas I met was an elderly Hispanic gentleman. I was speaking to an activist group in El Paso, and Ignacio came up afterward with his straw cowboy hat in his hand and introduced himself. He was silver-haired, still fit and spry, with that sun-fried face and neck that tells you he spent his life outdoors. Conservative cowboy shirt, silver belt buckle won at a rodeo, and expensive well-worn boots completed the picture. We spoke Spanish and Ignacio told me his story. For many years he knew he was gay. But he got married, conforming to the strict Catholic moral code that has ruled the old Southwest families of Spanish descent since colonial times.

"Finally," he said, "I got up the courage to come out to *mi familia*, including"—he grinned proudly—"all my grandchildren."

Around 1996, when I got acquainted with the gay rodeo circuit, it was amazing to see how our creative version of this sport had grown. Inspired by Ragsdale's event, LGBT rodeo producers had emerged in other states. Among them: Wayne Jakino and John King of Colorado, Linn Copeland of Kansas, Al Bell of California, Terry Clark of Texas. Their achievements can remind us that "gay pioneers in sports" are not always the athletes. Visionary producers like these women and men were the ones who sparked the formation of local rodeo associations across the country. They hooked up the LGBT rodeo movement with country-western gay bars, clogging and square-dance groups, equestrian centers, and so on. In short, they created the package that is familiar to gay rodeo fans today.

As gay rodeo grew, Reno remained a focus, with the International Gay Rodeo Association's National Finals held there. Today in 2006 its calendar lists rodeos in twenty-five U.S. and Canadian cities. The old Imperial Court connection is still strong. No gay rodeo is complete without high camp—meaning drag rodeo queens and truckloads of sequins! IGRA also pulls major sponsors like Anheuser-Busch and American Airlines.

Unlike pro rodeo, the rainbow circuit has stayed amateur by choice, so it is open to community participation. The old formula is pretty much the same: the core events, the announcer with his drawly patter, the colorful grand entry, the flags carried by galloping riders—Old Glory and Old Rainbow fluttering side by side. But the gender bars have tumbled here. Women get to ride broncs and bulls, while men get to compete in barrel racing, traditionally a female event. Last but not least, LGBT creative minds have created new events for tenderfoots—like "goat dressing," where you wrassle a pair of men's boxer shorts onto a goat.

Today few LGBT contestants work both circuits—after all, entering a pro rodeo means going back in the closet for a few days. Most of our champions have made their names exclusively in gay rodeo.

Notable example: Greg Olsen, the winningest cowboy in IGRA history so far. As a ranch kid born in Nebraska in 1960, Greg knew he was "different" when he was young. In high school he was out to a few gay friends, with whom he secretly went clubbing in the nearest big cities. Often he went to pro rodeos with his family but felt turned off by the heavy heterosexist atmosphere around the arenas.

Then in 1986, when he was twenty-six and moved to Phoenix, Greg heard about the Arizona Gay Rodeo Association's first regional rodeo. On an impulse he decided to enter. Once he caught the fever, there was no stopping him. He went on to be seven times IGRA All-Around Champion Cowboy. In fact, his success stirred up criticism that gay rodeo was getting "too professional."

Greg was a fashion rebel in his polka-dot cowboy shirt. To support his arena career, he tended bar in Charlie's, a popular Phoenix country-western bar, and also carried on a successful business as a farrier. His ranch near Phoenix was always crowded with friends and visitors. Even after injuries slowed him down, Greg continued to be a pioneering force in the sport till his untimely death in 1995, at the age of thirty-five.

Rodeo Today

The United States is no longer that beef-eating nation of 1900. Diet-conscious Americans switch to chicken, fish, and soy. So the cattle population has fallen from its record 175 million to just over 100 million. Today 98 percent of U.S. beef reaches the market via an intensive factory-feeding system that requires way less land and less of the traditional skills.

As a reflection of the new agribusiness scene, pro rodeo of 2006 is radically different from those cow-country contests of 1869. Fewer contestants are country kids now—the "urban cowboy" rules. City kids can overcome their fear of animals and learn bull riding in special schools, even college courses. Contestants train hard like any Olympic athlete. The familiar cowboy hat, which offers no protection against being kicked in the face, is giving way to a protective helmet with face mask.

Bull riding has gone so big that it's international, often a stand-alone event. Its association, Professional Bull Riders (PBR), is owned and operated by the ever-prickly contestants. Today's Jack Twist gets on the plane to ride bulls in Brazil and Australia. In his designer duffle bag, the bull rope and rosin are packed with a suit and tie. He has business cards and a Web site, and his bulletproof bull-riding vest is plastered with sponsor logos. Top contestants can win $250,000 a year, with a few individuals topping $1 million.

Despite efforts at safety, there are still catastrophic injuries, even deaths—captured on footage that gets aired on *Real* TV and *Sports Disasters*. The year 1994 was a bad one—five bull riders killed. Because of this, women are still barred from competing in the roughest pro rodeo events.

I asked Don what the attraction is—why any gay or straight rodeo rider would take these risks, when he could wind up not only broke but in a wheelchair.

"For those eight seconds, you're a star," Don replied. "The whole world is looking at you. If you ride the bull, you don't just win—you get the bragging rights."

Whether or not rodeo ever joins the Olympic Games, its future as a mainstream U.S. sport looks secure. Some Americans do complain bitterly that today's professional rodeo is too commercial, too divorced from its roots. But the grassroots rodeo is still out there in many towns, for anybody who wants to find it. The old-time "ranch rodeo" is being revived.

Gay rodeo, too, is as grassroots as it gets. The two-legged athlete out there on the back of the hoofed hurricane may be nonheterosexual, but he or she is still pitting human skills against the skills of a powerful animal athlete. And the old question is still out there to be answered— which of the two will win?

20 } Marx on the Mountain

Pleasure and the Laboring Body

VANESSA OSBORNE

Among the innumerable, predictably homophobic backlashes incited by Ang Lee's film *Brokeback Mountain*, the attack by Christian film critic Ted Baehr of movieguide.org is distinguished by its claim that the film constitutes "neo-marxist propaganda." While I take issue with the designation "propaganda" and acknowledge that Baehr deploys his terms haphazardly, I nonetheless concur that *Brokeback Mountain* is Marxist in its illustration of key conflicts that emerge out of Marxist theory's representation of capitalism. The film frames Ennis del Mar's struggle as a fundamental problem of the repression of the body under capitalism. Early in the film, Ennis, a low-wage seasonal worker, uses his body as an instrument of labor in the service of production. But through his relationship with Jack Twist, a bull rider who chafes at demands on his body and his time, Ennis, in a sense, discovers his body outside of its relationship to his labor. Jack embodies a divergence from productive imperatives because he actively seeks nonproductive bodily pleasure. On Brokeback Mountain, Jack and Ennis engage in a sexual relationship that temporarily frees them from the instrumentalization of the body and contests the mandate for productive labor enforced by a capitalistic society. After Ennis returns from the mountain, the film details his struggle to liberate his body from the confining sites of production and reproduction. Ultimately the film's final image, of the men's work shirts closeted and entwined in an embrace, is a poignant sign of an impossible hope of escaping from the imperatives of his life as a worker.

In the opening scene of *Brokeback Mountain* we witness a commercial transport truck driving along the road in the early morning hours. With its breaks squeaking, it halts to drop its cargo at an intersection in a small rural town. This truck has not stopped to deliver a load of supplies—feed or ranching equipment—yet it deposits something equally integral to a ranching operation. It delivers a worker. Ennis steps out of the cab of the truck, walks to the ranch office, and takes his position, leaning alongside the trailer door. This opening scene introduces the character yet yields very little in the way of characterization. We deduce little more than that Ennis has come to seek employment and that he does not have his own means of transportation. But with his arrival on the commercial transport truck the film subtly analogizes Ennis, the laborer, to the supplies these trucks deliver, the very instruments that enable the productivity of the ranching operation.

Ennis's personal history—he's a young man who was orphaned in his adolescence, with few financial resources and almost no education— reveals his early dependence on bodily labor and physical skills as a means of survival. Heath Ledger's acclaimed performance contributes to our understanding of Ennis as a corporeal instrument of labor. Early in the film he fails to meet the eyes of the other characters, particularly those of authority figures like Joe Aguirre. His downcast gaze communicates an ingrained sense of inferiority and a lack of connection with others. Ennis's avoidance of eye contact also invites others to perceive him as an automaton that lacks the subjectivity and interiority connoted by expressive eyes. He also rarely speaks. When he does speak, his sentences are short and simple. His muddled and often stuttering speech is nearly incomprehensible. In these early scenes, Ennis is fundamentally a corporeal presence, an obedient laboring body, represented as lacking capacity for meaningful self-expression and communication.

Ennis shares the fate of many who must sell their labor in a capitalist economy. Karl Marx's *Capital* offers a critique of the capitalist mode of production that centers on the antagonism between capital and labor and how that conflict results in the exploitation of the laborer's body. Marx analogizes the worker's sale of his labor to a literal alienation of the laborer's fleshly body; with trepidation the worker sells his skin to the capitalist (176). As a result of this alienating exchange, laborers suffer by becoming mere tools in the operations of capitalist production.

Capitalism thus transforms production into strategies of domination that "mutilate the laborer into a fragment of a man, degrade him to the level of an appendage of a machine, destroy every remnant of charm in his work and turn it into a hated toil" (645). The worker invests the better part of his day fusing his body to the machinery of the factory to acquire enough money for his subsistence so he may return the next day to repeat the process.

In the Workplace

When Aguirre dictates the job's terms and duties to Ennis and Jack, the film emphasizes the way he views these men as tools in the service of productive labor. The scene's composition illustrates Ennis's capitulation to this capitalist mandate. After being dropped off, Ennis leans just outside the door of the trailer, waiting silently with downcast eyes. He remains silent and very still until Aguirre arrives. Then he stands upright to follow him into the office. When the door swings shut, Ennis abruptly halts at the closed door. He lingers outside the office door until explicitly commanded to enter by Aguirre, who barks at the men to get their "scrawny asses" in his office. Aguirre's first words to Ennis and Jack objectify them as inadequate, as undernourished beasts of burden. During the moment when the laborers confront their employer, when the men should be empowered to negotiate the terms of their employment, he strips them of autonomy.[1]

Both men listen silently and attentively to the duties and obligations of the job, yet the differing postures of Ennis and Jack indicate a crucial distinction between the two men's dispositions toward their bodies and their employer.[2] Ennis presses his body against the wall with his eyes downcast, his legs together, his elbows compressed at his sides and his hat clutched in both hands on his chest. He constricts his body, making it as small as possible to yield the space and authority to Aguirre and his imposing desk. Ennis reproduces the traditional stance of the supplicant who stands with his head down and hat in hand before a superior, embodying humility and subservience. This early scene shows Ennis's capitulation to the instrumentalization of his body by demonstrating that, even before his official employment begins, Ennis presents himself as a motionless object ready to acquiesce to the demands of his employer. Though described later in the film, Ennis's strategy for coping with difficult situations—"if you can't fix it, you've got to stand it"—also affirms that his primary approach is one of capitulation to seemingly unchangeable forces.

Jack's markedly different stance underscores his defiance of the dictates and obligations placed on his body. While Ennis makes his body small and unstable, Jack appropriates as much space in the cramped room as he reasonably can. Jack's stance embodies stability, defiance, and readiness by replicating the pose of the cowboy gunslinger. Jack stands with his legs apart, his eyes fixed on Aguirre, and his hat in the hand he has placed casually on his hip. Similarly, the traditional gunslinger stands with his legs spread and grasps for the gun at his hip. Though neither Ennis nor Jack speaks while in the office, the scene's composition immediately reveals that, in the face of their employer, one character complies while the other resists. This early scene renders visible the two poles of the conflict that will emerge for Ennis; over the course of the film, Jack's defiance of the instrumentalization of the body and the mandate for productive labor will challenge Ennis's relationship to labor and his body.

Once the men begin their jobs on Brokeback Mountain, Jack frequently voices his opposition to his employer's regulations. He complains about the job's imposition on his free time—having to commute "four hours per day" to eat his meals and "spend half the night checkin' for damn coyotes." When the supply donkeys spill the food the men need for the upcoming week, Jack immediately proposes that they kill one of Aguirre's sheep. Ennis objects to consuming the very sheep they have been employed to protect. These differing responses reveal that Jack's instinct, when facing physical deprivation, is to flout the rules of his employer. Ennis, concerned about breaking the terms of his employment, substitutes a more challenging alternative—tracking and shooting an elk. The contrast in the men's attitude toward Aguirre and his restrictions reoccurs when their sheep mix with a flock of Chilean sheep, and Ennis proposes they "try to get the count right for Aguirre." In response, Jack retorts with an angry "Fuck Aguirre," focusing his frustration at the employer to whom he must answer.

Jack frequently verbalizes his frustration and dissatisfaction with

Aguirre's requirements in terms that describe how the job deprives him of autonomy. His complaints target his lack of control over his own body in response to Aguirre's rules that dictate what he must eat, where he must sleep, and where he must be. He is the first of the two men to protest the dietary limitations; before he rides off to his mountaintop camp, he barks, "No more beans" to Ennis. Though according to Aguirre's employee, it is "too early in the summer to be sick of beans," Jack firmly registers his disdain for their limited choices. He also angrily objects to Aguirre's arrangements regarding where and how he must sleep. Jack argues that Aguirre has "no right making [them] do something against the rules" with the "staying with the sheep no fire thing." Whether we understand this complaint as an objection to the conditions of the job or as a guarded admission that Jack wants to spend the night with Ennis, this statement ultimately represents an opposition to conceiving himself merely as an instrument of labor. In fact, reading his complaint as a hint that Jack wants to stay the night with Ennis identifies a conflict between Aguirre's mandate for productive bodily labor and Jack's competing unproductive, libidinous desire for pleasure.

Jack's resistance to mandatory labor consists of much more than surly complaints about how Aguirre handles his operation. Jack's choice of an unmanageable horse to ride up Brokeback Mountain reveals his resistance to the capitalist's appropriation of his body as a tool for labor. While Ennis warns him against the horse with the "low startle point," Jack ignores his advice, decides to ride the mare up the mountain, and eventually is thrown from his spirited mount. Jack's horse could jeopardize his summer's work by throwing and injuring him. Herding a large flock of slow-moving sheep, Jack has no need for an especially fast or energetic horse. A docile and reliable one would make a much better choice. Instead Jack chooses this high-spirited horse for the love and challenge of riding. While the possibilities for resistance to Aguirre's restrictions of the body and mandate for labor are few, Jack finds a way by engaging in challenging riding, something he enjoys.

At the Rodeo

Jack's self-professed occupation, rodeo bull riding, further demonstrates his resistance to productive labor. Ennis disparages bull riding and claims that he does not see the "point of riding some piece of stock for eight seconds." Bull riding in the rodeo is nonproductive labor; Ennis says it may "get [you] stomped" but it lacks a purpose. To Ennis it represents risk without productive yield. He describes the bull in terms of its commodity value, as a "piece of stock," and not as a challenging and difficult beast to be faced as a test of will or masculinity. He echoes his father's criticism that "rodeo cowboys was all fuck-ups." To hardworking ranchers like Ennis's father, rodeo cowboys carry a taint of immorality because they avoid productive labor in favor of wandering the country and gambling what little money they have on a chance to win the big prize. Furthermore, with the risk of extreme injury looming over each competition, they jeopardize their future productive labor each time they compete.[3]

Though Ennis's father criticizes the nonproductive, risk-taking rodeo cowboys, rodeos historically served as entertaining celebrations of the skill involved in the productive labor of cowboys, who first earned the respectability and folk hero status they enjoy in American culture through these demonstrations of their occupational skills. In his 1964 article "The American Rodeo," Mody C. Boatright, a folklorist of the U.S. West, claims that the skills that impressed the crowds included "picking up objects from the ground, shooting at targets from horses running at full speed, riding hanging by one leg from the saddle and firing under the horse's neck," steer wrestling, and bronco riding (196). In these early exhibitions the bronco riding elicited the most admiration from the spectators. In this event, a cowboy approached a horse that the local community had designated as unmanageable and therefore not useful; consequently, when he impressed it into service, he acquired the esteem of the spectators (198). The risk, excitement, and spectacle generated by the bronco riding exhibition necessarily designated this event a crowd favorite. Yet bronco riding also earned respect for the cowboy because it enacts humans' domination of nature in the service of productive labor. While the other events demonstrate humans' dominion over the natural world through labor, they do not enact the transformation of raw material, a wild horse, into both a productive tool, a working horse, and a marketable commodity, a salable horse, the way that bronco riding does.

But Jack is not a bronco rider; he does not tame wild mustangs and render them rideable, productive, and profitable. He rides bulls. This choice of occupation demonstrates his resistance to productive labor because bull riding differs from all the other rodeo events that celebrate cowboys' occupational skills. Bull riding frequently results in bodily injury in a demonstration of a skill that generates no productive yield. Cowboys compete to see who can impress the judges with their riding style while remaining astride a bucking Brahma bull for at least eight seconds. Bull riding not only causes the most injuries and fatalities of any event in the rodeo but also is the only event that does not correlate to ranch labor. There is no occasion for bull riding in the day-to-day life of the ranch hand. Most cattle ranches have little use for willful and fierce bulls; ranchers employ a very few for breeding purposes and castrate the rest of the male calves to render them more obedient beef cattle. The bull-riding competition even features a particular breed of bull not found on most ranches.[4] This event enacts the risks and the physical effects of hard cowboy labor, yet the bull rider endures this bodily harm, not in the service of compensated productive labor, but rather to entertain an audience and, very rarely, gain fame and fortune.

Jack identifies with the role of the bull rider as opposed to the hard-working laborer—the ranch hand or cowboy. He characterizes himself as someone who risks his body and his future earnings in a daring but fundamentally unproductive pursuit. Brokeback Mountain's costume designer, Marit Allen, and actor Jake Gyllenhaal communicate Jack's pride in his bull-riding career through the prominent display of his rodeo prize belt buckle. Jack exhibits it, pointing at it or standing with his shirt tightly tucked and his hands resting on his waist to draw attention to the shiny buckle. Even though, during the summer of 1963, Jack works on Brokeback Mountain as a wage laborer, his frequent assertions that he is a bull rider indicates his resistance to Aguirre's appropriation of his body as a tool for production. Moreover, the film presents Jack's bull riding as an additional way for him to control his own body and his labor, when Ennis confirms that Jack avoided the Army draft. Jack replies that, though he quit the rodeo while he "could still walk," he was "too busted up" to serve in the military. By choosing to end his bull-riding career when he does, Jack remains physically intact yet prevents the U.S. government from appropriating his body for military service in Vietnam.

Though Jack claims that money motivates his bull riding, he represents it as a pleasurable use of his body. Jack imitates bull riding when Ennis disparages it. Pretending to sit astride a bucking bull, Jack gleefully shouts, "I'm spurrin' his guts out! Wavin' to the girls in the stands!" and collapses in laughter. While the slim possibility of monetary reward may partially inspire Jack's bull riding, his enthusiastic inhabitation of the bull-rider persona reveals that he derives some pleasure from the competition and exhibition. Jack's bull riding and his subsequent playful reenactment exemplify a subordination of productivity that embraces play and advocates for pleasurable physical activity as an end in itself.

In the Campsite

On Brokeback Mountain Jack gradually awakens Ennis to a pleasurable use of his body, one that transforms his body from an instrument of labor to a source of pleasure. Since an account of the potential for liberation of the body that can be found in the free exploration of pleasure lies outside of Marx's scope in *Capital*, we can turn to Herbert Marcuse's investigation of the "juncture between the erotic and political dimensions" in *Eros and Civilization* (xxi). Marcuse laments that society has not used its growing productivity for reducing the repression of the instinct for pleasure. Rather, society has turned productivity "*against* the individual" as an "instrument of universal control" (93). By eliminating what he terms "surplus-repression"—repression of the instincts beyond what is necessary for the preservation and growth of civilization—Marcuse advocates not for a utopian abolition of labor, but instead for the end of the "organization of the human existence into an instrument of labor" (155). A society without surplus repression liberates the body by cultivating the pleasurable instincts, sexual and otherwise, and freeing the individual from the arduousness of alienating labor.

Marcuse's theory further resonates with the connections among alienated labor, productivity, sexuality, and the body in *Brokeback Mountain* when he aligns nonprocreative sexual activity with a resistance to instrumentalization of the body. In a society that "employs sexuality as a means for a useful end," Marcuse, citing Freud, claims that nonprocreative sexual practices "uphold sexuality as an end in itself" and therefore "threaten to reverse the process of civilization which turned the organism into an instrument of work" (50). Thus, nonprocreative homosexual sex acts represent a refusal of the reproductive imperative that characterizes heterosexual intercourse. The procreative possibility inherent in heterosexual intercourse links this type of sexual expression with production. By contrast, homosexual intercourse deliberately resists the regime of production because it lacks procreative possibility and thereby embraces sexual pleasure as an ultimate goal.

On Brokeback Mountain the men's sexual relationship exposes Ennis to an alternative conception of his body that liberates him from its instrumentalization and allows him to imagine his body as a source of pleasure to himself and to Jack. Juxtaposing two scenes in the tent telegraphs the gradual transition Ennis experiences. In the first tent scene, Jack orders the half-asleep, shivering Ennis into the tent. A little later, while they sleep, Jack places Ennis's hand on his erection. Ennis immediately responds by jolting upward, and then in a gesture fraught with violent energy, Ennis abruptly turns Jack over and penetrates him. Though Jack begins as the aggressor, Ennis's submission to his seduction is complicated by his eventual domination of the sex act. Ennis hastily capitulates and quickly achieves the desired result—sexual release. This brief scene indicates Ennis's changing relationship to his body; he is both exploited, by Jack's taking control of his hand's placement, and exploiter, by his dominant role in the sex act. Yet the next tent scene, with its mutual expressions of tenderness and affection, sweeps away terms like "aggressor," "domination," and "exploitation." In the tent Jack prepares to go to bed for the night. Looking at the fire, Ennis takes a moment to decide then he walks to the tent, shyly opens the flap, and joins Jack. First, Ennis is on top, then Jack, which highlights the reciprocal nature of their coupling. They affectionately caress one another, exploring erogenous zones beyond the genitals. Their lovemaking eroticizes their entire bodies, rendering them sites of mutual pleasure.

Ennis and Jack's sexual relationship contrasts with Ennis and Alma's heterosexual coupling, an activity that forsakes pleasure as an end in itself in favor of a productive intent. Ennis and Alma's early relationship is attuned to the reproductive imperative, as illustrated by the two children she bears in rapid succession. Yet the sexual relationship of the two men possesses no procreative possibility and therefore represents the free expression of the sexual instinct and the body for mutual pleasure. The film highlights the mutuality of their pleasure to indicate that the relationship fosters a shared experience of pleasure, instead of one man using the other's body as an instrument to provide individual sexual satisfaction.

Moreover the film emphasizes the opposition between productive labor and the men's sexual relationship by portraying their encounters as moments stolen from work's obligations. Each time they spend the night together, Ennis forsakes his place alongside the sheep, and problems ensue. After their first sexual experience, Ennis arrives where the flock grazes to find an eviscerated sheep, graphically rendered with its entrails hanging outside the corpse. This disturbing image, the only incidence of violence committed against the sheep, reinforces the notion that by spending time with Jack, Ennis has been remiss in his job. Another time when Jack and Ennis spend the night together while a hailstorm rages outside the tent, the sheep intermingle with a Chilean flock. Though the men try to disentangle the sheep, Aguirre later recognizes some Chilean sheep among his flock and voices his dissatisfaction.

In its representation of the twenty-year relationship between Jack and Ennis, the film highlights Ennis's struggle to negotiate between his obligations to alienated labor and his desire to spend leisure time with Jack. Ennis laments to Jack that "making a living is about all I've got time for now." Though with this statement, Ennis claims that he is nothing more than an instrument of labor, he always finds some time to spend with Jack. To go away into the wilderness with Jack, Ennis frequently breaks his commitments to his employers, quitting his low paying jobs or leaving without notification. The film visually renders the conflict between obligations to labor and pleasurable, nonproductive leisure by portraying the trips with Jack as picturesque moments in the vast and beautiful wilderness accompanied by a moving acoustic guitar score, while depicting Ennis's life with his family and in town with claustrophobic interior shots that emphasize demands on his body.[5] It is only on these trips with Jack, in the wilderness, away from labor and the obligations imposed on him, that Ennis can engage in play and freely indulge in a pleasurable use of his body.

In the Home

Though convention conceives of family life as a space free from the demands, self-interest, and obligations of capitalism, for Ennis, it is not a refuge from productivity. Rather, the home only relocates the productive and reproductive demands on his body. During intercourse, Alma interrupts Ennis's penetration with her plaintive concerns that commingle the economic and the pleasurable. She says, "As far behind as we are on the bills it makes me nervous not to take no precaution." Productive concerns that are both economic (they need more money) and sexual (babies result from sex) inhibit her bodily pleasure. Her request for precautions indicates an attempt to free their pleasure from the productive concerns of the economic and the reproductive by removing the procreative possibility from the act. He replies, "If you don't want no more of my kids, I'll be happy to leave you alone." Ennis's response reveals that he understands heterosexual intercourse to be exclusively reproductive rather than pleasurable. Though Ennis derives pleasure from homosexual sexual activity, heterosexual intercourse without the possibility of reproduction is completely meaningless to him.

Repeated images represent family life as a physical imposition on Ennis's body, akin to labor. In an early domestic scene, Ennis returns home to find a chaotic environment. At a washboard in their cluttered kitchen, Alma busily washes the clothing while their two daughters cry and scream from another room. Ennis lifts and tries to console the screaming baby while Alma Jr. clings to his legs. When Alma asks him to wipe Alma Jr.'s nose, he replies that he could "if [he] had three hands." This first portrayal of Ennis's experience of fatherhood connotes that this caretaker role replicates the demands on his body that work requires. His retort that he could satisfy his wife's request if he had "three hands" implies that he understands fatherhood as akin to physical labor; he could be more successful as a father if his body had a greater capacity for lifting and carrying. Thus, parenting necessitates a modification of his body in the service of greater efficiency and labor.

These scenes visually analogize the domestic sphere to the workplace by revealing that both spaces make arduous demands on his body. The image of Ennis carrying the children repeats in the film; he carries them again when he leaves them with Alma at the grocery store. This depiction links productive labor to Ennis's conception of fatherhood by reproducing an earlier scene of labor. On the trail up to Brokeback Mountain, Jack and Ennis both carry sheep. Jack hoists one on his shoulders and later one in front of him. In terms of the real logic of shepherding it makes little sense that the men would be carrying fully grown sheep up Brokeback Mountain. If these sheep must spend the entire summer exposed to the rough terrain and weather on the mountain, they must be healthy enough to make the climb up the mountain without human assistance. This illogical portrayal serves to emphasize the physicality of the labor on Brokeback Mountain. The very few times Ennis interacts with his young children, like the sheep he guarded, they demand this same type of labor; they require his supervision and constrain his movement. This analogy proposes that both the obligations to labor and to family life impose themselves on Ennis, literally obstructing the free movement of his body and constricting his options.

Furthermore, the film's use of spatial relationships underscores the way that domestic life stifles Ennis's body. In the aforementioned domestic scene, Ennis lives in a small, rustic house on the open range. The exterior shot emphasizes the spaciousness and quiet of the environment surrounding the property; it reproduces the panoramic camera shots employed to depict the men's time on Brokeback Mountain. The film then cuts to an interior shot of Alma and Ennis's home to reveal the contrasting inside of their home, which is cramped, dark, loud, and chaotic. As Ennis opens the door, a cacophony of screaming children, Alma's demands, and radio voice-over assaults him. The visual and auditory contrast differentiates between the freedom and peace on the open range that he experiences with Jack and the physical confinement and sensory assault that he experiences in his domestic life with Alma. The representation of Ennis's home life as an imposition on his physical body intensifies with the family's move to an apartment in town. At Alma's request, which she frames as for the children's benefit, the family relocates to an even more stifling apartment above a noisy laundromat. Even in the middle of a relatively spacious rural town, the Del Mar family resides in the most cramped circumstances.[6]

The juxtaposition of Ennis with Jack in spacious, peaceful, and beautifully captured exterior scenes on their "fishing trips" with the restrictive, chaotic, and unattractive interiors he and his family inhabit creates a visual analog to the fundamental conflict that Ennis faces in the film. The mandate for labor and its alienation of the body clash with his desire to liberate his body from the productive imperative by engaging in physically pleasurable yet nonproductive pursuits with Jack. Ennis's objections to an imposition of the logic of instrumentalization onto sexual pleasure emphasize this conflict. Ennis wants sexual pleasure to be free from the corrupting influence of the domination of the body and responds to challenges to his ideal with violence. At the Fourth of July fireworks show, Ennis and his family overhear some bikers who discuss their search for sexual satisfaction. They assert that there is "bound to be a lot of pussy on the hoof in a crowd like this" and then speculate about where they could find "the most pussy." Their statements distort Ennis's conception of pleasurable sexual expression by instrumentalizing the bodies of the women with whom the bikers copulate. Ennis reacts to this objectification, at first angrily and eventually violently.

Ennis's fierce insistence on separating pleasure from instrumental-ity culminates in his angry outburst upon learning that Jack has been soliciting male prostitutes. The film's editing emphasizes the notion that having sex with prostitutes grafts the logic of instrumentalization onto the sexual experience. In the Mexico scene Jack engages a male pros-titute, and then the following scene features the Twist family Thanks-giving. This chronology sets up a contrast between the gritty alleys of Mexico and the ideal of the wholesome family home at Thanksgiving, wherein the prior Mexico scene undermines our understanding of the family's unity. Yet it also analogizes the male prostitute to an object of consumption. After Jack walks into the shadows with the man, the following frame features a full-screen shot of the cooked Thanksgiving turkey displayed for consumption. This editorial choice jarringly jux-taposes the turkey with Jack's solicitation of prostitutes to indicate that he reduces these men to the status of inanimate meat to be consumed in the satisfaction of sexual appetite.

When Ennis reacts angrily to the implication that Jack has solicited prostitutes, Jack responds by explicitly blurring the lines between sex-ual pleasure and instrumentality. He refers to his desire for Ennis as "needing *something* I don't hardly never get" and "a couple high altitude fucks." Jack characterizes their sexual relationship as simply a means to satisfy a need. In contrast to Jack's description of their relationship earlier in the film—"when this thing grabs hold of *us*"—this later phrasing emphasizes individualistic pleasure by eliminating the "us" and replacing it with "I." This subtle shift in pronoun and Jack's reference to the "high altitude fucks" transform the relationship from a sanctuary of mutual pleasure away from the alienation of the body under capitalism to a replication of the capitalist's appropriation of the body of the laborer to yield a result. In response, Ennis explodes and then states, "I'm nothing," indicating his extreme alienation. In Jack's angry revision of their relationship, the bodies of Ennis and the Mexican male prostitutes serve as mere tools to produce Jack's necessary sexual release.

But the following scene, Jack's flashback, contradicts his previous description and reaffirms that Jack relishes the mutual pleasure and affection that forms the basis of their interactions. This imaginary retreat to the original summer on Brokeback Mountain recalls a moment stolen from the obligations of work, a tender evening embrace by the light of the dying campfire before Ennis heads off to his nighttime duties. This poignant memory of Jack enfolded in Ennis's arms washes away Jack's angry accusations and reimagines the possibility of corporeal freedom in a mutual expression of tender pleasure. The film's final scenes return to the men's embrace in the image of the shirts on a hanger with one shirt enfolding the other from behind, replicating the way Ennis held Jack by the campfire. The arrangement and rearrangement of the shirts symbolically express the mutuality of the men's pleasure. Jack arranges his shirt on the outside, enveloping Ennis's in a reversal of the fireside scene, and Ennis subsequently rearranges them to return Jack's affectionate embrace.

By reproducing the fireside embrace, the shirts symbolize the possibility of a pleasurable relationship liberated from the productive imperative. They are work shirts, and as work shirts, encase and confine the laboring body. Yet their surfaces are marked by an eruption of the body, by a commingling of the two men's blood spilled, not during labor, but during a playful fight that turned violent, a reaction that stemmed from both men's impassioned disappointment at Aguirre's command to come down the mountain early. Through their arrangement and their history, these shirts evoke an ideal of shared corporeal pleasure beyond the demands that Ennis's working life, especially, has placed on him.

But ultimately this final image of the men's entwined shirts represents the impossibility of corporeal freedom. The embrace is purely imaginary, and their bodies are absent. The empty shirts serve as mere surrogates for the men's fleshly bodies. The circumstances of Ennis's acquisition of the shirts affirm that the shirt substitutes for Jack's body. When Ennis leaves the Twist home with the shirts in his hands, Jack's father insists that Jack's body will remain in his possession and, against Jack's wishes, will be confined in a family plot. In lieu of scattering Jack's ashes on Brokeback Mountain, Ennis creates an imaginary Brokeback Mountain in his closet. With the postcard picture and the embracing shirts, Ennis invents a space of freedom and mutual pleasure, yet it is wholly devoid of corporeality. The film ends with Ennis living in one cluttered, small room in a trailer, a space even more stifling than any of the homes he shared with Alma. If we read Ennis's choice to relocate to a trailer park according to the spatial logic of the rest of the film, we recognize that he has chosen to surrender his struggle for liberation and has acquiesced to confinement of the body.

As mementos of pleasure free from productive imperatives, the shirts are comforting. Enshrined in an embrace in Ennis's closet, these work shirts have been liberated from the necessity and utility that they previously represented. As figures for the bodies of Ennis and Jack, the shirts become an inspirational and lasting reminder of a defiant gesture. But as mere shells without bodies they also recall the futility of that resistance. The tragedy of *Brokeback Mountain*'s final scene is not only the lost love but also Ennis's final capitulation to the loss of free pleasure.

Notes

1. Zeese Papanikolas's exploration of the underside of the cowboy myth in *Trickster in the Land of Dreams* confirms that the economic and social circumstances of real cowboys in the U.S. West looked more like those of the transitory migrant worker than the fiercely independent lone cowboy of Remington paintings and dime novels (73–77).

2. Jack's silence does not signify that he, like Ennis, sees himself as a laboring body without a voice or consciousness. We understand later that Jack had

no questions or objections for Aguirre because he worked for Aguirre's operation on Brokeback Mountain the previous summer.

3. In "The Rodeo Cowboy as an American Icon," Demetrius W. Pearson and C. Allen Haney cite research that suggests the incidence of injury in rodeo far exceeds that of most sports, including collegiate football. They contend that the potential for injury in rodeo is as high as 89 percent (17–19).

4. The Brahma bull was adopted for this event because its ferocity and its loose hide, which moves around its body, render it especially difficult to ride (Stoeltje 253).

5. Even the one interior scene that features Jack and Ennis together four years after their summer on Brokeback Mountain lacks the constricting quality that the other interior shots possess. While an exterior shot reveals that the men have gone to a motel together, the interior shot, of the two men lying with one another on a bed, resembles the earlier scenes in the tent. The full-screen shot of Ennis's and Jack's bodies obstructs the motel room background and thereby visually returns us to the tent on Brokeback.

6. After the divorce Ennis moves back out to the rural range. His sense of obligation to his family prompts his accommodation to Alma's request to relocate. Yet once Alma divorces him and he is no longer obligated to reside with his wife and children, he returns to the spaciousness and quiet of the rural environment.

21 } Personal Borders

MARTIN AGUILERA

Sitting at our kitchen table in the housing project where I grew up, while having breakfast one morning early in 2006, my father asks me about a movie he's been reading of in *Diario de El Paso*, the local Spanish-language newspaper. It's the one with a lot of Oscar nominations that season. About the two *vaqueros*. Have I seen it?

"*Sí*," I tell him.

Have I seen it?

I can't begin to express to him how much I have longed for *Brokeback Mountain*, how much it means to me, how elated I am that it even *exists*, this melancholy work of art, and not simply because I'm a film-obsessed aspiring filmmaker but because I am gay and stories about people like me aren't told often enough—not nearly enough—least of all through the medium I most love.

Certainly gays and lesbians had been featured in Hollywood movies, but as I'd become used to seeing them, they were there only as comic relief: confidantes to Reese Witherspoon or Julia Roberts in some straight romance where *they* get the guy. These images had begun changing over time, albeit slowly, and queers began to shake off their minstrel mantle to take center stage in popular entertainment—although primarily on television. There was *Ellen* on prime time and *Will & Grace* a few years later, if you liked it cute and sweet. Showtime's U.S. version of *Queer as Folk* came along after that, a polarizing no-holds-barred exploration of the different facets of modern GLBT life. Raw, honest, brutal, titillating—it portrayed the homosexual as a richer, layered, more textured individual *and* as a sexual being.

Movies had not been so bold.

I couldn't hope to walk into a cineplex and watch such a story unfold, preceded by hip-hop–fueled deodorant ads and previews for the latest thriller from M. Night Shyamalan. If you wanted to watch movies about gay men leading gay lives you had to go to the local video store and peruse the limited special interest section, or browse the gay and lesbian category with Netflix online. There you could find countless independent features (many of which were European) made available by TLA Releasing or similar distributors who'd cornered the straight-to-video queer market. The fact that a movie studio had put up a sizable chunk of change for a gay-themed loved story, acquired a director revered by cinephiles around the world to film an A+ script, and cast two bankable up-and-coming actors was a feat of epic proportions. I had waited my whole young life, it seemed, for a Hollywood moment such as this.

I'd been a child at the time of *Making Love* and *Parting Glances*, was as equally unaware of *Longtime Companion*, and although it made a profound impact on me, I was too young to fully appreciate the political effect of *Philadelphia*.

This baby called *Brokeback Mountain* was mine.

I want to say this to my father, and so much more . . . but I can't. And it's not just because of the language barrier (I speak fluent Spanish but communicate better in English—he speaks only Spanish), or because of the educational differences between us (he made it through sixth grade in Mexico—I put in a year and a half at an accredited U.S. university), or even due to the generation gap (he's thirty-eight years my senior). The problem lies much deeper than that, in a chasm of denial and things-not-said that's so prevalent in this culture and environment I was raised in. It is a void that his simple question—had I seen *Brokeback Mountain?*—created between us because it was a question that came loaded with the million-watt spotlight that lit up the white elephant in the kitchen: my homosexuality.

From time to time such questions will arise; simple, innocuous questions, but I feel like the answers to them carry the weight of the world.

The last time I can recall another awkward nondiscussion between us was when I came home from work one evening the previous November.

I'd thrown down my messenger bag, grabbed my voter registration card, and rushed to my neighborhood's polling station to vote against Proposition 2, which would (and did) amend the Texas constitution to define marriage as solely between a man and a woman. My father was perplexed that I'd run out to vote instead of sitting down to the dinner he'd prepared. Later that night after the news had announced the results of the proposition I had voted against and I finally sat down to eat, my dad asked me if I had run out to vote *for that.*

These father-son moments always seemed to happen in the kitchen. I froze, felt my heart skip a beat; my blood ran cold. I managed to nod. He understood. I understood. We just never spoke about such things. That November night I went to my room and sat in the dark for a while, hating myself for being a hypocrite. Everywhere else I had been actively vocal about Proposition 2, and yet the mere hint of my old man bringing it up turned me into a coward.

I had no excuse for such undignified silence, but in my father's presence I was frequently subject to those.

There was a time when cowboy movies didn't create immediate nervous tension between my father and me. I remember lying in bed with him when I was a little boy, head resting against his chest, feeling comforted and safe with every single beat of his heart. We were watching *Shane,* a movie he had seen when he'd been around the same age I was. Years later, in a moment of unguarded tenderness, my father told me that watching the film as a kid in a theater he had imagined himself to be Brandon De Wilde calling out "Come back, Shane!" to Alan Ladd. My grandfather had been absent in his life. It didn't take a genius to understand his longing for a patriarch.

I was very moved by this revelation.

My father was never one to wax nostalgic about things of the past. But I sensed a romantic in him, this salt-and-pepper-haired man who hummed "Moon River" and the theme from *A Summer Place* to himself often, this man who quite possibly had wanted bigger things in life but was never given the resources and opportunities to see any of them through, this man who believed in the magic of movies and TV.

While watching *Walker, Texas Ranger* one night and consuming her customary pork rinds and quart of beer in her room, my grandmother (with whom we lived)—a fan of martial arts action movies and TV programs—told me with dark amusement that as a boy my father had believed he could fly. He loved watching George Reeves as Superman soar through the air, so one afternoon he had grabbed one of their bath towels, tucked it into the back of his shirt, gone up to the rooftop of the two-story tenement they were living in, and flung himself off. He didn't get to fly. Instead, he got a bad concussion when he struck the pavement, hit his head, and blacked out.

"That's why he's a neurasthenic," my grandmother mused to me in Spanish, and chugged her Coors. "*Esta loco.*"

So it was my father, the stoic dreamer, who early in life instilled in me a love of movies of all kinds—the classic melodramas and grand spectacles of Hollywood's Golden Age, the Cantinflas comedies, the Pedro Infante tearjerkers, Hitchcock, even B horror flicks I was always begging him to take me to see. And with *Shane* he brought cowboys into my consciousness.

It was in 2000, possibly 2001, that I first read about the "gay cowboy movie" in development based on the short story by Annie Proulx. Gus Van Sant was going to do it. Then Joel Schumacher. Then nothing. One thing was certain, though: this was not going to be one of my father's preferred Westerns. And although Wyoming sheepherders were clearly far removed from my existence as a brown man in a moderately sized urban border city, my interest was piqued, and I sought out and read the short story.

It stayed with me for months. I thought about the characters of Jack and Ennis often. Who would they be? How would they be played? Who would make the movie? What would it look like? The desire for *Brokeback Mountain* to be big became, for me, an obsession.

All I know of ranch life is limited to what I've read in books or seen in movies, but I know what it's like to have sex with a man for the first time and to have been plagued with a sense of guilt and shame that came with such intimacy. It was something sprung from the homophobic drone I was surrounded with (*puto maricón joto puñete manflora marimacha*) at school, at times at home, all around. I understood how putting on a mask for the sake of others could whittle away at your soul, because even though I was living a public life in school and at clubs and bars that was very much out, loud, and proud, I would put on a mask for my father. I knew what it was like to live in a place where men are subliminally forced to adhere to a macho stereotype because of cultural and religious traditions. It was a suffocating environment for me for many reasons, some of which I brought on myself through fear and insecurity.

Others because that's just the way it was.

El Paso, Texas, is a city that's difficult to explain to someone who hasn't lived there because its rhythms, its cadences, its whys and hows are misunderstood even by the very people who reside within it. For me it seems to exist in a time warp where past and present collide in confusion. The city is a predominantly "Hispanic" southwestern-desert landscape where multilayered Mexican customs have become Anglicized. (In his fascinating book *Brown*, Richard Rodriguez argues there is no such thing as "Hispanic.") The poverty of the "sister city," Juárez, Chihuahua, found right across the fence, spills over on the humble shoulders of the many El Pasoans who have relatives residing there, or Juarences who cross the bridge into El Paso to come to work. Over the course of more than a decade hundreds of women, and more recently children and men, have been brutalized and massacred in Juárez amid a frenzy of multiple serial killers, corrupt politicians, drug lords, gangland turf wars, prostitution rings, underground sex clubs, slave trades, dirty cops, and the black market for human organs.

And El Paso—a literal stone's throw away—remains, at least on the surface, unaffected by the violence.

There is a duality to daily living here, a split identity passed on throughout the family and community from the mixed media of two different countries and cultures, the end result being a generated sense of disassociation from both in people who, like me, are "different."

If you can't fix it, you've got to stand it.

It is a laid-back city, ideologically Democratic but religiously conservative. People celebrate Fourth of July and Cinco de Mayo. They're as fanatic about Chico's Tacos as they are about Olive Garden. In the classroom our grandparents' Spanish becomes interchangeable with our teachers' English. Our teen cousins may be locked in their rooms blasting Nine Inch Nails in angst-ridden stupor while down the hall-way our *tía* sings along gleefully to Vicente Fernandez and vacuums the carpet. The Franklin Mountains are lovely in the hues of sunsets unparalleled anywhere else, yet at times their stillness can be unsettling, a stillness that has a tendency to drift over the city. It was no surprise to me when Cormac McCarthy told Oprah the idea for his novel *The Road* came to him while staring out at those mountains from a downtown El Paso hotel and imagining them in flames. Overwhelmed by a sense of dread. Of course. It was a dread I knew all too well, powerful enough that one of our greatest living American writers could tap into it and be inspired to pen a Pulitzer Prize–winning vision of a postapocalyptic hell.

I am sympathetic to the plight of Jack Twist and Ennis del Mar, because in the emotional contours of their story I feel my life. I don't experience a border between art and life. I think of Whitman: "Every atom belonging to me as good belongs to you." The best kind of visionary art can move, affect, and resonate with everyone from all walks of life, in any space and time. This is what *Brokeback Mountain* managed to achieve.

When the film opened in El Paso I stood in line with close friends and quipped that we didn't have to go to the local gay bar that night; it had come with us to the movies. A sense of pride overwhelmed me as I recognized a large number of men and women from the small, insular, typically apolitical gay and lesbian community in the city. This may have been "our" movie, but it was so much more, and for the first time ever—through the power of cinema, my everlasting love—I felt bound to my queer brothers and sisters. All of us had come together for this. All of us had joined with one single-minded purpose that felt more important than just "going to see a movie." Finally, our stories would be told, and Hollywood would at long last give us our place and learn that we, too, wanted our lives in wide-screen glory on par with the best of the best and of such technical grace and artistic mastery as *Casablanca, Out of Africa, Citizen Kane*. It felt like a beginning. It felt like revolution. It wouldn't last.

What blissful naïveté. As of 2009 the best Tinseltown was able to deliver on its promise of a "mainstream" gay cinema was Gus Van Sant's

Milk and, to a lesser degree, director Ang Lee's *Taking Woodstock*, which featured another gay male lead. Both films were from the noble Focus Features. And what of lesbian characters? They haven't put in an appearance in lead roles for studio product since Stephen Daldry's *The Hours*. The "floodgates" *Brokeback* had opened only led to . . . *I Now Pronounce You Chuck and Larry* and Sacha Baron Cohen's *Brüno*. The road to hell is always paved with good intentions. Pity. It is exactly at this moment in time, on the cusp of America redefining itself for the twenty-first century, that an influx of serious queer cinema for the masses could break through barriers and make for positive changes to help establish a promised equality long overdue.

Some things don't change.

There are personal borders that won't be crossed. Or simply can't be crossed. It would mean nothing if they were. It would mean everything if they were. I have come to know and shamefully understand that. Because if some personal borders could be crossed, I could have told my father everything that *Brokeback Mountain* was for me that morning at the table. But I didn't. I was scared of tearing through the veil of our denial, and what it would mean.

We just never spoke about such things.

Instead I muttered briefly that indeed I'd seen it and left the kitchen and went into my room and began the routine of getting ready for work, Jack and Ennis on my mind: their lives, their duality, my own.

Not long after that, within months, I had the opportunity to move to Los Angeles and begin the pursuit of my dreams and have had much time to mull over my life in El Paso, that flawed and broken city that I loathe and I adore, and what it did to me for better or worse. And sometimes it makes perfect sense to me and sometimes it does not, what I kept from my father, though like Jack's and Ennis's fathers, I am convinced that he knew. But all that was and all that could have been doesn't carry that much weight for me anymore, only what lies ahead and what *can* be.

Now that I am gone.

Part 6 } Sympathy, Melodrama, and Passion

22 } **Mother Twist**

Brokeback Mountain and Male Melodrama

SUSAN MCCABE

There are scenes in Ang Lee's *Brokeback Mountain* that won't let go. Perhaps what makes the film closely akin to melodrama is its deft orchestration of heightened emotional experience. Among the film's most haunting scenes is the charged emotional interaction of the star-crossed, or rather culture-crossed, characters Ennis del Mar (Heath Ledger) and Jack Twist (Jake Gyllenhaal) as they are about to part for what will be the last time, after twenty years of secret trysts disguised as "fishing trips." Lee transforms the buddy movie into male melodrama or, rather, exposes the former genre's disavowal of erotic and emotional attachment: that scene shows two aged men and the damage done to them by homophobia through a poignant flashback to when they were young and handsome. No matter how glorious, the landscape cannot save them from a condemning social world, which is made visible in another scene when Ennis spots, in a long shot sweeping from his point of view, a truck on the road in the distance. His terror of being seen— that everyone in town is looking at him "like they all know"—pervades his consciousness. Before sinking to his knees and weeping, Ennis says, "It's because of you, Jack, that I'm like this. I'm nothin'. I'm nowhere." Another wrenching scene, which I examine later in more detail, depicts a grief-stricken Ennis making his pilgrimage to Jack's parental home to ask for his lover's ashes.

I had the unusual experience of viewing *Brokeback Mountain* for the first time in Lund, Sweden, in a small theater after it had been playing for several months. The audience was almost entirely made up of women, mostly women with their women friends, and a few scattered heterosexual couples. The crowd left the theater tearstained, satiated with the melodramatic twist to this Western tragedy. The Swedish subtitles oddly contrasted with western cowboy idiolect, giving the words a denaturalized effect, revealing language and landscape as incommensurate with expression and desire.

Melodrama can radically realign a viewer's sympathies by allowing men to take on typically female roles through the "convergence of the perverse and the sentimental that melodrama allows," as Patricia White (94) writes of *Now, Voyager* (Irving Rapper, 1942). By no means does *Brokeback Mountain* have only women in mind for its audience; rather, it calls on the psychoanalytic and visual dynamics that have informed most melodramas or "weepies," *addressed primarily to* women and at odds with more apparently male-centered genres, such as the Western. By subordinating heterosexual romantic and erotic currents to homosexual ones, the film creates a distinct twist to the genre's usual imperatives.

Peter Brooks characterizes melodrama as a vehicle for "ethical recentering," for "a search for a new plenitude in reaction to the decentering of modern consciousness." Among the characteristics Brooks attributes to melodrama, several apply extraordinarily well to *Brokeback Mountain*, twisting the genre's "strong emotionalism," "moral polarization," "extreme states of being, situations, actions," and "inflated and extravagant expression" to suit its renewed ends (200). Melodrama, for Brooks, is a direct reaction against the nuclear bourgeois family. *Brokeback Mountain*, for its part, calls into question almost every aspect of "compulsory heterosexuality."

More specifically, the film's representation of women, especially Jack's mother (played by Roberta Maxwell), resituates the maternal as central to the desire between men. I first establish in broad strokes how the film fits in with melodramatic expectations and motifs. Next, I trace the maternal in the queer relationship developing in the first portion of the film until Jack and Ennis first consummate their relationship (the first thirty minutes). Jack most clearly incorporates the maternal, tending the orphan Ennis (seeing to his wounds, enfolding him in blankets). Further, I examine the film's range of women in their choral comment on the grafting of the maternal onto male-male eroticism. The final part of this essay scrutinizes the climactic "homecoming" scene with Mother Twist, who finally gives tacit permission to homosexual desire.

Male Melodrama

Within the traditions of melodrama, *Brokeback Mountain* presents two men who reciprocate each other's love but can't be together, who meet against the backdrop of a magnificent horizon, who struggle to maintain their relationship against all odds. "You're too much for me, Ennis, you son of a whoreson bitch. I wish I knew how to quit you," Jack berates Ennis (during the last rendezvous). In another scene, Jack drives away in his now half maroon-colored truck after learning that the newly divorced Ennis is unavailable for a spontaneous reunion. As Jack chokes with tears, he sings along with the cracking voice of Emmy Lou Harris in contrast to "King of the Road," the hearty tune he accompanied en route to visit Ennis. Both Jack and Ennis are men "of means by no means," living out their doomed and thwarted desire. Embodying the melodramatic aims that Brooks sets forth, the film points toward a possible plenitude (glimpsed in a natural scenery, often identified with the maternal) and attacks the moral prejudices that disallow free expression of desire.

Perhaps exemplifying these characteristics, Douglas Sirk's melodrama classic *All That Heaven Allows* (1955) invokes the natural world to legitimate an otherwise secret or illegitimate affair, apart from the artifice of the flawed social world. Indeed, while multiple undercurrents within melodramas point to divergent desire, these energies are not usually as overt, nor generally do we see male/male desire as the main focus. In the remaking of Sirk's film into *Far from Heaven* (2002), Todd Haynes transfers a widow's (Jane Wyman) class-violating relationship with a gardener into a wife's love (Julianne Moore) of a black man (Dennis Haysbert). Both Sirk and Haynes accentuate what is permissible from a small town's constrictive perspective. Haynes sets his film slightly forward in 1957, but retains, even intensifies, the oversaturation of colors. Yet his revisionist film ups the so-called perversion, with Kathy divorcing her husband Frank (Dennis Quaid) after he falls in love with another man. This subplot does not, however, represent inversion as redemptive: it persists in its stereotype of the casual and carnal homosexual. In another instance of melodramatic lineage, *Now, Voyager* (1942) portrays homoerotic desire as a form of a remothering, so that Charlotte Vale (Bette Davis) remothers herself through mothering her unavailable lover's daughter. This relationship with a surrogate daughter (after the death of her punishing mother) becomes more important to her than a heterosexual relationship. In fact, she remains a single woman but is no longer a repressed "spinster."

In *Brokeback Mountain*, Jack mothers Ennis. The latter is not typically masculine, despite his seemingly irresponsive, stoic demeanor ("If you can't fix it, Jack, you got to stand it")—a persona the film undercuts. After the men leave Brokeback the first time, Ennis breaks down in an alley, his weeping and vomiting turning to rage as a man walks by and observes him. His anger and grief are cinematically bound to his marriage. We hear the words of the Lord's Prayer ("Forgive us our trespasses") as a voice-over while Ennis collapses in the alley, preceding the image of him cleaned up and marrying Alma (Michelle Williams). The film proposes that marriage and reproduction are not essential spheres, but can be obligatory and compulsory forms that do not do justice to the natural forces of attraction, tenderness, and passion. Ennis, in fact, marries during a period when he might otherwise have been drafted (later we learn the army does not "get" Jack because he is too "busted up" from the rodeo). The rhythms of ranch life "naturalize" so-called wayward desire, while towns and offscreen cities disrupt it. Alma wants to move to town (over a laundromat) in part to counteract the loneliness of Ennis's childhood—but perhaps in part to be situated in an overseeing community. Eroticism emerges in melodrama in part through its frustration and detours, yet *Brokeback Mountain* depicts conventional heterosexuality as the detour within these men's lives.

The Pup Tent, or Melodramatic Mothering

Ennis and Jack are hired to perform two distinct roles: one man will be the "camp tender" and prepare the food; the other will be the "herder" and put up a "pup tent." The latter will sleep "100%" among the sheep, within the fold, against the regulations of the forest ranger. With this arrangement, the men set up, with Ennis as first tender, and Jack leaving for work and returning for his meals. There is one shot of Jack holding and nursing an ailing sheep. Another scene portrays Jack attempting to nurse his companion's wound, after scolding Ennis for coming home late for dinner after he was thrown from his horse. With Jack's growing frustration with the bad hours and "smell of piss" in the pup tent, the men reverse positions. Jack confesses to being a bad cook but "good with a can opener," thus once more making their roles unstable and reversible.

Of the pair, Jack is apparently first attracted to Ennis, studying and framing him in an early shot in a side-view mirror while shaving and then again when he is evidently aroused while Ennis washes himself. When Ennis ends up staying at the camp late into the night and falls into a whiskey-soaked doze outside the tent (this is the thirty-minute mark), Jack can't bear to see Ennis shivering and cold. In a maternal and affectionate gesture, he invites Ennis into his tent for warmth. One thing leads to another; desire sparks on both sides. The morning after the men deny they are "queer" and try to suggest their passion was merely situational: "This is a one shot deal we have going on here," says Ennis. The same morning up at the herding camp, Ennis discovers a gored sheep—the result of his neglect. (The gored sheep is the position usually assigned to women in mainstream film, where women represent the lack that men define their masculinity against.) This punishing image in this context casts the pair's consort as impossible and unlawful as well as a danger to the herd. (Watching the men in intimate play with his high-focus binoculars, Joe Aguirre [Randy Quaid] calculates that the men are a danger to the herd and construes them as effeminate ewes.)

The film's metaphors of tending and herding would border on heavy-handed cliché if they weren't used to break our habits in thinking about masculinity, desire, and the presence of the maternal, where we might least expect their combination. In a metaphoric pup-tent, the characters each become maternal caregivers, whether making meals, herding sheep, tending wounds, or keeping house. The presence of the maternal, so often set apart from the erotic, in itself marks this move as revolutionary. Masculine friendships often exclude women in buddy films, but here Lee gives many more dimensions to same-sex male relationships—in a way reminiscent of Adrienne Rich's delineation of the "lesbian continuum" that includes a whole range of emotional and erotic valence, from tender to genital (51). After the initial sex scene, with the men taking dominant/passive roles, later intimacies show several reversals, including an image of Ennis sleeping at Jack's breast (the earlier scene showed a postcoital Jack looking as satisfied as an infant after breast-feeding). The film is a necessary intervention into conceptions of male homosexuality. Indeed, the men engage in tenderness as well as violent horseplay. Jack lassoes Ennis and wrestles him to the ground. When Ennis bleeds, Jack tries to staunch his lover's wound. His comforting words only cause the grieving Ennis to hit Jack in an effort to diffuse his sorrow about leaving Brokeback. Jack's nosebleed spreads from his shirt to Ennis's plaid one. Unbeknownst to Ennis (and to us until much later), Jack preserves both shirts, his own enclosing the other ("the pair like two skins, one inside the other, two in one" writes Annie Proulx [*Brokeback Mountain* 52]). "[C]an't believe I left my damn shirt up there," Ennis mutters to himself as they part for the first time in front of Jack's pick-up. Jack's gesture of enfolding Ennis, along with the memorial shirt, intimates an ongoing maternal eroticism.

The film introduces the absent maternal most explicitly when Jack talks about his mother whose religion would doom their "trespassing" to exclusion from heaven. After flamboyantly singing lyrics from one of his mother's hymns, "I know I shall meet you on that final day," Jack says his mom "never explained it [the Pentecost]," but he speculates that it means "that fellas like you and me march off to hell." As much as his mother's beliefs remain inchoate or unexplained, Jack appears to have incorporated her as a central part of his object-relations or, rather, his ability to exchange tenderness, care, and emotional closeness. The fact that Ennis was basically brought up by his sister (until she got married) and brother (until he got a job on a ranch) makes him markedly alone. Jack becomes his maternal stand-in as well as male companion, revising the debilitating influence of his own father ("tough old bird" who kept his secrets close and never came to see Jack ride rodeo). Considering the ensuing portrait of both men's censorious fathers, it appears that the maternal is dominantly present in their desire for each other. Ennis does not speak of his mother while narrating his family history. His pivotal primal scene depicts his father dramatically exposing a nine-year-old Ennis (and his brother) to the spectacle of a castrated rancher in an irrigation ditch, punished for living with another man. This image, like the gored sheep, recurs in traumatic flashbacks and finally merges with the image of Jack's murder perpetrated with a tire iron.

The Choric Women

In generating audience sympathy and identification, how does *Brokeback Mountain* address the female spectator? Surely watching Ennis leave his wife for "fishing" trysts (the traditional alibi for male companionship) makes the woman viewer somewhat abject. The wife might well be construed as the paradigmatic neglected wife, but the twist in this plot is, of course, not another woman but a man. I am here more interested in how desire between men relies on identification with this more typically female abjection. To some extent, men have been cheated of melodramatic abjection in Hollywood cinema through its following the usual path marked out by oedipal narrative (i.e., by the father/son fight for dominance and the son's necessary turning away from the mother because of the threat of castration). In a conventional oedipal plot, the worst fate for men is that they might become like women (lacking a phallus), and thus (so the psychoanalytic argument runs) they incorporate sadism toward the feminine more broadly, within and without. This model of male development, with its anxiety surrounding identification with the maternal, has in fact shaped numerous mainstream films. The possibility that a man might not desire his mother but yet identifies with her can lead men into a masochistic position, associated with both female identity and with melodramatic desire. Here the film reclaims the possibility of maternal identification as one avenue of resistance to the twin monsters of homophobia and misogyny. As Tania Modleski argues, visual culture has often demanded not just a dead woman but also "the crime of matricide," as in Hitchcock's *Psycho* (14). Lee's handling of female characters, with Jack's mother casting a backward light on her son's development, is a means of rewriting the maternal in the context of desire between men.

Reversal of stereotypic gender roles shows characters—male and female—trapped by cultural expectations. Jack's wife, Lureen Newsome (Anne Hathaway), is the real master on the rodeo scene; later she also is squarely in the office, taking charge of the couple's business affairs, with Jack diminished and infantilized by his father-in-law as a rodeo "fuck-up." Further, Ennis's marriage to Alma is the prototypic fleeing of homosexual desire. His affection for Alma exists, yet it is the shadow of his real desire: the couple tumble in the snow in a muted version of the rambunctious rough play of the men. Notably, in this particular scene Alma could be a young boy, outfitted in ski clothes and a wool cap that disguises her gender.

When Alma first sees Ennis's pent-up desire and passionate kiss outside their apartment, she retreats in shocked silence as he packs up for his inaugural fishing trip. She holds her tongue, unlike Kathy in *Far from Heaven*, who when she discovers her husband kissing a man, demands he seek help. Years later, at a Thanksgiving dinner with her new husband, Alma confronts Ennis about getting married again, for apparently the whole family worries about his isolation. She then reveals, long after the fact, her knowledge of the sham fishing trips—he never brought home any trout and never found the note she attached to his tackle. This revelation meets angry denial and leads to the wronged wife's prototypic response to the "other woman" or femme fatale—she calls Jack Twist "Jack Nasty." Indeed, Ennis used Alma as a screen for his homosexuality. In this way the film reveals the intersection of homophobia and misogyny. For him, sex with her must lead to reproduction: her request for birth control had prompted the final dissolution of their marriage. "I'll have them if you'll support 'em," she asserts, inadvertently commenting on the way economics underpin compulsory heterosexuality. At one point Ennis defends Alma to Jack: "Shut up about [her] . . . this ain't her fault." His neglect of Alma is not personal. Nevertheless, we may not enjoy, especially as female spectators, the abusive treatment of Alma (the all-suffering "soul") or of the other women in the film, similarly cast aside, ignored, or abandoned. Yet there is a real attempt to link the female characters, in their disappointment and frustration, to both Ennis and Jack, particularly the latter, who wears his suffering and frustration more openly and believes, almost to the end, that the pair might live together somewhere. Both men are vulnerable in ways we don't usually see in men on the screen, thus allowing for transposing female identification with male characters.

Jack confesses to Ennis the extent of his longing: "You don't know how bad it gets." In this sense Jack is in a similar situation to Alma;

Cassie (Linda Cardellini), the waitress in love with an irresponsive Ennis; and even Jack's wife (whose voice suggests she is holding back her tears when she robotically narrates Jack's death framed as an accident). Women don't get what they want in the film any more than the men. Lureen wonders why men don't want to dance with their wives, and Lashawn (Anna Faris) responds, "We may not be sorority sisters, but we might have to dance with each other." The new couple in town (Lashawn's demur and soft-spoken husband is Randall Malone [David Harbour]) turns out to be another heterosexual ruse, for Randall, in the apparent manly after-dinner talk while the women "powder their noses," invites Jack to a secluded cabin. But Randall, like Lureen, is not the love of Jack's life.

Lee demonstrates how "straight" couples live alongside, or even within the context of, an unarticulated queerness. There are all sorts of background shots: for instance, a masculine-looking woman on stage plays in a band and the flitting image of a tattooed back locked in a dance at another bar. Even Jr., as Ennis dubs his daughter, reveals a fluid gender identity. She seems to identify with her father; she is as curt as he is: "You don't say much but you get your point across," the waitress tells Jr. after asking if she "is good enough" for Ennis. Like the son in *All That Heaven Allows*, she interviews the possible new mate, but in this case perhaps both "desiring" the father as well as "identifying" with him, contrary to the oedipal notion of sexual development that mandates one *or* the other, depending on the child's gender. The fact that Jr. (at age nineteen played by Kate Mara) visits her father in his secluded trailer in her new boyfriend's Trans-Am to announce her impending marriage to Kurt does not alter her masculine appearance (she sports no makeup on her serious face) along with the evident desire to mask deviance of any sort. She wears a frilly blouse under a rather masculine-coded sweater, which she leaves behind, prompting Ennis to carefully fold and smell it on his way to his dingy closet housing its double shirts (Jack's and his own) as well as a picture postcard of Brokeback.

Return of the Repressed: Mother Twist

Sigmund Freud writes that what is most familiar and strange or alien returns in the form of repetition; what has been repressed comes back to haunt (*Uncanny* 155). When Ennis returns to Jack's homestead, John Twist (Peter McRobbie) reveals Jack's "half-baked idea" to live with another man in a little house on the ranch. Ennis sits before the father, asking for the ashes Jack wanted scattered at Brokeback. In this denouement, Ennis says more words than he has in most of the sequences in the film. We first see the father at a distance, sitting (he never stands throughout the sequence), angrily dictating the fate of his son's ashes: "Tell you what, I know where Brokeback Mountain is. He thought he was too goddamn special to be buried in the family plot." Jack's wishes—both in life and in death—don't fit the heterosexual plot. Yet his father is unable, ultimately, to erase the meaningful intimacy and symbolic exchange manifest through Jack's cherished, bloodstained pair of shirts, a transitional object (one of those objects that represent loss of and connection to a loved person) that connects Mother Twist to both Jack and Ennis. In what is perhaps a fetishistic defiance of her husband's authority, the mother has herself attempted to maintain her bond with her son by keeping his room exactly as it was when he was a boy. This is reminiscent of the "perverse" Danvers in *Rebecca*, Hitchcock's 1940 melodramatic thriller and "woman's film," who keeps her beloved alive by preserving her objects and rooms exactly as she had left them. Danvers gives the unnamed new Mrs. DeWinter a tour of her lesbian eroticism, even putting her hand up the dead lover's semitransparent nightgown. Needless to say, Mother Twist is not on the same scale as Danvers, yet she preserves her intense attachment to her son's belongings.

These are instances of melancholy, what Freud would call a pathological form of mourning ("Mourning and Melancholia" 249, 258), because Danvers and Mother Twist, like Jack and later Ennis, refuse substitution for their loved ones. Even as Jack has attempted to find other outlets for his homosexuality, he nevertheless preserves the pair of shirts in his boyhood closet as a sign of enduring attachment. (Jack, we now realize, had purloined the shirt Ennis thought he had left at Brokeback.) The clothing, as the room's newest addition, summons what has been preserved in Jack's primary connection with his mother. Before discovering the shirts, Ennis puts himself in the place of Jack—picking up a rodeo miniature, opening a window, sitting on the room's small chair and looking out. This is one of the film's most intimate scenes, given the melodrama's demand that we *feel with* the lover's loss and the limits of desire. Similarly, Jack's mother anticipated this need to have such contact; after laying her hand on his shoulder, she invites Ennis to visit her son's room.

In the minimalist, barren home on the plains, Jack's mother *authorizes*, tragically after the fact, the love between Ennis and Jack. As Ennis descends the stairs from Jack's room, she provides a paper bag, an object that evokes the sad "remains" of lost love and the need to "hold" on to it. In her original version, Proulx doesn't have the paper bag; in fact, Ennis doesn't get to take the shirts at all. And the story's last image of Mother Twist is her using a serrated knife to prepare apples. (Perhaps Lee gives the electric knife to Alma's new husband—he uses it in carving the overcooked turkey—as a transfer of this compensatory phallic apparatus). The paper bag is a kind of "objective correlative" for the pair's wandering and unfulfilled love. From the first, the film shows Ennis getting off of a truck in Wyoming carrying a paper bag and later his duffel bag gains prominence. He has, in short, no proper home.

Along with Mother Twist's tacit understanding and anticipation of Ennis's desire for a paper bag, the script adds a significant gesture—small but resonant, which fits it into its larger repertoire of images used to refigure nonheterosexual desire. As Ennis reaches the threshold, he looks back at the scene: John Twist still sitting and staring in the background, and Jack's mother in the forefront making her last pantomime of connection. She puts her hand up to her throat, signaling in pantomime her own inability to articulate desire, her inability to speak. Jack's father, wanting to stifle the exchange of "illegitimate" grief, significantly doesn't see this gesture that enacts mutual repression and knowledge.

The film does not have a typical melodramatic bittersweet ending (here it is all grim), but it does dishevel the family plot. Like the other women in the film, Jack's mother remains unfulfilled. Yet her grief has somehow (miraculously) given her recognition of her son's queerness. She *knows*, as she has kept the stained garments hanging in the closet. Preserving her son's room is a means of enclosing *and* endorsing her boy's wayward desires. The tacit identification between Jack and his mother (and Jack's own ability to mother) exposes how the law of the father (made literal through the film's fathers) arbitrarily but insistently punishes deviations from heterosexuality, but through Lee's "twist" in the genre, has to some hopeful extent failed.

When Jack's mother puts her hand on her throat, strangling her cries, she provides a brilliant gloss on the silencing that takes place in homophobic culture. The secrecy and displacement that characterizes the queer relationship in the film points back to Lightning Flat where Jack grew up, a place that Jack fantasized might be far enough away from social ostracism. It is in fact the site of paternal dominance and stranglehold. The mother's choked speech and gestures of empathy with Ennis look backward to the unfulfilled, "illegitimate" relationship the men shared.

Much of the film qualifies as silent. And in fact, Ennis's film-long characteristic of curtness transforms, under Lee's direction, from stoic machismo to tender fragility, and scores his silences with an evocative stream of images. While the story is condensed and powerful, the film is epic, with a melodramatic score aimed at heartstrings. We respond to human longing set with and against fulsome clouds, open spaces, rhythms of light, rain, snow. Here, however, the tough westerner bearing his trained masculinity becomes subject to the fits of love and weeping that have more generally beset the melodramatic heroine. What can't be articulated operates with heightened proportions. The film's natural scenery, its expressive mountain ranges, embodies a grand yet perilous romance, one that by the dictates of melodrama must perish with its contact to a stunted human-scale culture where love between men and extended grief are not sustainable. Like Jack's mother, Ennis has to set up a private shrine in his trailer, far from everyone's gaze.

"The device of devaluing and debasing the actual figure of the mother while sanctifying the institution of motherhood is typical of 'the woman's film' in general and the sub-genre of the maternal melodrama in particularly," writes Linda Williams (3). In *Brokeback Mountain*, the maternal intersects with melodrama in aligning the feminine with the queer as the abject, silent, if powerful, agency of emotion and expressivity. Mother Twist does not deliver the moral judgment we are led to anticipate, given her religious orthodoxy. Instead, her physical gestures of understanding and of the unspeakable engender a significant disturbance to dominant heterosexual fantasies as well as to cinematic identifications.

23 } Passion and Sympathy in *Brokeback Mountain*

CALVIN BEDIENT

Erotic passion is a passion for union across the divide of two persons—a terrible thing to ask of Eros, who's but a child with a brain soft as an ovum and bones liquid as sperm, a child with a short life expectancy and a taste for tears and even for spilled blood. What passion lacks is a particularizing imagination, hence kindness. It clamors for an unimaginable totality, by multiplying x by y, me by you. Whereas sympathy is attentive and patient, passion is brute and impulsive. Passion itself, however, commands our sympathy for its hopeless raid on the infinite. Passion may even be born of sympathy as well as survive in it, if in infinite recess.

In Annie Proulx's short story "Brokeback Mountain," Ennis del Mar and Jack Twist, two nineteen-year-olds, come together as short-term sheep herders one summer high on a mountain in Wyoming. When the employment is over, they part, only to find that something in them can't do without the other. After going their separate ways when the seasonal work is done, they live in different states, marry, have children (Jack one, Ennis two) and then, after four years, sensationally fall on one another again, in a frenzy of mutual possession—the bucktoothed one, Jack, even tearing Ennis's face with his teeth.

When still married and even after his divorce, Ennis keeps putting Jack off, not as a lover but as what is now, unsufferingly, called a "partner," for he equates being identified as queer with being marked for extermination. He tells Jack that, when he was nine, his rancher-father led him to a country ditch to show him the mutilated body of another

rancher, to teach him what comes of two men living together as lovers—
"Hell," Ennis says, "for all I know he done the job" (29).[1] And so, you
see, he can't be queer; he's not one of *them*. This poor jerk, whom we're
weeping for well before the end of the great movie based on Proulx's
story, thus disrespects and fears his passion, suffering it involuntarily
and almost ignominiously. The situation is terrible. But if we trace the
passion to its beginnings on Brokeback Mountain we find sympathy,
insofar as anything other than a primordial Eros can be found. And
when we look at its grieving aftermath, we find sympathy again, a development of the same sympathy, now limpid and flowing quietly out of
the wounds passion has made.

The surprise is that the film, directed by Ang Lee and based on a
screenplay by Diana Ossana and Larry McMurtry, is a far more incisive
exercise of creative attention than Proulx's astonishingly original short
story is. Everything in the movie is sensitive and *on point*, like a tensed
bird dog or a prima ballerina. Its craft somehow surpasses craft; its aesthetic carefulness amounts to a great caring. It is engrossed, accurate,
patient, loving. By contrast, Proulx's style in "Brokeback Mountain" is
self-consciously whizbang and showy, her storytelling arch and all but
heartlessly rapid, her twist-and-skip style a stutter of notations, and her
descriptions often noisy.

What distinguishes her story nonetheless is material that the screenwriters were able to carry over intact: (1) the startling singularity of
its subject, its substitution of two Wyoming "losers" of the same sex
for the traditional protagonists of classic unhappy love stories—thus a
"queer" fiction thought up by a woman whose other stories and novels
show no interest in homosexuality; (2) her conjuring up, in particular,
of Ennis (for she has, in spades, the true storyteller's gift for giving life
to an imaginary character); and (3) hayseed dialogue that climaxes in
some tangy, occasionally heart-piercing utterances. What remained to
be done, though only great abilities could do it, was to bring a discovering love to the inherent or at least inferable and probable dynamics and
intricacies of the various episodes, in many of which, the film shows,
the emotional logic and the nuances had been skimped or were missing
in action in the story.

The film *Brokeback Mountain* gives Proulx's racy, racing narrative a radiant corporeality; a slowness of movement; and subtleties of expression, violent beauties, spatial metaphors, dramatic emphases, and intimacies that magnify its power and implications. The in-your-eye mountains (actually Alberta's, standing in for Wyoming's) are themselves emblems and teachers of a grave slowness, jutting up again and again in the midst of the action, prospiritual rocks that shout out the call to the blood of all things obscure in their origin but enormously present, as love is. Lee's film lets the progress and logic of scene after scene come to the viewer like rising bread, as opposed to being delivered already wrapped, a recurring "smart" fault of the story.

Take the film's unhurried opening action: headlights burrowing, a freight truck crosses a flat countryside held wide in the frame of the screen in a velvety, green predawn. It stops to let Ennis (Heath Ledger) off at the edge of a bleak small town, hopelessly named Signal. There, on an otherwise bare lot, sits an ugly trailer that serves as the local office of Farm and Ranch Employment. With his straw-colored hair and buckskin-colored coat—he'll remain dun and gold throughout the film—Ennis, waiting for the foreman to show up, leans against the rough wooden-plank side of the trailer and smokes and looks down, his face hooded by a dune-hued cattleman's hat. Then Jack Twist (Jake Gyllenhaal) drives up in his chirring, burnt-looking black pickup, gets out, and disgustedly kicks the rear fender. He lives up to his name by twisting around in the dirt for a while; glances at the tall stranger bent like a straw against the trailer, who's doing his best to ignore him; and then, evidently to provoke *some* recognition of his presence, twists a few steps in his direction with his hands on his hips, like a rather testy flamenco dancer impatient for the music to start. Smiling ever so slightly, Jack gives up (so, cowboy Blank Blank, that's your game, just fade into the setting?) and after a vacant look aside into vacancy (stopped profile of the nonengaged) returns to his truck. (It will be a few weeks before he calls Ennis out definitively, and almost disastrously, from his habit of hiding, at least from him.) Meanwhile, unsteady, the wind groans in that bare place, complaining against all that's hollow and fixed.

And so it goes. It's a Western moment, all right: it recalls what is virtually a little Western genre in itself, the charged wait across an empty street. But Ang Lee isn't out to evoke apprehension and menace; he's intent, instead, on exposing the niggardly vacancy of the lone masculine spirit, as concentrated in Ennis and reflected, perforce, in Jack. In *The New Yorker*, Anthony Lane proposes that the love story starts here, in this lull, these glances; but I think that, on the contrary, the scene establishes a sterile, masculine flatline above which the incalculable sum of the boys' homosexual love will later rise.[2] Ennis is an all but self-abnegating being (eyes cast down, he rocks nervously against the trailer, takes a puff, rocks nervously) and Jack's assessment of him is cool, knowing, ironic. The opening dramatizes the diametrical opposition of their temperaments: Jack with his basically erotic itch to connect with something, though he's already a bit uncertain about succeeding, and Ennis's barren standoffishness.

Proulx's account of their first meeting goes as follows:

That spring, hungry for any job, each had signed up with Farm and Ranch Employment—they came together on paper as herder and camp tender for the same sheep operation north of Signal. . . .

They shook hands in the choky little trailer office in front of a table littered with scribbled papers, a Bakelite ashtray brimming with stubs. The venetian blinds hung askew and admitted a triangle of white light, the shadow of the foreman's hand moving in it. Joe Aguirre, wavy hair the color of cigarette ash and parted down the middle, gave them his point of view.

"Forest Service got designated campsites on the allotments. Them camps can be a couple of miles from where we pasture the sheep." (254–55)

Facts, mostly, and not what Umberto Eco calls art's reproposal of Being's viscosity (*Kant* 34). It's this last that the movie goes for with its remarkable, loving patience—what the Italian critic Dario Zonta calls its "unusual balance and dauntless equilibrium." From Proulx's words, we learn more about the ashtray and venetian blinds than we do about Jack and Ennis. Characteristically, Proulx heads for the hard multiple thinginess of the visual scene, click click. The bang-on energy of her narrative style occludes Ennis and Jack as observing presences, as filters, as feathers hovering over their own gulfs, as beings. *Ashes* and a *triangle* of light—these may be thought of as latent symbols of, respectively, the patriarchal suppression of the heart's fire (witness Aguirre's ash-colored hair) and the as-it-were holy relation of mother and child (note how the precision-manufactured blind lets the triangular patch of light break through only because it's a bit disordered and how a masculine hand casts a shadow on it while signing a business document). But these objects come too early in the story to have real resonance; they're just accidental things, naturalism's gravel.

Proulx specializes in introducing local grit, implicitly presenting herself as a master-observer, someone who is really in the know. By contrast, the movie is free of a boast of worldly knowledge. It has a beautiful simplicity, a kind of humility. It washes Proulx's story clean of its underinvested hasty quality and leads one to see that Proulx tamped into short story form material that might better have been served in a novella. Her narrative is bound and determined to come off as dashing, even at the cost of being skittery and overexternal. Despite its visual medium, Lee's film is much more adept at taking us inside—inside itself and inside the characters. That Proulx got the risky story as right as she did is certainly a great distinction. But the story's greatest distinction is to have made the movie possible. The quality I want to stress in the movie is its extraordinary *sympathetic* understanding, which, as the contrast with Proulx's narrative helps one see, is an imaginative as well as a moral quality. It connects directly to the moral of the film itself: namely, the great and gentle goodness of sympathy. (The short story has the same moral, but as if seen in a bar mirror, smokily.)

The film's heightened sensitivity to the characters produces chains of precisely observed, subtle particulars. Take Jack's soapless shaving of his face in his truck's side-view mirror, using water from a mottled enamel cup, as he waits for Aguirre to arrive—an incident not found in the story. We see Jack's face, but not in the mirror: in the mirror we see Ennis sitting on the trailer steps. First, imputably, Jack in the mirror; then, plainly, Ennis in it; then, imputably, Jack again: in all, the Jack in the mirror serially brackets the Ennis in it, who distracts him from his contemplation of himself. Ennis is held in a silver circle but not idealized there—watched, rather, with a challenged curiosity. This aloof cowboy type with whom Jack has been employed to do a job and share meals in the thin, pure, unwritten air of a mountain—what manner of creature is he? In the small, the moment prefigures their summer together: of the two, Jack will be the one to draw Ennis into the circle of reciprocal sympathies.

This moment is too delicate to have made it into the short story. In large part, it fascinates for what it is in itself. Unlike so many moments in Proulx's narrative, it's not a mere node in a summarizing document. Still, it has a specific function in the film's design: it contrasts diametrically with Jack looking at Ennis in his side-view mirror when he drives away from Aguirre's office, the summer employment over—a moment that itself frames everything that comes between the two shots of the framing mirror. And what is his expression now? That of a man whose heart is being museumed by the glass. Ennis, getting smaller and smaller and flatter and flatter in the mirror (Ennis being, once again, the only figure we see there) is now Jack's Other being reothered, contrary to desire, in a kind of death by rapid and unremitting diminishment. Jack himself is not included in the mirror at all.

Proulx herself says nothing about Jack's emotions on parting from Ennis. Her Jack might be barely scathed by it. But isn't this the same Jack who, just hours before, as we learn later in the story, as also in the movie, secretly packed together one of Ennis's shirts with one of his to keep Ennis indefinitely beside him (the pair of shirts to be hung in Jack's closet "like two skins, one inside the other" [52])? Proulx doesn't prepare us to see that Jack has been torpedoed by passion.

She is bare-bones about Ennis's sensations: "Within a mile Ennis felt like someone was pulling his guts out hand over hand a yard at a time. He stopped at the side of the road and, in the whirling new snow, tried to puke but nothing came up. He felt about as bad as he ever had and it took a long time for the feeling to wear off" (18). "About as bad," "took a long time for the feeling to wear off"—as indirect speech, these phrases are appropriately stoic, but they give away too much to the hick, not to say the dumb animal, in Ennis. A touch corny, they don't quicken the sympathetic imagination.

By contrast, the film is *committed* to portraying Ennis's emotional devastation. For why should it be scanted? There is understatement, and there is too little statement. Ledger's Ennis dashes into a shed beside the road and tries to vomit up his unbearably spoiled insides while punching the wall. Still bent over, he lets out one choked sob, then dry-barfs some more. Always ready to beat someone up when he's hurt, he speaks scurrilously to a passing pedestrian who has stopped to look at him and maybe offer help. (It's the last time that Ennis will let a representative of the community see the extremity and "sickness" of his emotions.[3]) "Took me about a year," Ennis will later say to Jack, "a figure out it was that I shouldn't a let you out of my sights." Ledger's divinatory performance of this visceral crisis is astonishing—unimprovable. No actor could be more *inside* a character at the moment he is trying to evacuate everything he feels. The movie is blessed to have Ledger playing the moment. Whereas the short story barely has Proulx herself at work in it.

In the interim, passion has struck the boys like *lightning*: such is Proulx's barely disguised metaphor ("hot jolt," "brilliant charge," etc.). It's a cliché so naturalized by the storms on Brokeback and on the prairie that it doesn't embarrass. This is lightning that comes from out of their flesh and their histories, as actual lighting shoots up from the ground. Its charge (in both senses) seems to enter them from the very constitution of the physical world, which is essentially an unending rage of energy. Call it "demonic" (as Proulx herself does). How doubt the authority of a passion that takes two pieces of rusty farmyard junk, the lives of two profoundly discouraged country boys, and hurls them together and fuses them as if at a high temperature? "We got us a fuckin situation here," Jack says when, after four years, they meet again.

Each boy, now a man, has rejoined the other in the knowledge that his intervening marriage with a woman hasn't equaled the highs on Brokeback. It hasn't been, like their bond with each other, an incomprehensible connection. Now, not only does a "hot jolt" send Ennis down the stairs of his apartment two by two to seize the just-arrived Jack by the shoulder; an "electrical current" then snaps between them. And Jack, still shaking once he makes it up to Ennis's apartment, where he's introduced to Ennis's paltry and pasty wife, Alma, supposedly makes the floor vibrate. Are we, then, to understand that the story's physics is, say, Nietzsche's—quantum, vibratory, Dionysian?[4] Is passion a needle stuck into the arm by the wildness of the universe?

The movie doesn't have the luxury of invoking Proulx's quantum-pagan tropes. Yet on Brokeback, nature is visibly the boys' overseer. Inevitably, it is more plainly *there* and unreckonable than in Proulx's prose. As the boys of summer, the two are pre-Socratic (as is, of course, the film's very aesthetic, qua kinetic *motion* film, which makes for a happy accord). For a brief but life-altering interval, a quasi-sublime span of nature is their floor, ceiling, dilating space, firewood, kitchen, basis of employment, and means of transportation, responsibility, and sensual provocation. "Naturally" it calls to something huge and natural in *them*, even if the latter is usually half-hidden behind their torn and flapping human memories.

They even revert to hunting as well as herding, the most primitive male occupation. Sick of the cans of beans Aguirre's Basque assistant keeps toting up to them and after losing a food order when a bear on the trail makes the pack mules flee and shake off their loads, they provide for themselves by shooting an elk out of season—Ennis reluctantly doing it in place of Jack, who's a poor shot. For Ennis, it's a kind of coming out from the shadow of patriarchal law. Crouched side by side, the boys watch the magnificent wounded elk, its enormous rack of horns as jagged as Brokeback itself, stagger crookedly to the side, then sway undulantly back and fold to the ground, in a sort of anguish of slow motion. It is as if the forbidding majesty of the social Fathers, as well as the bestial vitality of the primordial, is thus brought down. For the male psyche, they are not entirely separate. Elated, Jack gives the still-crouching Ennis a way-to-go shove, knocking him off balance; and Ennis, never one to back away from a tussle, almost as playfully shoves back, mumbling about Jack's "dumb-ass misses." The dynamics of their first sexual encounter are thus prefigured—Ennis proving to be the shooter, Jack the one who initiates physical contact. At this point, of course, the contact is largely sportive, but as with all sport, there are undercurrents: they are like brothers who have just killed the primal father but don't know it. A rising wave of father-defying, father-replacing intimacy is set in motion by this perfect scene. (It has no counterpart in Proulx's story.)

On the one hand, nature necessarily separates the boys, as it does each individuated thing. Nature is not least those great distances:

sheep-tending Jack looking far down a greeny-dark mountainous gulf to Ennis's ember-sized campfire, and Ennis looking up from the river shallows in which he's just washed the coffee pot to where, on a sunny steep high meadow, a tiny horse bears Jack through still tinier lumps of grazing sheep ("as an insect moves across a tablecloth," Proulx says, with a characteristically hit-or-miss comparison [9]). But nature also throws the two together, so much so that they even try to root in it, as one, to bear up against it. Indeed, to try to *be* it, transformed by love's surprising irrational ardor.

Comes a bitterly cold night that makes it *sensible* for them to bed down together. Ennis, too drunk to make it back to night-watching the herd (for he has switched duties with the grousing Jack), rolls himself up in a blanket by the campfire while Jack retires to his tent. But, wakened and annoyed by Ennis's chattering teeth (a bit of a stretch, that), Jack orders him to come in out of the cold. Proulx:

> "Jesus Christ, quit hammerin and get over here. Bedroll's big enough," said Jack in an irritable sleep-clogged voice. It was big enough, warm enough, and in a little while they deepened their intimacy considerably. Ennis ran full-throttle on all roads whether fence mending or money spending, and he wanted none of it when Jack seized his left hand and brought it to his erect cock. Ennis jerked his hand away as though he'd touched fire, got to his knees, unbuckled his belt, shoved his pants down, hauled Jack onto all fours and, with the help of the clear slick and a little spit, entered him, nothing he'd done before but no instruction manual needed. They went at it in silence except for a few sharp intakes of breath and Jack's choked "gun's going off," then out, down, and asleep. (14)

The vulgarity of this jaunty, dodging, coy account of Ennis's shattering burst of sexuality with Jack is baffling: it's unworthy of the rest of the story, save for the other, less important vulgar bits that are unworthy of it. The tone's off-key, the prose hackneyed, the motivation blindsided, and the scene not palpated, not disclosed. On the contrary, the narrative is in a rage to be done with its meanly conceived task. Breezily, the scene comes and breezily it goes. This prodigal "full-throttle" Ennis is phony, trumped-up; he doesn't appear anywhere else in the story, except once, when he bounds down the stairs to batter Jack with his kisses four years later—by which time, however, he is after all already sexually freed up, if still closeted.

By virtue of Proulx's slapdash writing, one might assume that "as though he'd touched fire" (14) means that Ennis felt a fierce disgust or at least was shocked (as Heath Ledger's Ennis convincingly is); but what Proulx means, instead, is Ennis is instantly just too lustful, too fired up as a virile, active male, to toy with Jack's more or less irrelevant cock. The writing jerks about; nothing in it is seasoned or rings true, including "gun's goin off." No doubt advisedly, it avoids detailing the mechanics of the sex, except for one specific, which is tossed in with a typical mixture of apparent worldly knowledge and haste: "with the help of the clear slick and a little spit" (14). (Despite Proulx's nervous demurral, "no instruction manual needed," we have to wonder just how inexperienced this Ennis is.) In all, the passage is a narrative disaster.

Ang Lee & Co. beautifully ride to the rescue, revealing all that Proulx's scene ought to have been. (We can see it so clearly now!) The film initiates at this point a stunning sequence of significant moments. They whiz by, but their velocity is not the same thing as a skipping over: if viewers watch this part of the DVD in slow motion or with repeated windings-back, they'll find that nothing is even slurred. The sensational speed takes its cue from Ennis's shock and matches the maddened, whisky-sour surge of his lust.

Considering how important these moments are in the context of the film, not to mention in Hollywood film history, an analytical description of them may be warranted—not that any description could be equal to such minutely constructed, rapidly nuanced, and passionately enacted moments, even leaving aside the problem that our words for talking about such emotional matters seem too abstract and too used, and our words for talking about sexual matters too clean or too dirty. To begin with, the filmmakers override Proulx's wrong note "seized." Jack would be smart enough to know that Ennis, deeply self-defended Ennis, might well be frightened away by such peremptory boldness and might even get nasty. Much more convincingly, Gyllenhaal's Jack doesn't look quite awake as he gropingly reaches over, as if with a sleepwalking hand, to

hunt out Ennis's hand. (He doesn't at all come across as a sexual predator who, in full awareness of his intentions, has lured Ennis into his
lair.) Yet, judging by how quick this Jack is to, yes, seize hold of Ennis
in the following moment, against appearing confused by what has just
happened, he must indeed have at last been on the verge of waking.

In any case, his maneuver has a negative, reactive effect on Ennis.
Having wakened, Ennis bolts up on his knees and shrinks back and
faces Jack through a haze of alcoholic fumes, squinting at him as if he
were some unidentifiable being. But then Jack gets up on *his* knees,
after fighting off what seems a whole parachute's-worth of light-colored
bedding, and there in the full-moon glimmer of the tent, grabs Ennis by
the shoulder of his coat. In that transgression-abetting dim light, their
eyes focus in a mutual scrutiny—Ennis, his head a bit lowered, bull-like,
fighting through his stupor as he returns Jack's gaze. Ennis must face
the just thinkable in Jack's eyes—so Jack insists. Sensing that Ennis
has stalled somewhere short of outrage, Jack frees his hand from its
grip and pulls off his own jacket, thus encouraging Ennis to want him.

So, then, an emotionally logical *and* stunning series of instants, physically intense, clobberingly close-up—the total opposite of Proulx's clever
paragraph. And we're not to the end yet: when Jack reaches out for him
again, Ennis bats his arm away, but then as Jack comes back at him,
grasps Jack where the nape meets the shoulder, a defensive maneuver
that nonetheless half-rejects his own rejection, holding at a distance
but also keeping hold. After some scuffling, Jack reciprocates, cupping
Ennis's face between his hands, but as one who is not to be put off,
gently kneading and caressing it. There the two boys are now, clasping
one another by the head like classical wrestlers, Ennis already breath-
ing hard from the struggle. But their foreheads lean together less and
less like butting rams' horns and more and more as if to make a sudden shared dizzied bone-dam against the flood of sensations that may
be coming, is coming, cannot be stopped. Jack looks at Ennis, waits,
expects. By this point, in fatigue and incipient surrender, Ennis has
closed his eyes. And, suddenly, the push of his antagonism suddenly
converts into the pull of desire—the latter manifested with brilliant
minimalism when, without really shifting position, his hand, instead
of forcing Jack's head back, clutches his hair, in a spasmodic love-grip

(his hand, archaic, remembering something). The straight man is just now growing involute around Jack, like a grapevine. The moment is decided: Dionysus has entered the tent; Ennis *will* capitulate. With a wrestler's rapid deftness, Ennis twists Jack over and, as Jack himself has just done, hurriedly unbuckles his pants. He then yanks Jack's jeans down off his ass and, puffing and grunting, performs what could easily be mistaken for hate-sex, a sadomasochistic punishing of his own weak surrender to *wanting it*, but directed at a scapegoat, the groaning youth beneath him. For the father is up in him.

No kiss; just bang. For scrapping is the natural way in for these sons of son-of-a-bitchin' fathers, especially Ennis. The scene is a marvel; perfection.

With their great emotional intelligence, the screenwriters disregard Proulx's next narrative move, her superficial summary of the boys' sexual activities subsequent to that first night. For the night following, they create an intense, intimate scene in which the initial grappling, pounding sort of sex between Jack and Ennis is put aside in favor of their lying together in one another's arms. Ennis lingers by the campfire as Jack, stripped to the waist, settles himself in the tent. Will Ennis get on his horse and go tend the flock, as is his duty? After all, he had discovered that very morning, at the grazing grounds, a sheep eviscerated by a coyote, a bloody gaping carcass—in effect a warning of his social and sexual fate if he isn't careful. The "big son of a bitch" coyote, he tells Jack, had "balls on him size a apples"—effectively, again, an emblem of the castrating father. On this night Ennis is sober, but we know that he won't leave the camp; he sits by the fire and glances at the tent like someone who has only a single direction in which to move, if move he must. Something "unimaginable" is about to be asked of him. Is he ready? Is his conscience clear enough? Does he have the balls to act on the desire that Jack jump-started in him on the previous night?

If he enters the tent through those loose lip-flaps, it will signify that what he said to Jack earlier that day, namely, that "this is a one-shot thing we got goin on here," was accurate as to the "goin on," a signal of submission enclosed in a gesture of resistance ("one-shot thing"). The screenwriters switch these words from Proulx's Jack to their Ennis, from whom it promises more. In the same pitifully terse conversation, Ennis had said, "You know I ain't no queer," refusing to be classified, reclassified, see himself as degraded, turned around, and found out as a result of the previous night's fornication. Be that as it may, he now needs to be physically and emotionally comforted. So Jack will, in a moment, read him, exercising a mammalian instinct. If Ennis enters the tent, where Jack's white torso had visibly flickered as he finished undressing, it is on him, not on a fiery Dionysus. It's his acceptance of a destiny.

Once he stoops through the tent opening (having first covered his genitals with his cowboy hat, even though he's still fully clothed), he can barely stand to look that destiny in the face. Jack sits up from the waist and gently takes hold of Ennis's wrist as, feeling abashed, humbled, and in for more than he can fathom, Ennis (Ennis del Mar, who may now come in from the desolate sea) looks at him, looks down, looks at him again, looks slightly off to the side, looks back, looks off to the side again, and back, seeking his bearings. Everything here depends on Jack's perception of Ennis's almost sickened need for reassurance and on Jack's own instinctive ability to provide it—Jack being the more mother-brilliant, the more intuitive of the two. Here, the archaic maternal pattern of nourishment resurfaces, borne along in each of them in what Fernando Pessoa calls the sensations that "by a maternal paradox of time, [subsist] today, right here, between what I am and what I've lost, in my backward gaze that is me" (129).

We had already detected memory-traces of this warmth when Jack carried a sheep across a river and hefted another one up the river bank (charmingly, in the same scene, a lamb peeks out of a bag hanging from Ennis's saddle); and detected it again in Jack's hold-still-for-a-minute-won't-you grasp of a struggling lamb in his lap as he removed something sharp from its foot; indeed also in the slightly hurt, sympathetic aspect of his eyes at most times when he looks at the things of this world. Hence his previous easy submission to Ennis's bull-like charge. Jack is the caring one, the soother. Rescuer, now, of Ennis, whose being has for so long been coldly withdrawn from itself.

Jack takes Ennis's hat (flamboyant symbol of independent western masculinity, which the kneeling Ennis had been holding over his heart and abdomen) and lays it aside. He then puts his hand up to Ennis's jaw, cradling it, and whispers to a *very* attentive Ennis "it's all right . . . it's all right . . . it's all right," in sounds that rumble up barely articulated from the prelingual antiquity of his own being. (Movingly, the first faint utterance even sounds like "I'm sorry.") And slowly he coaxes Ennis's face close to his own for a kiss. Ennis submits. So it's all right. He's not queer, or if he is, it's all right or it *will* be all right. What is it, anyhow, but another way to be natural?[5] What he lets himself in for now—in the face of such a welcome—is, in any case, irresistible.

As Jack lies back, he draws Ennis with him, until the side of Ennis's head rests on his naked chest, like a child's on the mother's breast (a cushioned position echoed in the film when, after four years, the two are together again in bed in a motel, the back of Ennis's head on Jack's chest, Ennis smoking). And now Ennis runs his hand from Jack's temple on down to his chest and then, in a hooking curve, around it (once again, then, a tendrilling motion), somewhat shyly testing out Jack's shape and feel, which, of course, resemble his own but are remarkably, refreshingly, ontologically *other*. When Jack then rolls over on top of him, Ennis accepts his confident lead in the art of kissing, and, mobile and moist, the mouth rediscovers its primordial drive to incorporate whatever has left it outside, famished. At which point, the camera withdraws. All this in a few flashing moments of screen time.

Crucial to the film's moving persuasiveness about the growing strength and substance of Jack and Ennis's bond, this scene is, as intimated, not at all seeded by the story. Once more dispensing with the loving, divining obligations of the imagination, Proulx quickly dispatches the subject of the sexual experiences that follow that first night in the tent with the words: "They never talked about the sex, let it happen, at first only in the tent at night, then in the full daylight with the hot sun striking down, and at evening in the fire glow, quick, rough, laughing and snorting, no lack of noises, but saying not a goddamn word except once Ennis said, 'I'm not no queer,' and Jack jumped in with 'Me neither. A one-shot thing. Nobody's business but ours'" (15). This throwaway follow-up to Proulx's previous throwaway account of their sexual coupling grants neither Jack nor Ennis a due process of needing to reconcile himself to the stupendous advent of sexual love for another man, the acceptance of which, not least in the macho culture of the

American West, is no easy thing. It doesn't grant Ennis enough of the ordeal of his inevitable growing pains, his first tremulous steps forward as a queer who is, you know, not queer. It even obscures the chronology of their conversation about the business, though it's important to see that conversation as conducive to further sexual intimacy, an articulated clearing of the way.

More, Proulx's narrative is silent about, indifferent to, the qualities of the sex in those nights "in the tent" and then in "full daylight." It leaps from the punishingly intense sex in the tent to liberatory bouts of snorting and laughter, without any development. (The ventriloquism of "goddamn" makes Proulx one of the boys, but that isn't what we want from her; from her we want insight into them.) Such a cavalier report of such cavalier sex doesn't prepare for the drama of a hardly bearable bond that exalts and wrecks their lives and wrings from them a world of tears.

The physical and all but metaphysical beauty of the mountains themselves (first Brokeback, than unnamed others) forms an image of the infinity that the boys become attuned to, the one that passion craves: the mountains as blind, bold, enterprising, eruptions of matter into air. (You can't look at them without a catch at heart; the blood itself develops eyes to see them.) Brokeback, in particular, is like love's encounter with the air it finds *itself* in, high and equally lightning crazed. Despite the ominous note in its name, it seems to unfold without limitation, as passion would if circumstances didn't pierce and hurt it. In point of fact, the camera never quite tames and gathers Brokeback into a single recognizable thing, unlike the comparatively dull postcard of it at the end, so that, at once solemn and jetting, jagged and broad, it remains as untotalizable as love.

As a prompter of sentiments of infinite being, the equivalent of the mountain is maternal memory. Mountain and memory together constitute a third, in the musical sense, memory perhaps forming the tonic. In a passage that comes late in the story, Proulx herself introduces—in fact, labors—the notion of the maternal infinity that helps bind Jack and Ennis together on Brokeback. But Lee & Co. were right to demonstrate the same understanding early in the film. They show a surer grasp of the characters than Proulx does (for, even if Proulx invented them, they detach themselves from her; they exceed her). In portraying Jack as a more nurturing man than Proulx saw him as being, the film provides a reason why an Ennis might fall for him in the first place and explains how, by loving contagion, Jack induces in Ennis a much-needed softening of his character, which, let's face it, is, in the main and until the end, mean, selfish, and macho. Brilliantly, the movie furnishes Jack with not just an amphoric ass but a sympathetic soul and a need to embrace and caress, whose musical accompaniment is his murmured mother-haunted mantra: "it's all right; it's all right; it's all right."

Alas, no sooner does a mother-taught tenderness enter the boys' relationship on Brokeback than the roustabout idyll seems to speed to an end—a month sooner than expected because of an unseasonable turn in the weather. The mountain itself is, after all, no Eden. Comes down on it now the indifferent cold of the cosmos, its ice, not its fire. And *now* what will become of the boys' love? Great unpopulated outcrop in the land of the free, Brokeback had seemed to authenticate as natural their sensual impulses, but its rock and grass and trees and fish and game are in fact under the supervision of an invisible bureaucracy, much as the boys themselves are watched through Aguirre's "big-ass pair a binoculars" (27) when, waving their T-shirts about in the camp, they cavort together with such joyful freedom that Aguirre concludes they've been *stemming the rose*, an imported urban trope that, despite its witty mixture of the natural and the unnatural, its perfumery, leaves the boys pretty much just perverse. Now they must prepare to encounter a world of eyes. Loving each other on Brokeback was one thing, but down in the great prairie, with its tiny sheep-huddles of towns and stray ranches, the atmosphere—with its Christian suspicion of the passions, its fright-laden heterosexual straightjackets—will prove miasmal.

In a finely articulated sequence, the film illuminates the crisis they experience in having to leave Brokeback, a misery that the short story characteristically treats with short shrift. Like a biblical prophet, Proulx prefers to spread over their descent a forecast of doom: "they packed in the game and moved off the mountain with the sheep, stones rolling at their heels, purple cloud crowding in from the west and the metal smell of coming snow pressing them on. The mountain boiled with demonic energy, glazed with flickering broken-cloud light, the wind combed the grass and drew from the damaged krummholz and slit rock a bestial drone. As they descended the slope Ennis felt he was in a slow motion, but headlong, irreversible fall" (16–17). So comes a "fall," a paganized echo of the great mythic one, amid tendentious lurid associations— "demonic," "bestial." Rather than work out a visceral logic for what each boy might be feeling, Proulx indulges in flamboyant symbolism and metaphoric indirection. To explain the blood on the two shirts that Jack took down from the mountain and hid in his closet, she reserves her only important naturalistic detail until almost the very end of the story: "Jack, in their contortionistic grappling and wrestling, had slammed Ennis' nose hard with his knee" (51).

The screenwriters divine in this strangely uncommunicative report a narrative of the actions that sprang from the boys' reactions to the death of their idyll. Their brilliant sequencing of an inferred cathartic violence goes as follows: first, Ennis bitches about Aguirre's decision to shut down early; it deprives them, grumble, of a month's pay, grumble. Jack, packing up the tent, kindly offers Ennis a loan. Ennis: "I don't need your money, hunh? Hell, I ain't in the poor house. *Shit.*" What, then, *does* Ennis need from Jack? Well, Jack should know. Why does Jack seem to take this catastrophic turn of events so calmly? Plainly Jack Fuckin Twist (a name Ennis concocts later) doesn't really care about him. He kicks an empty tin can, picks up a piece of firewood, gouges the ground with it, tosses it away. (What good is an idyll writ in dirt?) Then he goes off into a meadow and sits holding his knees, long and long. Finally, Jack takes a rope, walks over to him, and lassoes him: "Time to get going, cowboy." Ennis is not amused. Freeing himself, he heads back toward the campground, whereupon Jack follows him and (now the devil is up in him) brings him down with a lasso deftly thrown around his ankles. Jack laughs, but by this point Ennis is *really* not amused: "This ain't a rodeo, cowboy." Is he Jack's plaything, to elevate or bring down, to seize or to let go, as he pleases? It's unbearable.

Ennis begins to wrestle with Jack (for he's like a barely verbal toddler, and fighting is his way of settling beefs) and in his anger almost immediately gets unmistakably rough. Thus provoked and in self-defense, Jack, too, becomes vicious and so they roll around until Ennis, on top, repeatedly slams Jack's upper back against the ground. It's then that Jack, fighting up to a standing position, bloodies Ennis's nose with what seems to be a lucky punch (Ennis's back hides the blow from the camera). Ennis has to be stopped. And suddenly Ennis does stop, smarting from the pain and astonished by the blood jetting onto his shirt cuff. The bloodletting is opportune: better a burst of blood than of tears.

Ennis wipes his bloody nose on his sleeve and Jack, ever ready to be the male nurse, rushes in to assist him. (Here, incidentally, the camera slips: Jack's right arm, which at first supports Ennis's head from behind, is in the next frame under his nose. Having somehow already soaked up quite a bit of blood, as the plot necessitates, his sleeve now soaks up some more. The bloodying of the two shirts is in effect a metonymic excruciation of their passion). But Ennis isn't pacified. Does Jack think that, like a good physician, he has lanced Ennis's sorrow in a timely manner? Wasn't Jack laughing at him only a moment ago? So he belts Jack in the eye, knocking him down.

In one of her off-pitch, facile images, Proulx writes, in an awkwardly placed late comment on the incident: "Ennis had suddenly swung from the deck and laid the ministering angel out in the wild columbine, wings folded" (51). She doesn't hint at the motive for this violence. Was it simply a brutal retaliation for what she herself suggests could have been an accidental injury to his nose? We can see that she's holding a good hand but she keeps her cards so close to the chest that she isn't really in the game. It's the screenwriters and the director and the actors who bring an exact and *interested* emotional intelligence to the scene.

The emotions expressed in the parting of the boys confirm that, of the two, Jack is the more adaptable, the more constitutionally optimistic, the less desperate about finding other ways of getting out of himself. It won't hit him until later that even he, almost reedy "cowboy" though he is, isn't resilient enough to get past this one, past the summer, past Brokeback, past Ennis. On the other hand, once he knows what his life wants of him, he's courageous and committed; unlike Ennis, he's of one mind, not given to tying himself into knots of self-justification (Ennis in the motel: "I was sitting up here all that time trying to figure out if I was—? I know I ain't" [26]). *Jack* doesn't regard his homosexual passion as a somehow necessitated exception to the disgustingness of being queer—as somehow sanctified because it's *his*. It just is what it is, and nobody else's business. It's Jack who dreams of their having a "sweet life" together; Jack who proves long-suffering in the face of Ennis's terror of being hunted out like a demon rat and killed, should he be publicly identified as being queer; Jack who, in various ways and at various times, makes it "all right," or at least comfortingly says it's "all right," even if mostly it isn't. ("You know, friend," he declares at one point, "this is a goddamn bitch of an unsatisfactory situation.")

In the movie Jack repeats the soothing phrase "it's all right" in their last scene together. By a little river where it crowds excitedly into a mountain lake, he had just been railing at Ennis for keeping him on a "short fuckin leash" and, to make matters worse, having become as hard to see as the pope: "you have no idea how bad it gets. I'm not you, I can't make it on a couple of high altitude fucks a year. . . . I wish I knew how to quit you." Only a moment before Ennis had warned Jack that the things he doesn't know about Jack's having sex with other men—Mexico has been brought up—"could get you killed if I should come to know them." Exasperated, Jack, who's no profligate, whines, "[You] tell me you'll kill me for needin' it and not hardly never getting it." Whereupon Ennis, in an emotional and physical collapse at which Ledger is indescribably brilliant—note how, crying through squinched-up eyes, he presses his thumb between his brows, as if to keep his forehead from blowing up— this crumbling Ennis says, in words not included in the short story, "Then why don't you—why don't you just let me be? It's because of you, Jack, that I'm like this. I'm nothin'. I'm nowhere." (The moment is truly awful: as Ledger performs him, Ennis is so deeply habituated to being nonverbal and otherwise inexpressive that his sudden articulation of wrenching feeling is devastating, more so for coming out in choked spurts, like rusty water when you first turn on a long-unused tap.)

It's because of you that I'm nothing: what does the accused say to *that*? Well, he could point out that Ennis had concluded too early in his life that he would never amount to anything and, self-punishingly, had taken only short-term ranch-hand jobs to guarantee it. But Jack's too kind to say anything of the sort and, besides, he believes in his own misfortune. After some typical Jack-and-Ennis grappling as Jack tries to embrace Ennis's slumping body, Jack says, in a terse whirl, "Sorry. It's all right. Damn you, Ennis."

Sixteen years earlier, Jack had made an equivalent if less urgent gesture, again by a river. At that time, Ennis rejected Jack's proposal that they have "a little cow-and-calf operation, your horses; it'd be some sweet life." It was then that Ennis told him about the incident mentioned earlier in this essay: how Earl, one of the two men who had ranched up together down home, was beaten with a tire iron and dragged around by his dick until it came off. (In this story, the tire iron is the homophobe's weapon of choice: Ennis will later surmise that one was used to kill Jack). He comes to the point: "two guys livin together, no way. Now, we can get together once in a while way the hell out in the back a nowhere." Jack (with sarcasm): "Ever four fuckin years?" Ennis: "If you can't fix it, Jack, you got a stand it." Jack: "For how long?" Ennis: "For as long as we can ride it. There ain't no reins on this one" (a slightly richer contextual placing of this image than in Proulx's narrative). At which moment, closing the discussion, a suddenly sorrowful long-faced Jack, an all-but-pushed-away Jack, doesn't sulk; rather, he reaches out, there in the fire-lit dark and runs his thumb slowly down Ennis's ear, then strokes his cheek with the back of his fingers—gestures that say "it's all right," and with the implication: "you're forgiven and there's nothing to forgive." In their last scene together, almost the same meaning wafts from "Sorry. It's all right," but now it's a weary, if not broken-hearted, statement.

So it is that Jack extends himself through acts of sympathy with Ennis; he gives solace, even when that means that he's packing up his own hopes. To say it again: at crucial times Jack is like a mother to Ennis, a mother remembered and imitated in a sexually passionate man's body. It's just how he is; it's not his purpose to make of Ennis—the frightened boy in Ledger's Ennis, whose very face is, like a boy's, not quite well defined—a more generous presence. Jack just wants to be and live and work with him.

Does Jack's example nonetheless "take"? Yes, already on Brokeback Mountain, Ennis responds gratefully to Jack's gentleness. But the scene that attests to his capacity for a maternal sweetness of being, there on

Brokeback, is curiously placed very late in the story. In Proulx's text, it comes to us as Jack's fond memory of a "dozy embrace":

> What Jack remembered and craved in a way he could neither help nor understand was the time that distant summer on Brokeback when Ennis had come up behind him and pulled close, the silent embrace satisfying some shared and sexless hunger.
>
> They stood that way for a long time in front of the fire, its burning tossing ruddy chunks of light, the shadow of their bodies a single column against the rock. The minutes ticked by from the round watch in Ennis's pocket. . . . Ennis's breath came slow and quiet, he hummed, rocked a little in the sparklight and Jack leaned against the steady heartbeat, the vibrations of the humming like faint electricity and, standing, he fell into sleep that was not sleep but something else drowsy and tranced until Ennis, dredging up a rusty but still useable phrase from the childhood time before his mother died, said, "Time to hit the hay, cowboy. I got a go. Come on, you're sleepin on your feet like a horse," and gave Jack a shake, a push, and went off in the darkness. (44)

The writing is crudely stocked with loaded metaphors. The filmed scene is simpler, though abruptly stuck in as the film's own memory, as it were, to contrast with what follows, the men's hurtingly cold final parting. Naturally, it dispenses with the flatly symbolic ticking watch in Ennis's pocket—a watch that Aguirre allocated to Ennis to use on Brokeback, ticking with Man-time, whereas what Ennis drifts into, as he begins to share Jack's sleepy trance, is Women's Time, heartbeat time, rocking time, the biomolecular time of a vibratory continuity: presymbolic time. The movie dispenses, also, with the (anyway inaudible) "steady heartbeat," indeed with all the smarmy elements that are in the scene; all of a sudden, it seems, Proulx has wakened to the possibility that a maternal peace and security and depth and eternity might once have blessed the men's togetherness on Brokeback.

The film also betters Proulx's version by beginning with the line "you're sleeping on your feet like a horse" and then having Ennis, his arm draped over Jack's shoulder and holding on to his woolly lapel, mumble-murmur that his mother used to say that to him and begin rocking them both back and forth ever so gently and sing something his mother used to sing to him, perhaps as she held him thus, a scarcely articulated music that in Ledger's swallowed version is agreeably vibratory, sleepy, and indistinct. In drowsily embodying his mother, Ennis calls her back semiotically and spreads her like a warmth from himself to Jack, until she's deep-humming in both of them. No coybowyish banality, such as "Time to hit the hay," jars the mood. (Still, the dialogue is awkward. Not even Heath Ledger can pull it off.)

Whatever the complete genealogy of Ennis's awakening to maternal memory, Jack is its catalyst and model. He calls Ennis back from his long retreat into nullity, from a "nothing" that, we are allowed to surmise, may have been created by his parents' death in an automobile accident when he was entering puberty, though we can imagine that he may always have lacked a talent for life. Who can reach him if not Jack? Jack, who was alone with him day after day in the wild and was reassuringly like him, and liked him. In Gyllenhaal's performance, Jack the charmer. Jack with his beautiful, ready mouth and long dark-auburn lashes under the black skate-winged brim of his hat, and his slender yet muscular body, which, like Ennis's, nicely meets the standards of Western iconography, notwithstanding that the film is otherwise iconoclastic vis-à-vis the Western. Jack with his clean-cut, picture-perfect profile (as camera close-ups note) and his nonetheless slightly long face with its earnest, crowding-together eyebrows; his hee-haw madcap outburst of yells and galloping when he suddenly turns "rodeo" on Ennis by the campfire; his somewhat endearing bouts of being manfully pissed about things; his sexual ease (even his implied previous homosexual experience); and, as already said, his capacity for sympathy? All these qualities help to explain how he draws Ennis out of himself, there on Brokeback, where lightning can strike him.

But what does Jack see in Ennis? The film's deeply reserved Ennis virtually requires the audience to stand in for him vis-à-vis Jack, to be his sensibility, to assume that he sees what *we* see. (Even Proulx's Ennis, though created in the potentially explicit, invasive medium of prose, isn't shown as responding to much of anything: we're told that both he and Jack are "glad to have a companion where none had been expected" [12], but he's almost entirely a puppet the narrator briskly moves around from the outside.) Several causes and components of Jack's attraction to Ennis can be inferred, not least the challenge of Ennis's stoic reserve. (Back to the opening scene: Jack *will* draw him out.) And even the film's more taciturn Ennis relates just enough about himself to awaken Jack's sympathy.

There is in Ennis a conflict, a contradiction, to which Jack is deeply drawn: on the one hand, a hardened loner's virile independence; on the other, a terrific if almost entirely repressed need to be befriended—indeed, virtually raised from the dead, brought through love into life. And Jack is gifted at assisting life to get on. He encourages Ennis to welcome his own being by welcoming it himself, coaxingly, attentively.

Ennis is a classic example of one of those lost-souled men whom certain people, usually women, can't help trying to rescue. In the film (but not in the story), a captivatingly forward, vivacious waitress (played with perfect pitch by Linda Cardellini) tries her hand at it and fails—this after Ennis's divorce from Alma. She tells Ennis that she just doesn't get him, while a tear travels down the Wyoming of her cheek, and when Ennis mumbles that he "probably wasn't much fun anyways, was I?" she says with a formidable conviction, "Ennis, girls don't fall in love with *fun*."

What, then, *do* they fall in love with? A man who visibly suffers, most times, from miles on miles of inner withdrawal from everything around him? Whose agreeable if almost blank face nonetheless bears a mouth arrestingly bracketed by displaced pouts, odd little disgruntlement-bumps? (At times, Ledger seems to be speaking through a stubby tongue-suppressor stuck sideways in his mouth.) A grown-up who, despite his manly build, is still a child in need of reassurance? All this is partly what Jack himself falls in love with—this in addition to Ennis's studly qualities (Proulx, in a vulgar contrivance, has *her* Jack say in that motel room: "Christ, it got a be all that time a yours ahorseback makes it so goddamn good" [24], a tacky chunk of dialog in which even the triplet of glottal *a*'s is too much.)

The telepathic sympathy that draws Jack to this forlorn Ennis is precisely a trait Ennis would do well to emulate. In fact, it will come to assuage as well as deepen his grief. In Jack himself, sympathy is associated with a certain ineffectuality. Naturally mild, Jack tends to *take* abuse (you can see Gyllenhaal's sensitive eyes take it)—even if, masculine after all, he'll lash out when he's pushed too far. Damaging his vertebrae and breaking his bones, he takes it riding bulls, partly because his dad was good at it and it's the one thing his dad might admire him for, if his dad could admire him for anything. He *took* it (and this is Proulx's Jack, not the movie's) when his father literally pissed on him for being a little kid who, when he pissed, missed the toilet. He takes it from the insolent Aguirre (a brilliantly hateful Randy Quaid), who, thick-necked ugly prick, needs to lord it over other men ("pair of deuces," he calls Jack and Ennis to their faces, on first meeting them; "scrawny assed," he adds). And he takes it (in the movie) when his father-in-law (who is also his employer) treats him as a pantywaist, until he's had it and asserts himself as master in, at least, his own home. Then, too, a couple of businessmen in his father-in-law's farm machinery office gossip about him as a "piss-ant" (couldn't ride *bulls*)—he attracts *that* sort of comment. But the softness in his nature is its merit. Complementing his "brilliant passion," it's a capacity to experience the sacredness of the other, the call of the outside to come inside. It's what keeps him from feeling what Ennis feels, that he's nothing.

And then we meet up with his mother who, in the film, in Roberta Maxwell's great bit performance, has the same quality in *her* eyes, even if her eyes have dulled from age if not also from looking around for so many years at the bleakness of the farm in Lightning Flat and at her husband's beyond American Gothic plainness, his long nose and parsimonious baldness. Eyes that nevertheless shine with a steady soft kindness, eyes like Jack's that, when they want to reach you, reach you.

This late scene helps us to account for the pure spirit-bubble in Jack's being, that to which Ennis seemed to respond as if it were water to drink from, a lake to bathe in. It is now confirmed that, if left gaping on the paternal side, Jack was at least maternally corroborated. It must have been from his mother that he derived his aquamarine sensibility, his acquaintance with the goodness of sympathy.

And Ennis, in his own enormously sympathetic meeting with her after Jack's death, effectively drinks from her love for her son. Never mind that she lives in an ascetically bare interior, which is painted a blued-white milk that has soured, with, for wall ornaments, grim old family portraits and one chunky wooden cross featuring Jesus' mild, glowing face at the join. She's a mediator, real as much as symbolic, of the final softening we see in Ennis's character in the film. Worn, slow, almost robotic, and understandably frightened of her husband (terrifyingly played by Peter McRobbie), she is nonetheless one of the deep ones. She is quick to sense the extremity of Ennis's grief over Jack's death (Ennis has come to Lightning Flat to try and retrieve some of Jack's ashes to scatter on Brokeback, as Jack had wished). And she divines its cause, whereupon she consolingly touches his shoulder after her husband has, with malice aforethought (for he's no dummy, either), as good as stoned him with the news that Jack was planning to move back to his childhood home with a rancher friend of his from Texas. So Jack had finally despaired of ever getting enough of Ennis, who had rationed his times with Jack for the sake of—of not being killed as Jack was! (The irony is cruel. Proulx's patterning of events distressingly validates Ennis's extreme caution.)

Touching his shoulder, her hand suddenly entering at the edge of the screen (the rest of her momentarily invisible, for here indeed appears a sort of "ministering angel," she encourages Ennis to go up to Jack's room, which she has kept as it was in his boyhood, something she says Jack appreciated, the boy in him having persisted in the man. It appears that she sends Ennis to discover in an alcove at the back of Jack's closet (a sequestered space a mother would know about) the two bloodstained shirts suspended from a single hanger, Ennis's under Jack's. Ennis duly finds them and, after smelling the collar of Jack's denim shirt for a lingering live trace of him, comes down with them loosely folded up together—at which Jack's mother shows no surprise at all. On the contrary, she takes a folded grocery bag from off the kitchen counter and silently hands it to him; once he's out the door, out of John Twist's murderous line of sight, he nods to her and lifts the bag ever so slightly, affirming the conspiracy of those who know how to love.

In the short story, Jack's mother isn't reported as seeing that Ennis makes off with the shirts (as if a mother, especially a grieving one, wouldn't notice). In fact, she's unnuanced, with one jarring exception:

when she says "You come again," she's coring an apple "with a sharp, serrated instrument," as if she were an amalgam of Eve and the punishing (castrating) angel in the Garden (52). True, the movie is somewhat suspect in making Jack's mother clairvoyant, not least because this development works so well in furthering Ennis's own development. Jack's mother is *so* understanding. She is here designed to give Ennis what he needs. All the same, this crucial element in the scene is kept admirably low-keyed—Maxwell's Mrs. Twist being as good at hiding feeling as Ennis himself is (and, for all her sensitivity, not really a warm presence; there's something too beaten back in her; her eyes are too peeled). But feeling she has; feeling is all she has. Ennis is, of a sudden, her virtual son, her son at one remove. So she urges him to come back, and there is meaning in her words—as opposed to Proulx's "You come again." There follows another of their eloquent exchanges of just-perceptible nods. The Ennis who leaves Jack's parents' house with the paired shirts feels more bolstered by maternal kindness than he has been for ever so long—say, since Jack reached up from his bedroll in the tent on Brokeback and touched his cheek, simply and utterly affirming him.

In tribute to Jack's memory he now welcomes and incorporates more than a little of Jack's gentleness into his beer-and-whisky-scented disposition. Not that the whole of the *difficult* Ennis can simply have disappeared: there's no certain vanquishing of the head-lowered bull in him. The Ennis who for all those years as an adult in Riverton, Wyoming, was pretty much a nothing, an emotional solipsist without friends, imagination, spit, conviction, or curiosity; the Ennis who created nothing, observed nothing, and, like a vegetable field of silences, said nothing; who would be startled if ever there should come a bounce into his own step; who stares at his little girls in their swings and asks them if they "want a push or sumptin"; who rolls his wife over and fucks her in the ass after a kiss and a feel or two and yells at her when she runs off to fill in for a fellow employee in the grocery store because a wife ought to stay home and cook dinner for her husband (besides, he's the unwilling prisoner of their marriage and so she owes him); the Ennis who seldom regrets anything (though Cardellini's waitress wrings a grunted "sorry" out of him), since there's not enough reflectivity in him to accept responsibility: in short, the Ennis who was a dud, a dud *except for Jack,* would still be one if it weren't for the alchemical effects of Jack's memory.

To the degree that Jack ceases to be an issue for Ennis (how to work him into his life?), he becomes a presence, and to follow Jack's example, however haltingly, is a form of fidelity to him. His final words in the story are "Jack, I swear." (With awkward literalness Proulx troubles to note that "Jack had never asked him to swear anything and was himself not the swearing kind" [54]. Thus she dodges emotion.) Significantly, in that last scene, Ennis addresses Jack as if he were near, could hear, is still alive to him.

The moviemakers are more decided about Jack's healing effect on Ennis after his death (especially then) and characteristically they pursue it with both more follow-through and more delicacy. They not only transform Mrs. Twist into an ally of Ennis's who recognizes his sorrowing strain of consideration; they also make his daughter Alma Jr. its grateful recipient when she visits him in his trailer house, which is parked together with a few others on a bare patch of land somewhere outside of town, and asks him to attend her wedding the following June. (He had just been placing magnetized numbers on his new metal mailbox out front of the trailer and was standing back to admire the total effect when she arrived. So, then, he is now prepared to be somewhere and perhaps even someone?) An almost total failure as a father, Ennis didn't know that she'd been dating a certain Kurt for the last year. (She's nineteen, Ennis's age on Brokeback, the age of liberation: "I guess you're nineteen; you can do whatever you want; is that right?") Ennis asks her if this Kurt fellow loves her. "Yes, Daddy, he does." Well (and here he echoes the kind of excuse he used to give to Jack), he thinks he's "supposed to be on a roundup down near the Tetons" come June. He looks about in his familiar dodging fashion, considers, makes an about-face: he reckons "they can find themselves a new cowboy." "My little girl getting married, hunh?" (and, for once, this diaphragm-punched subsyllable, which may be unique to Ledger, isn't indignantly deprecatory). Then he and his daughter toast her wedding-to-be with leftover wine. The episode is capped when he picks up the sweater that she absent-mindedly leaves behind (another, if lesser, affect-laden garment), tucks the neck-end under his chin, carefully folds it up like a flag, and places it on a shelf in his closet. To be returned and safe-guarded in the meantime.

The final scene in the film approximates the close of Proulx's narra-tive. Ennis tacks a photograph of Brokeback Mountain above the two shirts, which are once again hung one inside the other, the film's Ennis having made them handily visible, at least to him, in a sort of place of honor on the inner side of his closet door (yes, thus keeping a closeted love still closeted). At this point the movie refines on the short story by showing that Jack's blue denim shirt is now *inside* Ennis's pale, non-descript plaid one (a small, faded, permanent blood stain is just visible on the shoulder of the latter).[6] Whatever Ennis's previous failings at taking responsibility, he now conducts himself as Jack's symbolic guard-ian—guardian, at least, of his memory. Through tears of tenderness, he reaches out and buttons the top button (a classic western pearl button) of Jack's shirt, snugging him in. Another refinement. It may sound all too sweet, but it's not: it's devastating.

These shirts tell their own story. A story of loss: Ennis is bewildered by the disappearance of his shirt on Brokeback, just as he is by Jack's seemingly indifferent parting. A story of outdoor mountain glory: the blue shirt once held a complex of odors that Ennis tries to retrieve in Jack's closet, "smoke and mountain sage and salty sweet stink of Jack," as Proulx articulates it (281). A story, too, of an almost ritual spilling of blood for love's sake and despite it; of the reign of bad luck in a wash-and-iron, washed-out West; of lovers who want to keep the other as close, by means of their shirts, as the image of an eye on the inner side of an eye lid. Not least a story of the secret continuation of their secret bond after death. And a story of a late cleaning up, a symbolic righting of what had been dirtied and set awry. A story, then, of a hard-learned lesson in caring for a few near things that on the world's river are being borne away.

Notes

1. Unless otherwise noted, all quotations are from Annie Proulx's *Brokeback Mountain*.

2. Lane jumps the gun: "There is something wired and wary in their silence," Lane writes, "and the entire passage can be read not only as an echo of *Once Upon a Time in the West*, whose opening hummed with a similar

suspense, but also as an unimaginable change of tune. Sergio Leone's men were waiting for a train; these boys are falling in love" (117).

3. The next words we hear in the movie are those of the preacher marrying Ennis and Alma: "and forgive our trespasses."

4. It should be noted that in "Brokeback Mountain," Proulx's metaphysics consists *only* of flash-life hints. Proulx is not a visionary writer—in fact, unlike "Brokeback Mountain," her work usually lacks the vertical dimension: height, depth. What readers get from Proulx is not spiritual expansion but racy detail and hopes denied. She mirrors what Harold Bloom speaks of as "the Gnostic despair of society" that persists in the "American Religion," and her imagery of sparks may recall the divine "spark" or "*pneuma*" of Gnostic scriptures, but the positive side of Gnosticism, its precious regard of the *original* self, the spark-self, is missing (55).

5. The timing of the story's events (1963–83) places it just outside of the AIDS horror and, further, makes it potentially post-Queer, as well as pre-Queer and extra-Queer, by which I mean outside the most activist period of the gay sub-culture. The short story nonetheless profits from the activist struggle, as does the movie.

6. The stain is higher than any of the spots filmed earlier, but let that be. If the shirts tell the tale, their passion has been purged of its violent element. We may feel some disquiet at the just-held-off parallel with the religious paradigm of suffering, purification, and atonement, the abdication of sinful carnality. What impulse moves Proulx to situate Ennis and Alma's life together above a laundry? Evidently, the sacrificial paradigm—Greek, Christian, and so on—dies hard.

Selected *Brokeback* Bibliography

Beard, Laura J., and David H. J. Larmour, eds. Spec. issue of *Intertexts* 10.2 (2006): 105–79. [Contributors include Brittany R. Powell, Todd D. Kennedy, Kathleen Chamberlain, Victoria Somogyi, Kylo-Patrick R. Hart, Scott L. Baugh, Donovan Gwinner, Sara L. Spurgeon, and Alan O. Weltzien.]

Block, Richard. "'I'm Nothing. I'm Nowhere': Echoes of Queer Messianism in *Brokeback Mountain*." *New Centennial Review* 9.1 (2009): 253–78.

Campbell, Neil. "From Story to Film: *Brokeback Mountain*'s 'In-Between' Spaces." *New Centennial Review* 9.1 (2009): 205–20.

Herring, Scott, ed. "Moving Image Review." GLQ: *A Journal of Gay and Lesbian Studies* 13.1 (2007): 93–109. [Contributors include Dwight A. McBride, Martin F. Manalansan, John Howard, Michael L. Cobb, Corey K. Creekmur, and Dana Luciano.]

Le Coney, Christopher, and Zoe Trodd. "Reagan's Rainbow Rodeos: Queer Challenges to the Cowboy Dreams of Eighties America." *Canadian Review of American Studies* 39.2 (2009): 163–83.

Leung, William. "So Queer Yet So Straight: Ang Lee's *The Wedding Banquet* and *Brokeback Mountain*." *Journal of Film and Video* 60.1 (2008): 23–42.

Members of the Ultimate Brokeback Forum. *Beyond Brokeback: The Impact of a Film.* Livermore CA: WingSpan, 2007. [Members of a forum on Dave Cullen's Web site cull some of their many responses to the film (Cullen writes the preface). An intriguing array of often deeply personal responses to the film, the book's dedication is "For Jack and Ennis."]

Patterson, Eric. *On Brokeback Mountain: Meditations about Masculinity, Fear, and Love in the Story and the Film.* Lanham MD: Lexington Books, 2008.

Proulx, Annie, Larry McMurtry, and Diana Ossana. *Brokeback Mountain: Story to Screenplay.* New York: Scribner, 2005. [In addition to Proulx's story and the screenplay by McMurtry and Ossana, the volume includes three essays:

"Getting Movied" by Proulx, "Adapting Brokeback Mountain" by McMurtry, and "Climbing Brokeback Mountain" by Ossana.]

Stacey, Jim, ed. *Reading Brokeback Mountain: Essays on the Story and the Film.* Jefferson NC: McFarland, 2007.

White, Rob, ed. "Special Feature on *Brokeback Mountain.*" *Film Quarterly* 60.3 (2007): 20–67. [Contributors include Jim Kitses, Robin Wood, Chris Berry, Ara Osterweil, B. Ruby Rich, D. A. Miller, Joshua Clover, and Christopher Nealon.]

Works Cited

Film References

10 Things I Hate about You. Dir. Gil Junger. Buena Vista, 1999.

The 36th Chamber of Shaolin. Dir. Lau Kar-Leung. Dragon Dynasty, 1978.

All That Heaven Allows. Dir. Douglas Sirk. Universal Pictures, 1955.

Angels in America. Dir. Mike Nichols. HBO Films, 2003.

Australia. Dir. Baz Luhrmann. Twentieth Century Fox, 2008.

Back Street. Dir. David Miller. Universal Pictures, 1961.

The Ballad of Little Jo. Dir. Maggie Greenwald. Fine Line Features, 1993.

The Birdcage. Dir. Mike Nichols. United Artists, 1996.

Blazing Saddles. Dir. Mel Brooks. Warner Bros., 1974.

The Boys in the Band. Dir. William Friedkin. Paramount Pictures, 1970.

The Bridges of Madison County. Dir. Clint Eastwood. Warner Bros., 1995.

Brief Encounter. Dir. David Lean. Eagle-Lion/Universal Pictures, 1945.

Brokeback Mountain. Dir. Ang Lee. Focus Features/Universal Pictures, 2005.

Brüno. Dir. Larry Charles. Universal Pictures, 2009.

Butch Cassidy and the Sundance Kid. Dir. George Roy Hill. Twentieth Century Fox, 1969.

Calamity Jane. Dir. David Butler. Warner Bros., 1953.

Candy. Dir. Neil Armfield. Thinkfilm, 2006.

Capote. Dir. Bennett Miller. Sony Pictures Classics, 2005.

Casablanca. Dir. Michael Curtiz. Warner Bros., 1942.

Casanova. Dir. Lasse Hallström. Buena Vista, 2005.

The Celluloid Closet. Dir. Rob Epstein and Jeffrey Friedman. Sony Pictures Classics, 1995.

Chris & Don: A Love Story. Dir. Tina Mascara and Guido Santi. Zeitgeist Films, 2007.

Citizen Kane. Dir. Orson Wells. RKO, 1941.

City Slickers. Dir. Ron Underwood. Columbia Pictures, 1991.

Crash. Dir. Paul Haggis. Lions Gate Entertainment/Yari Film Group, 2005.

Crouching Tiger, Hidden Dragon. Dir. Ang Lee. Columbia Pictures/Sony Pictures Classics, 2000.

The Dark Knight. Dir. Christopher Nolan. Warner Bros., 2008.

Darwin's Nightmare. Dir. Hubert Sauper. International Film Circuit, 2004.

The Day after Tomorrow. Dir. Roland Emmerich. Twentieth Century Fox, 2004.

Desert Hearts. Dir. Donna Deitch. Samuel Goldwyn, 1985.

Destry Rides Again. Dir. George Marshall. Universal Pictures, 1939.

Donnie Darko. Dir. Richard Kelly. Pandora/Newmarket Films, 2001.

Far from Heaven. Dir. Todd Haynes. Focus Features/USA Films, 2002.

Forty Guns. Dir. Samuel Fuller. Twentieth Century Fox, 1957.

Gentleman's Agreement. Dir. Elia Kazan. Twentieth Century Fox, 1947.

Goodfellas. Dir. Martin Scorsese. Warner Bros., 1990.

Guess Who's Coming to Dinner. Dir. Stanley Kramer. Columbia Pictures, 1967.

Horse. Dir. Andy Warhol. Sherpix, 1965.

Hotel Rwanda. Dir. Terry George. United Artists, 2004.

The Hours. Dir. Stephen Daldry. Paramount Pictures, 2002.

Hud. Dir. Martin Ritt. Paramount Pictures, 1963.

Hulk. Dir. Ang Lee. Universal Pictures, 2003.

I Now Pronounce You Chuck and Larry. Dir. Dennis Dugan. Universal Pictures, 2007.

The Ice Storm. Dir. Ang Lee. Twentieth Century Fox, 1997.

Imitation of Life. Dir. Douglas Sirk. Universal Pictures, 1959.

Intermezzo: A Love Story. Dir. Gregory Ratoff. MGM, 1939.

Johnny Guitar. Dir. Nicholas Ray. Republic Pictures, 1954.

The Karate Kid. Dir. John G. Avildsen. Columbia Pictures, 1984.

Kiss of the Spider Woman. Dir. Hector Babenco. Island Alive, 1985.

A Knight's Tale. Dir. Brian Helgeland. Columbia Pictures, 2001.

The Last Picture Show. Dir. Peter Bogdanovich. Columbia Pictures, 1971.

The Living End. Dir. Gregg Araki. October Films, 1992.

Lonesome Cowboys. Dir. Andy Warhol. Sherpix, 1968.

Longtime Companion. Dir. Norman René. Samuel Goldwyn, 1989.

Lord of the Rings: The Fellowship of the Ring. Dir. Peter Jackson. New Line Cinema, 2001.

Lord of the Rings: The Return of the King. Dir. Peter Jackson. New Line Cinema, 2003.

Lord of the Rings: The Two Towers. Dir. Peter Jackson. New Line Cinema, 2002.

Love Is a Many-Splendored Thing. Dir. Henry King. Twentieth Century Fox, 1955.

Lovin' Molly. Dir. Sidney Lumet. Columbia Pictures, 1974.

Lust, Caution. Dir. Ang Lee. Focus Features/Haishang Films, 2007.

Madame X. Dir. David Lowell Rich. Universal Pictures, 1966.

Mädchen in Uniform. Dir. Leontine Sagan. Film Choice, 1931.

Magnificent Obsession. Dir. Douglas Sirk. Universal Pictures, 1954.

Making Love. Dir. Arthur Hiller. Twentieth Century Fox, 1982.

The Man in the Gray Flannel Suit. Dir. Nunnally Johnson. Twentieth Century Fox, 1956.

Milk. Dir. Gus Van Sant. Focus Features, 2008.

Mississippi Burning. Dir. Alan Parker. Orion Pictures, 1988.

Monster. Dir. Patty Jenkins. Newmarket Films/Media 8 Entertainment, 2003.

Monster's Ball. Dir. Mark Forster. Lions Gate Entertainment, 2001.

Munich. Dir. Steven Spielberg. Universal Studios/Dreamworks, 2005.

Nighthawks. Dir. Bruce Malmuth. Universal Pictures, 1981.

Now, Voyager. Dir. Irving Rapper. Warner Bros., 1942.

The Object of My Affection. Dir. Nicholas Hytner. Twentieth Century Fox, 1998.

The Order. Dir. Brian Helgeland. Twentieth Century Fox, 2003.

Out of Africa. Dir. Sydney Pollack. Universal Pictures, 1985.

The Outlaw. Dir. Howard Hughes. RKO, 1943.

Paradise Now. Dir. Hany Abu-Assad. Warner Independent Pictures, 2005.

Parting Glances. Dir. Bill Sherwood. Cinecom Pictures, 1986.

The Passion of the Christ. Dir. Mel Gibson. Newmarket Films, 2004.

The Patriot. Dir. Roland Emmerich. Columbia Pictures, 2000.

Philadelphia. Dir. Jonathan Demme. TriStar Pictures, 1993.

Posse. Dir. Mario Van Peebles. Gramercy Pictures, 1993.

Psycho. Dir. Alfred Hitchcock. Universal Pictures, 1960.

Querelle. Dir. Rainer Werner Fassbinder. Gaumont, 1982.

Rebecca. Dir. Alfred Hitchcock. United Artists, 1940.

Rebel without a Cause. Dir. Nicholas Ray. Warner Bros., 1955.

Red River. Dir. Howard Hawks. United Artists, 1948.

Reflections in a Golden Eye. Dir. John Huston. Warner Bros., 1967.

Ride the High Country. Dir. Sam Peckinpah. MGM, 1962.

Rocky. Dir. John G. Avildsen. MGM, 1976.

Schindler's List. Dir. Steven Spielberg. Universal Pictures, 1993.

The Searchers. Dir. John Ford. Warner Bros., 1956.

Sense and Sensibility. Dir. Ang Lee. Columbia Pictures, 1995.

The Sergeant. Dir. John Flynn. Warner Bros., 1968.

Shane. Dir. George Stevens. Paramount Pictures, 1953.

South Pacific. Dir. Joshua Logan. Twentieth Century Fox, 1958.

Stagecoach. Dir. John Ford. United Artists, 1939.

A Star Is Born. Dir. George Cukor. Warner Bros., 1954.

Star Wars. Dir. George Lucas. Twentieth Century Fox, 1977.

A Summer Place. Dir. Delmer Daves. Warner Bros., 1959.

Sunday Bloody Sunday. Dir. John Schlesinger. United Artists, 1971.

Taking Woodstock. Dir. Ang Lee. Focus Features, 2009.

Taxi zum Klo. Dir. Frank Ripploh. Promovision International, 1980.

The Terminator. Dir. James Cameron. Orion Pictures, 1984.

Terms of Endearment. Dir. James L. Brooks. Paramount Pictures, 1983.

Thelma and Louise. Dir. Ridley Scott. MGM, 1991.

Titanic. Dir. James Cameron. Paramount Pictures/Twentieth Century Fox, 1997.

Top Gun. Dir. Tony Scott. Paramount Pictures, 1986.

Toy Story. Dir. John Lasseter. Walt Disney Pictures, 1995.

Two Spirits. Dir. Lydia Nibley. Independent Lens, 2009.

Unforgiven. Dir. Clint Eastwood. Warner Bros., 1992.

Velvet Goldmine. Dir. Todd Haynes. Miramax, 1998.

The Wedding Banquet. Dir. Ang Lee. Samuel Goldwyn, 1993.

The Wizard of Oz. Dir. Victor Fleming. MGM, 1939.

Print and Online References

"Alberta Tourism: Quick Facts." Alberta Tourism, Parks and Recreation, Tourism Research Unit, Feb. 2009. 28 June 2010. http://industry.travelalberta.com/en/IndustryContent/Documents/Research/TourismQuickFactsFebruary2009Revised.pdf.

"Alberta: Unparalleled Diversity." Alberta Film Commission, Calgary Economic Development and Edmonton Film Commission. 2006. Advertisement.

Allmendinger, Blake. *The Cowboy: Representations of Labor in an American Work Culture*. New York: Oxford University Press, 1992.

Allor, Martin. "Relocating the Site of the Audience." *Critical Studies in Mass Communications* 5 (1988): 219.

"Alta. Film Crew Disappointed *Brokeback Mountain* Didn't Win Best Picture Oscar." *Canadian Press News Wire* 6 Mar. 2006.

Althusser, Louis. "Ideology and Ideological State Apparatuses." *Lenin and Philosophy and Other Essays*. Trans. Ben Brewster. London: New Left Books, 1971. 123–73.

Aron, Michele, ed. *New Queer Cinema: A Critical Reader*. New Brunswick NJ: Rutgers University Press, 2004.

———. "The New Queer Spectator." Aron 187–200.

Baehr, Ted. Rev. of *Brokeback Mountain*. *Worldnet Daily*, 15 Dec. 2005. 10 July 2010. http://www.wnd.com/index.php?fa=PAGE.view&pageId=33906.

Bawer, Bruce. *A Place at the Table: The Gay Individual in American Society*. New York: Poseidon, 1993.

Beckel, Graham. Personal interview by William R. Handley. October 2006.

Benshoff, Harry. "Reception of a Queer Mainstream Film." Aron 172–86.

Berry, Chris. "The Chinese Side of the Mountain." *Film Quarterly* 60.3 (2007): 32–37.

Berry, Michael. "Ang Lee: Freedom in Film." *Speaking in Images: Interviews with Contemporary Chinese Filmmakers*. New York: Columbia University Press, 2005. 324–61.

Bloom, Harold. *The American Religion*. New York: Simon and Schuster, 1991.

Boatright, Mody C. "The American Rodeo." *American Quarterly* 16.2 (1964): 195–202.

Boone, Joseph Allen. *Tradition Counter Tradition: Love and the Form of Fiction*. Chicago: University of Chicago Press, 1987.

Boswell, John. *Christianity, Social Tolerance, and Homosexuality: Gay People in Western Europe from the Beginning of the Christian Era to the Fourteenth Century*. Chicago: University of Chicago Press, 1980.

Bouldrey, Brian. *Monster: Adventures in American Machismo*. San Francisco: Council Oak Books, 2001.

"Box Office Mojo." *Brokeback Mountain*. IMDB.com, 2006. 6 June 2010. http://www.boxofficemojo.com/movies/?id=brokebackmountain.htm.

———. Gay/lesbian genre chart. IMDB.com, Aug. 2009. 15 August 2009. http://www.boxofficemojo.com/genres/chart/?id=gay.htm.

Boyle, Kevin. "Id." *A Home for Wayward Girls*. Kalamazoo MI: New Issues, Poetry and Prose, 2005. 44–45.

Bradshaw, Peter. "True Grit." *Guardian* 6 Jan. 2006, final ed., Film and Music sec.: 7.

Braudel, Fernand. *The Mediterranean and the Mediterranean World in the Age of Philip II*. Trans. Siân Reynolds. 2nd ed. Vol. 1. 1949. Berkeley: University of California Press, 1995.

"*Brokeback* Angels." Posted by EmbiggenX. *YouTube*, 3 Feb. 2006. 19 July 2010. http://youtube.com/watch?v=WP5gns_CKDE.

"*Brokeback* Fiction." Posted by NoSoup4U. *YouTube*, 9 Feb. 2006. 19 July 2010. http://youtube.com/watch?v=xqsrWDA8afU.

"*Brokeback Mountain* to Shine at Oscars: Alberta Film Crews Building Mountains of Acclaim." *Travel Alberta—What's New*. Travel Alberta, 31 Jan. 2006. 19 Sept. 2006. http://www1.travelalberta.com/whatsnew/details.cfm?whatsnewID=489.

"*Brokeback* Palance." Posted by elsantorobo. *YouTube*, 23 Feb. 2006. 19 July 2010. http://youtube.com/watch?v=ZiI5RMuCc2U.

"*Brokeback* Penguins." Posted by bluerocket23. *YouTube*, 28 Feb. 2006. 19 July 2010. http://youtube.com/watch?v=VaMr5TXNZic.

"*Brokeback* Stooges." Posted by bluerocket23. *YouTube*, 1 Mar. 2006. 19 July 2010. http://youtube.com/watch?v=d3ph0E9K700.

Brooke, Aslan, and Alexander Cho, eds. "The Best of Gay Los Angeles." *Frontiers* 24.23 (2006): 93.

Brooks, Peter. *The Melodramatic Imagination: Balzac, Henry James, Melodrama and the Mode of Excess*. New Haven CT: Yale University Press, 1976.

Brown, Mark, and W. R. Felton. *Before Barbed Wire: L. A. Huffman, Photographer on Horseback*. New York: Bramhall House, 1959.

Buchanan, Kyle. Rev. of *Were the World Mine*. *Advocate* 2 Dec. 2006: 56.

Buckendorff, Jennifer. "Get Off *Brokeback*'s Back Already, Would Ya?" *Seattle Times*, 27 Feb. 2006. 9 July 2010. http://community.seattletimes.nwsource .com/archive/?date=20060227&slug=gaycommentary27.

Burroughs, Alexandra. "Buzz and Debate Surrounding *Brokeback Mountain* Swirl in 'Redneck' Alberta, the Unlikely Location for Gay Cowboy Film." *CanWest News* 24 Dec. 2005: 1.

Butler, Judith. *The Psychic Life of Power: Theories in Subjection*. Stanford CA: Stanford University Press, 1997.

蔡登山 [Cai, Deng Shan]. 张爱玲 «色, 戒» [Eileen Chang's "Lust, Caution"]. 北京: 作家出版社 [Beijing: The Writers Publishing House], 2007.

Carman, Colin. "Heath Ledger and the Idolatry of Dying Young." *Gay & Lesbian Review Worldwide* July–Aug. 2008: 28.

Carter, David. *Stonewall: The Riots That Sparked the Gay Revolution*. New York: St. Martin's Press, 2004.

Chopin, Kate. *The Awakening*. 1899. New York: Knopf, 1992.

Chow, Rey. "Postscript (Inspired by *Brokeback Mountain*): 'The Juice'; or, 'The Great Chinese Theme.'" *Sentimental Fabulations, Contemporary Chinese Films: Attachment in the Age of Global Visibility*. New York: Columbia University Press, 2007. 197–200.

Cixous, Hèléne. "Extreme Fidelity." *Writing Differences: Readings from the Seminars of Hèléne Cixous*. Ed. Susan Sellers. New York: St. Martin's Press, 1988.

"Club Review." *Insight Out Books*, 7 May 2006. http://www.insightoutbooks .com/.

The Cody Statement: A Declaration of Uniting and Guiding Principles for the Republican Party in the 21st Century. Cody WY: Republican Unity Coalition, 2001.

"Conservatives Quick to Opine on *Brokeback Mountain*'s 'Agenda,' Slow to Actually See Film." Media Matters for America, 20 Jan. 2006. 19 July 2010. http://mediamatters.org/research/200601200005.

Coulter, Ann. "It's Hard Out Here for a Wimp." 8 March 2006. 17 June 2010. http://www.anncoulter.com/cgi-local/article.cgi?article=103.

Covert, Colin. "'Brokeback Mountain' a Spellbinding Story: The So-Called 'Gay-Cowboy Movie' Is Really a Classic Romantic Melodrama, Flawlessly Executed, That Happens to Feature Two Men." *Star Tribune* [Minneapolis] 16 Dec. 2005, Friday ed., Scene sec.: 8F.

"Cowboys Promote Brokeback 'Alberta' in Manhattan." *CBC News*. Canadian

Broadcasting Corporation, 24 Feb. 2006. 21 Sept. 2006. http://www.cbc.ca/story/canada/national/2006/02/24/20060224-albertatourism.html.

Cullen, Dave. "Ultimate Brokeback Forum." 10 Sept. 2005. 1 July 2010. http://www.brokeback.davecullen.com.

———. Various quotes. 17 June 2010. http://www.davecullen.com.

Cummings, Debra. "Alberta's *Brokeback Mountain* Snags Three Oscars." *Travel Alberta—Stories & Articles*. Travel Alberta, 6 Mar. 2006. 19 Sept. 2006. http://www1.travelalberta.com/Stories/index.cfm?action=display&storyID=180.

———. "'Brokeback' Opens Up Alberta's Sweeping Wilderness." *Travel Alberta—Stories & Articles*. Travel Alberta, 8 Feb. 2006. 19 Sept. 2006. http://www1.travelalberta.com/Stories/index.cfm?action=display&storyID=174.

Dargis, Manohla. "50's Pinup Lives Again at Toronto Film Festival." *New York Times* 15 Sept. 2005, late ed.: E1.

———. "Masculinity and Its Discontents in Marlboro Country." *New York Times* 18 Dec. 2005, New York ed.: AR13.

David, Larry. "Cowboys Are My Weakness." *New York Times* 1 Jan. 2006, late ed., sec. 4: 9.

Davis, Anthony A. "Ang's Angst." *Avenue* Nov. 2005: 66–75.

Davis, Natalie Zemon. *The Return of Martin Guerre*. Cambridge MA: Harvard University Press, 1983.

de Lauretis, Teresa. *Technologies of Gender*. Bloomington: Indiana University Press, 1987.

D'Emilio, John. *Sexual Politics, Sexual Communities: The Making of a Homosexual Minority in the United States, 1940–1970*. Chicago: University of Chicago Press, 1983.

Detrixhe, John. "An Interview with Annie Proulx." Dec. 2005. 4 July 2010. http://www.bookslut.com/features/2005_12_007310.php.

"Did You Hear the One about *Brokeback*?" *MSNBC.com*, 13 Feb. 2006. 19 July 2010. http://www.msnbc.msn.com/id/11206157/.

Dilley, Whitney Crothers. *The Cinema of Ang Lee: The Other Side of the Screen*. London: Wallflower, 2007.

Dinoff, Dustin. "Alberta Back on Oscar Mountain." *Playback* 20 Feb. 2006: 28.

Drudge, Matt. "Hollywood Rocked: 'Gay Cowboy' Movie Becomes an Oscar Frontrunner." *DrudgeReportArchives.com*. Drudge Report 2005, 6 Nov. 2005. 19 Sept. 2006. http://www.drudgereportarchives.com/data/2005/11/07/20051107_011200_flash3bm.htm.

Duggan, Lisa. "What's Right with Utah." *The Nation*, 13 July 2009. 10 July 2010. http://www.thenation.com/article/what's_right_utah.

Durbin, Karen. "Cowboys in Love . . . with Each Other." *New York Times* 4 Sept. 2005, late ed., Arts and Leisure sec.: 9+.

Ebert, Roger. "Forbidden Love: 'Brokeback Mountain' Tells a Powerful Story of Two Men and an Unforgiving World." *Chicago Sun-Times* 16 Dec. 2005: NC30.

———. Rev. of *Lust, Caution*. 5 Oct. 2007. 24 June 2010. http://rogerebert.sun times.com/apps/pbcs.dll/article?AID=/20071004/REVIEWS/710040306.

Eco, Umberto. *Kant and the Platypus: Essays on Language and Cognition*. Trans. Alastair McEwen. New York: Harcourt, 2000.

———. "Travels in Hyperreality." *Travels in Hyperreality: Essays*. Trans. William Weaver. San Diego CA: Harcourt, 1986. 3–58.

Edelstein, David. "Crash and Fizzle: Good Intentions, Lousy Delivery in *Crash* and *Kingdom of Heaven*." *Slate.com*, 5 May 2005. 3 September 2009. http://www.slate.com/id/2118119.

Edemariam, Aida. "Home on the Range." *Guardian Unlimited*, 11 Dec. 2004. 29 June 2010. http://books.guardian.co.uk/departments/generalfiction/story/0,6000,1371261,00.html.

Edmundson, Mark. "Freud and the Fundamentalist Urge." *New York Times Magazine* 30 Apr. 2006: 15.

Edwards, Steven. "Alberta Posse Hunts Tourists from Big Apple." *CanWest News* 25 Feb. 2006: 1.

———. "Alberta Rides Brokeback Success in New York Tourism Campaign." *CanWest News* 9 Feb. 2006: 1.

Elder, Robert K. "Lee Sees His 'Brokeback Mountain' as a Unifying Force." *Chicago Tribune*, 4 Dec. 2005. 29 June 2010. http://metromix.chicagotribune.com/movies/mmx-0512040442dec04,0,2208255.story?coll=mmx-movies_heds.

Ellsworth, Elizabeth. "Illicit Pleasures: Feminist Spectators and *Personal Best*." *Issues in Feminist Film Criticism*. Ed. Patricia Erens. Bloomington: Indiana University Press, 1991. 183–96.

Engels, Friedrich. *The Condition of the Working Class in England*. 1845. Oxford: Oxford University Press, 2009.

Fiedler, Leslie. "Come Back to the Raft Ag'in, Huck Honey!" *A Casebook in Critical Controversy: Mark Twain's Adventures of Huckleberry Finn*. Ed. Gerald Graff and James Phelan. 2nd ed. 1948. New York: St. Martin's Press, 2004. 519–25.

———. "Come Back to the Raft Ag'in, Huck Honey!" *Partisan Review* 15.6 (June 1948): 664–71.

———. *An End to Innocence: Essays on Culture and Politics*. Boston: Beacon, 1955.

———. *Love and Death in the American Novel*. Rev. ed. New York: Stein and Day, 1966.

Focus Features. "Brokeback Mountain." NBC Universal, 2006. 17 June 2010. http://www.brokebackmountainmovie.com.

Foot, Paul. *Red Shelley*. London: Sidgwick & Jackson, 1980.

"For Collector, 'Brokeback' Shirts Fit Fine." *Los Angeles Times*, 23 Feb. 2006. 19 July 2010. http://articles.latimes.com/2006/feb/23/news/wk-quick23.2.

Forster, E. M. "Terminal Note." *Maurice*. 1960. New York: Norton, 1987.

Foucault, Michel. "Body/Power." *Power/Knowledge: Selected Interviews and Other Writing 1972–1977*. Ed. Colin Gordon. New York: Pantheon Books, 1980.

Free Republic. Various quotes. 17 June 2010. http://www.freerepublic.com.

French, Peter A. *Cowboy Metaphysics: Ethics and Death in Westerns*. Lanham MD: Roman & Littlefield Publishers, Inc., 1997.

Freud, Sigmund. *The Ego and the Id*. Trans. Joan Riviere. New York: Norton, 1960.

———. *The Interpretation of Dreams*. Trans. A. A. Brill. New York: Barnes and Noble Books, 1994.

———. "Mourning and Melancholia." *The Standard Edition of the Complete Psychological Works*. Trans. James Stachey. Vol. 14. 1917. London: Hogarth, 1953–74. 243–58.

———. *The Uncanny*. Trans. David McLintock. 1919. New York: Penguin, 2003.

Frichtl, Ben. "Narnia Gets Lion's Share of Box Office, While Critics Hail Gay Cowboy Flick." *Concerned Women for America*, 13 Dec. 2005. 6 July 2010. http://www.cwfa.org/printerfriendly.asp?id=9689&department=cfi&categoryid=misc.

Gates, Gary J. *Same-Sex Spouses and Unmarried Partners in the American Community Survey*. Los Angeles: Williams Institute, UCLA, October 2009.

Gay Spirituality and Culture. Various quotes. 17 June 2010. http://gayspirituality.typepad.com.

Germain, David. "'Brokeback Mountain' Tests Oscar Waters." *AP Online*, 13 Dec. 2005. 9 Jan. 2006. http://www.cbsnews.com/stories/2005/12/13/ap/entertainment/mainD8EFIQO03.shtml. Available at http://www.encyclopedia.com/doc/1P1-116358604.html.

Gill, Alexandra. "Western Canada in the Spotlight." *Globe and Mail* 1 Feb. 2006: R1+.

Ginzburg, Carlo. *The Cheese and the Worms*. Trans. John Tedeschi and Anne Tedeschi. 1976. Baltimore: Johns Hopkins University Press, 1992.

Glaze, Violet. "The Searchers: Almost Classic Doomed-Love Story *Brokeback Mountain* Maps an Affair to Remember." *City Paper* [Baltimore], 28 Dec. 2005. 1 July 2010. http://www.citypaper.com/film/review.asp?rid=9732.

Gregory, Tom. Personal interviews by Chris Freeman. 10 May 2006 and 7 August 2009.

Guisnel, Jean. *Cyberwars: Espionage on the Internet*. Trans. Gui Masai. New York: Basic Books, 1999.

Handley, William R. *Marriage, Violence, and the Nation in the American Literary West*. Cambridge: Cambridge University Press, 2002.

Harte, Bret. "In the Tules." *Bret Harte's Gold Rush: "Outcasts of Poker Flat," "The Luck of Roaring Camp," "Tennessee's Partner," and Other Favorites.* Berkeley CA: Heyday Books, 1997. 146–63.

———. "Tennessee's Partner." *Bret Harte's Gold Rush: "Outcasts of Poker Flat," "The Luck of Roaring Camp," "Tennessee's Partner," and Other Favorites.* Berkeley CA: Heyday Books, 1997. 34–42.

Heffernan, Virginia. "*Brokeback* Spoofs: Tough Guys Unmasked." *New York Times* 2 Mar. 2006, late ed., final sec.: E1.

Henderson, William Haywood. *Native: A Novel.* 1993. Lincoln: University of Nebraska Press, 2010.

Herring, Scott. *Another Country: Queer Anti-Urbanism.* New York: New York University Press, 2010.

———. "*Brokeback Mountain* Dossier." GLQ 13.1 (2007): 93–94.

Hinton, Gregory. Introduction to screening of *Two Spirits.* "Out West: LBGT Stories of the American West" series. Autry National Center. LA Gay and Lesbian Center, West Hollywood, 28 June 2010.

Hirsen, James. "Tony Curtis Blasts 'Brokeback Mountain.'" *Newsmax,* 7 Feb. 2006. 30 June 2010. http://archive.newsmax.com/archives/articles/2006/2/7/221024.shtml.

Hoberman, J. "Stable Relationship." *Village Voice* 30 Nov.–6 Dec. 2005: 48.

Hollinghurst, Alan. *The Swimming Pool Library.* New York: Vintage, 1988.

The Holy Bible. King James version. New York: Meridian, 1974.

Hornaday, Ann. "Wrangling with Love on the Range." *Washington Post* 16 Dec. 2005, F ed.: T43.

Hsu, Hsuan L. "Racial Privacy, the L.A. Ensemble Film, and Paul Haggis's *Crash.*" *Film Criticism* 31.1 (2006): 132–56.

Hune-Brown, Nick. "The Cowboy Way." *Toronto Star* 5 Mar. 2006: D1+.

Hunter, Stephen. "Brokeback's Image Control." *Toronto Star* 5 Feb. 2006: C21.

Hutcheon, Linda. *A Theory of Adaptation.* New York: Routledge, 2006.

Internet Movie Database. *Brokeback Mountain.* 2005. 19 July 2010. http://www.imdb.com/title/tt0388795/business.

———. *Message Boards.* Various quotes. 17 June 2010. http://www.imdb.com/title/tt0388795/board.

Isherwood, Christopher. *A Single Man.* 1964. Minneapolis: University of Minnesota Press, 2000.

Jacobson, Harlan. "*Brokeback Mountain.*" *Film Comment* Nov.–Dec. 2005: 71–72.

Johnson, Colin R. "Rural Space: Queer America's Final Frontier." *Chronicle of Higher Education,* 13 Jan. 2006. 30 June 2010. http://chronicle.com/article/Rural_Space_Queer_America_s18513.

Kaplan, Amy. "Manifest Domesticity." *American Literature* 70 (Sept. 1998): 581–606.

Kinsey, Alfred C., Wardell B. Pomeroy, and Clyde E. Martin. *Sexual Behavior in the Human Male*. Philadelphia: Saunders, 1948.

Kreimer, Seth F. "Technologies of Protest: Insurgent Social Movements and the First Amendment in the Era of the Internet." *University of Pennsylvania Law Review* 150.1 (2001): 119–71.

Kushner, Tony. *Angels in America: A Gay Fantasia on National Themes*. 1995. New York: Theatre Communications Group, 2003.

Lacey, Liam. "Why Are Liberals Laughing?" *Globe and Mail* 5 Jan. 2006: R3.

Lane, Anthony. "New Frontiers." *New Yorker* 12 Dec. 2005: 117.

LaSalle, Mick. "Just Your Average Marlboro Men—Who Fall in Love." *San Francisco Chronicle* 8 Dec. 2005, Friday ed., Daily Datebook sec.: E5.

Leavitt, David. "Men in Love: Is *Brokeback Mountain* a Gay Film?" *Slate Magazine*, 8 Dec. 2005. 3 June 2010. http://www.slate.com/id/2131865. [Reprinted in this volume.]

Lee, Ang. "The Director's Cut: *Brokeback*'s Ang Lee on Jack, Ennis . . . & Other Outsiders." *Equality*. Human Rights Campaign Publication, Spring 2006: 6–9.

———. Interview by Carlo Cavagna. *AboutFilm.com*, Dec. 2005. 6 July 2010. http://www.aboutfilm.com/movies/b/brokebackmountain/lee.htm.

Leland, John. "Make Reviews, Not Boycotts." *Toronto Star* 26 Dec. 2005: c8.

LeRoy Ladurie, Emmanuel. *The Peasants of Languedoc*. Trans. John Day. 1966. Urbana: University of Illinois Press, 1976.

Lewis, Nathaniel. *Unsettling the Literary West: Authenticity and Authorship*. Lincoln: University of Nebraska Press, 2003.

Li Hongzhi. *Falun Gong*. English version. Rev. ed. New York: Universe, 2000.

Loffreda, Beth. *Losing Matt Shepard: Life and Politics in the Aftermath of an Anti-Gay Murder*. New York: Columbia University Press, 2000.

———. "Scheduling Idealism in Laramie, Wyoming." *Postwestern Cultures: Literature, Theory, Space*. Ed. Susan Kollin. Lincoln: University of Nebraska Press, 2007. 159–71.

Lubman, Sarah. "A Chinese Battle on U.S. Soil: Persecuted Group's Campaign Catches Politicians in the Middle." *San Jose Mercury News* 23 Dec. 2001, Sunday morning final ed., Front sec.: A1+.

Manalansan, Martin F., IV. "Colonizing Time and Space: Race and Romance in *Brokeback Mountain*." *GLQ* 13.1 (2006): 97–100.

Marcuse, Herbert. *Eros and Civilization*. Boston: Beacon, 1966.

Marx, Karl. *Capital*. Ed. Frederick Engels. Trans. Samuel Moore and Edward Aveling. Vol. 1. New York: International Publishers, 1967.

"Matthews Cited Savage's '*Bareback Mountain*' Characterization of *Brokeback Mountain*; Imus Cited Producer's '*Fudgepack Mountain*' Remark." Media Matters for America, 19 Jan. 2006. 19 July 2010. http://mediamatters.org/research/200601200002.

McClure, Helen. "The Wild, Wild Web: The Mythic American West and the Electronic Frontier." *Western Historical Quarterly* 31.4 (2000): 457–76.

McKinley, Jesse. "Marriage Ban Inspires New Wave of Gay Rights Advocates." *New York Times* 10 Dec. 2008: A22+.

McMurtry, Larry. "Adapting *Brokeback Mountain*." Proulx, McMurtry, and Ossana 139–42.

———. *Leaving Cheyenne*. New York: Simon and Schuster, 2002.

McMurtry, Larry, and Diana Ossana. *Brokeback Mountain: A Screenplay*. Proulx, McMurtry, and Ossana 29–127. [Paginated originally as 1–97.]

———. "*Brokeback*'s Big Secrets." Interview by Anne Stockwell. *Advocate* 28 Feb. 2006: 42–44.

Members of the Ultimate Brokeback Forum. *Beyond Brokeback: The Impact of a Film*. Livermore CA: WingSpan, 2007.

Mendelsohn, Daniel. "An Affair to Remember." *New York Review of Books* 53.3 (2006): 12–13. [Reprinted in this volume.]

———. "'Brokeback Mountain': An Exchange with James Schamus and Joel Conarroe." *The New York Review of Books* 53.6 (2006): 68–69.

———. *How Beautiful It Is and How Easily It Can Be Broken: Essays*. New York: HarperCollins, 2008.

Merriam Webster's Collegiate Dictionary. 10th ed. Springfield MA, 1993.

Midnight Diamonds. Various quotes. 16 May 2010. http://www.midnight-dia monds.com/brokeback. [Site now discontinued.]

Miller, D. A. "On the Universality of *Brokeback Mountain*." *Film Quarterly* 60.3 (2007): 50–60.

Modleski, Tania. *The Women Who Knew Too Much: Hitchcock and Feminist Theory*. New York: Routledge, 1988.

Moffat, Wendy. *A Great Unrecorded History: A New Life of E. M. Forster*. New York: Farrar, Straus, & Giroux, 2010.

Monette, Paul. "My Shirts." *No Witnesses*. New York: Avon, 1981.

Morgenstern, Joe. "'Brokeback Mountain' Brings an Open, Epic Sweep to Cowboys' Hidden Love." *Wall Street Journal*, 9 Dec. 2005. 8 July 2010. http://online.wsj.com/article/SB113408500737317852.html.

Myers, B. R. "A Reader's Manifesto: An Attack on the Growing Pretentiousness of American Literary Prose." *Atlantic Monthly* July/August 2001: 104–22.

National Marriage Forum. Various quotes. 17 June 2010. http://www.marriage .org.au/re_entering_the_circle_of_life.htm.

Nelson Limerick, Patricia. "Seeing and Being Seen: Tourism in the American West." *Seeing and Being Seen: Tourism in the American West*. Ed. David M. Wrobel and Patrick T. Long. Lawrence: University Press of Kansas, 2001. 39–58.

"No Gay Cowboys Here." *Xtra!* 2 Mar. 2006, Toronto ed., News Briefs sec.: 19.

Noveck, Jocelyn. "Flood of *Brokeback* Jokes Gets Mixed Reaction from Gays." *Seattle Post-Intelligencer*, 8 Feb. 2006. 8 July 2010. http://www.seattlepi .com/movies/258640_brokebackhumor08.html.

Osterweil, Ara. "Ang Lee's Lonesome Cowboys." *Film Quarterly* 60.3 (2007): 38–42.

Ownby, David. *Falun Gong and the Future of China*. Oxford: Oxford University Press, 2008.

———— "The Falun Gong: A New Religious Movement in Post-Mao China." *Controversial New Religions*. Ed. James R. Lewis and Jesper Aargaard Petersen. Oxford: Oxford University Press, 2005. 195–214.

Packard, Chris. *Queer Cowboys and Other Erotic Male Friendships in Nineteenth-Century American Literature*. New York: Palgrave Macmillan, 2005.

Paglia, Camille. Interview by Mark Adnum. *Outrate,* July 2006. 29 June 2010. http://www.outrate.net/?p=428 .

Palmer, David A. *Qigong Fever: Body, Science, and Utopia in China*. New York: Columbia University Press, 2007.

Papanikolas, Zeese. *Trickster in the Land of Dreams*. Lincoln: University of Nebraska Press, 1995.

The Passion of the Christ. New Market Films, 2004. 17 June 2010. http://www .thepassionofchrist.com/splash/htm.

Pearson, Demetrius W., and C. Allen Haney. "The Rodeo Cowboy as an American Icon: The Perceived Social and Cultural Significance." *Journal of American Culture* 22.4 (1999): 17–21.

People Can Change. 2005–8. 17 June 2010. http://www.peoplecanchange.com.

Pessoa, Fernando. *The Book of Disquiet*. Ed. and trans. Richard Zenith. London: Penguin Books, 2001.

Powers, John. "Hollywood's Newest Age of Liberal Cinema." *LA Weekly*, 12 Jan. 2006. 8 July 2010. http://www.laweekly.com/2006-01-12/columns/ hollywood-s-newest-age-of-liberal-cinema/.

Proulx, Annie. Afterword. *The Power of the Dog*. By Thomas Savage. New York: Little, Brown, and Company, 2001. 277–93.

————. "At Close Range with Annie Proulx." Interview by Matthew Testa. *Planet Jackson Hole*, 7 Dec. 2005. 29 June 2010. http://www.planetjh.com/ testa_2005_12_07_proulx.html.

————. *Bad Dirt: Wyoming Stories 2*. New York: Scribner, 2004.

————. "Biography." 2 Feb. 2006. 29 June 2010. http://www.huaren.us/dis pbbs.asp?boardid=358&id=172999&page=0&move=next.

————. *Brokeback Mountain*. 1997. New York: Scribner, 2005. [Bedient's, Freeman's, Hinton's, and McCabe's reference.]

————. "Brokeback Mountain." *Close Range: Brokeback Mountain and Other Stories*. London: Harper Perennial, 1999. 281–318. [Lo's reference.]

————. "Brokeback Mountain." *Close Range: Wyoming Stories*. New York: Scribner, 1999. 251–83. [Carman's, Handley's, Hunt's, and Sonstegard's reference.]

————. "Brokeback Mountain." Proulx, McMurtry, and Ossana 1–28. [Morrison's reference.]

————. *Close Range: Wyoming Stories*. New York: Scribner, 1999.

————. *Fine Just the Way It Is: Wyoming Stories 3*. New York: Scribner, 2008.

————. "Getting Movied." Proulx, McMurtry, and Ossana 129–38.

————. Interview by staff. *Missouri Review* 22.2 (1999). 29 June 2010. http://www.missourireview.com/index.php?genre=Interviews&title=Interview+with+Annie+Proulx.

————. *The Shipping News*. New York: Scribner, 1993.

————. *That Old Ace in the Hole*. New York: Scribner, 2002.

Proulx, Annie, Larry McMurtry, and Diana Ossana. *Brokeback Mountain: Story to Screenplay*. New York: Scribner, 2005.

Reynolds, Susan Salter. "Writer No Longer at Home on the Range; Writer Finished with Wyoming." *Los Angeles Times* 18 October 2008: A1+.

Rich, Adrienne. "Compulsory Heterosexuality and Lesbian Existence." *Blood, Bread and Poetry*. 1980. New York: Norton, 1986. 23–75.

Rich, B. Ruby. "Brokering *Brokeback*: Jokes, Backlashes, and Other Anxieties." *Film Quarterly* 60.3 (2007): 44–48.

————. "Hello Cowboy." *The Guardian*, 23 Sept. 2005. 8 July 2010. http://www.guardian.co.uk/film/2005/sep/23/3.

Rich, Frank. "Two Gay Cowboys Hit a Home Run." *New York Times* 18 Dec. 2005, late ed., sec. 4: 13.

"Ridin', Ropin', Redecoratin' and Jokin' on the Late Shows." *USA Today*, 25 Jan. 2006. 19 July 2010. http://www.usatoday.com/life/movies/news/2006-01-25-brokeback-side_x.htm.

Robinson, Marilynne. *The Death of Adam: Essays on Modern Thought*. New York: Houghton Mifflin, 1998.

Rodriguez, Richard. *Brown: The Last Discovery of America*. New York: Viking, 2002.

Rudé, George. *The Crowd in History, 1730–1848*. New York: Wiley, 1964.

Rushdie, Salman. *The Wizard of Oz*. London: BFI, 1992.

Russo, Vito. *The Celluloid Closet*. New York: Harper & Row, 1981.

Ryzik, Melena. "Go Retell It on the Mountain." *New York Times*, 22 Jan. 2006. 8 July 2010. http://www.nytimes.com/2006/01/22/movies22paro.html.

Savage, Thomas. *The Power of the Dog*. New York: Little, Brown, 1967.

Schamus, James. "Focus(ed) Debate." *Filmmaker*. IFP, 24 Mar. 2006. 4 June 2010. http://www.filmmakermagazine.com/blog/2006/03/focused-debated.php.

Schneider, Richard. "Not Quitting *Brokeback.*" *Gay & Lesbian Review Worldwide* May–June 2006: 10.

Schrobsdorff, Susanna. "Chick-Flick Cowboys: 'Brokeback Mountain' Has Stolen the Hearts of Women in Middle America." *Newsweek*, 20 Jan. 2006. 29 June 2010. http://www.msnbc.msn.com/id/10930877/site/newsweek/.

Sedgwick, Eve Kosofsky. *Epistemology of the Closet*. Berkeley: University of California Press, 1990.

———. *Touching Feeling: Affect, Pedagogy, Performativity*. Durham NC: Duke University Press, 2003.

Sefton, Dru. "Beating That Queasiness: Straight, Liberal, and Gun-Shy about Brokeback." *San Francisco Chronicle*, 15 Jan. 2006. 9 July 2010. http://articles.sfgate.com/2006-01-15/opinion/17276199_1_brokeback-mountain-golden-globe-awards-two-men.

Shallit, Gene. Rev. of *Brokeback Mountain* on "Critic's Corner." *The Today Show*, NBC, New York, 5 Jan. 2006.

Shank, Jenny. "Proulx, McMurtry and Ossana Discuss Adapting 'Brokeback Mountain.'" *New West*. Mountain Press Publishing Agency, 23 Nov. 2005. 21 June 2010. http://www.newwest.net/index.php/main/article/4463.

Sontag, Susan. "Notes on 'Camp.'" *Against Interpretation and Other Essays*. New York: Noonday, 1966. 275–92.

Spanbauer, Tom. *The Man Who Fell in Love with the Moon: A Novel*. 1991. New York: Grove, 2000.

Spines, Christine. "Western Union." *Entertainment Weekly* 853 (2005): 30–38.

Staiger, Janet. *Interpreting Films: Studies in the Historical Reception of American Cinema*. Princeton NJ: Princeton University Press, 1992.

———. "Reception Studies in Film and Television." *The Film Cultures Reader*. Ed. Graeme Turner. London: Routledge, 2002. 46–72.

Stein, Ruth. "At the Toronto Film Festival: Love, Real and Pretend, on 'Brokeback' Set." *San Francisco Chronicle* 13 Sept. 2005, final ed.: E2.

Stoeltje, Beverly J. "Rodeo: From Custom to Ritual." *Western Folklore* 48.3 (1989): 244–55.

Stone, Wilfred. *The Cave and the Mountain*. Stanford: Stanford University Press, 1966.

Sullivan, Andrew. "Gay Cowboys Embraced by Redneck Country." *Sunday Times* [London], 26 Feb. 2006. 30 June 2010. http:/www.timesonline.co.uk/article/0,,2092-2058537,00.html.

———. *Virtually Normal: An Argument about Homosexuality*. New York: Knopf, 1995.

Targ, William, ed. *The American West: A Treasury of Stories, Legends, Narratives, Songs, and Ballads of Western America*. Whitefish MT: Kessinger, 2005.

Taubin, Amy. "*My Own Private Idaho*: Private Places." Criterion Collection, 4

Mar. 2005. 7 July 2010. http://www.criterion.com/current/posts/596-my
-own-private-idaho-private-places.

Teo, Stephen. *Hong Kong Cinema: The Extra Dimensions*. London: BFI, 1997.

"The Towleroad Guide to *Brokeback Mountain* Poster Parodies." 18 Oct. 2005.
19 July 2010. http://towleroad.typepad.com/towleroad/2005/10/the
_towleroad_g_1.html.

"Toy Mountain." Posted by ADizzy. *Spike*, 28 Mar. 2006. 19 July 2010. http://
www.spike.com/video/toyback-mountain/2714461.

Trebay, Guy. "Cowboys, Just Like in the Movie." *New York Times* 18 Dec. 2005,
Fashion and Style/Sunday Styles sec.: 1, 6.

Trevor-Roper, H. R. "Fernand Braudel, the *Annales*, and the Mediterranean."
Journal of Modern History 44 . 4 (1972): 468–79.

Turan, Kenneth. "The New Frontier of 'Brokeback' Is Vast and Heartfelt." *Los
Angeles Times*, 9 Dec. 2005. 8 July 2010. http://articles.latimes.com/2005/
dec/09/entertainment/et-brokeback9.

Turner, Mark. "Brokeback Gotham." 2008. 30 June 2010. http://www.fanpop
.com/spots/batman/images/475902/title/brokeback-gotham.

Ultimate Brokeback Forum. Advertisement. *Variety*, 10 Mar. 2006. 10 July
2010. http://davecullen.com/brokebackmountain/img/ad-final.jpg.

"Utah Carroll." *Lone Hand Western: Journal of the Old West*, 2005. 17 July 2010.
http://www.lonehand.com/cowboy_songs.htm.

Warner, Michael. *The Trouble with Normal: Sex, Politics and the Ethics of Queer
Life*. New York: Free Press, 1999.

Warner, Tom. *Never Going Back: A History of Queer Activism in Canada*. Toronto:
University of Toronto Press, 2002.

Warren, Patricia Nell. "Real Cowboys, Real Rodeos." *Gay & Lesbian Review
Worldwide* (July–August 2006): 19–23.

Weltzien, Alan. "'Just Regular Guys': Homophobia, the Code of the West, and
Constructions of Male Identity in Thomas Savage and Annie Proulx." *All
Our Stories Are Here: Critical Perspectives on Montana Literature*. Ed. Brady
Harrison. Lincoln: University of Nebraska Press, 2009. 117–38.

Whalen, Tracy. "Camping with Annie Proulx: *The Shipping News* and Tourist
Desire." *Essays on Canadian Writing* 82 (2004): 51–70.

White, Dave. "The Straight Dude's Guide to *Brokeback*: Our Intrepid Gay Columnist Has Sage Advice for His Straight Brethren." *MSNBC.com*, 12 Dec.
2005. Nov. 2006. http://www.msnbc.msn.com/id/10342237/.

White, Edmund. *The Farewell Symphony*. New York: Knopf, 1997.

———. *My Lives: An Autobiography*. New York: HarperCollins/Ecco, 2006.

White, Evelyn. "5,000 See Dust Fly at Gay Rodeo: No Tinhorns in East Bay
Competition." *San Francisco Chronicle* 21 Sept. 1987, final ed.: A3.

White, Patricia. *Uninvited: Classical Hollywood Cinema and Lesbian Represent-
ability*. Bloomington: Indiana University Press, 1999.

Whyte, Murray. "When a Kiss Is Just a Kiss." *Toronto Star* 13 Dec. 2005: A3.

Wildman, Sarah. "In the Unlikeliest of Places." *Advocate* 16 Dec. 2008: 16.

Williams, Linda. "'Something Else Besides a Mother': *Stella Dallas* and the Maternal Melodrama." *Cinema Journal* 4.1 (1984): 2–27.

Wiltz, Teresa. "Divas of Disaster: People Just Can't Look Away from the Train Wreck Girls." *Washington Post* 6 Jan. 2007, Final edition, Style: C1, C8.

Winter, Jessica. "The Scripting News: Brokeback Writers on the Road from Page to Screen." *Village Voice* 30 Nov.–6 Dec. 2005: 33.

Wister, Owen. *The Virginian: A Horseman of the Plains.* 1902. Intro. Thomas McGuane. Lincoln: University of Nebraska Press, 1992.

Wloszczyna, Susan. "Film Spurs Culture of Gay Cowboy Jokes." *USA Today* 26 Jan. 2006, Life sec.: 1D.

Wood, Robin. "On and Around *Brokeback Mountain*." *Film Quarterly* 60.3 (2007): 28–31.

Yahoo!Movies. Various quotes. 17 June 2010. http://messages.movies.yahoo.com.

Yoshino, Kenji. *Covering: The Hidden Assault on Our Civil Rights.* New York: Random House, 2006.

Žižek, Slavoj. *The Parallax View.* Cambridge MA: MIT Press, 2006.

Zonta, Dario. "Western alla Lee." *Brokeback Mountain.* Italian DVD booklet. Milan, Italy: Giangiacomo Feltrinelli Editore Milano, 2006.

Contributors

MARTIN AGUILERA was a 2007 fellow of Film Independent's Project: Involve mentorship program. When he was fifteen, his play *The Derelicts* was produced by the Fourth Wall Players—for which he was awarded an Outstanding Achievement Award at the 1998 Young Texas Playwrights Competition. In 2004 his screenplay *The Image Consultant* was accepted at the National Association of Latino Independent Producer's Writer's Lab in New York City; he was the youngest writer to attend that year. His script *Miseducated* was one of the top three winners for the 2009 Slamdance Teleplay Competition.

CALVIN BEDIENT's most recent critical book is *The Yeats Brothers and Modernism's Love of Motion* and his most recent book of poems is *Days of Unwilling*. He is a coeditor of *Lana Turner: A Journal of Poetry and Opinion* and of the New California Poetry Series.

COLIN CARMAN holds a PhD in English literature from the University of California, Santa Barbara. He has taught at Colby College and Santa Barbara City College. His writings have appeared in the *Gay & Lesbian Review Worldwide* and *GLQ: A Journal of Lesbian and Gay Studies*. He currently teaches at Colorado Mountain College in Breckenridge and is working on a book on Percy Shelley and homophobia in nineteenth-century England.

ALAN DALE grew up in Indiana and earned a PhD in comparative literature from Princeton University and a JD from Yale Law School. He lives in Portland, Oregon, and is deputy legislative counsel to the Oregon Legislative Assembly. He has written two books, *Comedy Is a Man in Trouble: Slapstick in American Movies* and *What We Do Best: American Movie Comedies of the 1990s*. His article "To Crie Alarme Spiritual: Evelyn Waugh and the Ironic Community" appeared in *Modernist Cultures*. His movie reviews can be found at http://www.weirdprofessortype.com.

JON DAVIES is a writer and curator based in Toronto. His writing has appeared in *C Magazine, Canadian Art, GLQ: A Journal of Lesbian and Gay Studies, Animation Journal, Cinema Scope, Xtra!*, and many other publications. He has also curated numerous screenings for the artists' film and video exhibitor Pleasure Dome and for various venues in Toronto and internationally, as well as several exhibitions. He is currently the assistant curator of public programs at The Power Plant Contemporary Art Gallery.

CHRIS FREEMAN has a PhD in English from Vanderbilt University and teaches at the University of Southern California. He is coeditor, with James Berg, of three books: *The Isherwood Century, Conversations with Christopher Isherwood*, and *Love, West Hollywood: Reflections of Los Angeles*. He also edited and introduced *Under the Rainbow*, a memoir of Hollywood by John Carlyle. Most recently, he coauthored *Fine on Acting* with Howard Fine.

JUDITH HALBERSTAM is a professor of English, gender studies, and American studies and ethnicity at the University of Southern California. She is the author of *Female Masculinity, Skin Shows: Gothic Horror and the Technology of Monsters*, and *In a Queer Time and Place: Transgender Bodies, Subcultural Lives*. Halberstam has also written for *The Nation, Bitch*, and other magazines.

WILLIAM R. HANDLEY is the author of *Marriage, Violence, and the Nation in the American Literary West* and coeditor, with Nathaniel Lewis, of *True West: Authenticity and the American West*. He teaches at the University of Southern California and served as president of the Western Literature Association in 2005. Among his essays are "Belonging(s): Plural Marriage, Gay Marriage, and the Subversion of 'Good Order,'" in *Discourse*, and an examination of the silent film *The Vanishing American* in *America First: Naming the Nation in US Film*, edited by Mandy Merck.

ANDREW HOLLERAN has published four novels, including *Dancer from the Dance* and *Grief*, which won the 2007 Stonewall Book Award. He teaches creative writing at American University and frequently publishes articles in the *Gay & Lesbian Review Worldwide*.

GREGORY HINTON created *Out West* for the Autry National Center in Los Angeles. Sponsored by HBO, *Out West* is a historical program series dedicated to illuminating the contributions of the LGBT community to the history and culture of the U.S. West. An author and a filmmaker, Hinton's novels include *Cathedral City, Desperate Hearts, The Way Things Ought to Be,* and *Santa Monica Canyon.* His films include *It's My Party* and *Circuit.* Born in Wolf Point on Montana's Fort Peck Indian Reservation; raised in Cody, Wyoming; and educated in Boulder, Colorado—Gregory Hinton is a proud son of the rural American West.

ALEX HUNT is an assistant professor of English at West Texas A&M University. He has edited a collection titled *Annie Proulx and the Geographical Imagination* and has published numerous essays in western American literary studies, ethnic studies, and ecocriticism. He is a former bull rider.

DAVID LEAVITT is the author of eight novels, four short story collections, and a book about Alan Turing. His work has appeared in *The New Yorker,* the *New York Times,* the *Washington Post, Harper's, Esquire, Vogue,* the *Paris Review,* and other publications. He is a professor of English at the University of Florida, has taught at Princeton University, and is the recipient of fellowships from the National Endowment for the Arts, the Guggenheim Foundation, and the Institute of Catalan Letters in Barcelona, Spain. He was named a Literary Lion by the New York Public Library.

MUN-HOU LO received his PhD from Harvard University and teaches in the University Scholars Programme at the National University of Singapore. His work has appeared in *Modern Fiction Studies,* GLQ: *A Journal of Lesbian and Gay Studies,* and the anthology *Motherhood Misconceived: Representing the Maternal in U.S. Films.*

SUSAN MCCABE is a professor of English at the University of Southern California. Her books include *Elizabeth Bishop: Her Poetics of Loss, Swirl* (poems), *Cinematic Modernism: Cinema and Modernist Poetry,* and *Descartes' Nightmare* (poems). She is currently working on a critical biography, *Bryher: Female Husband of Modernism.*

DANIEL MENDELSOHN's international bestseller *The Lost: A Search for Six of Six Million* won the National Book Critics' Circle Award, the Prix Médicis in France, and many other honors. His other books include the memoir *The Elusive Embrace,* which explores themes of sexual awakening and family history through the lens of classical literature; an acclaimed two-volume translation of the complete poetry of C. P. Cavafy; and a collection of his critical writings, *How Beautiful It Is and How Easily It Can Be Broken,* named a Best Book of the Year by *Publishers Weekly.* His articles and essays appear frequently in the *New York Review of Books* and *The New Yorker.*

JAMES MORRISON is the author of *Broken Fever*, a memoir; *The Lost Girl*, a novel; *Said and Done*, a collection of short stories that was a finalist for a 2009 Lambda Literary Award; and several nonfiction books on film. Morrison lives in Southern California and teaches film, literature, and creative writing at Claremont McKenna College and in the Claremont Colleges consortium.

VANESSA OSBORNE is a lecturer at the University of Southern California and earned her PhD in English and critical theory at the University of California at Irvine. Her dissertation, "Consuming Objects, Consuming Individuals," argues that image-oriented marketing strategies that emerged in the late nineteenth and early twentieth centuries created the conditions for modern celebrity. She is the author of "The Logic of the Mannequin: Shop Windows and the Realist Novel" in *Display: The Places and Spaces of Fashion*.

ANNIE PROULX is a Pulitzer Prize winner and National Book Award winner (both for her 1993 novel *The Shipping News*) and the author of the story "Brokeback Mountain," which earned her the O. Henry Prize for best short story in 1998 (she also won the following year for "The Mud Below"). She won the PEN/Faulkner Award for Fiction for her first novel, *Postcards*. She is the author of six other books, including three short story collections about Wyoming and her most recent novel, *That Old Ace in the Hole*.

JAMES SCHAMUS is an award-winning screenwriter (*The Ice Storm*) and producer (*Crouching Tiger, Hidden Dragon*) and is a professor of professional practice in Columbia University's School of the Arts, where he teaches film history and theory. He is the CEO of Focus Features, the motion picture production, financing, and worldwide distribution company whose films have included *Lost in Translation, Milk, Eternal Sunshine of the Spotless Mind, The Pianist, Atonement, The Constant Gardener*, and *Coraline*. He is the author of *Carl Theodor Dreyer's Gertrud: The Moving Word*.

MICHAEL SILVERBLATT is the host of *Bookworm*, a weekly radio show dedicated to literature, created at KCRW in Santa Monica, California, and broadcast around the country. The twenty years of his interviews with writers around the world are archived at http://www.kcrw.com.

ADAM SONSTEGARD is an assistant professor of American literature at Cleveland State University and a former lecturer in the writing program at the University of California, Davis. His scholarly work in nineteenth- and twentieth-century American studies explores literary art's mediation of—and its mediation by—the visual arts. He has published in *Biography*, the *Henry James Review, Texas Studies in Language and Literature*, and the *Arizona Quarterly*.

NOAH TSIKA is a PhD candidate in cinema studies at New York University, Tisch School of the Arts. He is the author of the book *Gods and Monsters: A Queer Film Classic*, and his essays include "The Queerness of Country: Brokeback's Soundscape," in *Reading Brokeback Mountain*, and "'Compartmentalize Your Life': Advising Army Men on RealJack.com," in LGBT *Identity and Online New Media*. He is currently completing a dissertation on the American military training film.

KENNETH TURAN is a film critic for the *Los Angeles Times* and National Public Radio. He is the author of *Never Coming to a Theater Near You, Now in Theaters Everywhere*, and *Free for All: Joe Papp, the Public, and the Greatest Theater Story Ever Told*.

PATRICIA NELL WARREN grew up on the historical Grant-Kohrs ranch in Montana and spent many years working in the mainstream media. Over the years she has written best-selling gay-themed fiction and provocative political commentary, as well as extensive magazine coverage on the American West's past and present. Warren blogs at the *Huffington Post*, ACLU, Outsports, and the Bilerico Project. Today she lives in Los Angeles, where she co-owns her own independent publishing and media company, Wildcat International. Her personal page is at http://www.patricianellwarren.com.

DAVID WEISS is an assistant professor of media studies at Montana State University–Billings. He has published in scholarly journals, including *Popular Communication* and the *Howard Journal of Communications*, as well as in regional and national publications such as *The Advocate*. Prior to launching his academic career, Weiss spent two decades in the advertising industry in New York City, serving as a management executive at several of the world's largest ad agencies.

Index

Page numbers in italics refer to illustrations.

Abramoff, Jack, 233–34
Academy Awards, 2, 101–5, 115n1, 116n4, 140, 190
Adams, Ansel, 111
adaptation of "Brokeback Mountain," 3, 17, 29, 149, 153–76, 179–89
The Adventures of Huckleberry Finn (Twain), 81
Aguilera, Martin, 4, 11
Alberta, Canada, 5, 144, 249–63
Allen, Marit, 289
Allison, Dorothy, 87
Allmendinger, Blake, 147
Allor, Martin, 209
All That Heaven Allows, 168, 311, 317
Althusser, Louis, 127
Anderson, Corey, 233
Angels in America, 21, 45
Annales School, 164–65, 176n1
Araki, Gregg, 22n6, 207
Aron, Steve, 121, 122
Auni, Noelle, 259–60
Australia, 134n1
authenticity of *Brokeback Mountain*, 43, 44–45, 140–41, 143, 144, 149–50, 219, 249–63
Autry, Gene, 190
Autry, Jackie, 122
Autry National Center for the American West, 7, 116n6, 118–22
Avedeon, Richard, 111
The Awakening (Chopin), 19

Bachardy, Don, 112
Back Street, 168
Bad Dirt (Proulx), 160, 165
Baehr, Ted, 6, 283
Baldwin, Alec, 238
The Ballad of Little Jo, 200
Banderas, Antonio, 222
Bawer, Bruce, 87
Beckel, Graham, 20, 22n7
Beckett, Samuel, 125
Bedient, Calvin, 6
Bell, Al, 280
Beyond the Bull, 267
Black, Dustin Lance, 104
Blazing Saddles, 42
blogosphere, 208–27
Bloom, Harold, 349n4
Bogdanovich, Peter, 206

377

Boone, Joseph Allen, 83–84
Boswell, John, 124
Bouldrey, Brian, 141
Bowers, Hilary, 254
Bowie, David, 187
Bowles, Paul, 87
Boy George, 187
The Boys in the Band, 45
Bradshaw, Peter, 260
Brand, Max, 270
Brando, Marlon, 171
Braudel, Fernand, 164
The Bridges of Madison County, 39
Brief Encounter, 169
Brokeback Mountain: Story to Screenplay (Proulx, McMurtry, Ossana), 46
Brooks, Peter, 310
Brüno, 305
Buchanan, Kyle, 133
Buckendorff, Jennifer, 241
Buffalo Bill Cody's Wild West Show, 271
Burroughs, Alexandra, 257
Bush, George W., 81, 103, 187, 213, 233, 235, 243
Butch Cassidy and the Sundance Kid, 16, 191, 196
Butler, David, 199
Butler, Judith: *The Psychic Life of Power*, 127–28
Byrd, James, 149

Cage, John, 207
Calamity Jane, 199
Cameron, James, 197, 224
Campbell, Carolyn, 122
Canada. *See* Alberta, Canada
Candy, 135n7
Capital (Marx), 284, 290
Capote, 115n1

Cardellini, Linda, 182, 317, 343, 346
Carman, Colin, 5
Carter, David: *Stonewall*, 135n9
Carter, Jimmy, 187
Casablanca, 304
Casanova, 50
Cavagna, Carlo, 11
The Cave and the Mountain (Stone), 117n11
The Celluloid Closet (Russo), 95, 115
Chan, Jackie, 69
Cheney, Dick, 233, 235
Chopin, Kate: *The Awakening*, 19
Chow, Rey: *Sentimental Fabulations*, 78n7
Chris & Don: A Love Story, 112
Citizen Kane, 304
civil rights. *See* gay civil rights movement
Cixous, Hèléne, 123
Clark, Terry, 280
Clift, Montgomery, 192, 195, 197
Clooney, George, 222
Close Range (Proulx), 140, 153, 165, 189n1
the "closet," 18, 33, 41, 54, 108–9, 133, 211–12, 219–20, 274–76
Cody, Buffalo Bill, 271
Cohen, Sacha Baron, 305
Coke-Kerr, Derek, 259
Cole, Paula, 17
"Come Back to the Raft Ag'in, Huck Honey!" (Fiedler), 49, 81
The Condition of the Working Class in England (Engels), 128
Conway, Tim, 238
Cooper, Gary, 105, 270
Cooper, James Fenimore, 269–70
Copeland, Linn, 280
Costner, Kevin, 190
Coulter, Ann, 211, 213

Covering (Yoshino), 88
Covert, Colin, 32
Cowboy Metaphysics (French), 263n3
Crash, 101–2, 104, 117n12
Crawford, Joan, 199
Crouching Tiger, Hidden Dragon, 57, 60–61, 69, 72–75
Cruise, Tom, 222
Cukor, George, 215
Cullen, Dave, 11, 214
Cumming, Joan, 122
Curtis, Tony, 16

Daldry, Stephen, 305
Dale, Alan, 5, 6, 7
Damon, Matt, 222
Dandridge, Dorothy, 136n9
Dargis, Manohla, 2, 45, 264n6
The Dark Knight, 3, 103, 135n7
David, Larry, 244–45
Davies, Jon, 5
Davis, Anthony A., 264n5
Davis, Bette, 312
Davis, Geena, 15
Day, Doris, 199
The Day after Tomorrow, 222
de Lauretis, Teresa: *Technologies of Gender*, 116n7
DeLay, Tom, 233–34
De Leon, Yadhira, 122
Deluise, Dom, 42
D'Emilio, John, 92
Depp, Johnny, 222
Desert Hearts, 16
Destry Rides Again, 198
De Wilde, Brandon, 301
Diario de El Paso, 299
Dietrich, Marlene, 198
Dilley, Whitney Crothers, 60–61, 71
Dine, Jim, 207
Donnie Darko, 222

Drudge, Matt, 262
Duggan, Lisa, 8
Dylan, Bob, 49

Earle, Steve, 215
Eastwood, Clint, 193, 197
Ebert, Roger, 34, 55–56
Eco, Umberto, 324
Edelstein, David, 117n12
Edmundson, Mark, 125
Edwards, Steven, 255, 259
The Ego and the Id (Freud), 126
Elder, Robert K., 178n9
Ellen, 299
Ellsworth, Elizabeth, 211
El Paso TX, 303–4
Emmerich, Roland, 222
An End to Innocence (Fiedler), 84
Engels, Friedrich: *The Condition of the Working Class in England*, 128
Eros and Civilization (Marcuse), 290
Etbauer, Robert, 138

Falwell, Jerry, 243
The Farewell Symphony (White), 28
Far from Heaven, 311, 316
Faris, Anna, 317
Felchlin, Marva, 122
Fernandez, Vicente, 304
Fiedler, Leslie, 81–85, 91; "Come Back to the Raft Ag'in, Huck Honey!," 49, 81; *An End to Innocence*, 84; *Love and Death in the American Novel*, 84–85, 94
Fine Just the Way It Is (Proulx), 165
Flynn, John, 210
forbearance, 55, 63–70
Ford, John, 111, 194, 197, 198
Foreman, Matt, 247–48
Forster, E. M., 114, 117nn10–11; *Maurice*, 112–13

Forte, Will, 238
Forty Guns, 192, 199
Foucault, Michel, 135n4
Freeman, Chris, 5, 7
Freeman, Morgan, 193
French, Peter A.: *Cowboy Metaphysics*, 263n3
Freud, Sigmund, 191, 290, 317–18; *The Ego and the Id*, 271; *The Interpretation of Dreams*, 126

Garland, Judy, 107, 133, 135n9, 215
gay civil rights movement, 6, 18–19, 21, 82–83, 85, 88, 89–90
Gentleman's Agreement, 176
Gibson, Mel, 212, 222
Ginzburg, Carlo, 164
Golden Globes, 32, 50
Goodfellas, 240
Goodman, Andrew, 122
Gray, John, 122
A Great Unrecorded History (Moffat), 117n10
Greenwald, Maggie, 200
Gregory, Tom, 7, 105, 107, 109, 113–14, 120, 122
Grey, Zane, 270
Guess Who's Coming to Dinner, 176
Guiliano, Neil, 247
Gumby and Pokey, 236, *237*
Gyllenhaal, Jake, 206, 208, 254, 256, 273, 289, 309, 323; Annie Proulx on, 161; and *Brokeback Mountain* poster, 231–33; media attention on, 186, 213, 222–23; performance by, 2, 27, 29, 32, 47, 50, 85, 132, 149, 163, 171, 179, 205, 330; praise for, 221–22, 223, 226

Halberstam, Judith, 5, 6–7, 12
Hamer, Dean, 245

Haney, C. Allen, 298n3
Hanks, Tom, 115n1
Han Xin, 66–67, 71
Harbour, David, 317
Harper, Stephen, 250
Harris, Emmylou, 215, 311
Harte, Bret: "In the Tules," 12; "Tennessee's Partner," 12
Hartley, Mariette, 199
Hathaway, Anne, 20, 205, 233, 244, 258, 315
Haynes, Todd, 207, 311
Haysbert, Dennis, 311
Heffernan, Virginia, 238–39
Helander, Brian, 119, 122
Helgeland, Brian, 222
Henderson, William Haywood: *Native*, 13
Herring, Scott, 11, 22n4
Hinton, Gregory, 4, 7, 22n5, 116nn5–6
Hinton, Kip, 118
Hitchcock, Alfred, 315, 318
Hoffman, Philip Seymour, 115n1
Holleran, Andrew, 5
Hollinghurst, Alan: *The Swimming Pool Library*, 28
homophobia, 5, 13, 47, 84–85, 113, 149, 166; among audiences, 180, 218; in *Brokeback Mountain*, 123–34; external, 47, 95; institutionalized, 251–53; internalized, 5, 13, 47–48, 99, 137, 302–3; jokes and, 248; majoritarian, 82–85, 131–32, 166; misogyny and, 315–16; poverty and, 45; rodeos and, 278–79; rural, 47, 113
Horse, 255
Horseman, Pass By (McMurtry), 89
Hotel Rwanda, 246
The Hours, 305

Houston, Pam, 244
Hsu, Hsuan L., 117n12
Hud, 206
Hughes, Howard, 16, 200
The Hulk, 56
Hune-Brown, Nick, 253, 263n3
Hunt, Alex, 11
Hunter, Ross, 168, 172
Hurt, William, 115n1
Huston, John, 171
Hutcheon, Linda, 3

The Ice Storm, 56
Imitation of Life, 168, 169
Imus, Don, 243, 245, 247
I Now Pronounce You Chuck and Larry, 305
Intermezzo: A Love Story, 169
Internet. *See* blogosphere
The Interpretation of Dreams (Freud), 126
Interpreting Films (Staiger), 215
"In the Tules" (Harte), 12
Isherwood, Christopher, 117n10; *A Single Man*, 112

Jacobson, Harlan, 249
Jakino, Wayne, 280
Jarman, Derek, 207
Jefferson, Dick, 130
John, Elton, 133, 187
Johnny Guitar, 199–200
Johnson, Colin R., 173–74
Jones, A. Quincy, 105
Joplin, Janis, 187

Kaplan, Amy, 17
The Karate Kid, 69
Keister, Francis Scott, 149
Kelly, Richard, 222
Kidman, Nicole, 134n1

King, John, 119, 280
Kinsey, Alfred C., 174–75, 177n4, 187; *Sexual Behavior in the Human Male*, 174
Kiss of the Spiderwoman, 115n1
Klein, Ralph, 250
Knight, Robert, 201n1
A Knight's Tale, 222
Kohrs, Conrad, 269
Korman, Harvey, 238
Kreimer, Seth F., 212
Kupelian, David, 260
Kushner, Tony, 21

labor, 269, 274–76, 284–97
Ladd, Alan, 301
Ladurie, Emmanuel LeRoy, 164
Lane, Anthony, 324
Lane, Nathan, 238
LaSalle, Mick, 37
The Last Picture Show, 89, 206
Lau Kar-Leung, 67
Leaving Cheyenne (McMurtry), 177n5
Leavitt, David, 21, 173
Ledger, Heath, 208, 254, 256, 309, 323; accent used by, 181; Annie Proulx on, 161; and *Brokeback Mountain* poster, 231–33; death of, 3, 103, 132, 135n7; media attention on, 186, 213; performance by, 2, 3, 27–29, 32, 35, 47, 50, 124, 132, 149, 163, 170–71, 179, 205, 330, 339, 343, 347; praise for, 60, 221–22, 223
Lee, Ang: Academy Award won by, 116n4; as Asian filmmaker, 77n4; and "Brokeback Mountain," 131–34; cinematic style of, 55–57, 77n2, 167–68, 198, 305, 320, 323–24; as director of *Brokeback Mountain*, 2, 3, 11, 12, 20, 22, 27, 30, 32, 35, 40,

Lee, Ang (*cont.*)
  50, 52, 86, 104, 124, 153, 163, 168,
  179, 190, 195, 223, 229, 259, 283,
  309, 330, 335–36; on Ennis and
  Jack's love, 135n6; on repression,
  60, 62–63, 73–74, 252
Lehman, John, 117n10
Leno, Jay, 43, 243, 247
Letterman, David, 43, 49, 236, 242,
  247
Lewis, Nathaniel: *Unsettling the Literary West*, 140
Li Hongzhi, 64, 65, 71
Limerick, Patricia Nelson, 253
The Living End, 22n6
Lo, Mun-Hou, 5, 19
Loffreda, Beth, 8–9; *Losing Matt Shepard*, 149
Lohan, Lindsay, 136n9
Lonesome Cowboys, 46, 49, 190, 255
Longman, Andrew, 260
Longtime Companion, 300
Lord of the Rings, 240
Losing Matt Shepard (Loffreda), 149
Love and Death in the American Novel (Fiedler), 84–85, 94
Love Is a Many-Splendored Thing, 171
Lovin' Molly, 177n5
Luhrmann, Baz, 134n1
Lust, Caution, 56, 58

Madame X, 168, 169
Mädchen in Uniform, 87
Madden, Shane, 226
Magnificent Obsession, 168
Mahan, Larry, 277
Making Love, 27, 87, 300
Manalansan, Martin F., IV, 73
The Man in the Gray Flannel Suit,
  177n5

The Man Who Fell in Love with the Moon (Spanbauer), 13
Mara, Kate, 317
Marcuse, Herbert: *Eros and Civilization*, 290
Marshall, George, 198
Martinez, Fred, 2
Marx, Karl, 127; *Capital*, 284, 290
masculinity, 47, 59, 93, 138–41, 191–
  98, 270, 303–4
mashups, *Brokeback Mountain*, 3,
  231–41
Matthews, Chris, 245
Maurice (Forster), 112–13
Maxwell, Roberta, 310
McBride, Mary, 215
McCabe, Susan, 17
McCambridge, Mercedes, 199
McCarthy, Cormac: *The Road*, 304
McGreevey, Edward, 186
McKinley, Jesse, 134n1
McMurtry, Larry: Academy Award
  won by, 116n4; *Brokeback Mountain: Story to Screenplay*, 46;
  changes to "Brokeback Mountain"
  made by, 181–83, 322, 332; historical essays by, 156; *Horseman, Pass By*, 89; *Leaving Cheyenne*, 177n5; as
  screenwriter of *Brokeback Mountain*, 2, 6, 11, 29, 30, 35, 45, 47, 51,
  111, 132, 153, 156, 171, 179, 206
McRobbie, Peter, 318, 345
melodrama, 168–72, 309–20
Mendelsohn, Daniel, 19, 21, 39–41,
  57, 59, 62, 96, 108, 172–73, 177n8
Miles, Vera, 199
Milk, 103, 124, 305
Milk, Harvey, 134n1, 187
Miller, D. A., 60, 73, 76n1, 108–9,
  116n8
Mississippi Burning, 246

Modleski, Tania, 315
Moffat, Wendy: *A Great Unrecorded History*, 117n10
Monette, Paul: "My Shirts," 109
Monroe, Marilyn, 136n9
Monster, 115n1
Monster's Ball, 135n7
Moore, Julianne, 311
Morgenstern, Joe, 31
Moring, Mark, 256
Mormons, 7–8, 21
Morrison, James, 7, 21
Morse, Martin, 12–13
Munich, 102
Murray, Ty, 138
Myers, B. R., 141
My Lives (White), 112
"My Shirts" (Monette), 109

Native (Henderson), 13
Nelson, Willie, 42, 49, 99, 270
Newman, Paul, 196
Ney, Bob, 233–34
Nicholson, Jack, 104
Nighthawks, 28
Noveck, Jocelyn, 247
Now, Voyager, 310, 311–12

The Object of My Affection, 87
O'Brien, Conan, 242–43, 247
Olsen, Greg, 281
The Order, 135n7
O'Reilly, Bill, 245, 247
Oscars. *See* Academy Awards
Ossana, Diana: Academy Award won by, 116n4; *Brokeback Mountain: Story to Screenplay*, 46; changes to "Brokeback Mountain" made by, 181–83, 322, 332; as screenwriter of *Brokeback Mountain*, 2, 6, 29–30, 35, 45, 111, 132, 153, 156, 171, 179, 206

Ottinger, Ulrike, 207
The Outlaw, 191, 193, 195, 200
Out of Africa, 304
Ownby, David, 63–64

Packard, Chris, 140; *Queer Cowboys*, 12
Paglia, Camille, 173
Palmer, David A., 77n3
Papanikolas, Zeese: *Trickster in the Land of Dreams*, 297n1
Paradise Now, 102
parodies of *Brokeback Mountain*, 3, 230–48. *See also* mashups, *Brokeback Mountain*
Parting Glances, 300
The Passion of the Christ, 212
The Patriot, 222
Pearson, Demetrius W.: "The Rodeo Cowboy as an American Icon," 298n3
Peckinpah, Sam, 193
Penn, Sean, 104
Philadelphia, 45, 87, 95, 115n1, 300
Phoenix, Joaquin, 222
Pitt, Brad, 222
Plath, Sylvia, 136n9
Posse, 200
The Power of the Dog (Savage), 13
Powers, John, 230
Prieto, Rodrigo, 179
Prince, Richard, 111
Proposition 8, 7–8, 103, 116n2, 124
Proulx, Annie, 2, 6, 45, 46, 50, 121, 123, 198, 273, 277–78, 302, 314, 321; *Bad Dirt*, 160, 165; on the *Brokeback Mountain* shirts, 110–11; *Brokeback Mountain: Story to Screenplay*, 46; camp and, 141–42; *Close Range*, 140, 153, 165, 189n1; on cowboys, 270; *Fine Just the Way*

Proulx, Annie (*cont.*)
   It Is, 165; on homophobia, 128; and
   hyperrealism, 144; interview with,
   153–62; literary influences on,
   86–87; and naturalism, 168; other
   books by, 139–40, 144, 148–49,
   166; on the setting of "Brokeback
   Mountain," 91; *The Shipping News*,
   139, 166; *That Old Ace in the Hole*,
   139, 144, 148–49, 154; writing style
   of, 92–93, 143–45, 164–67, 174–75,
   177n3, 183–85, 322, 324–30, 341; on
   Wyoming, 126, 157, 158, 164, 252
The Psychic Life of Power (Butler), 126
Purdy, James, 87

Quaid, Dennis, 311
Quaid, Randy, 313
Queer as Folk, 299
Queer Cowboys (Packard), 12
Querelle, 87

racism, 117n12
Ragdale, Phil, 278–79
Rambo, Gene, 277
Rapper, Irving, 310
Ray, Nicholas, 199
Reagan, Ronald, 270
Rebecca, 318
Rebel without a Cause, 95
Redford, Robert, 196
Red River, 14, 191, 192–93, 195, 196,
   197
Reeves, George, 302
Reflections in a Golden Eye, 171
Remington, Frederic, 270
Rich, Adrienne, 313
Rich, B. Ruby, 3, 104, 207, 214
Rich, Frank, 45
Richardson, Jeffrey, 120, 122
Ride the High Country, 193, 196, 199

Ritt, Martin, 206
The Road (McCarthy), 304
Roberts, Julia, 299
Robertson, Pat, 244
Robinson, Marilynne, 91
Rocky, 69
rodeo, 40, 119–20, 122; creativity in,
   272–73; current state of, 281–82;
   gay, 278–81; Golden Age of,
   277–78; heterosexism in, 276–77;
   historical roots of, 268–72; and
   horses, 270–72; labor of cowboys
   in, 274–76, 287–90; masculinity
   and, 138–41, 270; recent popularity
   of, 267–68
"The Rodeo Cowboy as an American
   Icon" (Pearson), 298n3
Rodriguez, Richard, 303
Rogers, Roy, 270
Rozema, Patricia, 207
Rudé, George, 176n2
Rushdie, Salman, 107
Russell, Charles M., 270, 274
Russell, Jane, 200
Russo, Vito: *The Celluloid Closet*, 95,
   115

Salkind, Susanne, 247
Santaolalla, Gustavo, 50, 239
Sarandon, Susan, 15
Savage, Michael, 243
Savage, Thomas: *The Power of the
   Dog*, 13
Scanlon, Michael, 233–34
Schamus, James, 21, 60, 178n9
Schindler's List, 5, 211, 246
Schlesinger, John, 210
Schneider, Richard, 104
Schulman, Cathy, 102
Schumacher, Joel, 302
The Searchers, 194, 197, 199

Sedwick, Eve Kosofsky: *Touching Feeling*, 23n8
Sense and Sensibility, 56
Sentimental Fabulations (Chow), 78n7
The Sergeant, 210
Sexual Behavior in the Human Male (Kinsey), 174
Shadix, Scotty, 122
Shane, 12, 14, 301, 302
Shepard, Judy, 2
Shepard, Matthew, 2, 44, 47, 50, 149
The Shipping News (Proulx), 139, 166
shirts, *Brokeback Mountain*, 105–11, 114, 118–22
Shyamalan, M. Night, 300
Siamos, Xenia, 255
Silverblatt, Michael, 6
Simpson, Al, 118–19
A Single Man (Isherwood), 112
Sirk, Douglas, 46, 168, 311
Smith, Harry, 255
Smith, Ryan, 130
Sonstegard, Adam, 6, 19
Sontag, Susan, 141–42
South Pacific, 171
Spanbauer, Tom: *The Man Who Fell in Love with the Moon*, 13
Spears, Britney, 136n9
Spielberg, Steven, 102, 211
Stagecoach, 198
Staiger, Janet, 209; *Interpreting Films*, 215
Stanwyck, Barbara, 192, 199
A Star Is Born, 215
Stewart, John, 140
Stone, Wilfred: *The Cave and the Mountain*, 117n11
Stonewall (Carter), 135n9
Stonewall Riots, 18–19, 82, 90, 124, 135n9, 139n1, 174, 254
Stowe, Harriet Beecher: *Uncle Tom's Cabin*, 7, 93–94

Sullivan, Andrew, 46, 88, 173; *Virtually Normal*, 87
Sunday Bloody Sunday, 210
The Swimming Pool Library (Hollinghurst), 28

Taking Woodstock, 305
Taxi zum Klo, 28
Technologies of Gender (de Lauretis), 116n7
"Tennessee's Partner" (Harte), 12
10 Things I Hate about You, 135n7
Teo, Stephen, 69
The Terminator, 197
Terms of Endearment, 89
Terry, Patrick, 120
That Old Ace in the Hole (Proulx), 139, 144, 148–49, 154
Thelma and Louise, 12, 15–16, 18, 19
Theron, Charlize, 115n1
The 36th Chamber of Shaolin, 67, 69–70, 74
Tibbs, Casey, 277
Titanic, 3, 39, 178n9, 224, 252
Top Gun, 240
Touching Feeling (Sedgwick), 23n8
Towle, Andy, 236
Travolta, John, 222
Trebay, Guy, 260, 264n7
Trevor, Claire, 198
Trickster in the Land of Dreams (Papanikolas), 297n1
The Trouble with Normal (Warner), 88
Truman, Harry, 82
Tsika, Noah, 4, 11
Turan, Kenneth, 3, 31
Turner, Mark, 3
Twain, Mark: *The Adventures of Huckleberry Finn*, 81
Two Spirits, 2, 22n5

Uncle Tom's Cabin (Stowe), 7, 93–94
Unforgiven, 193, 201
Unsettling the Literary West (Lewis), 140
Utah, 8, 251, 267

Van Peebles, Mario, 200
Van Sant, Gus, 207, 302, 304
Vaughn, Vince, 222
Velvet Goldmine, 87
violence, 34, 52, 54–55, 94–95, 130, 145–47, 149
The Virginian (Wister), 9, 12, 13–14, 15, 17, 140
Virtually Normal (Sullivan), 87

Wainwright, Rufus, 99, 100, 133
Walker, Texas Ranger, 301–2
Warhol, Andy, 46, 49, 190, 255
Warner, Michael: *The Trouble with Normal*, 88
Warren, Patricia Nell, 4, 116n9
Waters, John, 207
Wayne, John, 16, 139, 190, 192–95, 197, 267, 270
Web sites. *See* blogosphere
The Wedding Banquet, 56, 70–71, 72
Weiss, David, 3, 5
Weltzien, Alan, 13
Western (film genre), 5–6, 11–12, 15–16, 111–12, 190–201, 301–2

Whalen, Tracy, 140
White, Dave, 244
White, Edmund: *The Farewell Symphony*, 28; *My Lives*, 112
White, Patricia, 310
Whittington, Harry, 233
Whyte, Murray, 258
Will & Grace, 45, 299
Williams, Linda, 320
Williams, Michelle, 177n6, 182, 205, 233, 312
Williams, Tennessee, 87
Winfrey, Oprah, 304
Wister, Owen: *The Virginian*, 9, 12, 13–14, 15, 17, 140
Witherspoon, Reese, 299
The Wizard of Oz, 105, 107, 133–34
Wloszczyna, Susan, 229
Wood, Robin, 55
Woolf, Virginia, 136n9
Wuorinen, Charles, 3
Wyman, Jane, 311
Wyoming, 8–9, 10, 44–45, 47, 118, 149, 150, 260; Annie Proulx on, 126, 157, 158, 164, 252; rural life in, 165–66, 174, 262

Yoshino, Kenji, 97; *Covering*, 88

Žižek, Slavoj, 125
Zonta, Dario, 324